Catholics across Borders

Catholics across Borders

Canadian Immigrants in the North Country,
Plattsburgh, New York, 1850–1950

MARK PAUL RICHARD

SUNY
PRESS

Cover Credit: Grey Nuns of the Cross and students in front of D'Youville Academy, October 1908. Courtesy of Archives des Soeurs de la Charité d'Ottawa, accession P-M5/10.

Plattsburgh's *petit Canada*, 1916, from J. L. Beers and C. J. Bord, *New Atlas of the City of Plattsburgh, NY, 1916*, section E. Courtesy of Feinberg Library Special Collections, SUNY Plattsburgh, atlas case G1254.P5 B4 1916.

Published by State University of New York Press, Albany

© 2024 Mark Paul Richard

All rights reserved

Printed in the United States of America

No part of this book may be used or reproduced in any manner whatsoever without written permission. No part of this book may be stored in a retrieval system or transmitted in any form or by any means including electronic, electrostatic, magnetic tape, mechanical, photocopying, recording, or otherwise without the prior permission in writing of the publisher.

For information, contact State University of New York Press, Albany, NY
www.sunypress.edu

Library of Congress Cataloging-in-Publication Data

Name: Richard, Mark Paul, author.
Title: Catholics across borders : Canadian immigrants in the North Country, Plattsburgh, New York, 1850–1950 / Mark Paul Richard.
Description: Albany : State University of New York Press, [2024] | Includes bibliographical references and index.
Identifiers: ISBN 9781438496214 (hardcover : alk. paper) | ISBN 9781438496238 (ebook) | ISBN 9781438496221 (pbk. : alk. paper)
Further information is available at the Library of Congress.

10 9 8 7 6 5 4 3 2 1

Contents

List of Illustrations vii

Preface ix

Introduction 1

Chapter 1　The Collaboration of the Irish and the French Canadians: Creating a Catholic Community, 1850–1870　7

Chapter 2　Oblate Priests, Grey Nuns, and Ethnic Institutions: Forging a French-Canadian Community, 1870–1900　33

Chapter 3　An Execution in Canada, a Murder in Plattsburgh, and *Le National*: Shaping Francophones' Political Consciousness, 1870–1900　63

Chapter 4　Religious Habits, Catholic Institutions, and the Champlain Tercentenary: Ringing in the Twentieth Century, 1900–1910　87

Chapter 5　The Contest between the Grey Nuns and Local Physicians: Founding Nonsectarian Community Hospitals, 1900–1920　119

Chapter 6　The Visibility of the Canada–US Border: Separating Nuns and Nations, 1910–1920　143

Chapter 7	The Era of the Second Ku Klux Klan: Pursuing Interfaith Collaboration while Expanding Catholic Institutions, 1920–1930	175
Chapter 8	The Depression Years: Collecting Nickels, Dimes, and Quarters, 1930–1940	207
Chapter 9	Plattsburgh during World War II and the Early Cold War: Retaining a Catholic Heritage, 1940–1950	229
Conclusion		255
Afterword		259
Appendix		265
Abbreviations		275
Notes		277
Index		335

Illustrations

Figures

1.1	St. Peter's Church	10
1.2	D'Youville Academy	16
2.1	Dr. J. H. LaRocque	49
3.1	Louis Riel in Keeseville, New York	65
4.1	Grey Nuns of the Cross and students	93
4.2	Our Lady of Victory Academy	108
4.3	Guard of Honor, St. John Baptist Association	111
4.4	President William Howard Taft and dignitaries during Champlain Tercentenary	112
4.5	Monument to Samuel de Champlain	115
7.1	Champlain Valley Hospital and School of Nursing	202
8.1	Community Advertisement for Minstrel Show	210
8.2	Brothers of Christian Instruction	217
8.3	Dominican Sisters	218
9.1	Sisters of Charity of St. Louis	238
9.2	Grey Nuns of the Sacred Heart	241

Tables

1	Nativity of the Oblate Priests of St. Peter's Parish	266
2	Nativity of the Grey Nuns of the Cross at D'Youville Convent	267
3	Nativity of the Grey Nuns at Champlain Valley Hospital	268
4	Nativity of the Brothers of Christian Instruction	269
5	Nativity of the Boarding Students of the Grey Nuns at D'Youville Convent	270
6	Nativity of the Diocesan Priests at Our Lady of Victory Parish	270
7	Nativity of the Diocesan Priests at St. John the Baptist Parish	271
8	Nativity of the Sisters of Mercy	272
9	Nativity of the Sisters of Charity of St. Louis at Our Lady of Victory	273
10	Nativity of the Dominican Sisters at St. Peter's Parish	274

Preface

This book is the result of an intellectual journey that began in the early 1990s. It was at the University of Maine, where I earned my master of arts degree in history, that I first started learning about the history and culture of Franco-Americans, the descendants of French-Canadian immigrants in the United States. The activities of UMaine's Franco-American Centre proved integral to my formation. During one panel presentation at the centre, I heard two French professors and a community person, all from New York's capital district, argue that our understanding of the Franco-American experience was too heavily focused on French-Canadian population centers of New England. I actually contributed to that trend by going on to research and write two monographs based in New England, both published while I taught at the State University of New York at Plattsburgh.

A mere twenty miles from the Québec border, Plattsburgh, like many French-Canadian population centers of New England, had had a *petit Canada* (Little Canada). Located among the French-named streets of Lafayette, Montcalm, and Champlain, this ethnic community had existed near Saint-Pierre (St. Peter's) Church (see cover). Shortly after arriving in Plattsburgh, I was intrigued to learn that the church sponsored an annual French festival, so I attended. But nothing I saw or heard at the festival struck me as French, except for the *tortière* (meat pie) served in the school cafeteria. Over the years, members of the community expressed an interest in my work, inviting me to make presentations and sharing with me bits and pieces of the French-Canadian heritage of rural upstate New York. One sent me a photograph taken locally in the 1870s of a Métis leader from Canada's Northwest Territories, along with the information that this person's correspondence with an important Franco-American leader could be found in the archives of a university library in Massachusetts where I had previously conducted other research. As I followed up on the leads, I redoubled my efforts to locate a copy of the French-language newspaper of Plattsburgh, published in the 1880s. After turning many stones on campus and in the community, I discovered that some issues had been preserved on a small reel of microfilm at my university's library and that a more extensive microfilmed collection of the newspaper existed back on my home turf at UMaine's Fogler Library.

The upshot is that a good deal of the information I have gathered to research and write this book eventually came from sources located outside of Plattsburgh. My travels took me to Orono and Alfred, Maine; Worcester, Massachusetts; Ogdensburg and Ossining, New York; Philadelphia, Pennsylvania; La Prairie and Lévis, Québec; and Ottawa, Ontario. A number of small research grants made possible my travel to the repositories in each of these cities. I am thankful for the funding I received from the Plattsburgh College Foundation John L. Myers History Endowment; State of New York / United University Professions Joint Labor-Management Committee Professional Development Awards Program; SUNY Plattsburgh Office of Sponsored Research; and the Ministère des Relations internationales et de la Francophonie, Government of Québec, which also came through with a subvention to assist SUNY Press with publication costs. The endnotes acknowledge the various repositories I visited in the Plattsburgh area and beyond. I am grateful to the many librarians and archivists who made available to me the resources in those collections so that I could piece together this community study. I wish to thank David Palmieri for commenting on several chapters of this manuscript and the external reviewers for their thoughtful remarks on the entire draft. One of the reviewers (Leslie Choquette) offered ninety-two suggestions for my consideration—a figure of symbolic importance in French-Canadian history, equal to the number of demands the *Patriotes* made of the British in the 1837–1838 Rebellion in Lower Canada! Their suggestions all helped to clarify and improve this book. Part of chapter three was originally published in Mark Paul Richard, "'Riel . . . vivra dans notre histoire': The Response of French Canadians in the United States to Louis Riel's Execution," *Journal of Canadian Studies / Revue d'études canadiennes* 51, no. 3 (Fall 2017): 697–724; it is reproduced with permission from the University of Toronto Press (https://utpjournals.press), doi 10.3138/jcs.2017-0035.r1.

As I conducted my research, it became clear to me that something different from what happened in New England took place in upstate New York. While there were certainly many similarities, the differences illustrate the importance of looking outside of defined spaces to pursue historical questions. This book distills many years of thinking and writing about the Franco-American experience in New England, and it shares what I have discovered that was different in the borderlands of New York State. This book is my answer to the New York panelists I heard at the Franco-American Centre several decades ago, and to the many New York residents I have since met, who have called for the inclusion of their French heritage into the larger narrative of the Franco-American experience in the United States.

Introduction

When French explorer Samuel de Champlain famously clashed with the Iroquois in 1609 near today's Ticonderoga, it was not the last incursion of French speakers into territory that became northern New York. There has been a French presence in the state since the colonial period, fueled by different waves of immigration. The largest influx of francophones took place from 1830 to 1930, the century before the United States applied immigration restrictions to continental migrants. Existing studies of French-Canadian immigrants in the United States have focused on the large industrial centers of New England, with little attention paid to the rural mill villages or to the borderlands shared by Québec and the northeastern states, including New York. Unlike previous works, this community study of Plattsburgh, New York, examines the evolution of a rural village into a French-Canadian population center of upstate New York.

The Five Nations of the Iroquois League controlled much of what became New York State at the time of Champlain's expedition. When Champlain joined forces with the Huron, the Ottawa, and the Montagnais to confront the Iroquois, they traveled along the large lake native peoples had named *Canaderi Guarante*, "the lake that is the gate of the country." A mapmaker and the lake's first European explorer, Champlain renamed it after himself. As a result of his 1609 expedition, the French laid claim to much of northern New York. They built—more than a century later—Fort Saint-Frédéric (today's Crown Point) in 1732 and Fort Carillon (today's Ticonderoga) in 1755, and they granted seigneuries on both sides of the lake. The French lost control of the Champlain valley in the French and Indian War, during which the Iroquois sided with the British against the French, a war that culminated with the British conquest of New France in 1760.[1]

When American rebels invaded British North America in 1775–1776, upwards of 150 French Canadians sided with them but had to leave after the failed invasion. In all, an estimated 1,800 French Canadians and Acadians helped the Americans in their war for independence from the British. The New York legislature in 1789 granted lands along Lake Champlain to French-Canadian refugees as compensation for supporting the Patriots. At the same time, it granted lands to the children of Acadian exiles, the French speakers who were deported from the Maritime colonies during the French and Indian War because they would not swear an oath of unconditional loyalty to the British crown. As a result of the land grants, approximately 250 French-speaking Acadian and Canadian families settled in northeastern New York by the early 1800s.[2]

French speakers were not the only recipients of land. The State of New York also offered grants to English-speaking veterans of the Revolutionary War. Parcels unclaimed by veterans were sold to individuals like Zephaniah Platt, originally of Poughkeepsie, one of the earliest settlers of what became Clinton County, located in the northeasternmost part of the state and bordering British North America. Drawn to the region by timber lands, iron-ore beds, and waterpower sites along the Saranac River, Platt received the Patent of Plattsburgh in October 1784. In 1815, Plattsburgh became incorporated as a village, following another military conflict between the Americans and the British, the War of 1812–1814, during which the Battle of Plattsburgh was fought on Lake Champlain.[3] As these historical examples illustrate, Plattsburgh and the Lake Champlain region stood at the nexus of important international events.

Beginning in 1816, steamships on Lake Champlain moved between Saint-Jean-sur-Richelieu in Lower Canada (now the Province of Québec) and Albany, New York, helping to facilitate the migration of French Canadians to lands formerly under French control. Plattsburgh, from its early settlement, was a diverse community, as families brought different ethnic and religious traditions. Those who came from the south tended to be English or Dutch Protestants, while those from the north were mostly French-Canadian Catholics. The French Canadians who settled in the vicinity of Plattsburgh by the early 1800s largely worked in the lumber industry and established farms.[4]

The Rebellion of 1837–1838 in Lower Canada precipitated another migration of French Canadians to Plattsburgh. After the unsuccessful revolt against the tight controls of the British Empire, exiled *Patriotes* (who borrowed symbols from the US Revolution) migrated to New

York and Vermont to avoid imprisonment or hanging. Of the leaders, Louis-Joseph Papineau went to Albany, Ludger Duvernay to Rouses Point, and Robert Nelson and Cyrille Côté to Plattsburgh. Although the US government chose to remain neutral, and Papineau advised against organizing an attack, Nelson and Coté persisted. In February 1838, they crossed the border at Alburg, Vermont, with 600 men and established in Napierville the Republic of Lower Canada. But the *Patriotes* were chased back into the United States and US authorities disarmed them. Charged with violating neutrality, Nelson and Côté were acquitted by a jury and resumed their hostilities against British rule. A number of *Patriotes* returned to Lower Canada after the amnesty of June 1838, while others remained in the United States with Nelson and Côté to form a secret society called the *Frères-Chasseurs* (Hunters' Lodges) to continue agitating for and fomenting political change. In November 1838, Nelson and Côté led another invasion of Lower Canada, this time with 2,000 men, but it also failed, and they retreated to the United States. The *Patriotes* subsequently dispersed throughout the United States, some as far west as California and as far south as Louisiana, while most moved to states in the Canada–US borderlands region, such as Michigan, Illinois, Wisconsin, Vermont, and New York.[5]

Médard Hébert and Pierre-Paul Desmarais settled in Plattsburgh, where they established a grocery store. Local accounts suggest there were other French Canadians who chose to stay in Plattsburgh following the rebellion. They were not farmers but urban dwellers who included artisans, "former clerks, merchants and factory workers [who] went into our flouring mills, sawmills, tanneries, glass factories and into many other fields of endeavor," writes Roswell Hogue.[6]

Local sources also suggest that the migration of French Canadians to Plattsburgh increased after the Rebellion of 1837–1838.[7] These migrations were part of a larger movement of people during the century from 1830 to 1930, where upwards of one million French-speaking Canadians emigrated to the United States. After the uprisings ended, the emigration of French Canadians to the United States was not tied to political causes or strife. During the second half of the nineteenth century, Québec experienced such demographic and economic challenges as a growing rural population that lacked sufficient access to arable land, indebtedness incurred with the specialization and mechanization of agriculture, and an urban industrial development that did not proceed at a rapid enough pace to absorb the province's surplus rural population. These conditions produced unemployment, prevented advancement, created distress, and precipitated their emigration. Most francophone immigrants ended up in such northeastern industrial centers as Lewiston and Biddeford, Maine; Manchester, New Hampshire; and Lowell, Lawrence, and Fall River, Massachusetts, as well as the mill towns and mill villages of the Blackstone River Valley in Massachusetts and Rhode Island and of the Quinebaug River Valley in Connecticut.[8]

Less known are the migrations of French Canadians to New York State or to the Midwest and West.[9] Plattsburgh, New York, therefore presents an interesting community study. French-Canadian immigrants constituted at least one-third of Plattsburgh's population in the mid-1800s.[10] It lies just 60 miles south of Montréal, the largest French-speaking population center in North America. As a French-Canadian demographic cluster in the rural borderlands of upstate New York, Plattsburgh offers some fascinating contrasts with the textile mill centers of New England.

Among other themes, this community study highlights processes of acculturation and assimilation in US society. Plattsburgh's French-Canadian immigrants and their Franco-American descendants became integrated in US society in ways that occasionally differed from their counterparts in other northeastern communities. A central argument of this book is that, unlike in many of the industrial centers of New England, interethnic cooperation rather than conflict served as the prevalent pattern in upstate New York from the mid-nineteenth to the mid-twentieth centuries.

This study also sheds light on the evolution of the Canada–US border over historical time. It considers how the border, a relatively porous construct to 1930, became politicized over time, affecting the populations on either side. In the same vein, this work demonstrates how international events between Canada and the United States played out at the local level, particularly those that had bearing on the French-Catholic identity of the Plattsburgh community.

This monograph similarly contributes to American religious history, in which Catholics have often been viewed as outsiders. As it sheds light on the history of Catholicism in the United States, which has largely excluded French-Canadian Catholics, it traces the evolution of religious establishments in the borderlands region. Through the extensive use of sources from religious and other archives that have rarely been tapped by scholars, this book provides considerable insight into the inner workings of Catholic institutions. It teaches us a great deal, for example, about the labors of priests, nuns, and brothers, many of whom were immigrants, as it explores the movement of religious personnel across the Canada–US border—a topic that has attracted little historical attention. The women and men religious who emigrated from Canada to found and staff Plattsburgh's Catholic institutions were not all French-Canadian descendants but also consisted of individuals of Anglo- and Irish-Canadian descent as well as natives of France. This work particularly looks at how they shaped the French-Canadian population of Plattsburgh.

This study highlights the significant contributions of lay and religious women in creating and supporting Catholic establishments. It also teaches us much about gender relations within Catholic institutions. The women religious who conducted schools and hospitals had access to professional positions and authority that many lay women did not. Sometimes this brought them into conflict with priests and bishops in the Roman Catholic hierarchy. As early feminists (who probably would not have recognized themselves that way), the nuns who served in Plattsburgh blazed trails that later opened pathways to lay women.

Finally, in the contemporary period, much political and journalistic attention focuses on the large, mostly Catholic, groups that cross the southern US border. This study looks at Catholic migrations across the northern US border in an earlier period of time, thus providing a historic perspective to aid in our understanding of the present. Transnational Catholic migrants helped shape local, regional, national, and even international history by their activities in Plattsburgh and beyond. In short, the history of Plattsburgh's Catholic migrants forms part of the larger narrative of the US immigrant experience.

Chapter One

The Collaboration of the Irish and the French Canadians

Creating a Catholic Community, 1850–1870

Before 1827, missionary priests, including clergy from Lower Canada, served Catholics of northern New York. Some itinerant clergy preached in French and others in English. From 1827, English- and French-speaking Catholics in Plattsburgh worshipped together—presumably in English—first in a private residence and then in a store, before building a church named "the First Roman Catholic Church of Plattsburgh" on a site that later became City Hall Place. The congregation of Irish and French descendants "had little in worldly goods" and mostly consisted of farmers, according to a parish publication from 1943. To raise money for the church, Rev. George Drummond traveled to Canada where he visited parishes in the fall of 1839 to ask for their financial support. By 1850, French-Canadian immigrants constituted 32 percent of Plattsburgh's household heads; they had enough critical mass to withdraw from the First Roman Catholic Church in 1853 to form a parish of their own, directed by the Order of Mary Immaculate, or Oblate priests.[1] The early cooperation between the Irish and French Catholics of Plattsburgh in religious matters was typical of many other communities in the Northeast, but over time ethnic rivalries surfaced in those communities, leading to significant divisions. Events did not play out in the same way in Plattsburgh. The Oblates played a critical role in creating a community among Plattsburgh's French-Canadian population during the 1850s and 1860s;

the Sisters of Charity of Ottawa contributed significantly to the process and, surprisingly enough, so did the village's Irish population.

By the mid-1800s, Plattsburgh's French Catholic population nearly equaled the number of English-speaking Catholics, and the former began asking for francophone priests. A house-to-house survey in January 1853 revealed that a majority of the village's French-Canadian residents favored a parish of their own. Twenty-five French-speaking Catholics traveled from Plattsburgh to Montréal to prevail upon the Oblates to send them priests. Founded in Aix, France, in 1816, the Order of Mary Immaculate began its work in Montréal in 1841 at the invitation of Bishop Ignace Bourget, who had met the order's founder during a trip to Rome the same year. In 1842 and 1843, Oblate priests traveled to northern New York to preach missions of up to 4 weeks to 500 Catholic families near Rouses Point, just north of Plattsburgh, and that probably is how Plattsburgh Catholics came to learn of the order. In July 1853, the Oblate Provincial from Montréal signed a contract with the Roman Catholic Bishop of Albany, John McCloskey, who authorized the religious order to serve "the Canadian Catholics of Plattsburgh in a stable and permanent way." The next month, the Oblate Provincial signed a contract in Plattsburgh with five representatives of the city's French-Canadian population.[2] For their part, the five trustees agreed to provide the Oblates within two years a property on which to build a church, a rectory of stone or brick, and enough space to have a garden. According to the contract, the Oblates could collect pew rentals and make other collections to maintain the church.[3]

A historical account compiled by the Oblate order reveals its reasons for agreeing to go to Plattsburgh. They believed that not having a priest who spoke French could lead to the loss of Plattsburgh's French-Canadian population from the Catholic Church. As francophone men religious, the Oblates understood that a connection existed among French-Canadian descendants between the French language and the Roman Catholic faith, something they acknowledged implicitly when they announced at masses in October 1856 that "the [French-] Canadian school to preserve the [French] language and [Roman Catholic] faith will open on Monday." Serving the 2,000 or so *Canadiens* from the Plattsburgh area would enlarge the Oblate organization in North America. In addition, the Oblates liked Plattsburgh's proximity to Montréal, and they foresaw having to make no financial sacrifice to establish the order in Plattsburgh.[4]

After settling in Plattsburgh, the Oblates completed the first census of St. Pierre parish in January 1854. In all, there were 600 families: 200

of them in the village and 400 in the countryside within 15 miles of the church site. Many of the household heads, reports Roswell Hogue, were "struggling farmers and laborers." Most of the latter found work in the lumber, paper, and mining industries. However, the population was poor and consisted of "veterans of the Papineau rebellion" of 1837–1838, as the Oblates noted in their historical account. In adding that they were not used to saving money or to donating to the priests or church, the Oblates appeared to make a veiled reference to the anti-clericalism of some of the *Patriotes*.[5] To build a church, then, was a substantial feat. It necessitated significant assistance from outside the ethnic and local communities.

The trustees purchased a property from Roswell Weed of Plattsburgh for $1,418 and signed a mortgage with him for $1,218 in August 1853. An Anglo-American benefactor of Plattsburgh's French-Canadian population, Weed thus contributed $200 to the new parish. During the construction of St. Pierre Church and rectory, the trustees had to rent a house for the Oblates, provide them $600 yearly, and rent a church building, but the contract allowed the trustees to retain the revenues from pew rentals and other collections until the new church was completed. In the interim, French Catholics worshipped in the building of the former Universalist Church and worked to raise funds for their new church. French-Canadian women organized a bazaar in December 1853 that raised a reported $320.[6] Like Drummond before them, the Oblate priests visited parishes in Québec to seek their financial assistance; Rev. Jean-Pierre Bernard, the first pastor of St. Pierre, reportedly raised $1,700 during a monthlong tour of Québec parishes in 1854. Demonstrating interethnic cooperation, Irish Catholics of Plattsburgh also contributed money, labor, and supplies for the new church. The Oblates noted that some Irish men transported wood about fifteen miles to frame the church, while others made about eighty trips to deliver sand and stones for its construction.[7]

In July 1854, Plattsburgh witnessed the laying of the cornerstone for the new church of St. Pierre (see fig. 1.1). Reflecting a pattern that would typify public celebrations, the ceremony was a bilingual affair. A clergyman who represented the Diocese of Montréal spoke in French, and Rev. Louis De Goësbriand, Bishop of Burlington, made his remarks in English. Native-born residents of Plattsburgh regarded the ceremonies with curiosity. The *Plattsburgh Republican* commented that the proceedings were "solemn, and to most of our citizens, novel ceremonies." Reflecting a theme and concern that found expression in subsequent reporting over

Figure 1.1. St. Peter's French Catholic Church, Plattsburgh, NY, founded in 1854 and administered by the Order of Mary Immaculate, or Oblate priests. Courtesy of Holy Cross Catholic Parish, as shared by Richard B. Frost.

time, the English-language newspaper also pointed out that "everything was conducted with much order and propriety."[8]

Although recognized as a French Catholic church, St. Pierre from its earliest days served a bilingual parish community. Proximity to bilingual Montréal perhaps influenced these linguistic roots. In November 1855, a concern arose about the validity of the elections of the trustees, so on three consecutive Sundays in 1855 an announcement read in French and English notified the congregation of a December 17 meeting of "male persons of full age who have statedly worshipped in this house and with this Church and have been considered as belonging thereto" for the election of trustees.[9] To meet the needs of Plattsburgh's bilingual community, as early as 1856 the Oblates serving Plattsburgh were French and Irish in origin.[10] As we will see, this had a significant impact on ethnic relations in Plattsburgh and on the development of its French-Canadian community.

Because the population of St. Pierre parish lacked sufficient means, the Oblate order ended up contributing some of the funds needed to construct the church, and they wanted to hold a mortgage on the building to protect their investment. The bishop permitted this action, and he warned the French-Canadian population of Plattsburgh that they might lose their religious personnel if they did not live up to the terms of their 1853 contract with the Oblates. In May 1856, the trustees of St. Pierre presided over a parish assembly to discuss that contract. Those who attended the meeting resolved that the Oblates remain in Plattsburgh and that the trustees be granted the authority to meet the terms of the original agreement with the order. However, the opposition of part of the congregation to the proposed financial arrangements led the bishop to suggest another solution in July 1856 and, following the December election of trustees, the financial disagreements between the parish and the Oblates were settled amicably, as the Oblates noted in their historical account.[11]

In 1857, J. E. Guigues, the Bishop of Ottawa, who was himself a member of the Oblate order, thanked the Bishop of Albany for supporting the Oblate priests in Plattsburgh in managing temporal affairs with the parish trustees. To ensure that the Oblates in Plattsburgh would have sufficient revenue, he asked the bishop to consider placing the Irish parish in the village under the direction of the Oblate order as well. Then there would be three Oblate priests living in the village who could attend to the needs of *Canadiens* dispersed widely in the North Country between the dioceses of Albany in central New York and Burlington in northwestern Vermont.[12] Several years later, the Bishop of Albany approved the appointment of an Irish Oblate priest to serve the Irish Catholic population of Plattsburgh.

Once established in Plattsburgh, the Oblate priests turned to the Sisters of Charity of Ottawa in 1860 to staff the parish school. Founded in 1737 by the French-Canadian widow, Marguerite d'Youville, the Sisters of Charity of Montréal split into four autonomous branches in the mid-1800s, with one group forming in St. Hyacinthe in 1840, one in Ottawa in 1845, and another in Québec in 1849. Commonly known as the Grey Nuns, the Sisters of Charity joined forces with the Oblates in different locations in British North America. When the Grey Nuns traveled to the Northwest territories in 1844 to work with Native peoples and the Métis (the descendants of French fur trappers and Native women), the Oblates followed them in 1845.[13]

In that same year, Rev. Pierre-Adrien Telmon, an Oblate priest, established a Catholic parish in Bytown (renamed Ottawa in 1855) and asked the Grey Nuns of Montréal to send sisters to establish a school and hospital and to work among the sick and poor in their homes. About half of Bytown's 6,000 residents were anglophone and half were francophone. In response to Telmon's call, Elisabeth Bruyère, the twenty-six-year-old superior, brought four professed nuns, a novice, and a postulant to Bytown in February 1845; three of the women were French-speaking and three English-speaking—"exactly what was needed to satisfy the Bytownians," writes the historian Sr. Paul-Emile. The following month, the Grey Nuns opened Bytown's first bilingual school. A printed commendation form for its students appeared in English, with blanks completed in French by Mother Bruyère in July 1860, suggesting that the order functioned in both languages.[14] As we will see, these developments in Bytown presaged some that took place in Plattsburgh.

The Oblates also worked with the Grey Nuns in the United States. Oblate priests administered Holy Angels parish in Buffalo, New York, and they asked the Sisters of Charity of Ottawa to come to Buffalo in 1857 to teach and to care for the city's poor and sick. So close was the working relationship of the Oblates with the Grey Nuns of the Cross, as they were also known, that their foundress in Ottawa wanted to put the order under the direction of the Oblates. Bruyère wrote the head of the Oblate order in France in January 1860: "You should find it natural that, having been founded and directed since our foundation at Bytown by the Oblate priests, our most fervent desire is to assure ourselves forever of their leadership; we are well resolved not to neglect any means to achieve this end."[15] Given their close ties and past collaboration, the Oblates naturally turned to the Sisters of Charity of Ottawa to work with them in Plattsburgh.

Bishop Guigues secured in his role as Oblate provincial the permission of Bishop McCloskey for the Grey Nuns to establish a boarding school in Plattsburgh. He also presided over the General Council (the governing apparatus) of the sisters that named the eight nuns who would serve in Plattsburgh. In September 1860, Rev. André Garin of Plattsburgh arrived in Ottawa with McCloskey's letter in hand to meet the sisters who would serve his parish community. Mother Bruyère gave him some items for the bazaar that would be organized to assist the sisters financially. At Garin's request, two sisters departed Ottawa in mid-October to prepare the newly built convent, and about fifteen women from the parish assisted them with sewing. By their various efforts, the religious and laywomen proved instrumental in helping establish French-Canadian institutions in Plattsburgh. Anticipating the arrival of the Grey Nuns, the parish women had organized a bazaar in December 1859 to raise money for a convent school to educate girls. When Plattsburgh's French-speaking population organized a celebration of Saint-Jean-Baptiste Day in June 1860 to honor the patron saint of French Canadians, they noted in their newspaper advertisement that "the Canadian Ladies," or parish women, would prepare the dinner and that the proceeds from the event would benefit the new convent being built for the Grey Nuns.[16]

In November 1860, using the train tickets Garin had provided, Mother Bruyère escorted six more nuns to Plattsburgh. After the benediction of the convent, the sisters entertained large numbers of visitors. French-Canadian, Irish, and Protestant women paid homage to Bruyère and the eight founding sisters. The nuns were particularly struck, as were the Oblates, by the numerous Irish visitors, noting in their convent's chronicle, which was written entirely in French, "it is a mark of the affection that a large number of Irish men and women are showing us."[17]

The sisters had much work yet to do. Prior to their arrival, Catholic children of Plattsburgh "only had Protestant schools to attend," they noted.[18] The sisters went house-to-house to recruit students to the parochial school of St. Pierre and to their boarding school for girls. Provided directions by one of the priests, Mother Bruyère and Sr. Eléonore Lavoie (the founding superior of D'Youville Convent), headed one way, while Sr. Amelia Robillard and Mary Dufresne (the housekeeper at the Oblate rectory) proceeded in another.[19]

Meanwhile, sisters with Irish and Anglo family names recruited Irish children in other areas of Plattsburgh and its vicinity. Sr. Marie de la Conception (née Rachel Curran) and Sr. d'Youville (née Emelia Walling) recruited students among the Irish parishioners of Rev. Richard Moloney. An Oblate priest from Ireland, Moloney resided at the rectory of St. Pierre Church with the other Oblates of Plattsburgh, Rev. André Garin and Rev. Claude Sallaz, the latter two originally from France. Just a few months before the arrival of the Grey Nuns, Moloney had become pastor of the church at which the French Canadians and the Irish had previously worshiped together. It became reincorporated in 1863 as St.

John the Baptist Church. The sisters recorded that they established "a current of fine kinship" with the Irish church based on a shared faith tradition and a devotion to the Roman Catholic Church.[20]

The sisters also received assistance from important Irish benefactors, Elizabeth and Bernard McKeever. Both born in Ireland, the McKeevers were a pious couple of means.[21] They brought the Grey Nuns in a stagecoach pulled by two horses to the Irish Settlement located a few miles from the village of Plattsburgh so that the sisters could recruit students for the parish and boarding schools. For McKeever, religion trumped ethnicity. He told the Grey Nuns: "Your presence here," recorded the sisters in French, "will be like in Plattsburg, the best form of propaganda in favor of Catholic instruction." The nuns the McKeevers assisted apparently were a force to be reckoned with. The chronicler of the convent noted in November 1860, "My Sister Marie de la Conception exerts all her strength to persuade parents to place their children in the convent [school] and several touch her hand as a sign of promise." Thus, the Grey Nuns recruited "among the faithful from the two languages" for their two schools.[22]

When St. Pierre parish school opened under the Grey Nuns in mid-November 1860, there were about 100 students, 20 of whom were anglophone, the sisters recorded. While the large majority of students were French-Canadian, Irish pupils made up a sizeable minority. The academy the sisters began in their convent initially enrolled fifteen girls as day students, and a few boarding students joined them after it opened. Some of their initial teaching supplies came from Bruyère, who sent religious books for their library, and from Garin, who procured textbooks and two globes during a trip to Montréal.[23]

Besides teaching, the Sisters of Charity stationed in Plattsburgh were also expected by their foundress to engage in charitable works. As the Grey Nuns wrote in their own historic account, "Mother Bruyère considered that the Grey Nun teacher should remain, wherever she goes, a sister of charity, and that besides children to teach, there will be some poor and some sick to visit in Plattsburgh as in Ottawa and in Buffalo." Indeed, from their arrival in Plattsburgh, the Sisters of Charity of Ottawa visited the poor and sick at their homes, for there was no hospital in the village.[24] Sisters [Rose?] Leblanc and Amelia Robillard began their visits during the first week of November 1860, and the order made fourteen visits to the sick during their first two months in Plattsburgh. For the remainder of the 1860s, the Grey Nuns visited each year anywhere from

59 to 134 different members of the community at their homes, treating them for a wide variety of conditions, such as fever, burns, flu, asthma, ulcers, broken bones, and inflammation, among others. These figures underrepresent the amount of work undertaken by the sisters, because they actually made multiple visits to the sick; for example, they point out in their register, "The sick are regularly visited daily until the figure for healing or death indicates the end." While the large majority of the people in their care had French surnames, their register reflects that some had Irish, Jewish, and Anglo-American family names.[25]

The Grey Nuns recorded in their chronicle during their first month in Plattsburgh that many different members of the community in turn assisted them. The sisters noted that Plattsburgh's French-Canadian population was poor, but its members demonstrated goodwill and proved helpful in different ways. French-Canadian women would wash floors and do laundry for the nuns, boys would cut wood and bring them water, and the men would also assist according to their means. Irish men and women from the village of Plattsburgh and from the Irish Settlement brought the sisters various provisions. As plans for a bazaar became publicized, people with French, Irish, and American surnames stopped by the convent to donate articles.[26]

Among their many skills, the Grey Nuns of the Cross were fundraisers. Dowries from the families of young women entering the order constituted one means by which they generated money. When the Sisters of Charity of Ottawa needed to repay a loan from the Sisters of Charity of Montréal, Mother Bruyère wrote the superior of Montréal that she could not do so in 1861. But Bruyère indicated that she would meet the order's obligation the following year, if the father of one of their novices came through with the dowry he had pledged. "Sister [Agnès McMillan] will enter the novitiate next year; I promise you her dowry, should she persevere," Bruyère wrote, continuing, "If he [Mr. McMillan] makes me a payment as I hope, you will have it at once." Bruyère thus promised her counterpart the dowry of a woman who later served at the Plattsburgh convent.[27]

Throughout their first decade in Plattsburgh, the Sisters of Charity relied heavily upon the assistance of community members, but they were not passive—they were active in soliciting the funds or provisions they needed. Their chronicle indicates that they particularly worked the countryside. In December 1861, for example, the superior and another sister visited farmers in the Irish Settlement, stayed overnight at the home of a

Mr. Fitzpatrick, and continued their collections the next day. In February 1864, the sisters visited farmers for provisions to help them get through the winter, recording that "the good farmers of this place, especially the Irish," were generous with them. The Grey Nuns also collected for the poor from the village of Plattsburgh. In January 1862, Sr. Robillard and a Mrs. Miron collected $8 in funds as well as unnamed provisions for the destitute.[28]

The sisters and many of the children they served lacked financial resources. Mother Bruyère sent Rev. Sallaz a letter informing him that the mother house in Ottawa had to provide the sisters in Plattsburgh their shoes, religious garments, and other clothing, since they lacked the means to acquire them on their own. She also indicated to Sallaz that the sisters could not accept all the poor children of the parish because they lacked a suitable building. The sisters had been teaching 100 to 120 parish children yearly at their convent.[29]

The families of the girls who attended the private academy of the Grey Nuns (see fig. 1.2) paid tuition for them to receive their education in D'Youville Convent's day and boarding programs. Bruyère expressed

Figure 1.2. D'Youville Academy, administered by the Sisters of Charity of Ottawa, or Grey Nuns of the Cross, early 1900s. In the background are St. Peter's Church and rectory (left) and St. Peter's Academy (right). Courtesy of Archives des Soeurs de la Charité d'Ottawa, accession P-M5/4.

her belief that the sisters could only attract students of well-to-do families by providing separate locales for their education: "If we wish to have the children of the rich, we need to separate them entirely from the poor. To receive a larger number of the latter it would be necessary to place them in the interior of the convent and consequently to resign ourselves to see them move away from all the others, that is to say, those [girls] who support the house." To this end, Bruyère proposed to Sallaz that the sisters rent the convent for their academy for girls and that they work together to find another convenient location to educate the parish children.[30]

To benefit their academy, the sisters organized musical and dramatic productions put on by their students. General admission to the program in June 1867, for example, cost 35 cents, but 50 cents if one wanted reserved seats. The sisters also offered private music lessons to raise money. When the sisters arrived in Plattsburgh in November 1860, two Anglo-American women visited them to discuss their teaching methods in music and contemplated sending their children for lessons.[31] The nuns were willing to serve a clientele from different ethnolinguistic backgrounds as they raised the money needed to support themselves in Plattsburgh's French-Canadian parish.

Mother Bruyère shared some interesting observations about the French-Canadian population the Grey Nuns encountered in Plattsburgh. Many had become acculturated in US society to the extent that they lacked knowledge of Catholic traditions and had lost their French language. Bruyère wrote of Plattsburgh's residents: "These poor people are quite uneducated, particularly the children who do not even know for the most part how to make the sign of the cross." Bruyère also noted: "The majority of the [French] Canadians have forgotten their mother tongue; they do not know how to speak without using English."[32] This loss of native language may seem surprising, given the proximity of Plattsburgh to Canada East (formerly Lower Canada, later Québec province) and to its largest city, Montréal, but the wave of *Patriote* immigrants had already had a generation to acculturate before the arrival of the Grey Nuns and before the mass migration of economic immigrants who followed.

Proximity to Canada East undoubtedly encouraged forms of cultural persistence, such as celebrations of Saint-Jean-Baptiste Day. The earliest-known celebration in Plattsburgh took place on Sunday, June 24, 1860, when French speakers organized a high mass at St. Pierre Church and a clergyman from Montréal preached. Afterward, the parishioners paraded with representations of St. John, the French explorer Jacques Cartier, a young Indian, and an Iroquois chief, the latter likely denoting the Native leader against whom Samuel de Champlain had fought in upstate New York in 1609. Plattsburgh's French-Canadian population also planned speeches and to sing national songs at the event to which "our friends from Canada are cordially invited," they stated in their newspaper ad.[33]

The francophone population organized similar celebrations over the next few years on or around June 24, the feast day of St. John the Baptist, but by 1864 they moved the date of the festivities to July 4, Independence Day. This shift in date signified a measure of acculturation, representing a blending of traditions from the sending and the receiving societies, as Plattsburgh's French-Canadian population chose to celebrate its ethnic holiday along with the independence of its adopted country. On the Fourth of July 1864, French speakers celebrated both holidays with a mass at St. Pierre Church, a picnic, music and French songs, and speeches in French and English. A Mr. Boucher spoke in French about "their moral duty, to God and man but their obligations to their adopted country, America," noted the *Plattsburgh Republican*. Many from Canada participated in the festivities, the newspaper revealed, with the Grey Nuns recording, "the streets are filled with Montréalers." The activities raised over $300 to benefit the building of the church, which was not yet complete.[34]

In 1865, the Saint-Jean-Baptiste celebration also took place on the American holiday, July Fourth. The trustees of St. Pierre Church recorded in their minutes their decision to celebrate "the St. John the Baptist national holiday of French Canadians, July 4, only as American citizens and subjects of the Government of Washington." By this statement, they indicated their desire to retain their ethnic traditions while simultaneously embracing those of their adopted country. The *Republican* commended its French-Canadian population, beginning its reporting of the event with the statement, "Our Nati[o]nal Anniversary was celebrated in an appropriate manner by our citizens of French extraction." The St. Pierre band led the procession from downtown to the church; a dinner followed mass, with speeches given in English by dignitaries and in French by the Oblate priests and other unnamed guests. As usual, parish women supplied the refreshments. Near the end of its column, the *Republican* commented: "The greatest decorum, harmony and peace was observed through the day."[35]

Plattsburgh's celebrations of Saint-Jean-Baptiste Day on the Fourth of July in the 1860s preceded a similar conjoining of holidays in French-

Canadian communities of New England by nearly a quarter century. The historian Yves Roby has noted that the practice was not common prior to the 1890s. It was only in 1899, for example, that French-Canadian descendants of Southbridge, Massachusetts, first celebrated the feast day of their patron saint on July 4.[36]

When Plattsburgh's French-Canadian population planned its Saint-Jean-Baptiste celebration on Independence Day in 1867, the *Plattsburgh Sentinel* chided readers with the news that "our Canadian friends" appeared to be the only ones from the village planning a proper celebration of the Fourth of July.[37] The newspaper recognized implicitly that Plattsburgh's French-Canadian population was demonstrating its acculturation and patriotism in the host society.

Another celebration highlights interethnic connections in Plattsburgh. Shortly after their arrival, the Grey Nuns forged important ties to the village's Irish parish. Evidence of that, the nuns point out in their own historic account, can be found in their celebration together of St. Patrick's Day on March 17, 1861. On that day, the sisters escorted their students to Rev. Moloney's church, where they found that Bernard and Elizabeth McKeever had reserved pews for them and their younger pupils. The older students helped with the music by singing two pieces, and Rev. Garin sang a high mass, assisted by Rev. Sallaz and Rev. Moloney, who were Oblate priests from Plattsburgh's two Catholic churches. When the sisters returned to the convent, they discovered that Moloney had sent candy for the children. They commented in their historical account: "This exchange of courtesy and religious fraternity will repeat itself from year to year"—and their chronicles attest to that. In 1865, the sisters brought their boarding students to celebrate high mass on St. Patrick's Day at St. John Church, and they were met at the door by Bernard McKeever who ushered them to the front pews. In 1868, the sisters escorted nearly 500 day students to the 8:00 a.m. mass at St. John's to celebrate St. Patrick's Day, where they sang hymns in English. Moloney addressed the children in English and French, and they were given candy after mass. On St. Patrick's Day 1869, when the sisters again brought their students to the 8:00 a.m. mass at St. John's Church, their pupils carried the banner of Ireland. Rev. Moloney again addressed the students in French and English, and they found candy awaiting them when they returned to their classes.[38]

Ethnic isolation, then, did not characterize the development of Plattsburgh's French-Canadian parish, as it did in some northeastern industrial communities, such as St. Pierre parish of Lewiston, Maine, in its formative years.³⁹ This ethnic intermixing in Plattsburgh can be attributed in large part to the orders of women and men religious who served in the village. Both the Oblate priests and the Grey Nuns had Irish members, and both orders helped facilitate the mingling of Irish and French-Canadian Catholics in the community.

The schools administered by the Grey Nuns also demonstrated intermixing, particularly of Canadian and US customs. In late December 1860, the sisters had their boarding students write New Year's letters to their parents, commenting in their chronicle, "It is not common practice in the States, but they are happy to conform to this reverent custom of Canada." By 1863, the sisters had to adjust the school calendar for the day and boarding students to allow for a vacation from Christmas through New Year's Day, as was customary in the United States. In previous years, the women religious had tried to continue classes during the holiday season "so as to conform to the practices of the Mother house; but since the majority of the children left classes, we were obliged to conform to the practice of the States by giving the children several days of relaxation." Celebrating Christmas with a midnight mass was a cherished French-Canadian tradition. Sometimes the boarding students chose to delay the visit to their families so they could participate in midnight mass on Christmas Eve.⁴⁰

In some years, the Oblate priests said midnight mass at the chapel of the sisters, but in other years, they chose not to do so. The chronicler of the convent wrote one terse line on Christmas Day, 1867: "We did not have the good fortune to have midnight mass at the convent." In 1869, Rev. Charles Bournigalle surprised the sisters by offering midnight mass at their chapel on Christmas Eve, despite being ill and despite the fact that the Oblates had refused this privilege for a number of years for unspecified reasons.⁴¹

Sometimes priests withheld sacraments from sisters in order to discipline them, reveals the historian Margaret Susan Thompson, who also argues that patriarchy defined the relationships between priests and nuns during the nineteenth century. The refusal of the Oblates to say midnight mass for the Grey Nuns in Plattsburgh on Christmas Eve appears to have been an assertion of patriarchal authority by the men religious; perhaps the refusal centered on some unresolved dispute with the sisters. The treatment of the Grey Nuns by the Oblates came into question not long after the sisters arrived in Plattsburgh. In 1862, Mother Bruyère wrote Bishop Guigues to complain that Rev. Édouard Chevalier mistreated the sisters by his conduct to the point that the order might have to consider leaving Plattsburgh, and she asked that Guigues intervene on their behalf.[42] As we will see, during their more than six decades of service to St. Pierre parish, the Grey Nuns periodically found themselves in conflict with the Oblate priests as each group tried to carry out its Catholic ministry.

The sisters, of course, practiced Catholic traditions at their convent school. The Grey Nuns admitted Protestant students to their boarding school, and those students participated equally in Catholic observances. In February 1864, both Catholic and Protestant boarding students celebrated the Feast of the Purification, where they paraded a statue of the Virgin Mary through each room of the convent, offering a prayer to Mary at each stop. The following month, there was a similar procession through all the rooms of the convent school in honor of Mary and Joseph in which Protestant students also took part. The sisters subsequently recorded in their chronicle that the Protestant students showed no signs of religious prejudice, commenting: "Among them there is not any fanaticism; in the devotional exercises, they conform well to our customs for the ceremonies of outside worship." Never did the Protestant girls say or do anything in front of the sisters that could be interpreted as disrespecting "our holy religion," the sisters recorded.[43]

The lack of anti-Catholic sentiment noted by the sisters in their convent school in the 1860s might be attributed in part to the demographic composition of Plattsburgh. In 1860, the village's population numbered 3,648, and by the mid-1860s, Catholic church membership far exceeded that of individual Protestant denominations. According to the *Plattsburgh Sentinel*, in June 1866, Plattsburgh's four largest Protestant churches together had nearly 600 congregants, whereas St. John's Catholic Church had 1,000 and St. Pierre Catholic Church had 1,800, while the Plattsburgh Jewish congregation had a mere 30 members.[44] Catholics in Plattsburgh therefore far outnumbered Protestants and Jews.

Exhibiting numerical superiority, Plattsburgh's French-Canadian churchgoers became a social force in the community. Men of St. Pierre parish formed an association called the Canadian Union in April 1866. All members of the association were Catholic, a requirement to join the society.[45] Although the society lasted only about six years, its brief history sheds considerable light on Plattsburgh's French-Canadian population, demonstrating such themes as its integration into US society, the rise of a political class, and divisions within the ethnic community.

By the end of 1866, the Canadian Union consisted of 180 "mostly young men" and, like the parish institutions, organized a festival and oyster supper to raise money to furnish the hall they planned to rent. The English-language press kept a cautious eye on the organization. In February 1867, the *Plattsburgh Republican*, which favored the Democratic Party despite its name, reported that the Canadian Union was not a political organization but a mutual-benefit society, "so we are informed." Ethnic mutual-benefit societies functioned as early forms of insurance companies. When the Canadian Union celebrated its first anniversary in a hall decorated with evergreens and American flags, both the *Plattsburgh Republican* and the *Plattsburgh Sentinel*, the latter Republican in its politics, commented on the event. The *Republican* stated that "we hear" the society has grown to 275 members and has $600 in the bank. The *Sentinel* commented that the anniversary celebration began and ended with a prayer, calling attention to its status as a confessional association. It also noted that Joseph Delorme, an honorary member of the society, spoke of the benefits its members receive, and that Francis Good of the nearby community of Schuyler Falls spoke on "the Progress of the Canadian Nationality in the land of their adoption." These topics imply that, in their own ways, Delorme and Good each addressed the issue of ethnic solidarity in the Canadian Union to benefit French-speaking members in the United States. It is clear that this was a French-Canadian society because the *Sentinel* closed its report in French with a few words, albeit unaccented and misspelled, for the benefit of the association's members: "Nos amis Canadiens voudront bien nous pardonner si nous n'avons pu reproduire au long les discours qu ils ont ecoute avec tant d'attention. Notre connaissance de la langue Francaise nous limite a ne donner que le sujet de chaqe discours" ("Our [French-] Canadian friends will well [meaning, *please*] excuse us if we have not reproduced at length the speeches they listened to with such attention. Our understanding of the French language limits us to giving only the subject of each address").[46]

The growing numerical and financial strength of the Canadian Union attracted the continued attention of the English-language press throughout 1867. By November, the society had 350 members and $950 in its treasury, reported the *Sentinel*. The following month, it stated that the Union had assets of $1,000 and commented particularly on how the group was shaping the citizenship skills of its members: "Its influence is most beneficial upon its members, instructing them in rules of order and propriety, and making them a most useful class of citizens." For its part, the *Republican* had articles on the oyster supper and ice cream social the Canadian Union held at its hall to raise money for the "poor and needy" in the society. The *Sentinel* reported that the festival drew a large crowd and that "every one, whether Canadian or American, seemed to enjoy themselves largely."[47] Festivals and other public celebrations organized by French-Canadian descendants in Plattsburgh appeared to be the principal means by which many native-born Americans came to know them.

When the Canadian Union celebrated its second anniversary in April 1868, T. H. N. Lambert of New York, who planned to publish the newspaper *L'Union Canadienne* at St. Albans, Vermont, wrote both the *Sentinel* and the *Republican*. Lambert informed the readers of these newspapers that the Canadian Union had its own band with 14 musicians, led by Edward Mayo, and that its membership stood at 400 persons and its assets at $1,365. Lambert emphasized that the society "strives to be a successful national, as well as social and benevolent association." By a "national" association, Lambert meant an ethnic society. Thus, the Canadian Union served to advance the interests of Plattsburgh's French-Canadian population while providing aid in times of illness and death. Lambert went on to describe Edward Erno, who had been elected president of the society in November 1866, as "the real soul and right hand of the Union, and on whom, [*sic*] our American friends have helped us to confer the most envied positions in this village."[48] Lambert therefore intimated that the Canadian Union was cultivating a leadership class among the French-Canadian descendants of Plattsburgh.

Lambert also summarized some of the speeches made at the second anniversary celebration, possibly because Anglo-American reporters could not translate the proceedings well enough into English. Lambert noted that Joseph Delorme explained to young women in attendance the significance of the motto "L'Union fait la force" ("Strength through Unity"), namely that the association provided benefits for widows and orphans. A Mr. LaBonne of Schuyler Falls, described as a "staunch Canadian and an admirer of republican institutions," set about "cursing 'Old John Bull' and wishing to see Canada a free, prosperous and respected State amongst the United States of America." The idea of annexing Canada to the United States had gained currency among some Canadians and Americans. Franco-Americans who supported the concept hoped to connect French Canadians under one nation—not by depopulating Québec through mass migration to the United States, nor by repatriation to Québec or other parts of Canada, but by Canada's annexation to the United States.[49]

Interestingly enough, none of the speeches made reference to Canadian Confederation. Thus, the celebration functioned as a forum for French-Canadian descendants to contemplate geopolitical issues affecting their homeland as well as their existence in the receiving society.

In the host society, the Canadian Union showed elements of acculturation. It became incorporated in the State of New York in July 1869 so that it could conduct business just like other bodies that received incorporation certificates from the Secretary of State.[50] While adopting some of the customs of the receiving society, the association retained its French Catholic traditions.

This was evident in the celebration of funerals. When members of French-Canadian associations like the Canadian Union died, the surviving members would attend the funeral as a group wearing their regalia. After Charles Charron Jr. died at age 24 in June 1867, the *Sentinel* reported that 200 members of the Canadian Union gathered to form a procession led by Mayo's Band.[51]

But in 1869 they could not enter St. Pierre Church as a body to attend funerals, they complained in the press. This exacerbated a conflict between the Canadian Union and the Oblate priests who had charge of St. Pierre Church; it also led to an internal division within the association. Historical notes compiled by an Oblate priest in 1953 indicate that the Canadian Union had come into conflict with Rev. Sallaz, who served as the secretary of the church trustees, and that the Union had written the Oblate Provincial seeking Sallaz's transfer in December 1868. Following the prohibition on entering St. Pierre as a group, the notes further reveal, the Canadian Union sought revenge by interfering with the work of the trustees and of the parish and even dragged Sallaz into a civil suit filed in Schenectady, New York, in August 1869.[52] By Easter Monday 1870, Rev. Charles Bournigalle, the Oblate superior, had secured the bishop's condemnation of the Canadian Union "because of its liberalism and its lack of submission to ecclesiastical authority."[53]

William LaMoy and Edward Erno were elected president and vice president, respectively, of the Canadian Union in May 1870. Along with Joseph Mignault, they formed a committee that traveled to Albany, about 150 miles south of Plattsburgh, to discuss the prohibition for several hours with the vicar general of the diocese, Rev. Edgar Wadhams. They asked Wadhams to send a priest to mediate the dispute between the Canadian Union and the Oblates. The vicar general told the men he would either visit Plattsburgh during a planned trip to Ogdensburg or write Bournigalle.

Wadhams assured the men, they shared in a letter to the editor, "that he could not see what was the trouble, as all societies were admitted in church, except Free Masons." Bournigalle was a native of France, as were most of the Oblates serving St. Peter's parish in the late 1800s (see Table 1 in the Appendix). It was not uncommon for clergy from France to clash with French-Canadian immigrants in the United States.[54] Typically these clashes centered on French clergy pushing acculturation or assimilation in the host society at a more rapid pace than their parishioners wanted, but that does not appear to have been the case in Plattsburgh.

As the conflict within Plattsburgh's French-speaking community became public, so did its separate plans to celebrate the Fourth of July in 1870. The *Sentinel* publicized the Canadian Union's plans on June 24, the feast day of St. John the Baptist, adding: "We are happy to say they announce no intoxicating beverages will be allowed upon the grounds! As an ample police force will be provided, we assume that this will apply to spirits brought on the ground[s] after having been imbibed in some other quarter!" The *Sentinel* reported that the Canadian Union organized a parade featuring a band and 100 youth carrying banners; a local attorney read aloud the Declaration of Independence; and LaMoy, Erno, Mignault, and other members of the association made short speeches. In addition, the Union hosted a dinner at the town hall, provided ice cream as refreshment outside of its meeting place, and put on a fireworks display in the evening. While the *Sentinel* indicated that the fireworks were disappointing, it commented that the other activities of the Canadian Union went off well "and reflect credit upon the patriotism, independence, enterprise and perseverance of the organization."[55] Thus, the Anglo-American press of Plattsburgh praised the devotion that some of its French-Canadian population exhibited on the US national holiday.

The St. Joseph Society organized a separate celebration with a religious component. The society had been founded by the Oblate priests of St. Pierre parish in 1863 as a charitable organization of men to aid the sick. In 1870, members of the St. Joseph Society traveled with Bournigalle to Burlington, Vermont, on June 24 to celebrate the feast day of Saint-Jean-Baptiste; in Plattsburgh, however, the society and most French Canadians of the village again conjoined this celebration with the Independence Day of their adopted country, noted the Grey Nuns. Among the organized events was a high mass at St. Pierre Church and a procession to the train station to meet arrivals from Montréal. Railroads reduced their rates for the day, allowing French Canadians from Montréal and other communities to participate in the festivities, which included a parade of 2,000 individuals that ended at St. Pierre Church. The Grey Nuns noted in their chronicle that Americans holding prominent positions joined the parade, while other Americans watched the procession from streetcorners, their homes, and their shops. The sisters also noted that the women of the parish had worked for eight days in a large room the nuns made available to them, preparing the thousands of meat dishes and pastries served during the picnic that took place behind the church.[56]

The afternoon speeches and evening program reflected US and Canadian themes. Joseph Royall, an attorney and the editor of the Montréal newspaper, *Nouveau Monde*, spoke of the roles of Canadians in the United States and in North America, and "he mentioned [Marquis de] Lafayette and others as heroes of the Independence," reported the *Plattsburgh Sentinel*. Editors of other French-language newspapers, such as *La Minerve* of Montréal and *Le Protecteur Canadien* of St. Albans, Vermont, also spoke during the picnic. Evening entertainment at Palmer's Hall included musical and dramatic productions, with Burlington's six-year-old St. John the Baptist representative garnering three cheers after singing "Vive la Canadienne." This was the national song of Québec before the French version of "O Canada" replaced it in popularity. L. O. David, a Canadian attorney and journalist, "reviewed the lives of [Louis-Joseph] Papineau, [Louis-Hippolyte] Lafontaine, [Augustin-Norbert] Morin and other great men of Canada, and was applauded," reported the *Plattsburgh Republican*. Papineau, La Fontaine, and Morin were *Patriotes* of the 1837–1838 Rebellion in Lower Canada. The evening program ended at midnight with the band playing "Vive la Canadienne" and "Yankee Doodle," reflecting musical selections of French Canada and the United States, a fitting end for the blended celebration of Saint-Jean-Baptiste Day and Independence Day.[57]

The nature of the St. Joseph Society's combined holiday celebrations in Plattsburgh in 1870 was reproduced in French-Canadian population centers of New England in the 1890s. Yves Roby has pointed out, for example, that the activities for Saint-Jean-Baptiste Day and Independence Day were virtually the same: "In the Little Canadas, the Fourth-of-July festivities commenced with celebrating High Mass, to be followed by a parade of allegorical floats commemorating the milestones of the French fact in America; finally, the day ended with a picnic and a banquet."[58] In Plattsburgh in 1870, the separate celebrations organized by the Canadian Union and St. Joseph Society marked significant division among the community's French speakers.

Over the next year, the Canadian Union's internal divisions revealed additional fractures within Plattsburgh's French-Canadian community. The Canadian Union sued Edward Erno, William LaMoy, and others in the Circuit Court in Plattsburgh to recover personal property, or its value of $400, plus court costs, and the plaintiffs won. As the *Sentinel* revealed in late March, by publishing a letter to the editor signed "A Member of the Canadian Union," a group had separated from the Union and had taken money and property despite "the remonstrances of a large portion of the said Society." The writer continued: "And they commenced removing the furniture with the intent of delivering the same to the proposed rival Society, and made an order to withdraw the money from the bank." The lawsuit resulted as "regular members of the Union" sought to retrieve the funds and property taken from the society.[59]

The Canadian Union member wrote this letter to the *Sentinel* to challenge as untrue a report he had read that the Union had merged with the St. Joseph Society to form a new organization called the St. John Baptist Association. P. Girard, the recording secretary of the Association of St. John Baptist, indicated in a letter to the editor that the merger had begun the previous summer, 1870, but had been delayed on account of the lawsuit filed among some members. Girard pointed out that the fusion of the societies had been controversial, and he expressed his hope that those who opposed it might ultimately join the new organization. The merger took place "for the purpose of uniting the Franco-Americans for the betterment of moral, spiritual and intellectual welfare," noted the St. Pierre parish yearbook of 1931–1932. This undoubtedly was an important goal of the Oblate priests serving the parish. Rev. Bournigalle demonstrated his support of the merger of the St. Joseph society with the Canadian Union by meeting with and addressing the newly formed association and its elected officers.[60]

The writer challenging the report of the merger argued that expelled members of the Union were the ones who joined the St. John Baptist Association and that the Canadian Union still existed in 1871. But the association did not survive. The Canadian Union appears to have lasted only one more year, making its final public appearance during Plattsburgh's Fourth of July celebration in 1872.[61]

The conflict between the Canadian Union and the St. Joseph Society in Plattsburgh mirrors to some extent a similar conflict that took place in Montréal during the same period between the *Institut canadien* and Roman Catholic clergy. The *Institut canadien* was a cultural organization that established a library and reading room as well as an educational program to discuss and debate political and economic ideas from Europe and North America. The institute's liberal ideas, such as the separation of church and state, clashed with those of conservative clergy. As the Roman Catholic Church of Québec grew in power and prestige in the nineteenth century, especially after Confederation in 1867, it worked against modern, liberal ideas, particularly under Ignace Bourget, the bishop of Montréal from 1840 to 1876. Similar to what happened in Plattsburgh, Bourget fought against the institute in part by founding another society to compete against it, and conservative clergy ultimately emerged victorious in their struggle to destroy the *Institut canadien*.[62]

Those who sought to dissolve the Canadian Union, a member alleged, were "men who seek self aggrandizement and high political and religious position in the Canadian circle of our town, and would thereby destroy the happiness of widows, orphans, and sick brethren, for the sake of their own private aspirations." These were "men who style themselves the leaders of the Canadian population of this town to use them either for political or religious purposes." These comments published in the press point to a potential political division among naturalized citizens of French-Canadian descent in Plattsburgh. An ad announcing a "Grand Inauguration Meeting" of the "French Canadian Grant and Colfax Club" in September 1868 indicated that "several able French Speakers from abroad will address the meeting," and that the club's leaders were William LaMoy, president, and P. Girard, secretary. Three years later, in October 1871, the group refashioned itself as the "French Canadian Union Republican Club" with William LaMoy as president and P. Girard as secretary.[63] Differences centered on clerical influence over the organization and partisan politics appear, therefore, to have been the fault lines leading to the demise of the Canadian Union.

As French-Canadian immigrants in the northeastern United States became naturalized citizens and voters, they typically joined the political party that offered them the influence they desired. Or they made their selection based upon whether the native-born Yankees in the Republican Party or the Irish in the Democratic Party posed the lesser threat to their interests.[64] If the experience of the Canadian Union's former leaders is any indication, in the post–Civil War era, Plattsburgh's French-Canadian movers and shakers viewed the Republican Party as the medium to represent their interests in the host society.

The French-Canadian Union Republican Club adopted at its October 1871 meeting a number of resolutions consistent with other New York

State Republicans. They accepted, for example, the resolutions of the state Republican convention as an expression of their own sentiments. They chose not to support Democratic Republicans or Tammany Democrats. Moreover, to advance the interests of their ethnic group in the host society, they adopted a resolution recommending that unnaturalized French Canadians declare their intention to become US citizens and, for those who had done so, to take out citizenship papers at least ten days before elections.[65]

In summary, the rise and fall of the Canadian Union organization in Plattsburgh reflects the growing strength of the French-Canadian community in the mid-nineteenth century. It also reflects elements of its ethnic retention as it became more integrated into US society. That integration occasionally precipitated conflicts within the French-speaking community, especially as some of its members sought to exercise leadership roles and to engage in the political process.

The growing social and political strength of Plattsburgh's French-Canadian population led to a unique arrangement with the village's board of education, which first formed in 1867. But it also reflected the significant financial challenges of the parish school. An elderly nun wrote of the school's early years that it often lacked firewood in winter. "On such occasions I went to my class and requested the first boy who came in to announce to the others we would have no school because we had no wood. Immediately there was a rush home and soon the principal ones were back carrying wood on sleds," she stated. "Fire was made and school began and ended as usual—only the boys taking precautions that there was wood for [the] next day." In May 1867, the trustees of St. Pierre Church worried about how to meet the financial obligations of the parish. They decided to organize a July Fourth picnic to raise money to pay the salaries of the nuns teaching in the parish school, and they chose to have special collections beginning in August to make payment on the mortgage held by Roswell Weed. The financial situation of the parish was dire enough in 1867 that the Oblates considered closing St. Pierre School. But the Grey Nuns resisted and raised money to keep the school alive by organizing séances, musical and dramatic productions typically performed by their academy students.[66]

In February 1869, the Grey Nuns recorded in their chronicle that they had not received their small salaries from the parish for several years and that the priests could not raise the money to pay them because of "the inability of the Catholics to support" the school financially. Consequently, the Oblate priests placed St. Pierre School under the direction of the local public-school board.[67]

Doing so involved visits and meetings with state and local officials and quiet politicking over a couple years' time. Lucius Robinson, a former state comptroller who later became governor of New York, visited St. Pierre School in autumn 1867 and expressed his belief that it should receive state aid, and he procured a grant for the school. In spring 1868, Rev. Lori Smith, a Protestant minister who served as the state superintendent of schools, visited the sisters and was complimentary of their work. Smith commented that the Grey Nuns attended to children in the Plattsburgh community who would otherwise "be still running to perdition," the sisters recorded. The following year, Smith made an official visit to the parish school, which then had 750 students, to observe the classrooms and the teaching methods of the sisters. In addition to Rev. Sallaz, the organizers of the superintendent's visit included school-board members, such as William Hartwell, the president of the school board from 1867 to 1878, and Smith Weed, an attorney and state representative who eventually served on the board for nearly half a century. The visit's purpose, the sisters noted, was "to obtain for the sisters government wages like in other public schools." During the visit, Smith conducted an examination of the Grey Nuns at their convent and granted eight sisters teaching certificates.[68]

A special committee of the Plattsburgh Board of Education visited St. Pierre School to determine how it might be placed under the board's supervision. The committee reported in a letter to the *Sentinel*, ostensibly to cultivate public support for the move, that the current teachers at the school had certificates issued by the superintendent of schools. But it stated that the Catholic school utilized different textbooks than the ones the board had authorized in the village's other schools, noting in particular that it made use of some French-language books, whereas only English texts were used in the district's schools. Because changing the books would present a financial burden on impoverished families, the committee suggested that the board cover their cost to ensure that all elementary schools engaged the same textbooks. The committee further recommended that Plattsburgh manage the school for one year, rent the parish school building for $150, and pay each teacher $200 per year. The board of education accepted the subcommittee's recommendations.[69]

An informal transfer of St. Pierre School to the village of Plattsburgh took place on February 20, 1869. The unwritten agreement between the

Catholic parish and the public-school board entailed the village paying $150 for rent and fuel for the use of the school building and the state paying at least $1,200 in salaries for six sisters retroactively to September 1868. This sum represented a significant increase for the sisters who, in the years the parish paid them, had each received only $100 annually for teaching at St. Pierre School.[70]

The incorporation of St. Pierre into the district schools did not compromise the religious or ethnic character of the school, referred to as the Cornelia Street Primary in historical sketches. "Nothing is sacrificed of the religious or national interests of the children," noted the Grey Nuns. They continued to give their exams in English and French, but they acknowledged that the transfer to public education would entail a change of textbooks and other forms of "assujettisements" ("subjugation/control"). In fall 1869, the principal of the local public schools visited the classes of the sisters and began changing their textbooks "so that they adopt those of the public schools to keep one system in all of the classes overseen by the government," noted the sisters. This step, plus the certification of the sisters, completed the transfer to public education.[71]

By February 1870, the sisters followed the daily schedule imposed by the public schools, beginning the academic day at 9:00 a.m., stopping at 12:00 p.m., and running afternoon classes from 1:30 to 4:30 p.m. Following this schedule apparently was one of the forms of "assujettisements," for it disrupted their traditional order of exercises and the routine of their boarding program, but Mother Bruyère wrote them a letter telling them to comply, and they did.[72]

The Grey Nuns were well aware of the individuals responsible for effecting the transfer of the parish school to public education. Their records identify them and suggest the important connections the priests and nuns had made in Plattsburgh with Anglo and Irish benefactors. Besides Rev. Sallaz, the individuals responsible included William Hartwell, not only the president of the board of education but also of many civic organizations; Smith Weed, the lawyer and assemblyperson who, although Episcopalian, was "like his father a patron of Catholic institutions"; Moss Platt of the board of education; Everett Baker, the secretary of the board; and Bernard McKeever, the Irish friend of the sisters and "the only Catholic on the Board." When McKeever died in 1885, the Sisters lamented his passing, noting: "In him we lost a devoted friend because being one of the members of the board of education he had always pleaded our cause in the meetings held for the schools."[73] The ties that the St. Pierre trustees, the Oblate priests, and the Grey Nuns had cultivated in the Plattsburgh community, and in particular with the Weed and McKeever families, stood them in good stead at critical junctures as they worked to fashion a Catholic community in the village.

Creating that community in the Canada–US borderlands region was an arduous task. This chapter has highlighted the significant role of lay and religious women in creating parish institutions, facilitated in large part by their fundraising abilities. The Oblate priests oversaw and guided their efforts and sometimes came into conflict with the Grey Nuns and churchgoers, such as Canadian Union members. The Oblates and Grey Nuns each promoted elements of ethnic retention in the parish community while also facilitating its acculturation into US society. The blending of US and Canadian traditions can particularly be seen in the conjoined celebrations of the feast of Saint-Jean-Baptiste and the Fourth of July, and of the St. Patrick's Day observances in the 1860s, as well as the assumption by the local school board of the direction of St. Pierre School in 1869. Unlike in most other northeastern communities with French-Canadian populations, Irish descendants in the Plattsburgh area contributed substantially to the formation of the French Catholic community, especially by supporting the schools of the Grey Nuns. The Irish parish of Plattsburgh had no school of its own; in its support for Catholic education, it demonstrated that religion trumped ethnic sentiment. As we will see, Plattsburgh's Catholic history differs from other northeastern communities in the extent to which the initial cooperation between ethnic groups continued through the late nineteenth and early twentieth centuries.

Chapter Two

Oblate Priests, Grey Nuns, and Ethnic Institutions

Forging a French-Canadian Community, 1870–1900

From the 1870s through the 1890s, as French Canadians of Plattsburgh continued building their ethnic community, conflicts erupted. At times, those conflicts surfaced within St. Pierre parish between the Oblate priests and the Grey Nuns, who were helping parishioners to create a French-Canadian community, or between the priests and the parishioners. At other times, tensions arose from pressures coming from outside of Plattsburgh. Forging a French-Canadian community in rural upstate New York proved to be a difficult, sometimes messy, process.

In April 1871, the Grey Nuns became incorporated in the State of New York. The stated objectives of the Sisterhood of Grey Nuns were "the education of persons, as well those able as those unable to pay, the visiting [of] the poor and the sick, and the dispensing medicines to them, the foundation of an industrial school for girls out of employment, and general missionary and benevolent work." The act thus codified into law the work the Grey Nuns had been doing in Plattsburgh as well as in Buffalo and Ogdensburg, New York. The legislation incorporating the Grey Nuns also allowed them to purchase, mortgage, and convey real estate.[1]

Incorporation, Margaret Susan Thompson has noted, enabled Dominican nuns in Kentucky to enter into contracts in the nineteenth century without priests signing for them. Prior to incorporation, the Grey Nuns in Plattsburgh engaged in real-estate transactions as individuals and a priest also signed. For example, in July 1865, Sisters Julienne Bertrand, Emelia

Walling, and Marie Eléonore Lavoie, along with the Oblate priest Rev. Claude Sallaz, purchased a property on Cornelia Street in Plattsburgh for $1,500. Following the incorporation of the Grey Nuns, each sister transferred the one-fourth share of property she held in her name to the Sisterhood of Grey Nuns, with Bertrand selling her share to the order for $100 in November 1871 and Lavoie and Walling transferring their shares for $1 each in October 1877. The parish school that came under the administration of the Plattsburgh Board of Education sat on this property, for Lavoie's deed made clear that the property she conveyed was the one "upon which the public school is located, and which said school is taught by the members of the Sisterhood of Grey Nuns"; Walling's conveyance contained a similar reference. Sallaz transferred his one-fourth share in the property to the Oblate order in May 1871, following their incorporation in New York State, and they, in turn, sold it to the Grey Nuns for $100 in November of that year.[2]

While incorporation in New York State appears to have obviated the need for the Grey Nuns to have a priest as cosigner, the bishop still retained control over the transactions of the sisters. According to the language of the April 1871 articles of incorporation, if the Grey Nuns sold any real-estate holdings, the proceeds would have to go to the bishop: "In case of sale of all of such property, all moneys contributed or collected for the purposes of this act and invested in said property, shall be paid from the proceeds of the same to the Bishop of the Diocese in which said property is located, to be applied by the Bishop to the purposes of this act."[3] This language suggests the patriarchal influence exercised by Roman Catholic bishops over orders of women religious, and it likely came from the Bishop of Albany, John Conroy, whose headquarters were in the state capital.

Correspondence within the Oblate order in January 1872 adds weight to the impression that the Bishop of Albany pressured the Grey Nuns to make him the beneficiary of their properties in the event that they left the diocese. When the Oblates in Plattsburgh came into conflict with Conroy (described later), the Oblate Provincial expressed his belief that the bishop might also want to force the Grey Nuns out of his diocese. "These good Sisters in forming their corporation," the Provincial commented, "have they not allowed the insertion of an article that leaves to the bishop all of their properties in the case where they withdraw."[4] This was not a question, but an acute observation.

In May 1872, the New York State legislature amended the act incorporating the Grey Nuns. It replaced the sentence directing the proceeds of property conveyances to the bishop with language allowing the Grey Nuns to retain monies acquired from the sale of their properties. It read: "In case of the sale of any or all of such property, the proceeds thereof shall be applied by said corporation, the Sisterhood of Grey Nuns, to the purposes of this act, or be invested in other real estate for the use of said corporation." The sources are silent about what precipitated this change. Given the agency of the Grey Nuns, as described in the last chapter, it is possible they asserted themselves to seek this modification in the law. They may have gained the support of Rev. Edgar Wadhams, who became the first Bishop of Ogdensburg in May 1872. According to the historian Émilien Lamirande, Wadhams proved more sympathetic to the men and women religious in Plattsburgh than the Bishop of Albany.[5]

In April 1871, less than a week after the Grey Nuns, the Oblate priests themselves became incorporated in the State of New York as the "Oblate Missionaries of the Immaculate Conception." They formed this corporate body to pursue "the religious instruction of the people, especially of poor and neglected persons; the formation and direction of parishes; the education of clergymen; the work of missions in the country, cities and villages in this State, and the imparting [of] moral and religious education to poor and orphan children." The legislation incorporating the Oblates also allowed them the authority to sell and convey real estate and to sue or be sued in courts of law.[6] Unlike the initial incorporation of the Grey Nuns, that of the Oblates made no provision for the bishop to receive any proceeds from the sale of their properties.

Prior to incorporation, the Oblate priests purchased and sold property as well as took out mortgages in their own names. Clinton County court records document the transactions of individual clergymen Edward Chevalier, Claude Sallaz, John Bernard, André Garin, and Richard Moloney in the 1850s and 1860s. Following the incorporation of their order, these priests transferred their shares to the Oblate Missionaries of the Immaculate Conception, most doing so in May 1871.[7]

As the leaders of the French-Canadian parish of Plattsburgh, the Oblate priests were at the center of various conflicts, several of which must have also grated John Conroy, the second Bishop of Albany, who served in that role from 1865 to 1877. Relations between the French Oblates and the Irish bishop had strained by the early 1870s to the point that the prelate contemplated having the Oblates leave the diocese and replacing them with secular (diocesan) priests. In February 1872, Rev. Charles Bournigalle informed the superior of the Grey Nuns that the Oblates could not celebrate functions nor administer any sacraments in the parish on order of the Bishop of Albany and that they would not be allowed to continue their ministry. The priests and sisters received no explanation for why the bishop had suspended the faculties of the Oblates, recorded the Grey Nuns. The Irish Oblate pastor of St. John's Church, Richard Moloney, traveled to Albany in mid-February, ostensibly to resolve the situation with the bishop. A few days later, the bishop sent a telegram to the Oblates granting them the authority they once had to administer St. Pierre parish, noted the sisters in their chronicle.[8]

Oblate records provide far more detail on the intricacies of their dispute with the Bishop of Albany. As Florent VandenBerghe, the Oblate Provincial in Canada, explained in a January 1872 letter to Pierre Aubert, the assistant to the Superior General in France, Bournigalle had received notice from the bishop to pay the *cathedratium*, an annual assessment to support the diocese of Albany. None had been solicited for the previous year, but in 1872 the bishop requested $300 for the two parishes administered by the Oblates, St. Pierre and St. John. Bournigalle responded by asking for a delay, given the poverty of Plattsburgh's Catholic population, to which the bishop responded that Bournigalle's report did not conform to that of his predecessor's, and "that since the poverty is so great, the community [Oblate order] had the liberty to withdraw" from St. Pierre parish, VandenBerghe reported. In addition, the bishop proposed replacing Moloney at the Irish church with a diocesan priest. The Oblate Provincial expressed his belief that the bishop was intentionally making things difficult out of a desire to rid his diocese of religious orders like the Oblates and to replace them with diocesan priests. Presumably the bishop could exercise greater control over secular priests who answered only to him rather than those from religious orders who had their own hierarchy and internal rules to follow. VandenBerghe raised the question to his superior of whether this might be an opportune time for the Oblate order to leave Plattsburgh, since he felt the mission had languished for years and the bishop would continue antagonizing the Oblates. If the bishop removed the order from the Irish church, the Provincial stated, it would make the financial situation of the Oblates in Plattsburgh more precarious.[9]

One month later, VandenBerghe wrote Aubert that he had drafted a response to the Bishop of Albany, but that Bournigalle thought it too polite and had modified it, thus exceeding his instructions. Shocked by the tone of the letter, Bishop Conroy interdicted the priests in Plattsburgh. VandenBerghe considered traveling to Albany himself to meet with the bishop, but he chose instead to send Moloney for ethnic reasons: "Rather than going to Albany myself, I sent Father Moloney, knowing that matters sort themselves better between the Irish." Moloney was not well received initially, VandenBerghe reported, but he made some felicitous remarks to the bishop, and the latter restored the authority of the Oblates to perform their religious duties. In the meantime, the Provincial Council met for two days in February 1872 and concluded it would be best for the Oblate order to leave Plattsburgh, but news of the formation of the diocese of Ogdensburg changed the situation, and the Oblates decided not to withdraw from the village.[10]

Besides the Bishop of Albany, the Oblates also managed to run afoul of some in the parish community. As detailed in the last chapter, they came into conflict with members of the Canadian Union when they refused to allow them to enter the church as a group to attend the funeral masses of departed members. While that controversy spilled into the public domain, parishioners also pushed back in more subtle ways. In 1871, the Oblates complained that youth were tossing buttons into the collection baskets, girls who belonged to the religious society of *les Enfants de Marie* (Children of Mary) were going to dances, and over 10 percent of the parishioners of St. Pierre did not observe Easter services. From the pulpit, Bournigalle lamented that there were 110 children old enough to receive the sacrament of Communion who had not, 18 couples who were wed by a minister rather than a Roman Catholic priest, 12 women who were living apart from their husbands, 22 families who were apostate and not practicing their faith, and 9 couples living in public concubinages. Taken together, these examples suggest that the French-Canadian population of Plattsburgh was not clergy-dominated, a criticism often made of French-Canadian immigrants in the United States, particularly from the late nineteenth to the early twentieth centuries.[11]

The Oblates also came into conflict with the Grey Nuns over their salaries. After the village of Plattsburgh agreed to support financially the parish school of St. Pierre, and the state of New York agreed to pay the salaries of the sisters who taught there, the Oblate pastor arranged to pay each nun only $100 annually and to keep the difference. He tried to justify his actions by pointing out that the Oblates had given the Grey Nuns their convent and the land they used. As the Oblate Provincial in

Canada explained it to the assistant to the Superior General in France, the $100 salary for each nun fulfilled the obligation of the Oblates, "because the <u>academy</u> for which they had been given a house separate from the parish schools assured them a reasonable existence." The Oblate Provincial indicated that the order was using the remaining funds as reserves to prepare for the eventuality that the public school system no longer continued its arrangement with the parish, to construct buildings, and to found a school for boys. The Grey Nuns did not accept this level of paternalism. They insisted that they be given their entire salaries, pointing out to the men religious that each teaching nun had signed a contract with the board of education. They "maintain that all the money belongs to them," wrote the Oblate Provincial, "because we need the signature of the teachers, that is to say, of the sisters to collect the subsidies granted." While the Grey Nuns did not have a written contract with the Oblates for their work in Plattsburgh, the sisters had expected to be provided the resources they needed to carry out their mission. Although Bournigalle merely sought to continue the arrangements initiated by Sallaz, as the Oblate Provinicial pointed out, his brusque approach aggravated the situation: "By misfortune this matter became more involved by Father Bournigalle's manner of doing things which was neither kindly nor fair with regard to the Sisters: he unfortunately has the habit of rushing things and to appear too ardent in his antipathies." Bournigalle's eventual transfer in October 1873 helped facilitate the resolution of this dispute. Rev. Claude Sallaz, who had initiated the transfer of the parish school to the local school board in the late 1860s, returned to Plattsburgh after serving for several years as the superior of the Oblates in Buffalo, and he made amends with the sisters, according to Lamirande.[12]

Available sources do not make clear exactly how Sallaz, who died in February 1873, resolved this dispute with the Grey Nuns. Nor do the sources make clear how Rev. Moloney, who served as the superior of the Oblates in Plattsburgh from 1873 to 1879, did so. Mother Élisabeth Bruyère, the Superior General, had suggested a compromise whereby the Oblates would consider the sums withheld as installments on the price of the convent. The Oblates did execute deeds in 1877 and 1878 to the Grey Nuns for property to which Sallaz had previously held title—property located on Cornelia Street where their convent stood. But the dispute with the Oblates over the title to the convent persisted until the late 1880s, when the sisters noted in their chronicle, in November 1888, "that we have given a plot of land in Buffalo (of considerable value today) to the Reverend Fathers who, in payment, ceded us the Plattsburgh convent."[13]

Some of the problems of the St. Pierre parish community smoothed out, suggests Lamirande, not only with Bournigalle's departure but also following the division of the diocese of Albany. Formed by papal decree in 1872, the diocese of Ogdensburg encompassed the northern portion of New York State, with Vermont to the east, Lake Ontario to the west, Canada to the north, and the dioceses of Syracuse and Albany to the south.[14] The installation of Edgar Wadhams as Bishop of Ogdensburg in May 1872 shifted the ecclesiastical control of upstate New York from the capital district to the North Country.

Catholics of Plattsburgh warmly welcomed the new prelate. When Wadhams made his first official visit to Plattsburgh as bishop in June 1872, the village was adorned with US, French, and Irish flags, as well as with the banners of the St. John Baptist Society. Irish and French-Canadian residents joined together to meet the new bishop. Catholics from the Irish and French parishes of the village gathered at their respective churches, and then those from St. Pierre marched to St. John's, whereupon they formed a procession and marched as a group to the train station, where close to 4,000 people greeted Wadhams. The St. John Baptist Association participated in the procession, escorting Wadhams through the streets of the village to St. Pierre Church. Bournigalle still had charge of St. Pierre parish and was on hand to greet the prelate, and he addressed Wadhams in French "in the name of the Roman Catholics of this place," reported the *Plattsburgh Sentinel*, and Wadhams responded in English. The bishop presided over confirmation ceremonies the next day at both St. Pierre and St. John Churches.[15]

The participation of French-Canadian Plattsburgh residents in the parade to welcome the new bishop, as well as in community parades on Decoration Day and the Fourth of July in the 1870s, reveals that they were not an isolated ethnic group. When the village of Plattsburgh celebrated Decoration Day for the first time in 1871, the procession included disabled soldiers from the War of 1812 and the Civil War, members of the Grand Army of the Republic (GAR), city officials, clergy, grade-school students and their teachers, and 150 members of the St. John Baptist Association. On Decoration Day, the procession visited different cemeteries in the village, including the Catholic cemetery; at each cemetery, the ceremony consisted of laying flowers and wreaths and putting crosses on graves.[16]

Reflecting a lack of religious tension in the community, Protestant and Catholic deceased soldiers were honored equally on Decoration Day.

During the 1870s, as the St. John Baptist Society became integrated into such community celebrations, it also organized some of its own. In a departure from the recent past, the newly formed St. John Baptist Association decided in 1871 to hold the Saint-Jean-Baptiste celebration on June 24, the actual feast day of their patron saint. The association announced its intentions in an ad in the local press one full month before the event, perhaps in an attempt to get a jump on any plans the Canadian Union might propose. The St. John Baptist Association organized a long parade with nine bands. Delegations from the nearby communities of Redford and Schuyler Falls rode about forty teams of horses in the parade. The procession featured an eight-year-old boy representing St. John the Baptist next to a pet lamb in a vehicle adorned with flowers and evergreens. "Behind him was an Indian Chief all feathered and painted, and with bows and arrows in hand, and by his side" were Jacques Cartier and twelve young boys as his entourage, reported the *Sentinel*. Participants proceeded to the railroad station and steamboat landing to await arrivals from neighboring communities, as well as from Montréal and Vermont. Three railroad cars from Montréal carried the St. Peter's Montréal band. Arriving from Vermont by steamboats that crossed Lake Champlain were the St. John the Baptist societies of Burlington, St. Albans, Vergennes, and Montpelier, as well as the Union Catholic Society of Winooski and the St. Joseph Society of Burlington. One steamer carried not only the St. Albans Brigade Band but also the Hibernian Societies of St. Albans, all of which joined the parade. The presence of the Irish societies from across the lake made the event an intercultural celebration. Following the two marshals on horseback were "the American and French flags," reported the *Sentinel*, symbolizing the evolving identity of Plattsburgh's *Canadiens* as French and American.[17] The red ensign was nowhere to be seen, revealing that Plattsburgh's Franco population identified with France rather than Canada.

Once assembled, the various societies marched in regalia to St. Pierre Church, which "was highly decorated with red, white and blue draperies, flowers and banners," noted the *Sentinel*. As the Irish pastor of St. John's Church, Moloney was among the clergy present to greet the marchers. Following the mass, the procession formed anew and headed to the fairground for a picnic lunch served by the women of the parish. In the late afternoon, following the speeches by clergy, lawyers, and society presidents, the procession formed again and marched to the wharf from which some societies departed. An evening program featured the French drama *Vildac* and the comedy *Cobble and Financier*.[18]

The *Sentinel* marveled at the event. "Seldom, if ever before, has Plattsburgh witnessed such a display as that of Saturday, the 24th," it opined. The newspaper also commented "that the day passed off with general order and good behavior on the part of the whole, considering the immense gathering, which was at least 5,000."[19] The St. John Baptist Association thus made its grand debut in Plattsburgh with the public celebration of the feast day of its patron saint in 1871. By disentangling the celebration from the Fourth of July festivities, the association highlighted its role as an ethnic society.

The association had work to do, however, to establish a strong financial footing so that it could survive. In July 1871, P. Girard, the recording secretary of the society, gave notice in the newspaper that payments in arrears by members of the two organizations that had fused together to form the St. John Baptist Association had to be remitted by early August if they wanted to remain in good standing and not forfeit potential disbursements. The association was a French Catholic mutual-benefit society. Its minutes, all of which appear in French, reveal it was also a confessional organization, which began and ended its meetings in prayer. By its third year, the society had 302 members and $1,574 in assets and had made nearly $1,200 in disbursements to widows with children.[20]

When the St. John Baptist Association organized celebrations in honor of its patron saint in the late 1870s, they tended to be smaller affairs than the 1871 festivities described earlier, and they were not combined with Independence Day, as they had been from the mid-1860s. In 1877, for example, there was a mass at St. Pierre Church, which was decorated with red, white, and blue streamers, as well as banners, flags, and wreaths, followed by an address in French by Rev. Bournigalle.[21] The following year, the plans for the celebration consisted of a morning mass with an evening meal and concert.[22]

For their part, the Grey Nuns continued to organize their students to support activities at Plattsburgh's Irish church through the 1870s. Not only did the students of the Grey Nuns participate in the bazaars of St. Pierre Church, but they also attended those of St. John's Church. When the Irish church held its bazaar in December 1870, a majority of the boarding students of the sisters performed at the event. "They showed much kindness in working indifferently for the two bazaars—without distinction to nationality," recorded the sisters. They added: "Their generous conduct greatly pleases the Reverend Fathers."[23]

The sisters also continued to celebrate St. Patrick's Day by bringing their students regularly to the Irish church for masses until 1879. In October of that year, Bishop Wadhams decided to relieve the Oblates from the administration of St. John's Church and turned it over to diocesan priests. Following Moloney's departure, only on St. Patrick's Day 1882 was there any mention in the chronicle of the sisters of their attending mass at the Irish church with some of their boarding students, who were given the day off "like usual." Census records for the years 1880, 1892, and 1900 reveal that the pastors of St. John's Church who succeeded Moloney had also been born in Ireland. While there is some evidence of interchurch cooperation, such as the choirs of each parish singing at the other church on two occasions in 1882, the kinds of collaboration that existed during Moloney's tenure at St. John's appear to have waned with passing time.[24]

The Grey Nuns continued in the 1870s to take part quietly in civic events in the host society. When the United States celebrated its centennial in 1876, the sisters decorated the steeple and windows of their convent in a manner comparable to the homes of the village. "It seems that we are obliged to get on well with our American compatriots," they noted in their chronicle. "Our good Father [likely the pastor] warned parishioners not to drag behind in showing themselves generous and we are obliged to do like everyone else."[25]

The Grey Nuns also continued their work in the community by ministering to the ill. The sisters' register reflects that they assisted from 90 to 213 individuals in each year during the 1870s. The lowest number, 90, occurred in 1874, the year Plattsburgh faced a smallpox epidemic. It is not clear what role, if any, the Grey Nuns played during this epidemic, but their chronicle gives us a sense of what the local community experienced. On January 7, 1874, the sisters recorded that "a large panic reigns in the village": three people had already died of smallpox, boarding students who had gone home for the holidays had not returned, and parish schools had not reopened yet after the holidays. "Our [French-] Canadians, like our Americans, fear letting their children go out," they observed. Several days later, the sisters recorded that it was Sunday, but churches in the community were closed. Typhus had also spread, and everyone afflicted during the epidemic died within a week's time. Only on January 19 did the public and parish schools reopen, and nearly all children had been vaccinated, stated the sisters.[26]

The youth who attended the parish and boarding schools of the Grey Nuns in Plattsburgh during the 1870s received a bilingual education. The D'Youville Convent boarding school offered, among other classes, reading and writing instruction with English and French grammar. The sisters also offered both English- and French-language instruction at St. Pierre parish school in the 1870s. Not only did the sisters offer exams in both English and French, but they also, in the séances they organized, had their students present plays "in the two languages." When aspirants to *les Enfants de Marie* from the parish school participated in a ceremony presided over by Rev. Alexander Trudeau, "he speaks to them in English," noted the sisters.[27] Thus, the bilingual education the students received allowed them to function in both English and French. This facility in both languages helped to promote the acculturation of the children of French-Canadian descendants into US society.

On Christmas Eve 1873, communicants gathered at midnight at St. Pierre Church for the celebration of a high mass, at which Trudeau preached a sermon in English and French. While Trudeau may have in part been catering to the large number of Americans who attended the celebration, his bilingual comments also suggest that the parish community continued to function in both languages in the 1870s. Incidentally, in a notation reminiscent of the comments of the English-language press on the comportment of Plattsburgh's French-Canadian population at public celebrations, the Grey Nuns recorded in their chronicle that the Americans who attended that midnight mass in 1873 "behaved well, and appeared well attentive and silent."[28]

While relations between the Anglo-American population of Plattsburgh and the Grey Nuns generally were good in the 1870s, there were points of friction that occasionally surfaced during the decade. They demonstrate incipient forms of religious tension in the community. In 1871, some school-board members tried to get students to leave the boarding school of the sisters to attend the local high school, noted the Grey Nuns. The principal, Sr. Mary Kelly, met personally with the board to address unspecified false reports implicating her in pressuring students to study at the convent school rather than at the Protestant Academy, as the sisters referred to the public high school. The school-board president, William Hartwell, sided with the sisters, as did some others who were unnamed. The chronicler expressed hope that the matter was resolved: "Now the difficulties are overcome, we hope that all will go for the best on the subject of our schools."[29]

This was not the only episode of friction the sisters had to contend with, however. In 1875, the New York legislature amended the 1871 act incorporating the Sisterhood of Grey Nuns to allow the order to grant diplomas to its students, who subsequently could apply to the Superintendent of Public Instruction for teaching certificates to work in the common schools of New York. The *Sentinel* reproduced in December 1875 an article published in the *Albany Journal* that criticized this amendment and the original act incorporating the sisterhood. The *Journal* complained that the Grey Nuns who served as trustees of the order were not required to be US citizens. It alleged that, contrary to past practice, state officials did not have the authority to inspect the schools of the sisters. It also objected to the amendment allowing graduates of the schools of the Grey Nuns to teach in New York, because their schools were independent and were not regulated like the public schools and Normal Schools (teacher training colleges) of the state. In essence, the central complaint of the *Journal* was that it felt the Grey Nuns were receiving special treatment. The *Plattsburgh Republican* weighed in on the controversy by arguing that the amended legislation put the schools of the Grey Nuns on a par with the state's Normal Schools. The newspaper also contended that the Republican Party was responsible for proposing and supporting this "mischievous work."[30]

This school issue affecting the Grey Nuns of Plattsburgh got caught up in the village's partisan politics. The *Sentinel* struck back at the *Republican*, accusing it essentially of inciting religious prejudice. It asserted: "We are glad the *Republican* has put itself on record on this question, as it cannot now accuse us of dragging the school question before the public for the purpose of exciting sectarian prejudice." The *Sentinel* argued that the amendment had its origins in Democratic circles in Plattsburgh, had been passed by a Democratic assembly, and had been signed by a Democratic governor, "and then this Democratic newspaper of Clinton county attempts to throw the whole responsibility and odium onto the Republican party!" The *Sentinel* further countered the *Republican*'s objections by stating that legislation enacted in June 1875 provided that the Superintendent of Instruction could grant teaching certificates only after examining candidates, a measure "which completely nul[l]ifies the provisions of the Grey Nun act."[31]

In early January 1876, the *Sentinel* reported that the first bill introduced in the New York State Assembly in the New Year called for the repeal of the amendment to the act incorporating the Sisterhood of Grey

Nuns. It also reported that Governor Samuel Tilden essentially agreed with the *Sentinel*'s position that other legislation counteracted the amendment in question. The *Sentinel* asserted that Tilden must have signed the original amendment and was now being "'a little lame' in his apology!" In his address, the *Sentinel* stated, "the Governor refers to the Grey Nun Act, and attempts to slip his neck out of responsibility for signing it, by citing the general law which we published last week, and which it is claimed annulled the former act." Neil Gilmore, the New York Superintendent of Public Instruction, picked up the baton and, in his annual report to the legislature, recommended that it repeal the Grey Nun Act and amend the state's constitution to ensure that a "free, public and nonsectarian system of education shall be maintained." While the legislature appears not to have pursued these issues any further, the controversy highlights the seeds of religious friction that existed in Plattsburgh and in the state.[32]

Controversies over education also revealed some sources of ethnic tension in the community. William C. Fellows discovered while reading letters published in the *Republican* that some members of the local community blamed French-Canadian immigrants in 1876 for high illiteracy rates in Clinton County. In that year, a local teacher wrote to challenge the conclusion of an earlier article linking illiteracy in the county to poorly qualified teachers. The educator offered an alternative explanation, pointing the finger at French-Canadian immigrants in the area. "In my opinion the illiteracy is on the outside rather than the inside of the schoolroom," the individual wrote. "Our proximity to a province where education is at a low ebb, and the inducements afforded by our iron mining and lumber operations for poor laborers to seek employment in our country is the sole cause of the illiteracy of its inhabitants."[33]

In brief, while occasional sources of tension existed from outside of the French-Canadian community of Plattsburgh in the 1870s, the historical record largely points to peaceful coexistence and cooperation among the village's ethnic groups. The same was true for most of the 1880s and 1890s.

Until the 1880s, the post–Civil War migrations of French-Canadian descendants to the northeastern United States did not usually lead to permanent settlement and population stability. Of the French Canadians listed in the 1870 US census for Lewiston, Maine, 67 percent did not appear again in the 1880 census, the historian Yves Frenette finds. The French Canadians who migrated to Lewiston before 1880 typically moved on to other industrializing cities of the United States or back to the province of Québec. Consequently, northeastern communities like Lewiston did not have a stable francophone population until the final two decades of the nineteenth century, after they had created their own institutions, argues Frenette.[34]

Unlike Frenette, the historian Susan Ouellette asserts that Plattsburgh's French-Canadian population was not transient but instead showed cultural persistence, "since virtually all of the family names that appeared on the 1850 census can still be found in 1880." She discovered that the proportion of French-Canadian household heads increased from 32 percent in 1850 to 38 percent in 1880. Although Ouellette contends that Plattsburgh's French-speaking population experienced economic decline in the late nineteenth century, her own data reveals measures of upward mobility. From 1850 to 1880, the proportion of Plattsburgh's French-Canadian population working as unskilled laborers dropped from 62 to 45 percent, while those serving as artisans jumped from 37 to 53 percent, those working in professional/business occupations increased from 0 to 17 percent, and those engaged in white-collar occupations climbed from 7 to 18 percent. These figures stand to challenge her debatable conclusion that "French Canadians found themselves suppressing their cultural/linguistic heritage to gain access to the economic life of the larger community."[35]

The establishment of a French-language newspaper in Plattsburgh by Benjamin Lenthier in 1883 serves as but one piece of evidence to refute Ouellette's conclusion. Born in Beauharnois, Canada East, in 1846, Lenthier emigrated to the United States in 1867 and settled in Glens Falls, New York, where he oversaw a lumber operation that employed up to 300 men. Lenthier began his career as a journalist by cofounding the newspaper *Le Drapeau National* and then later founded *Le National* of Plattsburgh.[36] *Le National*'s weekly publication spanned seven years, until Lenthier moved the newspaper to Lowell, Massachusetts, in 1890. Beginning with the first issue, *Le National* declared on its masthead that it was "LE LIVRE D'ECOLE DE CEUX QUI N'Y VONT PLUS" ("the textbook for those who no longer go to school"). Besides educating *Canadiens*, Lenthier used the newspaper to advocate for and to defend the rights of French Canadians in upstate New York. In April 1885, when the Saint John Baptist Association accepted twenty-three new members, *Le National* wrote: "That proves that the [French-] Canadians of Plattsburgh understand that there is strength in unity. Very well, compatriots, unite yourselves, that is the only means to force the heterogeneous nationalities in the middle of which we live to recognize our rights."[37]

Le National established a place for itself in the 1880s among newspapers like *Le Travailleur* of Worcester, Massachusetts; *L'Indépendant* of Fall River, Massachusetts; and *Le Messager* of Lewiston, Maine, that resisted assimilationist forces in the US Northeast. Like them, *Le National* advocated for and defended French-Canadian immigrants in the United States. When Carroll Wright, the Massachusetts Commissioner of the Bureau of Statistics of Labor, issued his famous polemic in 1881 calling French-Canadian immigrants the "Chinese of the East," French speakers resoundingly objected to that characterization. Two years later, in its first edition, *Le National* bristled when a labor-union official echoed Wright's sentiment. Speaking to a Massachusetts senate committee on relations between labor and capital in 1883, F. K. Foster, the secretary of the Federation of Organized Trades and Labor Unions of the United States and Canada (the predecessor of the American Federation of Labor), similarly alleged, according to the French-language newspaper, that "the French-Canadians are in New England what the Chinese are in California." *Le National* countered that 40,000 French-Canadian descendants in the United States had supported the Union cause during the Civil War, that they had created educational institutions in their country of adoption, and that many had become property owners, naturalized citizens, and even holders of important government positions. The French-language newspaper argued for a higher regard for the *Canadiens* in US society, contending that they were far from being like the Chinese, "men without morals and principles."[38] While advocating for a higher standing for the *Canadiens* in the host society, the newspaper revealed its own ethnic and racial prejudices.

In its first issue, *Le National* stated unequivocally what it stood for. It acknowledged it was "openly Catholic" and supportive of French-Catholic schools "for the preservation of our faith and our language." It also indicated that it was not aligned with any political party but wanted to discuss questions by keeping in mind "the needs of our nationals."[39]

To that end, Plattsburgh's French-language newspaper helped organize and participated in conventions of French Canadians in the United States. In its first edition, *Le National* announced that the sixth convention of French Canadians of New York State would take place in Plattsburgh, "the largest French-Canadian center in the state." Delegates from communities throughout the state descended on Plattsburgh in August 1883 for activities that included a pontifical high mass, at which Bishop Edgar Wadhams officiated at St. Pierre Church, and an elaborate parade.[40]

The parade featured the city band; Grand Army of the Republic; uniformed men from the fire-hose companies Horicon and Lafayette; the St. John Baptist societies from Plattsburgh, Champlain, Troy, and Whitehall, New York, marching in regalia; and allegorical chariots.[41] One chariot contained a representative of Saint-Jean-Baptiste with a live lamb "accompanied by two wild Indians, showing that Christianity can subdue the wildest natures," stated the *Sentinel*. Another vehicle, sponsored by the village of Champlain, carried the likeness of Samuel de Champlain, two French soldiers, and twenty friendly Indians "representing the party who explored Lake Champlain." Following the fire-hose companies in the procession was "a band of thirty Iroquois Indians in their war paint and war costumes, with hatchets and bows and arrows. They were intended to represent the band who encountered the first white man, the explorer Samuel de Champlain, near what is now Ticonderoga," explained the *Sentinel*. A Plattsburgh resident led the band, and "a genuine Indian, Joseph Sky, chief of the Caughnawagas, accompanied this party," noted the newspaper. Another allegorical chariot carried "the Goddess of Liberty seated above the globe and presiding over its destinies, while seated at her feet were 38 beautiful girls representing the States of our Union." Other vehicles carried displays by local businesses or contained clergy and local officials. Schoolboys from the public school conducted by the Grey Nuns carried the US flag, the *Sentinel* added.[42]

In the afternoon, there was a sham fight between Champlain's group and a band of Iroquois Indians, with Champlain "of course coming off victorious, the sound of his arquebus putting the savages to precipitate flight," wrote the *Sentinel*.[43] Presided over by Dr. J. H. LaRocque (pictured in fig. 2.1), who had migrated to Plattsburgh from Saint-Jean-sur-Richelieu, Québec, in 1878 and who was elected president of the St. John Baptist Society of Plattsburgh in 1881, the convention's other events included music, speeches attended by thirty priests, a supper, and an evening fireworks display.[44] The convention thus wove together historical themes important to French-Canadian residents of Plattsburgh and New York State, including the explorations by Champlain of upstate New York and his conflict with the Iroquois. It also reflected important symbols, such as the patron saint of French Canadians, the Roman Catholic Church, and of course the United States. Thus, while promoting French-Canadian history and culture, the festivities also acknowledged the Americanness of its participants.

Figure 2.1. Dr. J. H. LaRocque, c. 1907. Courtesy of Clinton County Historical Association.

Le National found it difficult, however, to generate much enthusiasm among Plattsburgh residents for French-Canadian conventions held elsewhere. In July 1885, for example, when it announced that the eighth convention of New York's French-Canadian population would take place in Rochester, the newspaper argued against those who dismissed such conventions as unimportant. *Le National* contended that they elevated the ranks of the *Canadiens* in the United States, and it pointed to their successes, such as the establishment of French-Canadian schools and societies and gaining membership in political bodies like the Maine state legislature. One month later, *Le National* chided French-Canadian residents of Plattsburgh, and it singled out the St. John Baptist Association and St. Pierre parish for not nominating a delegate to attend the Rochester convention. Apparently, *Le National*'s editor and proprietor, Benjamin Lenthier, sufficiently goaded local priests that St. Pierre parish nominated him to represent Plattsburgh at the convention.[45]

The lack of reception to Lenthier's call for delegates from Plattsburgh to attend the Rochester convention should not be interpreted, however, as a lack of interest in French-Canadian culture or heritage, especially on the part of Plattsburgh's major ethnic society. Throughout the 1880s and 1890s, the St. John Baptist Association promoted by its various activities the cultural heritage of the city's French-Canadian population. Most notably, it participated in celebrations honoring the patron saint of French Canadians. In some years, the society traveled to Montréal or to Burlington for Saint-Jean-Baptiste Day. In other years, it organized festivities in Plattsburgh and brought speakers from those and other communities to help celebrate the event locally.[46]

In 1889, trains from Canada and steamers from Vermont transported at least 5,000 visitors to Plattsburgh. An arch over Bridge Street, decorated with cedar branches and the portraits of US President Benjamin Harrison, Vice President Levi Morton, and New York Governor David Hill, greeted visitors, as did the sign "Welcome to All," written in both English and French. Earlier in the decade, the Oblate priests had promoted respect for civic authority by recommending that parishioners decorate their homes to mourn the passing of President James Garfield; following suit, the Grey Nuns had decorated their convent door with Garfield's picture and with black-and-white funeral hangings. The portraits of US government officials on the 1889 Saint-Jean-Baptiste Day decorations similarly served as, in the words of *Le National*, "evidence of our loyalty to the government of our country of adoption." In that same year, although not connected by the French-language newspaper to the local celebrations, France commemorated in style the centennial of the French Revolution with the Paris World's Fair and Eiffel Tower. In Plattsburgh, flags of the United States and France adorned the city and symbolized by their presence and colors a profound intertwining—"the stars and the tricolor mixing together their pleats and marrying their brilliant shades," commented *Le National*.[47]

The St. John Baptist Society, accompanied by the city band, escorted the visitors to St. Pierre Church, where they celebrated a high mass. The church was decorated by the Grey Nuns with evergreens and with "the blended colors of the French and American flags being conspicuous throughout," reported the *Republican*. Following mass, the participants marched through Plattsburgh's streets in a parade featuring an allegorical vehicle with Jacques Cartier, St. John the Baptist, and Native Americans, most of them sporting costumes created by the Grey Nuns. Other carriages transported Catholic clergy and local officials.[48]

In the afternoon there were speeches by Dr. J. H. LaRocque, president of the St. John Baptist Society, who made the opening remarks in French, followed by George Weed, who spoke on behalf of his father, Smith Weed, the president of the corporation of the village of Plattsburgh. The presence of Weed's delegate not only highlighted the connection of local government officials to the French-Canadian population of Plattsburgh but also his family's longstanding ties to the French-speaking community. Judge Charland of Saint-Jean-sur-Richelieu, Québec, spoke in French of Canada's early martyrs and beseeched "his compatriots to keep the memories of the glorious past and the love of their native land warm in their breasts," translated the *Republican*. Addressing participants in their native tongue, Rev. D. J. O'Sullivan of Burlington spoke "in a stirring speech in French, alluding to the common interests of Irishmen and French Canadians in this their chosen country, and bespeaking unity for the trials which the future might have in store," reported the *Republican*, which also noted that he ended with a few words in English.[49] O'Sullivan's presence and remarks served to call attention to the interethnic cooperation that had existed between the French Canadians and the Irish in Plattsburgh since the mid-1800s.

Several journalists from Montréal also addressed the gathering. One of them, Joseph Tassé, the editor of *La Minerve*, remarked on his connection to Plattsburgh, commenting on how he had begun his career as a law student of Smith Weed. The journalists were followed by Rev. Joseph Fournier of St. Pierre parish who made the closing remarks, complimenting participants for their good appearance and behavior and "reminding them that the best Christians were the best patriots." An evening concert rounded out the day's activities, which ended with the playing of the "Star Spangled Banner."[50] The songs, speeches, and flags on Saint-Jean-Baptiste Day 1889 all reflected the French, Canadian, and American identities of Plattsburgh's francophone population.

This was evident at festivities in the 1890s as well. During the 1899 celebration, the *Plattsburgh Daily Press* noted that the bridge was decorated "with cedar, and the American and French colors," and that, at St. Peter's Church, "the red, white and blue of France and the United States are prominent."[51] The English-language newspaper clearly recognized the symbolism these overlapping colors conveyed. Anglo-Americans also recognized the importance of the French fact in the United States. Charles Johnson, president of the corporation of the village of Plattsburgh, participated in the procession that took place after mass and made the welcoming remarks, during which he mentioned the contributions of Frenchmen like Samuel de Champlain, "the discoverer of our lake," and Marquis de LaFayette, the supporter of the US Revolutionary War. Johnson's mention of Champlain and LaFayette by name drew applause from an audience that celebrated a blended French and American identity on this feast day.[52]

The participation of French speakers in local celebrations in the 1880s and 1890s reflects their integration into US society and their intermixing with non-Catholics. The St. John Baptist Association, for example, regularly joined the parade on Decoration Day/Memorial Day, a procession that typically visited the Catholic cemetery, the United States cemetery at the garrison, and Riverside cemetery.[53] In 1883, soldiers from the local garrison, veterans from the Grand Army of the Republic, men from the local fire houses, clergy from the Catholic churches, and the choir of St. Pierre Church all joined the parade. At the Catholic cemetery, graves were decorated, the priests held a religious service, the St. Pierre choir sang, and a missionary priest from Montréal gave an address in French; after three volleys by the soldiers, the procession moved to the garrison cemetery, where graves were also decorated, prayers said, and volleys fired, before all proceeded to the Riverside cemetery where flowers were laid and a hymn sung. Protestant ministers carried out services at the non-Catholic cemeteries.[54] These celebrations of Decoration Day/Memorial Day demonstrate an intermixing of Protestants and Catholics not typically witnessed in New England during the late nineteenth century.

The St. John Baptist Association received invitations to participate in other public celebrations as well, such as Fourth of July parades. The society had over 200 members by June 1885, and 80 of them marched in the Independence Day parade that year, which also commemorated the centennial of Plattsburgh. In 1886, *Le National* on its front page translated into French the Declaration of Independence for its readers. The French-language newspaper encouraged *Canadiens* to join Fourth of July celebrations. In 1889, it expressed its wish: "That all our compatriots dispersed throughout this vast territory [USA] unite on this day in [joining] the demonstrations of our brothers of this grand republic!"[55] Even the French-language newspaper of Plattsburgh, then, showed an openness to the traditions of the host society.

As Plattsburgh's French-Canadian community learned about its country of adoption and continued intermixing with Irish Catholics and Protestant Americans, it faced financial and other challenges. In March 1881, the Grey Nuns commented in their chronicle that "a good number of parishioners from the Canadian congregation have caused trouble for the Reverend Oblate Fathers" and have asked the bishop "to give them a secular [diocesan] priest, wanting to say in this manner to get rid of the good Fathers." The bishop sided with the Oblates in this dispute, the details of which are not known, but they appear to have centered in part on financial concerns. The sisters noted, for example, that the bishop met with a parish committee after high mass "in order to settle things in a manner in which the church revenue and that of the Reverend Fathers is much larger." Apparently the meeting went as the bishop had hoped, and the sisters added: "It is presumed the rebels' spirit is cooling down in recognition of their wrong." When Bishop Wadhams returned to Plattsburgh in May 1881 to administer the sacrament of Confirmation, he publicly stated his confidence in the Oblate priests, they recorded in their historical notes.[56]

The administration of parish finances occasionally led to bitter disputes in French-Canadian communities in the northeastern United States. In New York State, church properties came under the control of parish corporations, consisting of the bishop, vicar general, pastor, and two parishioners appointed by the bishop or vicar general. In the early 1880s, St. Peter's Church adopted this system. In October 1880, it filed for incorporation in Clinton County with the signature of the Oblate pastor, Louis Lebret, and with the mark of trustee Eusêbe Chauvin (who could not sign his own name.) In August 1881, thus following the controversy described above, Rev. Thomas Walsh, the vicar general of the Diocese of Ogdensburg, and Lebret filed paperwork appointing Eusêbe Chauvin and Edward Trembly to serve with them as trustees of St. Peter's Church.[57] States like Maine modeled their legislation after New York's parish corporation system, which actually gave the bishops control over parish funds, quite unlike the self-managed *fabriques* (parish corporations) of Québec. In Maine, this precipitated a bitter controversy between French-Canadian descendants and Irish bishops over the control of parish resources.[58] That kind of diocesan-level ethnic conflict apparently did not transpire in upstate New York. In Plattsburgh, the disputes over parish funds tended to play out at the local level between parishioners and priests.

Following the incorporation of St. Pierre Church, financial tensions continued to linger, and the parish apparently struggled to meet some of its obligations. During the 1880s, pew rentals typically ranged from $6.00 to $10.00 yearly, depending upon the choice of seating, with pews closest to the front of the church and nearest the center aisle commanding the highest rents. Around 1882, the Oblate priests added a surcharge of $1.50 to the price of pew rentals, in part to cover heating costs. Unsurprisingly, the Oblates found that pews did not sell so readily thereafter.[59]

Clearly the parish community needed other revenues, and they organized several activities to generate them. The church sponsored steamship excursions on Lake Champlain to destinations such as the picnic grounds of Willsboro to raise funds. Nearly 800 tickets were sold for a July 1882 excursion, and the organizing committee of the French church publicly acknowledged the support of non-parishioners, noting in the *Sentinel*, "We also thank our American and Irish friends who patronized us."[60] As in earlier years, the financial support of non-French Canadians provided necessary funds to St. Pierre parish.

In the mid-1880s, St. Pierre Church had about 3,500 members. Women continued to organize fairs to raise money for the church. In 1885, when St. Pierre Church became the first building in the village to install a steam heating system, it turned to the parish women to organize a bazaar to help raise the funds to pay for it. When the annual bazaar raised nearly $1,500 for the church in December 1886, *Le National* suggested it was a good outcome given the time of year when people had to devote funds to protect themselves from cold weather.[61]

But the newspaper chided parishioners in other years for not being more generous. In January 1887, *Le National* reported that a recent bazaar in Champlain had netted the French Catholic church over $2,600, and it asked, "What do the [French-] Canadians of Plattsburgh think of this result?" In that same month, the French-language newspaper pointed out that *Canadiens* in Fitchburg, Massachusetts, contributed $227 to the Christmas collection (a collection that typically constitutes a gift for the priests), adding: "We regret not being able to say the same of the [French-] Canadian congregation of Plattsburgh, which is nevertheless so much larger." The following year, *Le National* encouraged the *Canadiens* of Plattsburgh to give generously to the Christmas collection, noting: "This will be a meaningful way to address the devotion of the Rev. Father Superior who works so actively for the moral well-being of the parish."[62]

By 1893, if not earlier, St. Peter's Church capitalized on the large attendance at the midnight mass by selling for 10 cents each up to 300 reserved seats for the Christmas Eve service. In 1893, the growing parish had 830 families consisting of 4,150 individuals. It relied on its parishioners to generate the funds to cover improvements that cost a reported $6,000 in the previous year, including the installation of incandescent electric lights, the addition of one hundred pews, and the replacement of outside doors. Besides relying upon bazaars to raise money for church expenses, St. Peter's in the 1890s, as in the past, established monthly collections to help recoup the cost of the expensive improvements.[63]

During the 1880s and 1890s, the village of Plattsburgh continued its arrangement with St. Pierre parish whereby the board of education rented the parish school and public monies paid the salaries of the Grey Nuns who had charge of it, an arrangement that continued into the early twentieth century. This, of course, helped the parish financially. In 1883, the Grey Nuns taught 161 boys and 123 girls at the elementary school and probably around 20 more girls at their boarding school.[64] In the early 1880s, the sisters decided to erect a new three-story school building for the French-Canadian youth of Plattsburgh, reported *Le National*. The Grey Nuns adroitly secured the support of the Oblate priests, their Superior General and governing council, and the Plattsburgh Board of Education. To obtain the board's support, Sisters [Marie] McMillan and Adélaide Bertrand visited Smith Weed to discuss their schools and how to approach the other men on the school board. Weed offered guidance and encouragement, even contributing $50 for their new building, known locally as the Red Brick School. The school board also assisted financially, agreeing to rent the new building for $150 annually, bringing its total annual rent payment to the parish to $300, and it agreed to furnish three classrooms at the request of the sisters, who staffed them to 1907.[65]

The Grey Nuns also raised money for their new school by borrowing from wealthy residents and by organizing fundraising activities. The sisters borrowed $4,000 from M. J. Ayer, a Protestant woman, whom they paid 5 percent interest and repaid $1,000 yearly on the capital. They borrowed $2,500 from Gilbert Durand, the father of one of their students, agreeing to pay him 6 percent interest and to repay the capital when they could.[66] A December 1883 benefit featuring entertainment provided by the Plattsburgh City Band raised $270 for the new school building. The sisters also held a raffle for a gold watch and a fancy table, both of which could be viewed at the pharmacy owned by J. C. Smith and Dr. J. H. LaRocque, with the drawing taking place at the halls of the St. John Baptist Association. In conducting the raffle, the sisters tapped the ethnic networks of their parish and the goodwill of the larger community. Besides paying for the expenses of the new school building, the sisters also had to raise funds for repairs to their convent school to make better accommodations for their boarding students.[67] Thus, the sisters continued in the 1880s to demonstrate their strong political and entrepreneurial skills, while helping the parish meet important educational and financial objectives.

As in the past, the sisters actively sought out students to attend D'Youville Academy in the late nineteenth century. Beginning in the 1890s, the Grey Nuns began recruiting young women from Lowell, Massachusetts. The Oblate Fathers had invited the Sisters of Charity of Ottawa to take charge of schools in two different French-Canadian parishes there in the early 1880s. A decade later, the Grey Nuns would regularly travel to Lowell to enroll girls at their boarding school in Plattsburgh, escorting them to upstate New York at the start of the new academic year and then back to their families at the end of the school year.[68] In this way, they demonstrated their entrepreneurial skills and historical agency, running and financing their own bilingual academy in Plattsburgh.

One development within the Roman Catholic Church of the United States nearly brought an end to the arrangement with the Plattsburgh School Board by which the Grey Nuns also taught for the public school system. In 1884, US bishops met in Baltimore, Maryland, and called for each Catholic parish in the country to develop its own parochial school as a means of countering the growing attendance of Catholic youth in public schools. The year following the Council of Baltimore, the eighth convention of French Canadians of New York took up as its main issue the establishment of French Catholic schools where they did not exist in the state. *Le National* subsequently pushed for the formation of one for boys in Plattsburgh. As the newspaper's owner, Benjamin Lenthier noted that girls had access to a French Catholic education at D'Youville Convent, but that boys in the village did not have a comparable opportunity. A letter to the editor of *Le National* clarified the issue, noting that boys could only obtain a parochial education in Plattsburgh until ages ten to twelve, and the individual called for a parish meeting to address "this big problem."[69]

The issue went unaddressed for a couple of years. In February 1887, when *Le National* announced in its columns the date for a parish meeting, it urged all who were interested in "the future of the [French-] Canadian nationality in this country" to attend. "For a long time the [French-] Canadians of Plattsburgh whose population numbers 760 families have been accused of indifference with respect to education, for a long time we are accused of lacking patriotism, of favoring anglicism," it commented, challenging readers, "let us endeavor therefore to prove for once to outsiders that we have been loosely maligned, that the fire of patriotism burns today more steadfastly than ever in the hearts of the [French-] Canadians of Plattsburgh." About 250 to 300 "of the principal citizens of the [French-] Canadian congregation of Plattsburgh" turned out one Sunday evening in late February 1887 to meet with the Oblate pastor, Rev. Antoine Amyot, about creating a secondary school for boys—a school Amyot contended would help preserve the Catholic faith in the community as well as "our language." Among the others who spoke at the gathering were Dr. LaRocque and Benjamin Lenthier. In addition, the director of an academy conducted by Marist brothers in St. Athanase d'Iberville, Québec, addressed the gathering to explain their educational system. Those in attendance agreed on the need to create a separate school for boys under the direction of a religious order of brothers, while maintaining the school for girls under the Grey Nuns, reported *Le National*.[70]

St. Pierre parish subsequently made plans to separate from the public school system of Plattsburgh. The Grey Nuns and the Oblate priests concurred in 1887 that the sisters would no longer receive government-paid salaries and would no longer have to conform to the decisions of the public-school board, bringing their schools in line with the decisions of the Council of Baltimore "and to the desire of the Rev. Oblate Fathers who care to have schools entirely separated from a Protestant board," noted the sisters. Because the local school board had not been given enough notice, as prescribed by law, the separation did not take effect in 1887. In fact, the separation did not take place for a couple more decades. Bishop Wadhams decided in 1889 that the parish schools of St. Pierre would remain under the direction of the board of education, and the arrangement continued with some modifications until 1906.[71]

While St. Pierre considered taking back from the public school system the administration of its parish schools, the St. John Baptist Association contemplated its secularization. In June 1888, the association voted to remove religious clauses from its constitution. *Le National* advocated for the confessional nature of ethnic societies like this one, and it came out strongly against the actions of the society, characterizing them as a revolt against ecclesiastical authority. *Le National* commented that the association had not only rid its constitution of religious clauses but had also chosen no longer to have a chaplain. The French-language newspaper asked, "Will the St. John Baptist Society of Plattsburgh preserve the word *Saint* that forms part of its name? If it wants to be consistent with itself, we believe it should call itself THE JOHN BAPTIST SOCIETY, quite simply!" The newspaper's reporting reveals that it viewed the actions of the St. John Baptist Association as a crisis within Plattsburgh's French-Canadian community. While little is known of the reasons for the actions of the society, in February 1889 *Le National* pointed out that Rev. Fournier had succeeded Rev. Amyot as the superior in the Oblate rectory and that Fournier reached out to the society, discussed issues it misinterpreted, and asked it to reverse its decision to become a secular organization. The association unanimously rescinded its earlier actions and "became again a society openly and absolutely Catholic," reported *Le National*, with evident pleasure. When Fournier addressed the Saint-Jean-Baptiste Day gathering in June 1889, he commented: "On this day, all the wrongs of the past were forgotten, in fact, they were nobly redeemed," paraphrased *Le National*.[72]

As the pastor of St. Pierre Church, Fournier helped keep the St. John Baptist Association a confessional organization. Although the parish school did not similarly revert to the Catholic fold in 1889, Fournier took steps to increase both the presence of the Catholic nuns and the teaching of French. He asked the principal to press the public-school board to allow more French instruction in the schools the sisters conducted and to allow them to teach some higher grades, such as fourth. Fournier had been born in Canada and, like other French-Canadian clergy in the northeastern United States, he undoubtedly wanted to promote the preservation of the French language. During the 1880s, the sisters had continued to conduct their academy's classes and celebrations, such as graduations, in French and English. When the Grey Nuns celebrated their silver jubilee in Plattsburgh in 1885, formal remarks were made in both French and English. Given the interethnic cooperation that characterized the work of the sisters during the quarter century since their arrival in Plattsburgh, it is unsurprising that the high mass celebrated to honor them drew together the "the two congregations, [French-]

Canadian and Irish." Besides teaching, the sisters had ministered to the sick by home visits and to the poor by assisting with meals, clothing, and money in each year they served in Plattsburgh.[73] In short, they had functioned for a quarter century as representatives of the Catholic church in the Plattsburgh community—as a bilingual, intercultural religious order that ministered to all groups in the village, while helping the parish to preserve its French Catholic lifeways.

But the pastor wanted to increase French-language instruction in the parish school. After Fournier made his request to the sisters, A. McKeefe, the only Catholic member of the school board in 1889, stopped by to see them, and he recommended that the sisters speak directly with William Mooers, the president of the board of education. The sisters had already consulted with Smith Weed, "a very influential man and one who has always shown favor towards our community."[74] Weed told the sisters the pastor's request was reasonable and gave them hope that it would be granted. When the superior of the Grey Nuns and the school principal visited Mooers, he "told us that he will speak on our behalf to the other board members so as to get them on our side before the committee meeting." A couple of days later, after working behind the scenes, Mooers informed the sisters that the proposal would almost surely succeed. When the school committee met in August 1889, it agreed to allow the sisters to teach the fourth grade in their schools and to teach French in all grades.[75] This concession from the public-school board demonstrates the skills and the persistence of these Catholic nuns in advocating and negotiating for their schools in a male-dominated school administration of the late nineteenth century.

It of course helped that the sisters also acceded to the demands of the public educational system, thus building public trust in themselves and in their schools. The bilingual nature of the instruction at D'Youville Academy did not apparently arouse concern, and the sisters in fact received local and state recognition for their work. In 1896, the *Daily Press* commented, "This institution is sustained by a splendid public opinion in the village of Plattsburgh itself, and for this reason, if none other, it is a matter of congratulation to our citizens that the Grey Nuns are doing such a splendid work for the advancement of our American youth."[76] Their academy students took New York Regents exams just like public-school students did. The superintendent of Regents visited the institution in 1896, and in that year the Board of Regents of the University of New York granted it "an absolute charter as an academy," noted a Plattsburgh souvenir history publication the following year. The sisters aided their cause by seeking state certification. Twelve Grey Nuns, for example, went to "the Protestant Academy" to take their teacher certification exams in August 1896.[77]

As a group, the Grey Nuns connected with important civic and religious leaders not only as needed but also as opportunities arose. As a community in the Canada–US borderlands region, Plattsburgh received occasional visits from both Canadian and US officials. When President William McKinley and Vice President Garret Hobart visited Plattsburgh in 1897, all the Grey Nuns from D'Youville Convent attended a reception for them at the nearby Catholic Summer School, which organized theological instruction for Catholics at its site on Lake Champlain along the lines of the Chautauqua lecture series for Protestants. The sisters shook hands with the president and vice president, they noted in their chronicle. When Monsignor Paul Bruchesi, Archbishop of Montréal, called upon Catholic clergy in Plattsburgh in August 1899, he also visited the sisters at their convent after dining with the Oblate priests and viewing the church and new organ.[78] The Sisters of Charity of Ottawa based in Plattsburgh, then, were not a cloistered order isolating themselves from the larger world, but were instead actively a part of the community and the country in which they resided. They served in many respects as the public face of Plattsburgh's French Catholic community.

In conclusion, while the schools of St. Pierre parish taught by the Grey Nuns continued to be administered by the public-school board of Plattsburgh in the late nineteenth century, they did not relinquish their cultural and linguistic heritage. Nor did the village's larger French-Canadian community. This language retention during the early phase of mass migration to the United States stands in contrast to the impression the Grey Nuns had upon their arrival that French had been lost. Plattsburgh's French-Canadian population in the late 1800s continued intermixing with the Irish Catholic and Protestant American populations, celebrating its own history and culture as it learned of those of the host society. Conflicts within and outside of the French-Canadian parish community made clear that its evolution in upstate New York was a contested process. Pecuniary challenges were at the root of some of the conflicts that resulted. As we have seen, women of the parish performed significant labor to help the parish community to meet some of those financial challenges. Among those women, the Grey Nuns advocated for and managed their schools, negotiating political and economic challenges with finesse. As they did so, they guided the acculturation of younger generations of French-Canadian descendants into US society. The Grey Nuns, the Oblate priests, and institutions like the St. John Baptist Association and *Le National* all helped to create a French-Canadian community in Plattsburgh.

But the process was not unidirectional. Plattsburgh's francophone population of the 1870s, 1880s, and 1890s became more integrated into its country of adoption as it cultivated and maintained some of the traits that made it distinctive. At the end of the nineteenth century, French-Canadian elites in the US Northeast started to use the term "Franco-American" to describe French-Canadian immigrants in the United States. In doing so, they were trying to assert their French and American identities, just as Plattsburgh's francophones did, particularly in their public celebrations from the 1870s through the 1890s. By their actions and symbols, French-Canadian descendants in Plattsburgh demonstrated a blended identity as French and American, as their clerical and secular leaders helped them forge an ethnic community through the end of the nineteenth century.

Chapter Three

An Execution in Canada, a Murder in Plattsburgh, and *Le National*

Shaping Francophones' Political Consciousness, 1870–1900

Le National, the French-language newspaper of Plattsburgh from 1883 to 1890, evolved during this period of time into a newspaper that promoted Democratic partisanship. *Le National* believed that the Democratic Party served better than the Republican Party to advance the interests of French-Canadian descendants in upstate New York as well as in the greater United States in the late nineteenth century. The newspaper also helped to connect local French speakers to larger continental issues affecting North America's francophone populations, such as the controversy in Canada over the execution of Louis Riel. In addition, a widely discussed local murder case involving a French-Canadian man, Joseph Chapleau, and the French-language newspaper's lack of reporting on it provide insight into the sociopolitical environment affecting Plattsburgh's francophone population in the late 1800s. It notably revealed a lack of intercultural tension in the community. During its brief period of publication in Plattsburgh, *Le National* helped the village's French-Canadian population become more integrated in United States society and politics as well as in North American francophone society.

The controversy in Canada over Louis Riel's execution in 1885 exposed deep religious and ethnic divisions within the young federation. Some of those divisions also existed in the northeastern United States, attracting the attention of Plattsburgh's French-language newspaper. Riel had studied for the priesthood before leading the insurrections of the

Métis, the descendants of French fur trappers and Native women, in Canada's Northwest Territories. Catholic French Canadians of Québec became convinced that Protestant Anglo-Canadians of Ontario wanted to punish Riel because of his French and Catholic background. Across the border, French-Canadian immigrants in the United States also sympathized with Riel. Like their counterparts in Québec, many of them faced ethnic and religious rivalry in the late nineteenth century as a French Catholic minority in an Anglo Protestant nation. Riel's execution led them to question the perceived place of francophone Catholic minorities not only in Canada but also in the United States.[1]

While the life and death of Louis Riel in Canada have attracted significant scholarly attention, much less is known about Riel's forays into the northeastern United States (see Riel pictured in fig. 3.1). The contacts Riel cultivated among French-Canadian immigrants in New England and New York shed considerable light on ethnic and religious transnationalism in the nineteenth century. In addition, Riel's friendship with Major Edmond Mallet, a prominent francophone and Civil War veteran, demonstrates the continental dimension of the North American Franco identity. The oppression of French-speaking Catholic minorities in North America found a symbol in Louis Riel and his hanging. The responses of French-Canadian immigrants in the northeastern United States to Riel's execution served moreover to challenge social and political boundaries as well as the limits of citizenship in nineteenth-century America.

Approximately 120,000 French Canadians from Québec emigrated to the United States in the 1870s, and another 150,000 emigrated in the 1880s. Louis Riel was familiar to French-Canadian immigrants in the northeastern United States because they continued to follow news from Québec and because of the Métis leader's visits to francophone population centers in the 1870s. During the Red River rebellion of 1869–1870, Riel organized the Métis resistance to federal government incursion and expansion into the Northwest Territories, established a provisional government, and negotiated a compromise with the federal government of Canada that led to the creation of Manitoba as a province with English and French as its official languages. Riel also allowed the execution of Thomas Scott, a member of the anti-Catholic society of the Orange Order, for armed revolt and because Scott's foul and abusive heckling of the Métis while imprisoned by them had led to exasperation. Scott's execution provoked the animosity of Ontario's Anglo Protestant population, which viewed Scott as a martyr to the French Catholics of the Northwest. Following the uprising, Riel was elected to the federal parliament in October 1873 but, heeding the caution of friends, decided not to take his seat. Afterward, Riel visited the French-speaking clergy serving French-Canadian congregations in Plattsburgh and the nearby community of Keeseville, New York. From New York, Riel ran again for parliament in February 1874, but the body expelled him.[2]

Francophones on both sides of the international border discussed Riel's plight, but their views diverged. At the time of Confederation in 1867, French Canadians did not concern themselves about the minority rights of French speakers living outside of the territory that became Québec, argues historian A. I. Silver. He points out that residents of Québec did not initially recognize the Métis as their own people but rather regarded them at the time of the Red River uprising with "hostility, indifference, or bare tolerance." French-Canadian immigrants in the United States apparently saw them differently. In early June 1874, *Foyer Canadien*, a French-language newspaper of Worcester, Massachusetts, published a letter from St. Paul, Minnesota, calling Riel "the brave champion of the rights of

Figure 3.1. Louis Riel in Keeseville, NY, during one of his northern New York stays between 1873 and 1878. Courtesy of the late Raymond Allard, as shared with/by Julie Dowd.

our coreligionists and compatriots of the North-West." When the Société Saint-Jean-Baptiste of Montréal celebrated its fortieth anniversary in June 1874, more than 10,000 French Canadians from the United States joined in the festivities. They participated in discussions concerning Riel, who was not present at the convention, and largely supported amnesty for the Métis leader. But the convention's delegates were divided over the issue and did not adopt a formal resolution on Riel's behalf.[3]

Differing political organizations may help to explain the divergent attitudes of French Canadians in the United States and Canada toward Riel and the Métis. As the result of Confederation, French Canadians gained their own province with its own legislative assembly, and Québec thereafter could function as a nation within the country of Canada. Québec could thus serve as a homeland for Catholics of French descent. The large majority of French speakers in the United States, however, were scattered widely among the six New England states and New York and therefore were not concentrated in one subnational political unit. In addition, by the 1870s, they had not become naturalized citizens and voters in sufficient numbers to wield much political clout in the communities where they resided. As a French Catholic minority, French-Canadian immigrants in the northeastern United States could readily sympathize with the situation of Riel and the Métis in Manitoba.

Riel capitalized upon this sympathy, tapping his networks in the United States to raise awareness of and to gain support for the Métis. During summer 1874, Riel visited in Washington, DC, the Civil War hero Major Edmond Mallet, who had attended the Montréal convention in June. Born in Montréal, Mallet had emigrated with his family to Oswego, New York, when he was young; after serving in the Civil War, he earned a bachelor of laws degree and worked in the US Treasury Department. Riel went back to Washington to see Mallet in December 1874 following the condemnation of his assistant, Ambrose Lépine, for his actions at Red River. As we will see, Riel formed an important connection to Mallet. The Métis leader continued cultivating his ties with other French-Canadian immigrants by also visiting New York and New England in December 1874.[4]

It was not until February 1875 that Riel gained amnesty for his role in the Red River uprising. At the same time, however, he was banished from Canada for five years, beginning in April 1875. Riel therefore returned to Keeseville, but he did not stay put. Although exiled, he made occasional trips to and spent brief periods of time in Canada before going back to Keeseville, as he indicated in his letters to Major Mallet in May and July.[5]

By December 1875, Riel was again in Washington, DC, where he stayed with Mallet. Rev. Fabien Barnabé, the pastor of l'Immaculée-Conception Church in Keeseville with whom Riel had stayed, had written Mallet a year earlier (1874) to encourage his efforts on behalf of "the noble cause of the Métis," and to express his view that it would be important to gain the sympathies of US government officials. Mallet undoubtedly used his federal government connections to facilitate meetings between Riel, President Ulysses Grant, and Senator Oliver Morton, during which Riel raised the question of the United States financing an invasion of western Canada.[6]

During Riel's stay with Mallet, his host found him acting irrationally and became concerned about his mental state. Mallet later wrote: "Riel was certainly insane here in December 1875, and in order to prevent his enemies from knowing it I took ch[ar]ge of him." Mallet watched over Riel for a week and then accompanied him to New England. For the next few months, Riel spent time with his network of French-Canadian clergy who, like himself, served as pioneers organizing communities of French Catholics. Mallet initially brought Riel to the rectory of Rev. Jean-Baptiste Primeau, the founding pastor of Paroisse Notre-Dame-des-Canadiens of Worcester, a mutual friend of the two men and one with whom Riel had stayed during previous visits to the city. Like Mallet, Primeau was concerned about Riel's mental health and brought him about a week later to the Suncook, New Hampshire, rectory of Rev. Evariste Richer, the founding pastor of Paroisse Saint-Jean-Baptiste, a clergyman Riel knew from Manitoba. Probably uncertain how to help Riel, his hosts continued to shuffle him around. In January 1876, Riel was brought to Keeseville, but his mental health did not improve, so he was transported to Montréal and committed in March to a psychiatric hospital, the St. Jean de Dieu asylum at Longue Pointe, where he had spent some time in 1875. Because of overcrowding, or because the quality of care did not meet his needs, or due to concerns about safety (lest the Orangemen of Montréal discover Riel's whereabouts), or a combination of these reasons, he was subsequently transferred to the Beauport asylum, and he remained there until January 1878. Riel was registered at these asylums under assumed names, presumably not to call attention to a potential violation of the terms of his amnesty, which included exile from Canada. After leaving the Beauport asylum in January 1878, Riel again returned to Keeseville, where he stayed with the Barnabé family for about one year.[7]

Barnabé wrote Mallet in October 1878 that Riel was tired and in need of rest, but his mental health was good. Barnabé tried to help Riel find work in New York and in the western United States, recommending Riel, for example, to the Archbishop of St. Paul as a founder of Catholic colonies. In November 1878, Riel moved to St. Paul, Minnesota, and then to St. Joseph in the Dakota Territory, where he spent a year. From there, he moved to St. Peter, Montana, settled in a Jesuit mission, became a teacher, and married a Métis woman. Riel apparently decided to put down roots in the United States. The basic requirements for US citizenship were residency for a period of five years, declaring one's intention to become a citizen at least two years before naturalization, and renouncing allegiance to foreign leaders or governments. While in Montana, Riel declared his intention to become a US citizen in May 1880. At Helena in March 1883, he became a naturalized US citizen.[8] But he did not remain in the United States for long.

After a Métis delegation visited Riel in Montana in June 1884, and prevailed upon him to lead their efforts against the federal government of Canada, he returned to the Northwest Territories. Because the Canadian federal government had not honored its agreements with the Métis of Manitoba, they had moved further west to what became Saskatchewan. Riel orchestrated an insurrection there of the Métis and Crees and was formally charged with high treason in July 1885. A month later, a jury of six Anglo-Saxon Protestants found Riel guilty, and although it recommended clemency, the judge, also of Anglo-Saxon descent, sentenced him to hang, and Riel was executed in November 1885.[9]

Riel's hanging created bitter division in the Dominion of Canada. Anglo-Canadian Protestants viewed Riel as a traitor and advocated his execution. French Canadians of Québec knew Riel was insane but felt execution was an especially harsh punishment, one imposed by an Anglo-Protestant majority over a French Catholic minority. From Confederation until Riel's hanging, French Canadians had become aware of ethnolinguistic conflicts outside of Québec, such as the struggle of French-speaking Acadians of New Brunswick to gain public funding for Catholic schools. As they learned of such conflicts, residents of Québec came to regard themselves as defenders of Canada's French and Catholic minorities, including the Métis. While Catholic priests had helped mediate between the Métis and the federal government in 1869, the relationship between the Catholic clergy and the Métis became damaged in the mid-1880s as tensions rose in the Northwest.[10] Consequently, support for Riel remained lukewarm among French Catholics until his capture and execution in 1885. Thereafter, public sympathy for Riel in Québec led to a major and long-lasting political realignment from support for the ruling Conservative Party to support for the Liberals, a transition that has had a significant impact on provincial and federal politics for well over a century.

French-Canadian immigrants of the northeastern United States learned of the events that transpired in the Northwest Territories through articles their French-language newspapers regularly published throughout 1885.[11] After Riel received his sentence, *Le Messager* (Lewiston, Maine) questioned the justice of executing him, argued for clemency, and insisted that future relations between anglophones and francophones in Canada depended upon it. Plattsburgh's *Le National* also weighed in on the controversy. It contended that Riel did not deserve to be hanged and that imprisonment would be a more humane consequence. The newspaper suggested that Canada consider the example of how the United States dealt with Jefferson Davis, the leader of the Confederacy during the Civil War, whose sentence was imprisonment: "The Riel Affair is of little importance compared to that of Jefferson Davis and nevertheless the American authorities did not erect a scaffold for the latter." *Le National*'s editor called upon its readers in August 1885 to organize meetings to protest Riel's impending execution, something French speakers were doing elsewhere in that month in Biddeford, Saccarappa (now Westbrook), and Lewiston, Maine.[12]

French-Canadian immigrants in various upstate New York communities advocated strongly for Riel. Sixty-three French-Canadian Catholics of Malone signed a petition during a parish assembly to protest Riel's planned execution. Sixty-nine French Canadians of Rochester signed a similar petition that Attorney Ambroise Choquet sent to the US Secretary of State, Thomas Bayard, along with a copy of Riel's naturalization certificate. Choquet wrote that he knew Riel personally, was convinced from information he had received that "Riel is now insane," and requested that the US government intercede to prevent the hanging of one of its own citizens abroad. The secretary of state assured Choquet that Riel's citizenship had been considered. "Such citizenship, however, it must be remarked, even if beyond doubt, would not secure the possessor any immunity from Canadian law," wrote Bayard, "when, as it is definitely certified to this Government in the case in the present instance, the offense was committed within the territory of the Dominion."[13]

Riel's US citizenship certainly complicated matters. "The difficulty in Riel's case arose from the fact that British law of the period held that a person born a British subject could not lose that status later through naturalization in another country," noted Bob Beal and Rod Macleod. "To satisfy Canadian law Riel had to be charged as a British subject, but the United States had always strenuously objected to this doctrine and the two countries had actually gone to war over the issue in 1812, when the British persisted in impressing American seamen into the Royal Navy on the grounds that they were British subjects. To avoid diplomatic complications," Beal and Macleod explained, "the charge against Riel consisted of two sets of three identical counts, one of which named Riel as a subject of Her Majesty, the other simply as 'living within the Dominion of Canada and under the protection of our Sovereign Lady the Queen.'" In essence, then, according to J. M. Bumsted, "Louis Riel had been tried both as a British subject and as a resident of Canada, with his American citizenship implied but not stated. In either persona he was legally liable to be found guilty of treason."[14]

Newspapers serving French-Canadian immigrant communities reported Riel's execution. Immediately following the announcements, at least forty-one public protests in the United States were held in November and December 1885, as documented in the French-language press. The large majority (26) of the protests took place in the six states of New England: Massachusetts (14), Maine (3), New Hampshire (3), Vermont (3), Connecticut (2), and Rhode Island (1); outside New England, protests took place in New York (5), Michigan (3), Minnesota (3), Kansas (1), Missouri (1), Illinois (1), and the Dakota Territory (1). The public protests consisted of having masses said for Riel, gatherings to vocalize disapproval of his execution, and passing resolutions to express their disapprobation in a more formal manner, resolutions typically published in the press. As examples, the Saint-Jean-Baptiste society of Champlain, a village located north of Plattsburgh on the Canadian border, held a special meeting to condemn Riel's execution and unanimously viewed "this act of cruelty iniquitous as a formal violation of divine and human laws." At a meeting in Plattsburgh, presided over by Dr. J. H. LaRocque, participants heard an account of the history of the Northwest Territories, the complaints of the Métis, and the Canadian government's treatment of them. The editor of *Le National*, Benjamin Lenthier, served as the secretary of the meeting and proposed resolutions, adopted unanimously, identifying Riel as "our compatriot" and condemning his execution. In Glens Falls, a community south of Plattsburgh Riel had visited in March 1878, and where Lenthier had founded his first newspaper, French-Canadian residents passed resolutions declaring that Riel's execution was politically motivated and that it represented the vengeance of Orangists and of Prime Minister John Macdonald. They organized a mass for the repose of Riel's soul and planned to send their resolutions to Riel's widow, to the press, and to Macdonald himself. Some communities even took up collections for Riel's wife and children.[15]

The discourse of French-Canadian immigrants reflected their historic ethnic and religious challenges in the sending societies. In a display of cooperation comparable to that experienced in Plattsburgh since the mid-1800s, Irish and French-Canadian Catholics from Champlain unanimously passed resolutions concerning Riel's execution. One resolution emphasized the interethnic nature of their sentiments: "We, French Canadians and Irish Catholics, sons of those families that have had to suffer similar cruelties during the unrest of 1837 in Canada, and in Ireland for three centuries, reprove and condemn energetically the conduct of the Canadian government, in executing Louis D. Riel."[16] The *Canadiens* of Champlain thus viewed Riel's contemporary handling in the context of past conflict in Canada.

An anonymous contributor from Champlain, who signed his letter to the editor "Franco-Canadien," proposed erecting a monument to Riel, an idea that gained support from French Canadians in other northeastern states. Not all US French speakers viewed Riel as a hero, however. *Le Travailleur*'s editor, Ferdinand Gagnon, cautioned against elevating him to that status because of his role in the Northwest rebellions.[17]

In June 1886, an estimated 20,000 delegates from New England, New York, Michigan, Minnesota, and Canada assembled for a convention in Rutland, Vermont, wearing "on their chest the Canadian beaver and the maple leaf." Despite some squabbling in the press prior to the Rutland convention, the delegates who attended unanimously supported the resolution Major Edmond Mallet put forward to condemn the Canadian federal government's treatment of the Métis and particularly of Riel.[18]

Two years after the Rutland convention, francophone élites did not forget Riel. In 1888, the Riel Affair became an issue among francophone voters during the US presidential election. By the 1880s, French-Canadian immigrants were forming stable communities in the northeastern United

States and increasingly becoming naturalized citizens and voters. In 1888, voters had to choose between the Democratic incumbent, Grover Cleveland, and his Republican opponent, Benjamin Harrison. As it had done several years earlier, *L'Indépendant* (Fall River, Massachusetts) criticized Grover Cleveland for not having protected Louis Riel as a US citizen abroad, something it claimed the president had done in the past for naturalized citizens of Irish and German descent. As *L'Indépendant* saw it, Cleveland had recognized the electoral power of those ethnic groups and had discounted French Canadians. The newspaper categorically blamed Cleveland for Riel's death and contended that he should be taken to task for it as he made his bid for another term as president. *L'Indépendant* alleged that some Democratic French-Canadian voters who sided with Cleveland had even changed their views on Riel, having regarded him two years previously as a martyr and not as a criminal. The Democratic newspaper, *Le National*, was among them, charged *L'Indépendant*, a Republican newspaper.[19]

Le National tried to deflect the criticism that *L'Indépendant* heaped on President Cleveland. It also tried to unite French speakers behind the Democratic Party, arguing that the party stood up for workers and that it promoted equality in religious and civil rights; the newspaper asked francophones to support another Democratic victory in 1888. During the Gilded Age, when few differences distinguished the major political parties and presidential elections were very close, the votes cast in swing states like Indiana and New York determined the outcome of the contests in 1880, 1884, and 1888. Because New York was a swing state with thirty-six electoral votes, *Le National* attributed Cleveland's win in 1884 to French-Canadian votes: "In 1884, the [French-] Canadian vote of New York State was in favor of the Democratic Party, and it has to be admitted without contest that Cleveland's victory was due to our weight [tipping] the scales." The newspaper was concerned that another Democratic victory might not be imminent in 1888 because there were more Republicans than usual in that election year among "our compatriots." The lack of steadfast support for either major political party also helped make French-Canadian descendants a swing vote in other northeastern states before 1920.[20]

In the United States, French-Canadian immigrants equated the federal government's lack of action on Riel's behalf as a lack of regard for French Catholic minorities, as a palpable demonstration of the limits of citizenship in the nation-state in which they, like Riel, resided in the late nineteenth century. As demonstrated through the French-language press, through correspondence with government officials, and through public protests, French-Canadian immigrants were well aware of Riel's US citizenship. They also understood their rights in the host society and demonstrated knowledge of historical precedents by highlighting them to assert those rights. In doing so, they pushed the social and political boundaries of their era. What they encountered in the United States, in the person of Riel, however, were tangible limits to citizenship in the late nineteenth century. As Lauren Basson writes, "A long-time resident of the United States who became a naturalised citizen in 1883, Riel challenged the sociopolitical boundaries that limited full political membership in the US nation to white English-speakers who shared a Protestant, Anglo-Saxon heritage and cultural values." Whereas in Canada the Riel Affair led to long-term political realignment by French speakers, in the United States the shift of enough French-Canadian voters in 1888 from the Democratic to the Republican Party may have cost Grover Cleveland his bid for reelection.[21]

Through *Le National*'s editorial leadership in its reporting on and support of Louis Riel, the newspaper demonstrated its preeminent role as a defender of the interests of continental French speakers. In contrast to its extensive reporting on Riel and the aftermath of his execution, the French-language newspaper provided little coverage of the Chapleau-Tabor murder case that rocked Plattsburgh in the late 1880s. The historian Altina Waller has argued that the case served to illustrate ethnic and class divisions in the local community.[22] *Le National*'s apparent lack of interest in the Chapleau case suggests, however, that there was little to no ethnic interest at stake.

On January 31, 1889, *Le National* headed one of the articles on its third page "Un meutre" ("A murder"). For three and a half columns out of eight, the French-language newspaper provided a factual account of Joseph Chapleau's murder of his neighbor, Irwin Tabor.[23] The account made no mention of any ethnic tensions in the Plattsburgh community. Thirteen months later, *Le National* reported on the third page in its local news column that Chapleau's lawyers had succeeded in preventing his execution by electric chair following his March 1889 murder conviction.[24] Again, *Le National* remained silent on what this meant for the French-Canadian community of upstate New York. Plattsburgh's English-language newspapers provided far more coverage of the case than did the French-language newspaper. A review of the kinds of issues that attracted *Le*

National's attention during its publication in Plattsburgh will illustrate that it would not have shied away from addressing ethnic tensions in the community or the adverse treatment of *Canadiens*, had it perceived any in the Chapleau-Tabor murder investigation or trial.

When *Le National* began its third year of publication in June 1885, it announced to readers: "Our newspaper will remain, as in the past, attached to the principles that have guided us to the present and will always be ready to fight the good and large battles of the French-Canadian nationality," and, it added, "to defend at all times and in all places its religious and national interests." The newspaper pointed out that it was "openly [French-] Canadian [and] has no other goal than that of working and fighting towards and against all for right, justice and to assure the triumph of truth."[25]

While *Le National* defended French-Canadian interests on its pages, it did not do so at the expense of the Roman Catholic Church. Religion apparently trumped nationality for the newspaper, and it occasionally spoke out against French Canadians in their struggles with the Catholic hierarchy of the United States. In Fall River, Massachusetts, French speakers struggled with the Irish bishop, Thomas Francis Hendricken, who precipitated bitter controversies with them by appointing Irish pastors to French-Canadian parishes in the diocese. French Canadians of Massachusetts were concerned that the bishop's administrative actions would result in their forced assimilation into US society, and they demanded priests of their ethnic background during a convention held in 1885. *Le National* sided with church authority in this case, arguing that "our compatriots" were in the wrong and that church law should prevail. "As [French-] Canadian journalists," the editor explained to readers, "we have duties to fulfill towards our nationals; as Catholics, we submit to the canons of the holy [Roman Catholic] Church, our mother."[26]

Like other French-language newspapers of the northeastern United States, *Le National* helped promote naturalization among French-Canadian immigrants and encouraged their entry into the US political process. "One should not believe that in naturalizing ourselves we lose our national character," *Le National* stated in 1886. "No, we stay always at heart and in sentiment the sons of Canada and of France." This attachment to the French language, Roman Catholic faith, and French-Canadian traditions need not worry our American "fellow citizens," *Le National* indicated, for *Canadiens* were loyal to the governments under which they lived, whether in Canada or the United States.[27]

By the mid-1880s, *Le National* advocated Democratic partisanship as the means to advance the interests of French Canadians in the United States. During the 1885 elections, the newspaper made a pitch for the party of President Grover Cleveland and listed the Democratic nominees for various offices at the local and state levels as well as a short biography of each Democratic candidate. In promoting the reelection bid of New York's Democratic governor, David Hill, *Le National* struck at Republicans: "Today, the ideas of banishment and intolerance that the Know-Nothings cherish appear behind the transparent curtains of their disappointed illusions." The Know-Nothings had favored immigration restrictions on Catholic groups in the mid-1800s and, when the movement collapsed, many in it subsequently joined the newly formed Republican Party. The Know-Nothing movement's ideas were outdated, *Le National* explained in February 1886, because targeted groups like French-Canadian immigrants had become attached to their adopted country. "They are naturalizing American citizens and, fulfilling the duties of citizens, they have [the right] to share in the favors of the country," contended the French-language newspaper.[28]

Among the benefits French Canadians expected in the host society were patronage jobs, *Le National* made clear. The newspaper periodically mentioned in its columns that it was keeping track of the names of *Canadiens* appointed to various posts from the local to the national level. When it acknowledged in January 1886 that the Democratic Party seemed to offer more jobs to *Canadiens* than the Republicans had done in the past, it warned Democrats not to take the support of *Canadiens* for granted. In February, *Le National* complained that French Canadians were the largest ethnic group in Clinton County but that they were not getting their fair share of government jobs. The newspaper asserted that *Canadiens* were loyal Americans who paid their taxes, some had given their lives for the country, and the group, in turn, wanted public positions/jobs. In March, the newspaper announced that the local post office had hired a new employee, and it lamented, "We do not need to say that it is not one of our compatriots." When Charles Spear got the customs job in Plattsburgh, the newspaper commented: "The turn of [French-] Canadians has not arrived yet. Have patience, compatriots." But at the same time, it warned euphemistically: "There will come a time where they will need us and at that time we will thumb our nose at those who today hold the razor and the cake of toilet soap." By June, the newspaper emphasized that its political positions would favor French Canadians: "In politics, our newspaper as its name indicates will be above all national. We will favor the men who, in our humble opinion, will be the most disposed to safeguard and to protect the interests of our compatriots and the better qualified to fill honorably the functions to which they will be called." The newspaper added: "But above all, we will always be happy to lend a strong hand and to defend our own and the national cause with as much courage and energy that it has pleased Providence to give us."[29]

When *Canadiens* gained election to local offices, such as constable, inspector of elections, and clerk of courts, *Le National* pointed this out in its columns with evident pride. It did the same when *Canadiens* made inroads into businesses that had been dominated by Anglo-Americans, such as cutting and selling ice from Lake Champlain for home refrigeration. "We are happy to see that several of our good [French-] Canadians of Plattsburgh, among others Misters Archambault & Sons, Chabot, Bousquet, Desjardins, David, Lafosse, Philippe, etc.," it noted, "are competing with the American men for part of the riches of our mine of ice from Lake Champlain." The French-language newspaper even advocated for *Canadiens* in the Roman Catholic Church of the United States. After *Le National* learned that Bishop Edgar Wadhams had asked the Vatican in Rome for an assistant, given his advanced age and his infirmities, it expressed its hope that a *Canadien* would be considered for the position of the coadjutor bishop of Ogdensburg, noting that *Canadiens* made up a sizeable number of the diocese's Catholics: "It is to be hoped that, this time, our national element will not be neglected."[30]

When President Grover Cleveland nominated Major Edmond Mallet in 1888 to the post of inspector of Indian reservations, *Le National* expressed its great pleasure, and it explicitly mentioned to readers that Cleveland was a Democrat. As the French-language newspaper supported Cleveland's reelection bid in 1888, it evolved into a publication that promoted Democratic political partisanship. In August 1888, *Le National* reported that some influential *Canadiens* had gathered at the offices of Dr. J. H. LaRocque to organize a Democratic club; it expressed its support and its wish that Plattsburgh-area French Canadians would join the club, "which is destined to give to our compatriots an influence and prestige that they would not have by staying scattered and without cohesion."[31] At one meeting of the club, Lenthier spoke in favor of Cleveland and the Democratic Party, a party he claimed was sympathetic to French Canadians. The newspaper encouraged *Canadiens* to join le Club

Démocratique Canadien in order to prove "to the other nationalities that they are studying the politics of their adopted country and that they do not intend to vote blindly."³²

Following Cleveland's defeat, the Republican administration of President Benjamin Harrison replaced Mallet in 1889, and *Le National* went on the offensive to denounce the move in a series of articles, some of which it reproduced from other newspapers. Initially, *Le National* attributed Mallet's removal to Republican politics, but later it ascribed the action to anti-Catholicism, indicating that all Catholic employees of the Bureau of Indian Affairs had been replaced with Protestants. *Le National* shared with its readers articles from other French-language newspapers protesting against Mallet's removal, and it encouraged those newspapers to continue doing so until Mallet regained his post in order "to demand our rights as citizens of the grand republic."³³

Le National's owner participated in a meeting at the office of Dr. LaRocque to discuss a local response to Mallet's removal. It is unclear how many *Canadiens* attended the meeting over which LaRocque presided, but Lenthier recorded their resolution in *Le National*. "The French Canadians of Plattsburgh, N.Y., gathered in a meeting to this effect, protest in the strongest possible way against the arbitrary action of the Harrison administration," the statement read, "and consider as an insult to the French-Canadian race, that numbers a million loyal subjects of the American republic, the dismissal of the only representative it has in the offices of the Indian Department."³⁴ Despite the vociferous complaints made in the French-language press, Mallet did not regain his high-level government position.

Nonetheless, it is clear that *Le National* loudly exercised its voice on issues affecting *Canadiens* from the local to the international level. It might seem curious, then, that this French-language newspaper had so little to say about the Chapleau-Tabor murder case.

A native of Montréal who had been born in 1850, Joseph Chapleau migrated to the United States as a young man in 1870. After living initially in Grand Isle, Vermont, Chapleau moved around 1872 to Plattsburgh, New York, where he served for five years in the US Army, stationed at the Plattsburgh garrison. Chapleau also worked as a tenant farmer for a number of years on the property of William Jones, near Irwin Tabor, where he met Eliza Cassidy, an Irish domestic servant who also worked for Jones before she married Chapleau. In 1876, Chapleau purchased a one-acre parcel of land in Plattsburgh that he and Eliza sold a decade later, before acquiring another property of about forty acres in 1887, across from Tabor.[35]

By establishing a farm on land of his own in Plattsburgh, Chapleau gave evidence that he was setting roots in his country of adoption. He also did so by demonstrating various measures of acculturation in the host society. He married a woman outside of his ethnic group, he spoke English (albeit broken English), he had a subscription to an English-language newspaper (the *Plattsburgh Sentinel*), and he became a naturalized US citizen.[36] Thus, Chapleau demonstrated various signs before his fortieth birthday of his acculturation and integration into US society.

On January 28, 1889, Chapleau shocked the Plattsburgh community by bludgeoning to death with a sled stake his neighbor, Irwin Tabor. There had been a long-running feud between the two men. During the coroner's inquest, Chapleau contended while on the stand that Tabor had poisoned his cows and had threatened him. Chapleau maintained that he had acted in self-defense. Speaking without the aid of an interpreter, Chapleau stated in imperfect English at the inquest: "He jump on my sled, he had something in his hand, I couldn't tell zackly what he had, he came to strike me with it. I got a stake and hit 'im."[37]

Testimony presented during the coroner's inquest in January 1889 and at the murder trial a year later undermined Chapleau's account. Henry Hicks stated that Chapleau had asked him in August 1888 to help skin one of his cows, and they had found no signs of poison but nails, zinc, and a piece of bone inside the animal's stomach, which had been pierced by the nails. Hicks reported that Chapleau was present when he opened up the cow. In addition, Hicks indicated that a couple of weeks before the murder, Chapleau had told him he would shoot Tabor with a .32-caliber revolver if Tabor poisoned any more of his cows.[38]

The testimony of Chapleau's French-Canadian neighbors, the Browns, also did not corroborate his own. Peter Brown, a farmer, and his wife, Lena, were French-Canadian immigrants who had moved to the United States as minors. Prior to their migration, the Brown family name most likely was Lebrun. At Brown's home the night before the murder, Chapleau recounted a negative verbal exchange that had taken place between himself and Tabor in which he had threatened Tabor. When Tabor greeted Chapleau on the road, Chapleau called him "Cow doctor Vermonter," Brown related, a reference to Tabor's Vermont origins and to Chapleau's persistent belief that Tabor had poisoned his cows. When Tabor replied,

"Shut up your head," Chapleau told Tabor, as Brown repeated, "I will not shut up my head, but I am going to shut up your head for you, and when I shut it up it will stay shut." Mrs. Brown cautioned Chapleau, warning him he could be hung if he followed through on his threat, but he brushed off her concern and, as he headed out the door, noted that a new method of execution had replaced hanging, Brown testified during the murder trial.[39]

Although Peter Brown was illiterate, he could speak English and there was no indication that he provided his testimony through interpreters. His wife, Lena, was also illiterate but, unlike her husband, could not speak English. It is quite likely, then, that French was the language of their household, and it helps to explain why their sons Nelson and John, despite their English names, had a limited facility with the English language, even though they had both been born in the United States.[40]

Both Nelson and John Brown had witnessed Chapleau's assault on Tabor. Nelson, twenty-three, and John, sixteen, had been traveling by sleigh behind Chapleau when the assault took place. The coroner's inquest was scheduled on two separate days, the Tuesday and Thursday immediately after Tabor's murder. During the Thursday proceedings, with the aid of interpreter Joseph Gallant, the Brown brothers acknowledged having heard Chapleau threaten Tabor on several occasions, and they admitted seeing Chapleau strike Tabor from behind, knocking him out of his sleigh to the ground on the day he died.[41]

This testimony was not consistent with what the Brown brothers had said during Tuesday's proceedings, when they had obfuscated. "For dense ignorance he must be awarded the palm," the *Plattsburgh Morning Telegram* wrote of John Brown. "He didn't know anything about the affair, as he said, and in trying to tell the jury so he got himself into such a tangle that he could not extricate himself, and finally broke down and began to cry." The English-language newspaper continued: "The young man was very much mixed and either could not or would not tell a straight story." Since neither John nor Nelson Brown appeared to be forthright during questioning, they were held in jail "as witnesses" and were released only after Thursday's inquest, when they came clean about what they had observed.[42]

What had happened between Tuesday and Thursday that would explain the Brown brothers' change of testimony? The short answer is that a prominent member of the French-Canadian community had intervened. When Dr. J. H. LaRocque visited Nelson Brown in jail, he learned that the Browns had discussed at their home Chapleau's assault of Tabor and that they had decided not to tell authorities what they knew of his past actions nor what they had witnessed on the day of the assault. LaRocque prevailed upon the Browns to share what they knew. Called as a witness for the defense during Chapleau's murder trial, LaRocque indicated during his testimony that Nelson Brown had not understood what an oath was. Nor had John Brown, who explained the inconsistencies in his testimony during the two days of the coroner's inquest by stating that "he was so excited on Tuesday, and not understanding English perfectly, did not know what he was swearing to at the time," reported the *Plattsburgh Sentinel*.[43]

As illiterate French-Canadian descendants in Plattsburgh, whose stronger language was apparently French, the Browns did not understand how the US legal system operated.[44] The intervention of an elite member of their ethnic community convinced them to express in a straightforward manner what they had witnessed on that fateful day in late January 1889.

Indicted for murder by a grand jury, Chapleau pled not guilty in April 1889.[45] When Chapleau's trial began in Clinton County in January 1890, twelve men from outside of Plattsburgh, nearly all with Anglo-American surnames, served as jurors. Nelson Brown and his father, Peter, were called as witnesses for the People during the trial. But John Brown did not live long enough. He committed suicide by hanging himself in his father's barn in June 1889, half a year before the trial began. The *Plattsburgh Republican* noted that he had exhibited signs of anxiety prior to his death, such as refusing to eat, and added: "It is said that he has of late shown signs of fear lest some harm might come to him as the result of developing the full facts in the case at the pending trial of Chapleau."[46]

The jury found Joseph Chapleau guilty of murder in the first degree, and Judge Frothingham Fish handed him a death sentence. Chapleau became the first person in New York State sentenced to die in the electric chair. Fish told Chapleau plainly "that said punishment of death [shall] be inflicted by causing to pass through your body a current of electricity of sufficient intensity to cause death, and continued till you are dead: and may God have mercy on your soul." Chapleau was spared the electric chair, however, when Democratic Governor David Hill commuted his death sentence to life imprisonment, citing support from "many of the leading citizens of Clinton County," including county officials, the county judge, and all twelve jurors in the case. Hill stated: "It is clear that all the evidence was not fully developed on [sic] the trial, and the defendant's case was to some extent prejudiced thereby."[47]

Newspaper articles, available court records, and even published historical accounts of the Chapleau-Tabor murder case are silent about the role of religion and religious leaders. Where were the Oblate priests? Why did they not minister to and offer counsel to Chapleau and his family in the aftermath of his arrest and conviction for the murder of Irwin Tabor? The chronicle of the Sisters of Charity of Ottawa shed some light here. Three days after Chapleau's deadly assault of Tabor, two Grey Nuns, Sr. Marie McMillan (the local superior) and Sr. St. Michel (née Green) visited Eliza Chapleau at her home. The Grey Nuns had been making home visits and ministering to members of the Plattsburgh community since their arrival in 1860, so this visit to Mrs. Chapleau was not out of the ordinary. The sisters learned during their visit that Chapleau's wife was Protestant, he had not been a practicing Catholic for many years, and their eight-year-old daughter had not been baptized. Leaving the Roman Catholic Church opened Chapleau to the possibility of committing such a heinous crime, the sisters implied in their chronicle: "It is not surprising that the poor wretch, deprived of the graces of a good Christian, has let himself go commit a loathsome crime." Several days later, Sr. St. Claire (née Poirier) and Sr. St. Michel visited Chapleau in jail, and the Grey Nuns noted in their chronicle: "He appears to realize his crime and begins to regret it." Sr. McMillan and Sr. St. Claire visited Chapleau about a week later at a time when he was refusing to eat; they tried appealing to his religious heritage by discussing God's forgiveness, and he accepted religious items from them, such as rosary beads and a scapular. A few days later, after visiting her husband in prison, Eliza Chapleau stopped by the convent of the Grey Nuns. She expressed concern that her husband would starve himself to death, and she also took the opportunity to inform the sisters that she had no objection to her husband practicing his Roman Catholic faith, despite the fact that she was Protestant. The sisters tried to console her and promised to continue visiting Chapleau. When two Grey Nuns visited Chapleau a few days later, they found that he was now eating a little.[48]

The chronicles of the Grey Nuns thus inject a religious dimension, heretofore unknown, into the case of Joseph Chapleau. They also highlight the behind-the-scenes work of women, in this case women religious, in the community. They demonstrate, for example, the continuing role played by the Grey Nuns not only in ministering to those in need but also in bridging different ethnic and religious traditions in the community, all the while doing their work to promote the religious values and traditions of the Roman Catholic Church.

That Chapleau had fallen away from the church suggests one of the ways in which he may have been an outlier in Plattsburgh's French-Canadian community. His exogamous marriage suggests another way. Although Chapleau had been educated at the Collège de Terrebonne, north of Montréal, as the Grey Nuns learned when they visited his wife at their home, this should not be interpreted to mean that he had acquired a college education or that he was significantly more educated than his peers.[49] French-Canadian *collèges* provided secondary-level training to young men from twelve to eighteen years of age. It is true that there was no similar institution in Plattsburgh in the nineteenth century for boys to gain an education beyond primary school from women or men religious; for secondary-level training, their families would have had to send them to the local public high school or to one of Québec's *collèges*, a common practice among French-Canadian families of sufficient means who lived in the northeastern United States from the late nineteenth century through the middle of the twentieth.[50] It is unclear how many of Chapleau's ethnic peers had received secondary-level training. What is known, however, is that he had developed a facility in English and that he showed signs of acculturation into the host society that may have exceeded some other members of his ethnic community, such as his French-Canadian neighbors, the Browns.

Possibly *Le National* no longer considered Chapleau a "compatriote" because he had stopped practicing his Catholic faith. Possibly it was embarrassed by Chapleau's actions. Whatever the reasons for its relative silence on the murder case, the French-language newspaper surely would not have ignored his being singled out by the US justice system if it had had any inkling that it was taking place.

The historian Altina Waller argues that Chapleau's murder of Tabor was not an isolated incident or an aberration but actually part of a broader pattern of social and cultural tension in the Plattsburgh community. "Tabor was the victim, not so much of a single murderous temperament, but of the social and cultural conflict simmering beneath Plattsburgh's outwardly calm surface," she contends. While occasional tensions in the community came to light in the late nineteenth century, as this and previous chapters have revealed, contrary to Waller's argument, the Chapleau-Tabor case does not demonstrate fissures or ruptures in ethnic or social relations in Plattsburgh in the late nineteenth century. According to the *Plattsburgh*

Morning Telegram, "Tabor was a well-to-do farmer and Chapleau one not so well off in this world's goods."⁵¹ Admittedly, Chapleau's ethnic and class differences from Tabor may have helped arouse the animosity he had for his neighbor. But the historical record does not support expanding that generalization to the larger Plattsburgh community or viewing this case as emblematic of cultural and class conflict in the village. If that had been the case, *Le National*, as a defender of French-Canadian interests in the North Country and beyond, would surely have had much to say about it on its pages.

In New York—and throughout the country—in the late nineteenth century, nativist currents were evident. In 1889, the same year that Chapleau murdered Tabor and that Edmond Mallet lost his federal government post, the *New York Times* published an article titled "The French Canadians" that reflected nativist sentiment. The newspaper pointed out that this ethnic group did not make up a sizeable proportion of the population of either New York City or New York State but that there were 25,000 French Canadians in Clinton County, located in upstate New York on the border of Québec. The *New York Times* explained to its readers the reasons for their migration and where they were settling: "The immigrants, tempted by a more genial climate than their own and a higher rate of wages, have swarmed into the factories and taken up the farms abandoned by the natives as unprofitable." At the same time, the newspaper expressed concern about the fecundity of French-Canadian immigrants: "They are so much more prolific than their neighbors that the proportion of them to the whole community, wherever they have established themselves, tends to increase with surprising rapidity."⁵²

The *New York Times* raised the question of whether French-Canadian migration to the United States was a positive or negative occurrence, and it responded by considering the goals of the native-born: "It may be summed up in the general statement that immigration is a source of strength to the country in so far as it is capable of being readily assimilated and Americanized." The newspaper contended that assimilated and Americanized immigrants were "sources of strength to the Republic, not only economically, but politically and socially." By this measure, French Canadians fell short, argued the *Times*: "Tried by this standard, it must be owned that the French Canadians do not give promise of incorporating themselves with our body politic." The newspaper reached this conclusion after French-Canadian immigrants had held a convention in New York City in which they expressed an interest in retaining their customs and traditions in the United States. In a statement reminiscent of Carroll Wright's famous polemic, the *New York Times* opined: "The French Canadians mean to retain in this country, as for two centuries they have succeeded in retaining in Canada, the religion and the language of their ancestors, as distinctive badges of their separation from their neighbors. Comparatively few of them become citizens at all," the *Times* continued, "and those who do rate their citizenship so low and understand its duties so little that the power of voting renders them much less acceptable members of the community than they would be without it."[53]

While the *New York Times* did not advocate restricting French-Canadian immigration, it did express concern that, if enough French speakers naturalized, they would gain political power and might use it in US communities to push for their special interests through legislation, something the newspaper felt would be adverse to the interests of the larger community. Consequently, the *Times* recommended that US communities stand on guard: "The danger has scarcely yet become imminent in any American community, but it is foreshadowed distinctly enough to make it a patriotic duty for all Americans, in communities in which the French[-]Canadian population is considerable, to insist upon maintaining American political principles against all assaults."[54]

The large-scale immigration of French Canadians after the Civil War sparked such nativist sentiment in the United States. During the 1880s and 1890s, a national political movement known as the American Protective Association (APA) sought to reduce the influence of immigrant Catholics, such as French Canadians, in labor and politics. The APA spread to different parts of the country false stories about French Catholics, and it distributed anti-Catholic literature in communities heavily populated by French-Canadian immigrants. The anti-Catholic sentiment of groups like the APA permeated all regions of the country, including upstate New York. After the second Bishop of Ogdensburg, Rev. Henry Gabriels, said mass at the chapel of the Grey Nuns in 1894, he visited their boarding and parish schools, where he encouraged the students to apply themselves in the sciences, "but, above all, in the science of our holy religion as being the more necessary in a century where people want to abolish Catholic schools."[55] The bishop's comment to the schoolchildren in Plattsburgh suggested a form of resistance to the anti-Catholic forces at work at the state and national levels.

At the local level, as French-Canadian descendants became involved in politics in Plattsburgh, they sometimes found themselves the objects of negative comments because of their ethnicity, but this appears to have been a rare public occurrence in the late nineteenth century. One such incident took place in 1897. In March of that year, the *Plattsburgh Daily Press* claimed that "French citizens like Mike Dupont, Zeb Desso and Israel Crate [*sic*]" have been slurred and that their detractors "make sport of their alleged inability to speak correct English." Each of these men was active in Republican Party politics in Plattsburgh. Crete, a Democrat-turned-Republican, served on the village's Board of Trustees, a group that came under fire when twenty-five taxpayers and freeholders, exercising their rights under the General Municipal Law, filed an affidavit with the New York Supreme Court alleging that the trustees had improperly expended village funds. The *Plattsburgh Republican*, a Democratic newspaper, reported that the matter was under investigation in the courtroom of Justice S. A. Kellogg, and it charged that village officials "through their thoroughly subsidized organ, the Plattsburgh Press, have, day after day, since this proceeding was instituted, done their utmost to belittle the issues, and to revile its authors, and to stave off the matter." The newspaper suggested that the actions of the officials implied their dishonesty.[56]

The *Plattsburgh Daily Press* defended the men in its columns. In its view, so-called reformers had a nefarious objective: "The idea all the way through has been that no Frenchman has any right to attain any kind of prominence in public affairs and that when he does he is a fit subject for brutal attack in the public prints." The *Daily Press* thus suggested that nativist sentiment underlay the actions of those bringing suit as well as that of its rival newspaper. It claimed that the *Republican* had disparaged the men, yet they "are all respectable, thrifty, law-abiding and intelligent citizens, and creditable representatives of our French-Canadian population."[57] It is notable that an English-language newspaper defended this ethnic group. The anti-French sentiment that surfaced in the reporting on the court case brought forward by Plattsburgh taxpayers does not, therefore, appear to have reflected widespread attitudes in the local community.

Similarly, the Chapleau-Tabor murder case does not reflect larger nativist currents at the local level. Although ethnic tensions did exist in the Plattsburgh community, there were no big clashes among the different cultural groups that resided in the village. Had they existed, the chronicles of the Grey Nuns and the pages of *Le National* would have recorded them. Astute women, the sisters were quite perceptive about community relations, and French-language newspapers like *Le National* were not shy about reporting intercultural antagonism, or even perceptions of it, in the late nineteenth century.

Prior to leaving Plattsburgh, *Le National* helped French speakers of upstate New York to forge a political consciousness. As we have seen in the case of Louis Riel, the newspaper helped French Canadians to fashion a continental francophone identity that was willing to criticize Canadian and US political leaders. *Le National* also pushed French speakers to form at the local, state, and national levels in the United States a political identity more closely aligned with the Democratic Party. Some of this ethnic activism increased tensions, even among francophones from different locales in the Northeast. But the historical evidence does not suggest that it precipitated such fissures in the Plattsburgh community that it found expression in the actions of a French-Canadian man who murdered his Anglo-American neighbor.

Chapter Four

Religious Habits, Catholic Institutions, and the Champlain Tercentenary

Ringing in the Twentieth Century, 1900–1910

As the nineteenth century gave way to the twentieth, Plattsburgh's population increased significantly. In the early 1900s, French Catholics of Plattsburgh became aware of how larger currents of anti-Catholicism could at times play out in their local community. Nonetheless, they founded additional institutions to accommodate their growing numbers and the needs of the community. Some of the Catholic institutions they created had a clear ethnic identification, while others did not. In the early twentieth century, even though French-Canadian descendants of Plattsburgh showed signs of loosening some ethnic ties and traditions, they also presented elements of ethnic pride and preservation. Most notably, their creation of "French Day" in a nearly weeklong celebration of the European founding of Lake Champlain highlighted their historic and contemporary influence in the region and their pride in their heritage. In the first decade of the twentieth century, as individuals of French-Canadian birth and background in Plattsburgh became more integrated into US society, they did not demonstrate a straightforward movement toward assimilation but rather various twists and turns that continued to underscore their ethnic identity and sentiment.

Plattsburgh's population in 1900 stood at 8,434 residents, a 20.3 percent increase from the 1890 population of 7,010. As in most northern communities of this period, few people of color lived in the village; those who did made up a mere 0.2 percent of its population. Immigration contributed to most of the village's growth, for 43.6 percent of Plattsburgh's residents in 1900 were either foreign-born or had parents who were born abroad. As previous chapters have documented, French-Canadian immigration had a substantial impact on the community, from its public celebrations to its educational system to village politics. That influence continued into the twentieth century. In 1902, for example, when Plattsburgh became incorporated as a city, it elected a US-born French-Canadian descendant, Albert Sharron, as its first mayor.[1]

Born in Ellenburg, New York, Sharron moved to Plattsburgh at age sixteen and later became the co-owner of a dry-goods store that evolved into one of the largest department stores of the North Country. Sharron was a member and trustee of St. Peter's Church and was active in the Franco-American mutual-benefit society, the St. John Baptist Association. But he did not restrict his participation to organizations inside his parish and ethnic group. Sharron also became active in the local Chamber of Commerce, served as a director of Plattsburgh National Bank, and was a member of the Rotary and Elks clubs as well as the Knights of Columbus.[2] Such participation in nonfrancophone societies reflected Sharron's mixing in the larger community.

But Sharron certainly benefited from his ethnic roots. When Sharron won election as the mayor of Plattsburgh in 1902, the *Plattsburgh Daily Press* noted that he was "a merchant in excellent standing" who won the race with the solid support of Franco-Americans in the city. As we will see, Plattsburgh Franco-Americans achieved their most notable successes in politics in the Democratic Party. Indeed, the city's first Franco-American mayor won the office as a Democrat. "The fight was hotly contested by both sides, but the sentiment among the French to vote for Sharron, a Frenchman, was overwhelming and carried the day," the *Daily Press* reported. The newspaper went on to assert that there was considerable pressure within the Franco-American community to support Sharron: "That a Frenchman must vote for a Frenchman or be for ever [*sic*] an outcast among the French was preached from the pulpit, talked by the priests, and argued in the French societies, until the sentiment among the French people to stand by Sharron became irresistible." The newspaper concluded, "Race and religious feeling carefully worked up was the cause of Democratic success."[3] By "race," the *Daily Press* did not mean contemporary notions predicated upon skin color, but a nineteenth-century notion based upon ethnic background. In highlighting the ethnic and religious dimensions of the contest, the *Daily Press* acknowledged the growing political influence of Franco-American Catholic voters in the community.

One of the organizations to which Sharron belonged, the St. John Baptist Association, continued functioning as an ethnic society in the early twentieth century. The *Daily Press* noted in 1908, for example, that "only French residents of Plattsburgh or near-by towns are eligible for membership." The society still sponsored occasional excursions to Montréal, and it participated in a parade there to celebrate the fiftieth anniversary of the Society of St. Joseph of Montréal in 1901.[4]

In 1904, the St. John Baptist Association and the City of Plattsburgh hosted nearly 500 members and friends of the Société Saint-Jean-Baptiste of Montréal. The visit highlighted the continued cross-border connection of these French Catholic societies as well as the civic ties the two cities had cultivated over time. Plattsburgh Mayor William McCaffrey welcomed the visitors, telling them of the demographic effect of Canadian immigration in his city: "You will not find yourselves among strangers here, for it is safe to say that at least half of our citizens are of Canadian birth or Canadian descent." The mayor also commented on the French influence in upstate New York, stating: "You will find the names of many of the distinguished pioneers of New France, who did so much to open up this section commemorated, in our towns, lakes, rivers and streets." Dr. J. H. LaRocque greeted the visitors on behalf of the local St. John Baptist Association and spoke briefly about the role of Frenchmen like Samuel de Champlain and Marquis de Lafayette in contributing to US history and liberty. L. G. A. Cresse, the president of the Société Saint-Jean-Baptiste of Montréal, responded in English and French. Cresse commented on the friendly ties that existed between the United States and Canada "and expressed the hope and belief that at no great distant future the imaginary line now existing between the two countries would be entirely obliterated and they would be as one, at least as far as trade relations and fraternal relations are concerned," reported the *Daily Press*. The international visitors spent the next few days sightseeing in Plattsburgh and nearby AuSable Chasm.[5] Their visit highlighted Plattsburgh's role as a borderlands community that continued to tout its French Catholic origins in the opening decade of the twentieth century.

Unlike earlier decades, local celebrations of Saint-Jean-Baptiste Day in the early 1900s seemed to lack fanfare and enthusiasm. The Grey Nuns noted in their chronicle, for example, that a high mass in 1905 on the feast day of Saint-Jean-Baptiste attracted only twenty people in addition to the sisters. During the first decade of the twentieth century, the St. John Baptist Association had somewhere between 300 and 400 members, estimated the local press.⁶ But they appear not to have been as actively involved in local celebrations of their patron saint as in the past.

Members of the St. John Baptist Society still participated in other local events in the early 1900s, but they do not seem to have been the major organizers of them. In 1903, the *Daily Press* wrote that there had not been in the city a Fourth of July celebration for several years. It did note, however, that the St. John Baptist Association was expected to join the parade organized in that year, and it joined the parade again in 1905 and 1906. The society also participated in local Memorial Day parades, along with the Grand Army of the Republic, to visit local cemeteries. In addition, it marched in the Labor Day parade in the city that the Trades and Labor Assembly of Plattsburgh organized in 1907.⁷ Whenever there was a parade, some members of the St. John Baptist Association usually appeared in the lineup reported in the press. Impressionistic evidence suggests, however, that the organization did not play as large a role in organizing public celebrations in the early twentieth century as in the late nineteenth.

Part of the reason may be that Plattsburgh Franco-Americans were also joining other organizations that were not based on a shared French-Canadian heritage, as the memberships of Albert Sharron suggest. Some like Sharron joined the Knights of Columbus. Founded by Catholics in New Haven, Connecticut, in 1882, the Knights of Columbus formed a council in Plattsburgh in 1897. Men of French-Canadian birth and background who joined the organization had the opportunity to intermix with Catholics of other ethnic backgrounds. Some Franco-Americans even joined non-Catholic societies like the Knights of the Maccabees of the World, a fraternal organization founded in London, Ontario, in 1878 that spread to the United States within two years. The Maccabees boasted 145,000 members in the United States and Canada in 1894, the year they formed a tent (chapter) in Plattsburgh. At least three of the thirteen founding local officers had French surnames. Incidentally, cross-border movements were not unidirectional, because the Plattsburgh council of the Knights of Columbus in 1897 founded a council in Montréal, which became the first Knights of Columbus organization located outside of the United States—and Canada's first.⁸ As French-Canadian descendants of Plattsburgh joined non-French Catholic societies like the Knights of Columbus and non-French, non-Catholic organizations like the Elks,

Rotary, and Maccabees, they provided evidence of their intermixing with other ethnolinguistic groups in the host society.

As Franco-Americans of Plattsburgh became involved with organizations that were not French and Catholic in orientation, they continued to support their parish and its institutions. By 1901, St. Peter's had 925 families and 4,500 souls. Bazaars continued to be a major source of revenue for the church, netting at times between $1,600 and $1,800 in funds, often for major projects such as an upgrade to the church's heating system.[9]

In the early twentieth century, the St. Peter's parish community still practiced various French-Canadian traditions. The church continued, for example, the custom of celebrating Christmas with a midnight mass. In Canada, large numbers of francophone families made pilgrimages to the shrine of Sainte-Anne de Beaupré, the most important sanctuary in the Province of Québec, usually bringing ailing family members to seek the intercession of Saint Anne to help them heal. French-Canadian descendants continued this custom after settling in Plattsburgh. In 1886, for instance, *Le National* reported that two Plattsburgh families made the pilgrimage with twelve- and fourteen-year-old children who started healing from their maladies following the visit to the shrine. They were among the 90,000 faithful who journeyed to this sanctuary in the late 1880s. In 1903, St. Peter's Church, particularly its pastor Rev. Joseph Pelletier, had the responsibility of organizing the trip to Saint Anne's shrine on behalf of the Diocese of Ogdensburg. To get there, Plattsburgh residents had to take a train to Montréal and then travel by steamship along the St. Lawrence River to Sainte-Anne de Beaupré. The St. Peter's choir and orchestra provided the music both at the shrine and on the return trip aboard the steamer in that year. This trip was a bilingual affair, with one sermon on the boat offered in English by a Rev. Holland of Port Henry, New York, and another in French by a Rev. Lefebvre, the Oblate Provincial, from Lowell, Massachusetts.[10]

Typically, however, Plattsburgh residents made their pilgrimage to the shrine of St. Anne in Isle La Motte, Vermont. Doing so required taking a steamship from Plattsburgh across Lake Champlain to the island. In 1907, St. Peter's Church organized its nineteenth annual pilgrimage to the site, administered by Oblates of the Sacred Heart, and over 800 from Plattsburgh participated. The priests who accompanied the faithful to the shrine preached their sermons in French and English.[11]

There are various other signs that St. Peter's parish continued to pursue bilingualism at the turn of the twentieth century. The Oblate priests established a library for members of the church, and their printed 1903 catalogue reflects this bilingualism. The catalogue's cover appears in English and French; the inside front cover lists the library rules in English, and the inside back cover lists the rules in French. Out of the total collection of 839 books, the large majority (483, or 58 percent) were English-language titles, and the rest (356, or 42 percent) were French-language texts.[12] While reflecting the bilingualism of the parish community, the preponderance of titles in English suggests a preference for the dominant language of the host society.

Parish activities also reflected this growing preference. When the Grey Nuns attended midnight mass on Christmas Eve in 1905, they found that the Oblate priest, Rev. L. V. Lewis, preached the sermon in English. Following a concert in 1909 by the Champlain Literary Musical and Dramatic Club at the parish hall, Franco-American attorney Victor Boire gave a lecture in English to an audience of about 400 people on Marquis de Montcalm. Even the St. John Baptist Association was changing: a membership booklet from the early 1900s, written mostly in French, provided its section on sickness benefits in both French and English.[13] Available sources suggest, then, that French-Canadian descendants of Plattsburgh were increasingly comfortable using the English language.

No doubt this was in large part due to the formation of the children by the Grey Nuns. Parish children educated by the sisters continued to receive a bilingual education in the early twentieth century. Their activities also reflect their facility in both languages. To celebrate St. Valentine's Day in 1905, the Grey Nuns organized an evening program during which their students made recitations in French and English. In November of that year, the young girls who served as the choir for the 9:00 a.m. mass at St. Peter's Church gave two performances at the parish bazaar, "one in English and the other in French, which pleases greatly the people who went to the bazaar," noted the Grey Nuns in their chronicle.[14]

In the early 1900s, besides administering the parish school under the direction of the public board of education, the Grey Nuns continued to conduct their own academy for girls (see fig. 4.1). Although D'Youville Academy had visits from Regents inspectors, and the sisters had to prepare their students for New York Regents exams, the Grey Nuns had considerable autonomy in managing the school. Among other activities, the sisters recruited their own students. A couple of sisters traveled every fall to Lowell, Massachusetts, to recruit boarding students, attracting in some years thirty or more young women from that city to D'Youville

Academy; at the end of the school year, the sisters escorted the young women back home. In 1900, D'Youville Academy had 55 boarding students, 63 in 1905, and by autumn 1907, probably the peak year, there were 75 boarders at the convent school, an important source of income for the Grey Nuns. But the numbers dropped to less than half of that (36 boarders) in the following year, after the sisters increased their rates. In 1910, at the end of the first decade of the twentieth century, there were 40 boarding students at the academy.[15]

State and federal census records shed additional light on these students. In the census years 1900, 1905, and 1910, the boarding students of the sisters ranged in age from five to nineteen. The large majority of these female students were US-born (see Table 5). Accordingly, relatively few of the students by the early twentieth century, as in the late nineteenth, were Canadian residents or Canadian immigrants in the United States. As in 1860, when the convent school opened, not all of the students were French-Canadian descendants. In 1900, just under one-third of the

Figure 4.1. Grey Nuns of the Cross and students in front of D'Youville Academy, October 1908. Courtesy of Archives des Soeurs de la Charité d'Ottawa, accession P-M5/9.

boarding students had French surnames; in 1905, that proportion jumped to two-thirds, as the sisters drew nearly half the student population in that year from the Franco-American communities of Haverhill and Lowell, Massachusetts; and in 1910, when the sisters had in residence only two students born in Massachusetts, the proportion dropped to under half with French family names (see Table 5).[16] Judging from surnames, the boarding students of the sisters in the early twentieth century—just as in the nineteenth century—came from different ethnic and linguistic backgrounds. Thus, it proved prudent for the sisters to offer a bilingual and multicultural education to attract applicants to their academy.

As in the late nineteenth century, the boarding students of the sisters did not have to attend classes on St. Patrick's Day and instead used their time to prepare for an evening performance of music, singing, and recitations. In the early twentieth century, the sisters no longer escorted their younger pupils to the Irish church to celebrate St. Patrick's Day, and they noted that the elementary students and their instructors did not likewise have the day off: "Our poor sisters from the parish school have been obliged to teach class."[17] At their own academy, the Grey Nuns could set their own academic schedule for their ethnically diverse student body.

Commencement exercises at D'Youville Academy tended to be bilingual events featuring members of the clergy as speakers. In 1909, for example, one member of the clergy spoke in English and another from Montréal spoke in French during the celebration. Commencement speakers were not always drawn from Catholic communities, though. In 1905, the Plattsburgh Normal School principal, George Hawkins, addressed the graduating students, congratulating them and the sisters who instructed them while also making a pitch for the graduates to attend his institution. The sisters were of course familiar with the Normal School, for those who moved to Plattsburgh from communities outside of New York took their exams there to obtain state teaching certificates in the early twentieth century.[18]

In the opening decade of that century, the Oblate priests continued to put pressure on the Grey Nuns to provide more French-language instruction. In 1904, Rev. Joseph Pelletier, the pastor, pressed the Mother Superior for another French-language teacher. The sources do not make clear whether this instructor was to serve in the parish school administered by the Plattsburgh Board of Education or, more likely, at Collège St. Pierre (described later) that the parish had founded the previous year. Exhibiting sharp business skills, the Mother Superior agreed on condition that each student pay 50 cents monthly for the French class, and if the sisters did not realize $200 yearly from their instruction, "the Father Superior commits to paying the balance," the sisters recorded. In 1908, when Rev. J. H. Driscoll, the Irish pastor of St. John's Church, joined other representatives of the clergy at the commencement exercises of D'Youville Academy, he addressed the five young women graduates in English about the role of educated women in elevating humankind; for his part, Pelletier spoke about the school's successes and "of the excellent instruction received by the pupils, especially in French, and closed by hoping that there would be more time devoted to the study of that subject in the future," reported the *Daily Press*. Two years later, when Pelletier left Plattsburgh due to declining health, the *Sentinel* commented: "He kindled in the hearts of his people a new love for their mother tongue and national history, and today, as a result of his labors practically every French child in the city is being educated in French."[19]

Pelletier, who had migrated to the United States from French Canada, had worried during his time in Plattsburgh about the growing tendency toward anglicization, and he worked to ensure the preservation of the French language in the parish.[20] He made the arrangements for the Brothers of Christian Instruction to come to Plattsburgh in 1903 to take over the education of boys at St. Peter's School. Founded in Brittany, France, in 1819 by the Roman Catholic priests Gabriel Deshayes and Jean-Marie Robert de la Mennais, the Congregation of Christian Instruction, as it was originally called, served as a charitable organization designed to promote teaching. In the nineteenth century, the brothers expanded beyond France to establish missions in French colonies, such as Guadeloupe (1837), Martinique (1839), and Haiti (1864) in the West Indies; Senegal (1841) in Africa; St. Pierre and Miquelon (1842) in North America; French Guyana (1843) in South America; and Tahiti (1860) in the South Sea. Anticlericalism in France led to laws in the 1880s prohibiting religious orders from teaching in the public schools of France and its territories. Consequently, the Brothers of Christian Instruction accepted an invitation in 1886 to staff a school in Chambly, Québec, their first foreign mission outside the rule of the government of France. From 1886 to 1902, ninety-three Brothers of Christian Instruction migrated from France to Québec, and five years after arriving in Canada, the order opened a novitiate in La Prairie, located near Montréal. In 1903, the Brothers were conducting eighteen schools in Québec. By that year, the order had 2,000 members, with the large majority of them (1,750) still located in France. When France expelled religious orders from its territories and confiscated their houses in the early twentieth century, all of the brothers' missions (except Tahiti) closed, and many of them relocated to Canada. In 1903, sixty additional Brothers and forty scholastics migrated from France to Canada, more than doubling the size of the La Prairie province.[21] This had direct implications for the francophone population of Plattsburgh, just fifty miles south of La Prairie.

The Brothers of Christian Instruction were interested in establishing a mission in Plattsburgh so that some men in their order could learn English and become future teachers of the English language. One of the brothers who had been expelled from France in 1903, Cyprius-Celestine Tregret, explained: "English was much in demand then in Canada even in country schools and was necessary to teach in the U.S.A. and Provinces of Western Canada." The Brothers of Christian Instruction learned from a former member of Plattsburgh's St. Pierre parish, who had relocated to Montréal, that its pastor hoped to open a school for boys. The brothers subsequently contacted Pelletier to offer their services, and they proposed in June 1903 that the Oblates consider having the order assist them, indicating that the brothers "will be like in Brittany happy to be the devoted assistants of the clergy." One month later, the trustees of St. Pierre Church accepted the offer of the Brothers of Christian Instruction to provide three men at a salary of $250 for each brother per year, for two to teach French during the day and one to teach in the evenings "the [French-] Canadians as well as the Americans."[22] Thus, the hiring of the Brothers of Christian Instruction to teach in Plattsburgh constituted part of the effort of the parish community to preserve its French language.

Through Pelletier as a conduit, the brothers purchased in August 1903 the former Vilas mansion and adjacent land in Plattsburgh. The Grey Nuns had previously considered the property as a possible location for a hospital but had decided not to purchase it. When the brothers made their offer to buy the estate, their efforts apparently aroused some anti-Catholic sentiment, for Protestants tried to outbid them. A decade and a half later, the brothers noted in their order's newsletter, *Écho des Missions*, that the site had been associated with previous acts of anti-Catholicism. Once known as "Gallows Hill," where criminals were hung in the early nineteenth century, Plattsburgh residents were loath to build there, "but the Catholics, less superstitious than their fellow citizens," considered erecting a church on the site at one point, the brothers recounted. This alarmed Protestants who did not want to have a Catholic church near their residences, so a rich banker bought the property, explained the brothers, "determined to frustrate the intention of the Catholics." After the banker died, his property lay abandoned until the brothers purchased it. "The former residence of a Protestant banker was to become a place of refuge for the persecuted religious," the brothers wrote in 1908. Because the Brothers of Christian Instruction bought this property on a hill on the date of the religious Feast of the Assumption, they named the building Mount Assumption Institute.[23]

Shortly after their arrival at the institute, the brothers realized they had their work cut out for them when they heard the French language spoken in the Plattsburgh community. "Few people spoke a recognizable French in the salad of slang and English which they seasoned it with," wrote Brother Cléonique-Joseph, who first came to Plattsburgh in 1903 and started teaching at the parochial school in 1905. To illustrate, he quoted a worker at Mount Assumption Institute who recounted the following story: *"Un tinsmith était occupé à nailer des shingles sur la roof et à couler du plomb dans l'gutter. I fit un side-step, est tombé sur la walk et s'est cassé la skull. Quand on l'a rel'vé, iétait dead, dead!"* This means of communicating informally in both English and French in the same sentence apparently could be heard among younger members of the community as well, for Cléonique-Joseph further commented, "I had in class some children who scarcely spoke better."[24]

During their first year in Plattsburgh, Brothers Ambrosio (né Joseph-Jean-Marie Lucas), Denis-Antoine (né Jean-Baptiste Gélinas), and Joseph-Désiré (né Joseph Crépeau) did not attract large numbers of boys to their classes. They began the school year in September 1903 with as few as ten boys (though some accounts stated the figure was closer to thirty), and they ended the school year in June 1904 with fifty boys in grades four to seven. The brothers were disappointed with these numbers. "How can we account for this lack of enthusiasm on the part of the parents?" they questioned. "The Brothers were relied upon by some to help check the decline of the French language among the children. They were expected to emphasize French in class and out of class," they noted. But the parish community had acculturated in US society to the extent that not all favored French-language retention. "These Franco-Americans had to earn a living among an English-speaking population; a knowledge of English was necessary to them," wrote Tregret. "Quite a few parishioners were concerned that the new teachers might not very well prepare their children to compete in the English-speaking world where they would have to live," commented the brothers, who added: "Hence, the dubious reception accorded the Brothers in their first few months."[25]

While parents may have questioned the value of educating their sons in French, the parish community as a whole warmly received the brothers. The Oblates made the brothers feel a part of their religious community. "They consider us like their own. We all form a united community," stated the brothers. When St. Peter's parish held a banquet in honor of the brothers in January 1904, the attendees included the bishop of Ogdensburg, the superintendent of schools for New York State, the principal of the Plattsburgh Normal School, a county judge, and the Brother Provincial. The program included the singing of both "O Canada" and "America." The brothers were touched by the event, which stood in sharp contrast to what they had experienced in France: "It was an unforgettable celebration; and, when we dream of France, it is a contrast that grips the heart."[26]

The Brothers of Christian Instruction found that Protestant Americans in the Plattsburgh community were not hostile to their order, yet they regarded the brothers with some suspicion. Ambrosio, the first superior at Plattsburgh, was born in France and migrated to Canada in 1888; after learning English at the Christian Brothers College in St. John's, Newfoundland, he taught English at the La Prairie house of formation before moving to Plattsburgh in 1903. He wrote in 1905 that "the Protestant Americans are not fanatics for the most part; they do not discuss the persecution that rages in France against the [religious] congregations; they would like to learn about religious life really to see if there is something in it that is a danger for the state [nation]." Religious difference was palpable to the French brothers missioned in Plattsburgh, however. They felt uneasy enough about being part of a Catholic order in a community with a large number of Protestants that it affected their choice of clothing. Like the Grey Nuns, the Brothers of Christian Instruction studied for the New York State certification exams, administered annually in August at the Plattsburgh Normal School, but, writes Tregret, "the Brothers, not to attract undue attention, chose to appear in secular clothes" for their exams.[27]

In November 1903, seventeen scholastics from the order enrolled at the Normal School to improve their English-language skills and to become familiar with state educational requirements. By 1905, there were twenty-one scholastics in residence with the brothers who taught at the parish school. While nearly all scholastics were between eighteen and twenty-one years of age, two of them were as old as twenty-eight, and all twenty-one young men were "alien," to use the terminology of the period, with seventeen having been born in France and four in French Canada.[28]

Tregret has written that sending the scholastics to the Normal School "was a daring, unprecedented move in our Congregation," a move against which conservative members of the order spoke, for they felt it might lead to a loss of religiosity among the men. This was a concern because the Normal School was not a Catholic institution. During its first decade in the 1890s, the large majority (66 percent) of its accepted students were Protestant, compared to a small fraction (less than 28 percent) who were Catholic. Thus, "the Normal School had a marked Protestant identity and orientation," writes the historian Douglas Skopp. But Bishop Henry Gabriels approved training the brothers there as "an emergency measure caused by the persecution [in France]," noted Tregret.[29]

The presence of these scholastics increased the proportion of students with French surnames who attended Plattsburgh Normal School in the 1900s. Few students of French or French-Canadian descent studied at the Normal School in its early decades, despite their large numbers in Plattsburgh and the North Country. William C. Fellows examined samples of students with French surnames taken from the school's registers between 1889 and 1920 and from college yearbooks to 1930. In the five-year period from 1890 to 1895, Fellows found that 3 percent of the students had French surnames, and 8 percent did in the period from 1900 to 1905, when the scholastics training to become Brothers of Christian Instruction attended. The proportions ranged from 7 to 9 percent in later sample periods: 1910–1915, 7.9 percent; 1920–1925, 6.9 percent; and 1930–1935, 9.3 percent.[30] Thus, the number of French-surnamed students increased modestly after the arrival of the scholastics in Plattsburgh.

The Brother Provincial in Canada informed the Superior General in France in November 1903 that the scholastics had been well received in Plattsburgh: "Protestants like Catholics make us most welcome." In another communication with his superior in the following month, the provincial wrote: "My strongest support has been from the Protestant Americans." But the Superior General remained steadfastly concerned about the presence of the scholastics in a nonsectarian environment, noting in 1905 that "it seems to us that there are too many dangers to begin a third year," overruling the provincial's desire for them to complete the final year of a three-year course of study at Plattsburgh Normal School. Consequently, the scholastics were recalled to Québec to meet the large number of requests to serve in the province's schools.[31]

One of the scholastics, Cléonique-Joseph, remained in Plattsburgh to teach at St. Pierre Academy and learned New York State educational standards. Exiled from France, he initially migrated to La Prairie, Québec, in 1903 and studied at the Plattsburgh Normal School from 1903 to 1905. He then had teaching appointments in Plattsburgh at St. Peter's parish school from 1905 to 1911, at the scholasticate of the brothers from 1911 to 1912, and then again at St. Peter's Academy from 1916 to 1918, before moving on to assignments in Canada for the rest of his teaching career. While teaching in Plattsburgh, Cléonique-Joseph began preparing for the New York State Life Certificate late in 1906 and gained it by August 1909. Just like the classes of the Grey Nuns, those taught by the brothers were also subject to state inspections, including their French-language classes, even though French did not occupy a large place in the New York State curriculum. A state official would come all the way from Albany to verify that the brothers, who were native speakers of French, were competent to teach the language, reported Cléonique-Joseph. "It was merely a formality in our case," he stated. "But we received official recognition. Grade: 100%."[32]

The brothers also became acquainted with New York State laws and pursued incorporation. When taxes on the Mount Assumption property proved to be a burden for the Canadian district of the Brothers of Christian Instruction, Bishop Gabriels helped the order to obtain in 1904 a charter of incorporation from the state, which granted them tax-exempt status. After the Committee on Charitable and Religious Societies reported a bill to form a corporation of the Brothers of Christian Instruction, the New York State Assembly passed it, and the governor approved the legislation, a process that Plattsburgh's English-language press monitored and reported to its readers. The objects of the corporation, according to the legislation, were "the religious instruction of the people, the establishment of novitiates, primary, model and academic schools, boarding schools, commercial colleges, manual labor schools and hospitals in the towns, cities and villages of this state, and the imparting of moral and religious education to poor and orphan children."[33] Thus, the work of the Brothers of Christian Instruction would serve to complement that of the Grey Nuns in Plattsburgh and, as Rev. Pelletier would have it, with special emphasis on French-language instruction.

The ethnic origins of the brothers made that possible. When New York State census-takers came around in 1905, there were six Brothers of Christian Instruction in residence in Plattsburgh. All were immigrants who had been in the United States from one to three years, with two of them originally from France and the other four from French Canada. In 1910, US census-takers found twelve brothers in residence. Each had immigrated to the United States in the period from 1903 to 1909, with five of them native of France and seven of French Canada. Census data thus suggests that the majority of the brothers serving in Plattsburgh during the first decade of the century were of French-Canadian descent (see Table 4).[34]

Not long after their arrival, the work of the brothers garnered the attention of the English-language press. In September 1905, the *Plattsburgh Republican* complimented the Brothers of Christian Instruction for their fine work. The newspaper reported that only eighth-grade students were allowed to take Regents exams, but seventh-grade students taught by the brothers at St. Peter's took the exam and passed. This "placed them one year ahead of all the other city schools of the same grade and won laurels for themselves and honors, for the school which, in its two short years of existence, has already surpassed the most sanguine expectations," the newspaper stated.[35]

The graduation ceremonies, like those overseen by the Grey Nuns, were bilingual events that reflected multicultural themes. When Collège St. Pierre, a secondary institution that the parish organized for boys in 1903, had its first commencement exercises, "the school hall was brilliantly decked with flags and the starred flag of the United States married itself admirably with the Canadian and French flags," the brothers wrote. But the event was largely one to celebrate the accomplishments of Franco-American young men. Clinton County District Attorney Arthur Hogue, "one of the notables of the Franco-American bar," served as the keynote speaker at the first commencement. Addressing the graduates in English, he encouraged them to bring honor to the Franco-American community. Those attending the graduation exercises were lay and religious, Catholic and Protestant. This kind of intermixing the brothers found in Plattsburgh greatly impressed them: "We had there a good example of the large ideas and liberal spirit that distinguishes all veritable Americans."[36]

But the kinds of liberalism to which the brothers alluded in their report of the first graduation of Collège St. Pierre did not necessarily exist outside of Plattsburgh. In 1906, the Grey Nuns encountered significant anti-Catholicism as the result of a complaint generated from outside of the Plattsburgh community about their teaching in schools administered by the public board of education. DeWitt Morrell, a New York City attorney, complained to A. S. Draper, the New York State commissioner of education, that the sisters wore their religious habits while teaching in the Plattsburgh public schools. Draper in turn wrote to the superintendent of schools in Plattsburgh to ask if Morrell's allegation was true; if so, the sisters had to stop the practice, Draper insisted, for public funds could not be expended to support schools that allowed it. The Grey Nuns had been teaching in their religious attire in Plattsburgh for thirty-seven years when they learned of the complaint through a phone call from and meeting with local attorney J. B. Riley.[37] The next day, the sisters proceeded as they normally did, noting in their chronicle on January 3: "Opening of classes; we continue for the time being as if nothing has arisen." But the sisters were clearly worried. A few days later, they began a novena to St. Joseph, "champion of desperate causes," and they commented in their chronicle, "May he hear our supplications and let us look after the school until the month of June." In exchange, "we made the promise to make thirty-three Stations of the Cross as a community, if we obtain [the grace] to continue administering the school until June," they wrote.[38] The Sisters of Charity of Ottawa, of course, faced the challenge of teaching in a country, unlike Canada, where there is a separation of church and state.

The Plattsburgh School Board wrote Commissioner Draper and asked his permission to continue the arrangement the board had made decades earlier with the Grey Nuns. They pointed out that, in 1906, the local board consisted of eleven Protestants, three Roman Catholics, and one Jew. They noted that the school the sisters conducted had begun as a Roman Catholic school but since the late 1860s had been under the supervision of the school superintendent and the board of education. The board further informed the commissioner that the eight teachers and the principal were all licensed to teach and were all Roman Catholic, as were the students, given the location of the school. "While these teachers dress in a manner peculiar to their own ideas and propriety," the board wrote, "it has never been made a subject of criticism on the ground that it carried with it an authority for religious example or instruction." Over the course of three and a half decades, the board of education had never received complaints from local citizens, taxpayers, or even students about the instruction of the sisters, it stated. In concluding its letter, the board alluded to the religious harmony that had prevailed in the Plattsburgh community for many years. "We are confident that any action by the department tending to sever the pleasant relations so long existing among our citizens of mixed nationalities and religious affinities," they asserted, "will result in great injury to all interested in the cause of Education and only gratify the Vindictiveness of some outside meddler."[39]

A committee of four men from Plattsburgh's board of education—E. C. Baker, Judge R. E. Healey, H. E. Barnard, and Smith Weed—subsequently traveled to Albany in late January to speak directly to Draper. The commissioner told the men of the New York City lawyer's complaint that it was a violation of state law for instructors to teach in religious attire in public schools. Healey argued against the Lima decision, as it was known, saying it did not apply to Plattsburgh. "He also made a strong plea for the continuing of the harmonious feeling which had so long existed in our community between the different religious denominations of our city," the subcommittee reported, "which he attributed more th[a]n anything else to the wise and conservative course of the Board of Education during the past, nearly forty years." Barnard extolled the work of the Grey Nuns, "depic[t]ing clearly the obstacles the teachers had been obliged to overcome in dealing with a class of people ignorant of our language and laws, and closing with a vivid reference to the moral and intellectual improvement in the French population since his childhood and the present generation," the subcommittee wrote, "naming scores of young men who are now occupying honorary positions in life through the helpful influence of that department." A couple of days later, the sisters were informed that they could continue as usual until the end of the school year.[40]

In mid-April, the sisters learned that the New York Court of Appeals had affirmed the decision of a lower court that allowing women religious to wear their habits in public schools was not lawful in the state. Consequently, their longstanding arrangement with the public-school board would only continue a couple more months, and they recorded in their chronicle: "In this way we will teach under the government until summer and then . . . Farewell." In June, the Plattsburgh Board of Education formally notified the sisters that they could not teach under public administration the following school year. At the same time, the board expressed its regrets and credited them with making good citizens out of a population that was disadvantaged and illiterate.[41]

With the end of the public-private arrangement, St. Peter's parish took over the school again and paid the salaries of the sisters. The Superior General of the Sisters of Charity of Ottawa came to Plattsburgh to negotiate directly with the Oblate priests. According to the terms of their agreement, the parish would hire four sisters at $200 a year, and the sisters would teach boys only in grades two and three, but girls up to grade six. The arrangement to teach boys in two grades was temporary, "while waiting until the brothers can take charge of them."[42] By the "brothers," the Grey Nuns of course meant the Brothers of Christian Instruction.

St. Peter's parish then focused its energy on erecting a new building for the academy for boys that it called Collège St. Pierre, and it opened with great fanfare in fall 1907. During the Labor Day parade of that year, the St. John Baptist Association, the fire companies, and various unions formed the procession in Plattsburgh. The *Republican* noted that union men had made a "substantial voluntary contribution" to the academy. The parade ended at St. Peter's parish for the dedication of its new school. Rev. Lewis spoke about the importance of education for success and argued that religious training was a necessary component of education, highlighting this point to explain how the new academy differed from the public schools. Brother Joseph Lacasse, the principal, spoke in French on education, labor, praying, and good citizenship. Visitors then had the opportunity to tour the new school building, and the Labor Day celebration continued in the afternoon with field-day activities at the fairgrounds.[43]

A couple of months later, the parish held a banquet to celebrate the opening of the new school. The celebration included the mayor and other guests. During his remarks, Rev. Pelletier noted that the Brothers of Christian Instruction were teaching the Regents curriculum to 275 boys and the Grey Nuns were teaching 300 girls. These roughly 600 students, Pelletier pointed out, were being educated at no expense to the city of Plattsburgh. "We have erected the present building," he stated, "not in any spirit of opposition to the public schools of the city, but because we firmly believe in the necessity of religious teaching in the schools."[44]

Other speakers at the 1907 banquet reflected clear ethnic themes. J. B. Riley, "representing the Irish portion of the community," indicated that he was proud of his Irish ancestry, but he commented that he was even prouder of his US citizenship; Riley then paid tribute to the French language and to the French population of the community, noted the *Daily Press*. Addressing the banquet-goers in French, Dr. J. H. LaRocque spoke of their history in Clinton County, the obstacles they had overcome, the respect they had earned, and how well regarded they now were in the community. As the general president of the Franco-American mutual-benefit society Union St. Jean Baptiste d'Amérique based in Woonsocket, Rhode Island, Felix Gatineau spoke on the history of the French in North America and encouraged the preservation of the French language.[45]

The press recognized that the academy was not just a Catholic institution, but a French Catholic school. When the *Sentinel* reported in 1909 that St. Peter's Academy had 300 students under the direction of the Brothers of Christian Instruction, it added: "The boys in their charge are thoroughly instructed in both English and French." When Pelletier left his position as superior in 1910, the *Daily Press* commented: "The buildings of St. Peter's college will long stand as a monument to his energy and zeal in the cause of religious training for boys and the preservation of their mother tongue by the young French people of this city."[46] The establishment of Collège St. Pierre represented, then, an effort to preserve the ethnicity of Plattsburgh's French-Canadian descendants, as they continued their integration into the host society.

Besides the secondary school for boys, Catholics of Plattsburgh established new mutual-aid societies. L'Union Saint-Jean Baptiste d'Amérique (USJBA) formed in Rhode Island in 1900 "to bring together as members of one great fraternity all Americans of French descent residing in the United States," noted the parish yearbook of 1931–1932. Its goal "has been to safeguard the French language and the customs of the Mother Country." This was a French Catholic organization; to join it, one "must be of French origin or recognized as such, and a practicing Roman Catholic." Plattsburgh established two councils in the early 1900s: Conseil Montcalm, No. 123, for men in 1905, and Conseil Sainte-Cécile, No. 177, for women in 1907.[47]

Plattsburgh Catholics also established new cemeteries. For more than half a century, Irish and French descendants in the city had buried their departed members in the same cemetery on South Platt Street. When it became overcrowded, St. John's Church opened a cemetery of its own called Mount Carmel. Similarly, St. Peter's Church purchased a farm in 1900 to open its own cemetery within the city limits.[48] The gates to this cemetery still bear the French name of the parish, making clear it was not simply a Catholic cemetery, but a French Catholic burial place.

French-speaking Catholics of Plattsburgh also had enough numbers to establish a new parish in the early twentieth century. They founded Notre-Dame des Victoires Church in 1907 for families of French-Canadian descent "and also for the mixed families of the rural part of that region, at their option," stated the publication *The Catholic Church in the United States of America* in 1914.[49] By the term "mixed families," the publication suggested that the community practiced exogamy, whereby

French-Canadian descendants were marrying outside of their ethnic group, one of the elements of acculturation in a host society.

Individuals of French-Canadian birth or background in Plattsburgh likely were intermarrying with Irish Catholics in the community to create the mixed marriages. Before the formation of Notre-Dame des Victoires, Plattsburgh's two existing Catholic parishes, St. Peter's and St. John's, were "national," or ethnic, parishes. They were not "territorial" parishes in which all Catholics living in certain neighborhoods had to attend the church designated by the bishop as their place of worship. St. John became an Irish church after French-Canadian descendants had founded St. Pierre in the mid-1800s.

St. John continued to retain its Irish character at the turn of the twentieth century, reflected in part by the Irish background of its clergy. Census records for the years 1892, 1900, and 1905 reveal that one of the two priests serving St. John's in each of those years had been born in Ireland (see Table 7). By 1910, both priests at St. John's were born in the United States, but the birthplace of their parents was Ireland.[50] Thus, in the early twentieth century, US-born priests of Irish descent led the community of the faithful at St. John's Church, helping the institution to retain its Irish character.

Geographically, St. John's Church lay between St. Peter's to the north and Notre-Dame to the south. The Catholic mixed households of Plattsburgh had to choose whether to worship at the Irish church or one of the French churches. When Notre-Dame parish built a chapel-school building, one member of St. John's parish was sufficiently annoyed to write a letter to the editor of the *Daily Press* in August 1907 to complain that the new church would draw from the congregation of St. John's. The writer contended that the action reflected an "antagonistic disposition" on the part of the community's French Catholic population.[51] Such public expressions of Irish-French tension in Plattsburgh remained relatively rare in the early twentieth century.

Following New York law, the initial incorporation of Notre-Dame des Victoires in 1908 consisted of the corporate body of Bishop Henry Gabriels, Vicar General Peter Larose, and Pastor Joseph Ludger Desjardins, who selected laymen Peter Malo and Israel Crete as trustees. Crete, a grocer who owned property on South Catherine Street, served as a conduit to help the parish purchase land for its buildings on the same street.[52] Like St. Peter's, and other French-Canadian churches in the northeastern United States, Notre-Dame des Victoires organized fairs to raise money. In November 1909, the new church netted $1,100 from its parish fair. In that same year, to raise funds to benefit the church, it also organized minstrel shows, a topic that will arise again as a phenomenon of both acculturation to American racism and assimilation into whiteness. Like St. Peter, Notre-Dame des Victoires practiced bilingualism from its origins. During the dedication ceremonies that took place in July 1908, the attending priests preached in French and English.[53]

Notre-Dame recruited the Soeurs de la Charité de Saint-Louis to conduct its school. Marie-Louise-Élisabeth de Lamoignon, an aristocratic woman whose husband was executed by guillotine during the French Revolution, subsequently became a nun and founded the Sisters of Charity, Daughters of St. Louis, in Vannes, France, in 1803. Renamed the Sisters of Charity of St. Louis, the order worked to educate poor girls in Brittany. Because of the hostility toward religious communities in France that took place from the 1880s to 1914, peaking with anticlerical legislation from 1901 to 1904, two sisters boarded the ship *Lake Champlain* to sail from Brittany to Québec in 1902 in search of new missions for the order. Québec was an attractive destination for the congregation due to its French Catholic heritage. In 1903, twenty-six sisters from France followed them to Québec, and in 1904, forty-one others continued the chain migration. These 67 Sisters of Charity of St. Louis made up a sizeable proportion of the 361 women religious who emigrated from France to Québec during those two years. Besides teaching in different villages in Québec, the Sisters of Charity also cared for the sick, set up homes for the aged, and established boarding schools and orphanages.[54]

As the pastor of Notre-Dame des Victoires Church, Desjardins made several trips to Pont-Rouge, Québec, to ask the provincial superior of the Sisters of Charity of St. Louis in Québec to send him some teaching sisters. Desjardins wanted to establish a bilingual, confessional school not administered by the state government. He believed starting a school would fill the empty seats in his new church. During discussions with the provincial superior, Desjardins pointed out that having an establishment in Plattsburgh would assist the order in forming English-speaking sisters, an important consideration for an order that had founded some houses in western Canada and in the western United States.[55]

Desjardins apparently asked the Sisters of Charity of St. Louis to buy outright the chapel school building. In April 1910, the governing council of the order in France authorized a loan of 20,000 francs as a deposit toward the purchase of the structure, with a balance of 55,000 francs payable in five years (for a total of 14,000 US dollars), so that the congregation could establish itself in Plattsburgh. The council stipulated that its province in Canada had to agree to reimburse the loan. The Sisters of Charity of St. Louis then purchased in June the chapel school building from the Our Lady of Victory parish corporation to establish their convent and school (fig. 4.2), and they paid off the purchase price in installments to July 1916.[56]

In August 1910, the Mother Provincial of Québec, under whose administrative direction the Plattsburgh mission would exist, escorted five Sisters of Charity of St. Louis to Notre-Dame des Victoires parish. This group of sisters was well prepared for bilingual education in Plattsburgh. Mother Marie-Stéphanie (née Françoise Caro), born in France and appointed superior, had migrated to Canada in 1903 and then served in Eagle, Illinois; to learn the language and customs of the United States, she studied at a university conducted by women religious in Indiana and served in one of the order's houses in England, before arriving to Plattsburgh in 1910. Sr. Marie-Véronique (née Eugénie Le Clère), a native of Brittany, had taught in England and had undertaken some coursework at Oxford University before moving to Plattsburgh. Similarly, Sr. St-Michel

Figure 4.2. Our Lady of Victory Academy / Convent of the Sisters of Charity of St. Louis, Plattsburgh, NY; in the background is the new church of Our Lady of Victory, built in 1915. Courtesy of Archives des Soeurs de la Charité de Saint-Louis du Québec, accession 3303–01–02.

(née Marie-Perrine Hervé) was born in France but spent several years in England before migrating to North America; she initially served in parishes in Québec before her appointment to Plattsburgh and eventually to western Canada, her obituary noting "English studies having already prepared her for the new needs of our Congregation outside of France." Another foundress, Sr. Saint-Fidèle (née Frida Seymour) was born in England, migrated to Canada in the early 1900s as a postulant, and served in Plattsburgh in 1910 before appointments to western Canada.[57]

Among the Plattsburgh foundresses, Sr. St-Clément (née Délia Nolet) presented a different profile. Unlike them, she was a native of Québec. She had also migrated with her family to the United States and worked in its textile mills at age eleven, a scenario repeated by many French-Canadian children in the late nineteenth and early twentieth centuries. Nolet returned to Canada in 1903 and joined the Sisters of Charity of St. Louis, making her profession in 1906 and serving at the order's house in Warsaw, Illinois, doing laundry and cooking, before moving to Plattsburgh in 1910 to do "all [sorts of] manual work." There existed in many orders of women religious a class division between the sisters who trained for functions like teaching and those who did the manual work of the convents. Like the other sisters appointed to Plattsburgh in 1910, Sr. St-Clément's English-language skills led to her initial appointment there. Her obituary noted: "In 1910, her knowledge of the English language prompted our Mothers [the Superiors] to send her to Notre-Dame des Victoires in Plattsburgh." At different points in Sr. St-Clément's career, the congregation assigned her to houses it established in Keeseville and Redford, New York, and then back to Plattsburgh, where she worked the farm the sisters had, served as bursar, and trained postulants to the order, using to advantage the English-language skills she had acquired.[58]

Two postulants joined the founding Sisters of Charity of St. Louis at Notre-Dame in October 1910. Célanire Larochelle and Marie-Anne Loiselle, both born in Québec, moved to Plattsburgh to continue their studies in English. Larochelle made her profession in 1915, became Sr. Saint-Henri, and spent about forty-eight years of her career in northern New York, serving in Keeseville, Redford, and Plattsburgh. Loiselle made her profession in 1916, became Sr. Émilienne-Marie, and went on to serve much of her career in the western Canadian provinces of Alberta and Saskatchewan. With the founding Sisters of Charity of St. Louis, the postulants moved into a multipurpose structure that functioned as a church on the second floor, two classrooms and a residence for the women religious on the first floor, and a parish hall in the basement.[59]

The growth of such Catholic institutions in Plattsburgh, especially French Catholic ones, in the 1900s attests to the growing impact of French-Canadian descendants in the city. So do the public celebrations to commemorate the discovery by Samuel de Champlain of the lake that bears his name. The celebrations began on July 4th, 1907, two years before the tercentenary, when about 300 Plattsburgh residents joined nearly 6,000 other visitors who gathered at Champlain, New York, to dedicate a monument to the French explorer, the first such monument in the United States. Rev. F. X. Chagnon, the pastor of St. Mary's Church in Champlain who had immigrated to the United States from French Canada and had become a naturalized US citizen, enlisted the assistance of Louis Fontaine, a resident of the village of Champlain and a Franco-American member of the Lake Champlain Tercentenary Commission of New York, to erect the monument on church grounds. Financed by "the French-Canadian people in New York, the New England States and Canada," according to the *Plattsburgh Republican*, its dedication and unveiling celebrated both US Independence Day and Champlain's discovery. As part of the festivities, residents of Champlain decorated their homes with flags of the United States and France, and Plattsburgh's Lafayette Hose Company and St. John Baptist Association joined the parade.[60]

In 1909, residents of Vermont and New York held elaborate festivities for nearly a week to celebrate the tercentenary of the European founding of Lake Champlain. On Sunday, July 4, the opening day of the commemorations, the steamer *Ticonderoga* carried nearly 700 congregants of St. Peter's Church to Isle La Motte, Vermont, for a mass offered by clergy from the provinces of Québec and Ontario and the states of Vermont, New York, and Rhode Island. The clergy preached their sermons in French and English. The St. Peter's Academy band performed, and the St. John Baptist Association of Plattsburgh functioned as a Guard of Honor (see fig. 4.3) and executed a military drill. Formed earlier in the year in anticipation of the tercentenary celebrations, the Guard of Honor was a paramilitary organization that carried sidearms.[61]

Monday, July 5, 1909, was designated "Fraternal Day" in Plattsburgh. Fraternal and industrial organizations turned out in number to form a large parade. Among those in the procession were a platoon of police; Elks; Knights of Columbus from New York carrying the US flag and the papal colors; Knights of Columbus from other cities; the St. John Baptist

Figure 4.3. Guard of Honor, St. John Baptist Association, in front of St. Peter's Academy, Plattsburgh, NY. Courtesy of Clinton County Historical Association, accession 95.033.6765.

Guard of Honor; the Horicon, Lafayette, and Reserve Hose Companies; a float by the Cigar Makers Union; 300 members of the Carpenters and Joiners Union; and members of the Painters and Decorators Union, as well as the Clinton County Pomona Grange. The St. John Baptist Association won the prize for "best general appearance." The grandstand set up at the courthouse block featured speeches by the dean of the New York State College of Agriculture, a US agriculture official from the District of Columbia, and the head of the state grange.[62] The lineup of union and grange members in the parade and on the grandstand, of course, showed evidence of the organizations that sprang up in reaction to US industrialization.

Tuesday, July 6, was designated French Day in the Plattsburgh tercentenary celebrations. Organized by Dr. La Rocque, they began with a morning mass at St. Peter's Church offered by the auxiliary bishop of Montréal, Monsignor Zotique Racicot, and the pastor, Rev. J. N. Pelletier. The parade thereafter began outside the church, with Dr. LaRocque as marshal. The procession included the St. Peter's Academy band, a delegation from the general bureau of Union St. Jean Baptiste

112 | Catholics across Borders

d'Amérique, the St. John Baptist Guard of Honor, clergy in carriages, the Elks, and floats of Samuel de Champlain and King Henry IV and of French officers in the American Revolution, Marquis de Lafayette and Comte de Rochambeau. The mayor and other city officials reviewed the procession in front of the courthouse. The *Republican* reported: "The French day parade was without doubt the finest of the kind ever seen in this city." The newspaper was particularly enamored by one group, commenting that "the Guard of Honor of [the] St. John the Baptist Society, the showily dressed vet coats and cocked hats, all lent a color and gaiety to the parade." The *Republican* heaped compliments on the floats, especially for the poignant images they created: "The handsome floats with their occupants correctly costumed in the picturesque garb of the time and their hideously painted savages were sights never to be forgotten." The parade ended at St. Peter's Academy, where speeches followed. H. A. Dubuque, the city solicitor of Fall River, Massachusetts, gave a talk in French attended by Franco-Americans from upstate New York and Vermont, as well as visitors from Canada.[63]

The Grey Nuns noted in their chronicle on Wednesday, July 7, that the last of the parades honoring Champlain was held that day. The procession formed in front of their convent, where the sisters heard the

Figure 4.4. Carriages carrying President William Howard Taft and other dignitaries during the Champlain Tercentenary celebration, July 7, 1909. Courtesy of Feinberg Library Special Collections, SUNY Plattsburgh, accession 73.2/739.

music of the French-Canadian "soldiers" as the men prepared to march. A platoon of police and various infantry and cavalry joined the procession, including the New York Militia, the Grand Army of the Republic, and the Canadian troops the sisters heard. This was "Plattsburgh Day," and special guests included US President William Howard Taft, New York Governor Charles Evans Hughes, ambassadors from France and England, congressmen, and state officials (see fig. 4.4). Smith Weed, considered the "Grand Old Man" of Plattsburgh, entertained the dignitaries at a reception at his home.[64] The St. John Baptist Guard of Honor escorted the president, who joined the parade. Besides the president, teams of horses also pulled floats through downtown, which was decorated with US flags and flags of the fleur-de-lis of France.[65] Thus, each day of the tercentenary celebrations highlighted in some manner French historic and contemporary influences on the Plattsburgh community.

The local celebrations to honor Samuel de Champlain culminated three years later with the erection of a monument to the explorer in Plattsburgh on the shores of Lake Champlain. In May 1910, the eleven members of the Tercentenary Commission of New York considered various sites for a publicly funded monument, including Isle La Motte in Vermont and in both Crown Point and Clinton County in New York. After the press published news that the commission, which included five residents of Clinton County, was leaning toward Clinton County as the proposed site, J. W. Harkness, a resident of the Clinton County town of Peru and a member of the Pomona Grange, argued in his letter to the editor of the *Republican* that the monument should be erected at Crown Point where Champlain had fought the Iroquois. Harkness contended that Plattsburgh had other local heroes who had not yet been honored with monuments. Since the French explorer had no direct ties to Plattsburgh, Harkness questioned: "But what did Samuel Champlain do for Plattsburgh that makes its people so anxious to honor him with a monument[?]"[66] The short answer, of course, and one that appears not to have found expression in printed sources, is that the city of Plattsburgh had a sizeable population of French-Canadian descendants who exerted increasing influence in the community and on the political process.

In November 1909, Plattsburgh elected Andrew Senecal—a Franco-American dentist, parishioner of St. Peter's, and "staunch Democrat"—as mayor. Senecal remained in office until September 1912, and it was during his tenure that plans for the Plattsburgh monument to Champlain moved forward. The New York Lake Champlain Tercentenary Commission decided in February 1911 that there would be a joint monument to Champlain, one in Crown Point and the other in Clinton County, either in Plattsburgh or at Bluff Point, and the press revealed that the commission favored Plattsburgh. The commission had $15,000 to expend on a monument for Clinton County. But Plattsburgh also had to make a contribution, and the city held a special election in June 1911, voting 265 to 16 in favor of a special tax to raise $5,000 for a public park on the lake on which to place the monument, thus sealing Plattsburgh as the Clinton County location for the statue. "Only a few 'tight wads' or those having an imaginary grievance opposed the proposition," commented the *Daily Press* after the landslide vote. Mayor Senecal and the Common Council then made the arrangements to purchase the selected site on Cumberland Avenue for the city.[67] Thus, unlike in the village of Champlain, the efforts to erect a monument to the French explorer in the city of Plattsburgh were not spearheaded by a Roman Catholic priest of French-Canadian descent, financed by private funds coming largely from French speakers, or erected on the property of a French-Canadian national parish. Instead, the larger Plattsburgh community took this on as a project of its own.

The final product was a twelve-foot bronze statue of Samuel de Champlain in a soldier's attire that stands atop a twenty-four-foot granite pedestal overlooking the lake that bears the explorer's name (see fig. 4.5). At the base of the statue, carved in granite, is a Native American man, described in the press in 1912 as a Huron Indian.[68] Champlain, of course, had allied himself with the Hurons and other Native groups against the Iroquois in the region.

Shortly after Independence Day in 1912, Plattsburgh unveiled the Champlain monument. It was a civic celebration, not one with a strong religious or ethnic dimension, and quite unlike the French Day celebration that took place in Plattsburgh during the tercentenary festivities three years earlier. In fact, the French presence and participation were rather limited. The Guard of Honor of the St. John Baptist Society joined the parade, as it did most other parades in the city, accompanied by the Horicon and Lafayette Hose companies. They were joined by the Fifth Infantry Band from the barracks, the Maccabees, the Grand Army of the Republic, and Spanish War veterans, as well as the visitors who drove their automobiles in the procession. Among the distinguished visitors were Governor John Dix and Lieutenant-Governor Thomas Conway, the latter of Plattsburgh. There was no mass at St. Peter's or Our Lady of Victory churches at the

Religious Habits, Catholic Institutions, and the Champlain Tercentenary | 115

Figure 4.5. Monument to Samuel de Champlain, erected at Plattsburgh, NY, in 1912. Courtesy of Archives des Frères de l'Instruction Chrétienne, La Prairie, Québec.

start or end of the parade. The Rev. H. P. LeF. Grabau, rector of Trinity Episcopal Church, gave the invocation at the dedication, and Rev. M. J. Lavalle of New York, the former president of the Catholic Summer School, gave the benediction. There is no indication that Catholic clergy from Plattsburgh's Franco-American parishes were involved or even present at the unveiling and dedication. No flags of France adorned the city or the monument to Champlain. The statue was draped just with the US flag, and the Fifth Infantry Band played only the "Star Spangled Banner" at the event.[69] Visual and acoustical dimensions of the ceremony therefore highlighted US themes.

A quick review of the speeches also reveals the civic nature of the event. H. W. Knapp, the chairman of the New York Tercentenary Commission, presented the memorial to Governor John Dix as New York's chief executive. Dix accepted the memorial on behalf of the state and then presented it to the City of Plattsburgh so it might preserve it for future generations. Francis Lynde Stetson, a former Plattsburgh resident and prominent New York City attorney, accepted the memorial on behalf of the city and on behalf of the mayor, who was not present. Stetson spoke of Champlain's accomplishments and made perhaps the only reference to Native peoples, noting, "For more than a score of years he [Champlain] ruled in justice and equity, winning the hearts of his countrymen and almost idolatrous affection of the savage tribes of Canada." Adjutant General Lee Tillotson of Vermont stood in for Governor Mead, who was ill, and spoke of the friendship that existed between Vermont and New York. Count Emmanuel de Peretti de la Rocca of the French embassy in Washington, DC, commented on the friendship between the two republics, France and the United States, which he indicated had been strengthened by the erection of memorials to Champlain. The *Daily Press* noted that "Count de la Rocca spoke a few words in his native tongue and the French portion of the assemblage cheered him loudly for the consideration thus shown them." This was the only reference to Plattsburgh's Franco-American population in any of the published accounts of the event. John Stewart of New York, the chair of the executive committee for the planned 1915 Celebration of the One Hundred Years of Peace among English-speaking people, did mention Canada, but not on the theme of Champlain as the founder of New France and of Canada. Stewart commented that 40,000 Canadians had answered President Abraham Lincoln's calls for volunteers during the US Civil War and that Canada would join the projected celebration of the century of peace in 1915. The final speaker, Job Hedges of New York, a Republican candidate for governor, spoke about Champlain's work and on how his memory had lasted for 300 years. "Can we find in history the name of another single individual, who regardless of circumstances, hewed his way through forests of uncertainty, alone, but undaunted, to greater success than Champlain[?]" he asked rhetorically.[70] No local Franco-American joined these men in making a speech or in playing a public role in the dedication.

In brief, the commemorations of Samuel de Champlain in Plattsburgh shifted markedly from 1909 to 1912. The 1909 tercentenary festivities included a strong religious and ethnic component organized by the local Franco-American Catholic population and its clergy. In contrast, the 1912 dedication of the Champlain monument represented a secular and civic observance, one organized and executed primarily by non–Franco-Americans and that focused on US over Canadian or even French themes. That this could happen suggests a lack of religious or ethnic tension in the Plattsburgh community that would otherwise have worked against such a commemoration to a French Catholic leader. It also suggests an interesting dimension to acculturation, where the host society adopted as its own a religious and ethnic figure from the sending society of its largest immigrant population.[71]

In conclusion, Franco-Americans of Plattsburgh in the early 1900s created a new Catholic parish, located between the Irish institutions of St. John's Church and Mount Carmel cemetery, and formed their own ethnic Catholic cemetery apart from the Irish. They also formed two new Catholic schools, Collège St. Pierre and Notre-Dame des Victoires, taught, respectively, by the Brothers of Christian Instruction and the Sisters of Charity of St. Louis, orders both expelled from France. While organizing their own French Catholic institutions, Franco-Americans demonstrated in their public celebrations their bilingualism as well as other connections to the host society, while not abandoning their ethnic pride and sentiment, as the French Day celebration during the Champlain tercentenary demonstrates. Although anti-Catholic currents in the larger society did have an impact on the Plattsburgh community, most notably leading to the termination of the longstanding arrangement of the Grey Nuns teaching in the public school system, the Plattsburgh community itself showed little evidence of ethnic or religious tension as it rang in the twentieth century.

Chapter Five

The Contest between the Grey Nuns and Local Physicians

Founding Nonsectarian Community Hospitals, 1900–1920

In the early twentieth century, the Sisters of Charity of Ottawa created a new institution in Plattsburgh when they founded a hospital for the growing community. After overcoming numerous organizational and financial challenges to create the first civilian hospital in Plattsburgh, the Grey Nuns faced a significant professional hurdle when some area physicians chose not to practice at their institution but instead to create a medical facility of their own. Undaunted, the sisters persisted, opened their hospital, and founded a nurse-training school at the same time. The enterprising Sisters of Charity of Ottawa not only provided needed medical services to the Plattsburgh area, but they also offered access to professional work to young women in the community.

During the nineteenth century, Catholic and Protestant women religious provided health care for the growing immigrant population of the United States. By 1900, Catholic nuns had founded several hundred hospitals in the country, institutions that served as suitable alternatives to almshouses for the sick, making a substantial contribution to the development of the health-care system for the growing immigrant and working-class populations during US industrialization and urbanization. The history of such women religious in the medical field has not attracted significant scholarly attention. Part of the challenge is that few records of the hospital work of Catholic nuns have survived. But vowed Catholic women "spent their lives establishing the social institutions that were to become critical to nineteenth- and twentieth-century society," argues Sioban Nelson. She contends that "nursing and hospital foundation was part of a gendered international movement—a movement that to a great extent was neither English nor Protestant." Canadian nuns, Nelson points out, have made huge contributions to the development of the nursing profession in both Canada and the United States.[1] A bilingual order, the Sisters of Charity of Ottawa were part of the "gendered international movement" to which Nelson refers.

As a non-cloistered order largely consisting of immigrants, the Grey Nuns were cognizant of Plattsburgh's needs because they taught its students, and they conducted their ministry beyond their convent and parish. The sisters were aware of the outbreaks of contagious diseases, such as the smallpox epidemic that led officials to close their schools temporarily in December 1901. Besides teaching, the Grey Nuns served Plattsburgh in the early twentieth century by making home visits to the poor and sick, just as they had every year since the order's arrival in the village in the mid-nineteenth century. From 1898 to 1902, for example, the sisters made 1,812 home visits and prepared 1,165 meals for the poor.[2] At the turn of the twentieth century, then, the Grey Nuns who taught in Plattsburgh provided essential services for a community with a sizeable immigrant population that lacked institutions to care for the sick and needy.

Mutual-aid societies provided financial assistance but not social services or institutionalized care for the sick. For example, in 1897, the St. John Baptist Association offered members $4 per week as a sickness/injury benefit if they were unable to work, and it covered funeral expenses by having each of the other 200 members of the organization pay the widow or family of a decedent $1. Fraternal organizations like the Maccabees also provided local residents with life and disability benefits.[3] While mutual-benefit societies like these offered a form of insurance for their members, their local organizations constituted a small proportion of the city's total population, and therefore their reach was relatively small. This left many Plattsburgh residents without a safety net if the family's provider became ill for an extended period of time, or became disabled, or died.

Although a hospital opened at the Plattsburgh barracks for military personnel in 1896, no local hospital existed for civilians at the turn of the twentieth century. Residents who needed hospital care often had to travel long distances to Montréal, Albany, or New York City.[4] Thus, the work of Catholic nuns like the Sisters of Charity of Ottawa was vitally important to communities like Plattsburgh that could not otherwise have met the needs of the infirm and ill.

Beyond understanding some of the needs of the village of Plattsburgh, the Grey Nuns had experience in institutionalizing social services, not only in Canada but also in the United States. They had arrived in Ogdensburg, New York, in 1863 at the invitation of the Oblates, just three years after establishing a mission in Plattsburgh. In Ogdensburg, the sisters took charge of parish schools, where they primarily served French-Canadian descendants. Like other Catholic and Protestant women religious in the United States, the Sisters of Charity of Ottawa shifted from visiting the sick poor to organizing health-care institutions. They purchased a mansion that became incorporated as the Ogdensburg City Hospital and Orphan Asylum in 1886. As early as 1899, the Grey Nuns also directed St. John's Hospital in Ogdensburg.[5]

In 1900, the *Plattsburgh Daily Press* highlighted the work of the Ogdensburg City Hospital that the late Bishop Edgar Wadhams had authorized, and which the Grey Nuns managed but which had a board of directors of different faith traditions. "All classes of citizens have united in its support," the newspaper noted, "and here Catholic and Protestant have joined together in the common purpose of helping those that are in need." When the *Daily Press* commented on plans for a new city hospital in Ogdensburg that the Grey Nuns would direct, it stated: "The same liberal policy will be followed in the administration of the new building as of the old and its doors will be opened to all denominations."[6]

By the early 1900s, the Sisters of Charity of Ottawa started formulating plans to establish a hospital in Plattsburgh. They enlisted the aid of Martin O'Brien, a local attorney who, in June 1901, informed the Superior General in Ottawa of the availability of and the terms for a property on which stood the former Vilas mansion. O'Brien also let the superior know he had spoken to Rev. William Kelley, the pastor of St. John's Church, about the possible purchase, that the priest was supportive, and that he planned discuss it with the bishop. Within a week's time, the Superior General contacted the Bishop of Ogdensburg to inform him that the Grey Nuns in Plattsburgh could borrow $5,000 to make the downpayment on the property and could raise the remaining funds needed from subscriptions and donations.[7] This quick action suggests that the sisters had been planning for some time the purchase and financing of a property suitable for a hospital.

The Grey Nuns did not end up buying the Vilas property, but they continued making plans to establish a hospital in Plattsburgh. Rev. Henry Gabriels, Bishop of Ogdensburg, encouraged them to do so, but he did not want the Catholic diocese to assume the financial responsibility for the hospital. In August 1902, the sisters missioned in the city recorded in their chronicle that discussions about building a hospital were underway in Plattsburgh and that Sr. Anne de Jésus (née Marie A. Whelan, a US-born nun) was "personally charged to see it" through. The General Council of the Sisters of Charity of Ottawa had appointed her to oversee the fundraising and construction of the Plattsburgh hospital. Sr. Anne of Jésus had previously worked at the Ogdensburg hospital and had served as the superior there. This Grey Nun continued her teaching duties in Plattsburgh while also taking on the added responsibility of organizing the city's first civilian hospital.[8]

Like the Sisters of Charity of Québec, who situated their hospitals on the outskirts of cities, reflecting a concept of hygiene then prevalent in the early twentieth century that distance from the city would help heal the sick, the Sisters of Charity of Ottawa in Plattsburgh purchased a property away from the city center in 1902. They bought from their longtime benefactor, Smith Weed, a parcel for $1,800 and another parcel from his abutters for $1,500, creating an eight-acre lot on which they could build their medical facility. "The consideration paid is $3,300," commented the *Plattsburgh Sentinel*, "a very low price for land of such a fine location, and shows that the owners were anxious to promote so desirable an institution." The newspaper went on to inform readers that county residents would be cared for at the hospital regardless of gender, religious affiliation, or ability to pay. The *Sentinel* expressed its pleasure at the news of the proposed facility, stating, it "will be a boon to Clinton county, and will in the true sense of the phrase, fill a long-felt want, and deserves the fullest support of the people." The *Plattsburgh Republican* noted that the Grey Nuns themselves paid the $3,300 purchase price. Indeed, the sisters did so by mortgaging their convent-school property in Plattsburgh to Patrick Hanlon, the parent of one of their students, who granted them a "loan on satisfactory terms."[9]

In establishing the Plattsburgh City Hospital, the Grey Nuns demonstrated their strong entrepreneurial, political, and marketing skills, and individuals from the community recognized these formidable skills. In 1916, when Sr. Anne of Jésus had completed two terms as the superior of the hospital, the Sisters of Charity transferred her to the Pembroke,

Ontario, hospital to become its superintendent, and the *Sentinel* remarked: "Rev. Sister Ann [*sic*] is a lady of remarkable business ability," and it credited her efforts and energy for the establishment of the city hospital, indicating that she persisted against significant odds. "When she first went among the leading men of this city and spoke of her plans for the erection of an institution such as the . . . hospital, she received but little encouragement but she continued her work," the newspaper stated. The nineteen men who formed the first board of trustees were prominent in business and professional circles, and they included men of the cloth. Among them were Rev. Henry Gabriels, Bishop of Ogdensburg; Smith Weed, a businessman, attorney, and former politician; Albert Sharron, the mayor of Plattsburgh; Rev. William Kelley, the pastor of the Irish Catholic church; and Rev. Joseph Pelletier, the pastor of the French Catholic church. The other men on the board were attorneys and businessmen, as well as cashiers, vice presidents, and presidents of banks; some were also active in local government.[10] In short, these prominent religious, civic, and business leaders were well positioned to assist the enterprising Grey Nuns in founding a hospital in Plattsburgh.

Noticeably absent from the hospital's board of trustees was Dr. J. H. LaRocque. LaRocque was highly esteemed in both French-Canadian and Anglo-American circles in Plattsburgh and in Clinton County. LaRocque had led the St. John Baptist Association and was affiliated with other Catholic societies. He had also been active in local politics. When LaRocque ran in village elections for the position of trustee in 1887, *Le National* promoted his candidacy to readers, identifying him as "our popular compatriot"; LaRocque won that election and went on to serve as the village trustee for six years. LaRocque had been a member of the Clinton County Medical Society for a decade when, in 1887, he was elected its president, an honor demonstrating his status in Anglo-American circles, the French-language newspaper pointed out with obvious pride: "It is an evident proof of the popularity and of the esteem that our friend has with his American colleagues. Honor to true merit!" *The Souvenir Industrial Edition of Plattsburgh, 1897* also wrote in glowing terms of LaRocque's reputation in the community since his 1878 arrival in Plattsburgh, stating: "He has since then ranked among the leading physicians of this place, having won a reputation for skill and science in his profession, unexcelled by any physician in this vicinity."[11] As we will see, LaRocque opposed the organization of the hospital of the Grey Nuns and helped found a rival institution.

The board of the Plattsburgh City Hospital met at the grand-jury room of the local courthouse in September 1902 to sign the institution's proposed articles of incorporation. Their request for incorporation indicated "that we have associated ourselves together for the purpose of erecting, establishing and maintaining a Hospital for the medical and surgical treatment and care of the sick without regard to the race, nationality or religious convictions of those who may apply for such treatment." The New York State Board of Charities approved the incorporation of the Plattsburgh City Hospital in January 1903.[12]

The nondenominational incorporation of the proposed hospital was important to its eventual success as an institution. Tensions between Protestants and Catholics in the United States in the nineteenth and early twentieth centuries led to the creation of separate hospitals in different communities. Public hospitals in many cities did not allow visitations by Catholic clergy, so Catholics concerned about receiving last rites chose to build their own medical facilities. Pawtucket Memorial, a Protestant and Masonic hospital that opened in Rhode Island in 1910, did not admit French-Canadian doctors. Consequently, individuals of French-Canadian descent either had "to forego hospital treatment or choose Protestant doctors with whom rapport was more difficult because of language and background," according to sociologist Sister Florence Marie Chevalier. As a result, francophones in Rhode Island funded their own hospital in Central Falls, which opened in 1925. In short, discrimination motivated the creation of many religious and ethnic hospitals in the United States in the nineteenth and early twentieth centuries.[13]

To allay possible anti-Catholic sentiment that might be fomented against the hospital of the Grey Nuns, Smith Weed solicited letters from individuals in Ogdensburg about the work of the sisters there, and he shared those letters in the press in September 1902. George Hall, the mayor of Ogdensburg, wrote Weed of his city's hospital, stating: "The incentive for building this hospital was that the Grey Nuns could handle it to better advantage than any other parties and at a very much less expense." Hall reported no evidence of discrimination against patients or doctors by the Catholic nuns and indicated that the local community was pleased by their work. Thomas Spratt, a prominent attorney, similarly informed Weed that the work of the Grey Nuns in Ogdensburg "has been most favorable, and it has the support of all our citizens irrespective of creed." People of different faith traditions could call upon their own clergy, Spratt noted, "and no distinction is made on account of the religious belief of the patients." Spratt highly recommended the sisters to Weed and to the Plattsburgh community: "I can assure you if the people of Plattsburgh have the same experience with the Sisters as the people of Ogdensburg have, they will never regret selecting them. I have no doubt whatever," he continued, "but it will be a success from the beginning, and will be a source of comfort to those who take an interest in the establishment of the same, especially the people who have occasion to enter its walls."[14]

Despite these commendations, some in the Plattsburgh community apparently raised questions about the fact that Catholic nuns would staff the health-care facility. "As there has been some misconception growing out of the proposition to have the sisters furnish nurses," commented the *Daily Press* in April 1903, "it is proper to state that the title to the property will be vested in a corporation known as 'The Plattsburgh City Hospital,' and will be controlled by a board consisting of twenty trustees." At the same time, the newspaper published letters from four Protestant clergy of Ogdensburg who attested to how easy it was to minister to the sick under the care of the Roman Catholic nuns serving their hospital.[15]

In August 1903, the board of trustees met at the county courthouse and decided formally to have the title to the land on which the hospital would be built transferred from the Grey Nuns to the hospital corporation. That transfer took place two months later and included the understanding that the hospital corporation would pay off the mortgage on the D'Youville Convent property that the sisters had granted Patrick Hanlon to finance the land purchase. The agreement also indicated that the Grey Nuns would staff the hospital and would help raise the funds needed to build and maintain it.[16]

The *Plattsburgh Sentinel and Clinton County Farmer* highlighted on its pages the need for the institution: "With each succeeding day the demand for a public hospital becomes greater and the need more urgent." The newspaper tried to drum up public support by pointing out that all members of the community had a moral obligation to support financially the building project, concluding that "it is a piece of public enterprise which is worthy [of] the unqualified and hearty support of every citizen."[17]

Generating the funds necessary to build the Plattsburgh City Hospital required the efforts of many individuals and groups. Members of the local council of the Knights of Columbus held a subscription drive in 1903 that raised $3,500 toward the building's construction. For their part, board members of the hospital canvassed nearby communities to solicit funds. Some of those communities held fundraisers for the proposed hospital.

The town of Saranac held a dance, the village of Dannemora organized a grand bazaar lasting several days, and the Peru Grange contributed $100 toward the building fund. Area banks made pledge forms available so individuals could make donations. The local government also supported the facility; the Plattsburgh Board of Supervisors agreed to appropriate $5,000 for the building fund on condition that the hospital treat at no cost the poor who were county charges.[18]

On February 5, 1905, Sr. Anne penned a note promising St. Joseph that she would name the hospital chapel after him, "provided you send us $5.000 [sic] before the end of March." On March 20, she penned another note, recording the news from Mr. Riley (most likely a local attorney) that a woman from Brooklyn planned to donate at least $5,000 to help finance the hospital's construction. "This is surely St-Joseph's work," wrote Sr. Anne.[19]

Women played a significant role in fundraising efforts. Sr. Anne met personally with potential donors, but she did not work alone. In May 1905, local women gathered at the courthouse to form a Women's Auxiliary to support the proposed hospital. Each woman paid $1 annually in dues to the organization.[20] By March 1906, the Women's Auxiliary had 649 members and had raised $1,134 for Plattsburgh City Hospital. A summer concert, a winter social at the Elks Club, and a cake sale by young women helped to generate these funds.[21]

Demonstrating strong organizational skills, the Women's Auxiliary held a charity ball in April 1906, which was attended by more than 200 guests. The program consisted of playing the card games of whist and euchre in the early evening, then dancing for four hours, followed by refreshments. To pull off this event, women from Plattsburgh, Port Henry, Saranac Lake, Rouses Point, Au Sable Forks, Willsboro, Chazy, West Chazy, Keeseville, Peru, Lyon Mountain, and Dannemora served as patronesses for the charity ball, which generated $450 for the hospital. The large number of communities involved demonstrates the countywide support that existed for the institution. In fact, towns such as West Chazy, Dannemora, Rouses Point, and Saranac organized their own branches of the Women's Auxiliary.[22]

When the women organized their second annual charity ball in 1907, the *Republican* noted that the patronesses constituted a "long list of names representing equally nearly all church denominations," something the paper felt would contribute to the success of the event.[23] Thus, area women of different faith traditions united for a common purpose.

From its origins, the Women's Auxiliary, by organizing members from various communities and religious backgrounds, exercised a key role in supporting the work of the Catholic nuns who founded and managed Plattsburgh City Hospital.

That name, however, raised questions among some. Attorney John Riley, the vice president of the hospital's board of trustees, indicated during the cornerstone-laying ceremony in 1906 that the institution's name would change from Plattsburgh City Hospital to Champlain Valley Hospital to counter a misconception that the facility would only serve Plattsburgh residents. Not until two years later did the hospital trustees take the legal steps needed to change the name, a change that only went into effect in August 1910, a couple of months after the hospital opened.[24]

Demonstrating the interfaith nature of the hospital, leaders from all of Plattsburgh's religious communities were invited to make brief remarks at the cornerstone-laying ceremony in July 1906. Rev. Charles Grismer of the Methodist Episcopal Church gave the invocation. Rabbi J. Lubin of Congregation Beth Israel commented on how the hospital would be a place "where pure humanity and true charity will be extended to all mankind without distinction of religion or creed." Rev. W. S. Kelley of St. John's Catholic Church noted that "this Champlain Valley Hospital represents the offerings of the rich and the poor, of Jew and Gentile alike." Kelley questioned rhetorically, "Why should there be religious hatreds amongst us to block this noble work? At the door of this Champlain Valley Hospital the question of race, color or creed will never be asked." Rev. H. P. LeF. Grabau, the rector of Trinity Episcopal Church, and Rev. O. E. Kendall, the pastor of Baptist Church, also offered remarks at the ceremony.[25] Curiously, no Oblate priest from St. Peter's Church spoke at the event.

Francis Lynde Stetson was the only speaker to mention French heritage or local French-Canadian descendants in his remarks. Stetson commented on the contributions of the French in the field of medicine by his references to individuals like Louis Pasteur and Jean-Martin Charcot and to the development of hospitals such as Hôtel Dieu in Paris. Given that historic context, Stetson stated: "It is with great satisfaction that you must recognize the deep interest taken in this Hospital by your fellow-citizens of French extraction, of whom your worthy treasurer is one." Stetson also expressed "hope that this institution continuously will command their support as it affords relief to suffering in body, without regard to any other condition, or to race or creed."[26]

At the ceremony, the work of lay and religious women was appropriately acknowledged. The Women's Auxiliary was given due credit for its fundraising activities and "for keeping up enthusiasm" for the hospital building project. Work on the hospital had stalled after the basement was in place because of a lack of funds. At that time, Stetson came through with a contribution of $5,000. He commented during his address that the labor of another group of women, the Grey Nuns, made the hospital possible and ensured its future. As he put it, the sisters would provide "the Hospital with skillful service for an annual stipend so absurdly low as at once to bring the maintenance of the Hospital within the possibilities of the future." With these words, Stetson publicly acknowledged both the pioneering work and the self-sacrifice of the women religious. Although the Sisters of Charity of Ottawa, a Canadian order of nuns, would staff the facility, there is no indication that the ceremony reflected any Canadian themes. The event concluded with the singing of "America."[27]

Because of insufficient funds, it took longer than expected to build the hospital, but members of the board of trustees, community members, and the Women's Auxiliary redoubled their efforts to ensure its completion. As these efforts were underway, the Women's Auxiliary had to warn the public about a potential fundraising scam. In contemporary society, we hear almost daily about various ploys designed to part people from their money. Such activities also took place in earlier periods when the public did not have such ready access to information as we do today. After Helen Smith, the president of the Women's Auxiliary, learned that some women were posing as members of her organization to collect funds in Plattsburgh and nearby towns, she issued a warning through the local press in August 1907 about these "unauthorized women" and published in the newspaper the names of the local membership committee to gain the public's trust. A year later, the *Sentinel* reported the arrest of "a middle-aged, respectably-dressed woman" using the aliases of Mrs. Ward and Mrs. Manning to solicit money and clothing under false pretenses for hospitals in Plattsburgh and Saranac Lake; after speaking to the swindler, the judge let her off with a suspended sentence.[28]

Among the legitimate fundraising efforts was the accrual of significant donations. A. W. Emery, a member of the hospital's board of directors, donated a building lot valued at $1,000 to raise money for the facility, and a customs officer on the Canadian border won the parcel in a lottery. Loyal Smith, a multimillionaire who left much of his wealth to Clinton County institutions and charities, bequeathed $25,000 to Champlain

Valley Hospital for its construction and improvements, and he endowed the facility with a grant of $200,000, the income from which would finance five free beds at the hospital, with the remainder allotted to the hospital's general purposes.[29] In a final push to raise another $40,000 to complete the hospital construction, John Haughran, the treasurer, and John Moffitt, a member of the hospital's board of directors and the president of Plattsburgh National Bank, announced the sale of eighty gold bonds at $500 apiece. Yielding 6 percent interest payable each year on the first of January at Plattsburgh National Bank, the bonds would be repaid in full either on January 1, 1915, or on January 1, 1920, depending upon the decision of the hospital trustees. To secure the bonds, the hospital granted a mortgage to Plattsburgh National Bank. As Champlain Valley Hospital neared completion, the heirs of James Cavanagh agreed to furnish all of the operating-room equipment.[30] The early benefactors of Champlain Valley Hospital thus came from a cross-section of Plattsburgh and the surrounding communities, and not from one particular gender, ethnic, religious, or economic group.

The US federal census for 1910 provides a window into Plattsburgh's demography in the year Champlain Valley Hospital opened its doors. By that year, Plattsburgh's population had grown to 11,138, a 32.1 percent increase during the first decade of the century. In all, 3,756 residents, or 33.7 percent of its population, were foreign-born or had parents born abroad. Unsurprisingly, the large majority (54.7 percent) of the foreign-born white population had immigrated from Canada. Not all were French Canadian, however, for Anglo-Canadians made up slightly more than one-third (36.0 percent) of Plattsburgh's Canadian-born population in 1910.[31] The women religious who administered Champlain Valley Hospital were among the Anglo-Canadian migrants to Plattsburgh, and their migration to the city, as this and previous chapters have documented, had a substantial impact on its development.

Financial obstacles were not the only ones the Grey Nuns faced in creating Champlain Valley Hospital. A significant professional challenge arose when more than twenty physicians declined appointment to the medical and surgical staffs of the facility, because its board of trustees refused the request of the Clinton County Medical Society to appoint five doctors to the board. While a majority of the doctors were from Plattsburgh, the others came from surrounding communities. Some of the doctors announced their decision through a letter published in the press directed to the hospital board's secretary, A. W. Emery. Among them were J. H. LaRocque and Cassius Silver, two doctors who became founding directors of the rival institution.³²

As the president of the Champlain Valley Hospital's board of directors, Smith Weed likely requested the letter Francis Lynde Stetson wrote him, which Weed had published in the press. Stetson served as the governor of New York Hospital and indicated in his letter that physicians did not serve on its governing board because it is "generally agreed by the medical profession here in New York that such membership often leads to differences and contentions rather than to advantage of administration." Instead, Stetson advocated for the formation of a medical advisory board distinct from the board of trustees, rather than expanding the current board by five members, as the Clinton County Medical Society had requested, because having a few doctors on the board of trustees "would be likely to constitute a continuing cause and element of disaffection, especially as this small delegation would be ineffective for purposes of control."³³ The disaffected doctors opted instead to organize a hospital of their own, just as Champlain Valley Hospital was opening its doors to the public.

The opposition that the Grey Nuns faced from Plattsburgh-area doctors was not new to women religious who founded hospitals. "We felt instinctively the deep aversion of these old Puritans at the mere thought [that] the first institution for the care of the sick would be entrusted to ladies whose names and habits aroused suspicions," recorded the Sisters of Charity of Saint-Hyacinthe, Québec, in their chronicle when they organized a hospital in Lewiston, Maine, in 1888. Not only religious prejudice but also ethnic discrimination led to the formation of a rival institution by Protestants and nonfrancophones, including the Irish, in the Lewiston community. Given the interethnic and interfaith groups that rallied to support Champlain Valley Hospital, there is no evidence that the Grey Nuns in Plattsburgh had to confront the religious or ethnic prejudices the Grey Nuns of Lewiston had faced. But the latter group also faced gender discrimination, for it appears that doctors were not comfortable seeing women enter the male sphere of medicine as the managers of a medical institution. This same gender bias may have helped motivate male doctors in the Plattsburgh area to found Physicians' Hospital to compete against Champlain Valley Hospital. The chronicle of the sisters at D'Youville Convent shows no indication that Dr. LaRocque harbored any personal animosity toward the Grey Nuns; in fact, it suggests that he held them in warm regard. In the early twentieth century, LaRocque was among the well-wishers who regularly paid his respects in person to the sisters at D'Youville Convent at the start of the new year. But he apparently chose not to work at the hospital the order founded.³⁴

In June 1910, the Grey Nuns, who had had charge of the parish school for half a century, opened Champlain Valley Hospital. Just a few days before the facility admitted patients, the Superior General of the Sisters of Charity of Ottawa arrived in Plattsburgh with several sisters who joined the hospital staff. The initial personnel consisted of Sr. Anne de Jésus as the superior, four sisters to handle nursing functions, and a novice to work in the kitchen. To acquaint the community with the facility, which consisted of fourteen rooms to care for the sick, the sisters hosted a visitor's weekend, and a steady stream of people stopped by to view the physical plant.³⁵

The board of trustees announced in the press the hospital rules. To prevent against the possibility of uncollected debt, and to help ensure the solvency of the institution, the first rule required patients to provide the hospital superintendent with one week's pay and then thereafter to pay for their stay one week in advance; any remaining balance would be refunded when the patient left the hospital. While the hospital did accept "charity patients," it required the approval of the superintendent and of the executive committee for anyone who stayed longer than two months. The superintendent, of course, was the female hospital administrator, Sr. Anne.³⁶

As a nonsectarian institution, managed by an order of Catholic nuns, Champlain Valley Hospital had rules that reflected religious sensibilities. The tenth rule for patients stated: "Patients admitted to the hospital are forbidden to use profane or indecent language; to express immoral sentiments; to play cards or any game of chance for money." According to this rule, patients were also not allowed "to smoke tobacco in the house without the permission of the attending physician or surgeon or procure for themselves or others any intoxicating liquors." The sixteenth rule for patients made clear that Champlain Valley Hospital, although administered by Catholic nuns, was open to patients and clergy of all faith traditions: "Clergymen and the authorized representatives of religious bodies shall be admitted to the wards (upon terms of equality), for the purpose of visiting and extending religious ministrations to the sick inmates of their own creed or denomination," but they had to do so at times that did not interfere with their care. Writing of the work of the Sisters of Charity who served as nurses at the Baltimore Infirmary in the mid-1800s, Christopher J. Kauffman maintains that "American pluralism tended to foster both a self-consciously Catholic attitude and a consideration of Protestant sensibilities."[37] The Champlain Valley Hospital bylaws suggest that the same was true of the efforts of the Sisters of Charity of Ottawa.

One major difference between the work of Protestant and Catholic women religious in health care during the era of mass migration, argues Judith G. Cetina, was that Protestants actively pursued evangelization, seeking the religious conversion of immigrants as a form of social control. In contrast, she contends, "Catholic women religious simply desired to alleviate the suffering of the sick, including men, women, and children, and to bring them spiritual consolation during times of illness and impending death." This appeared to be the intended goal of Champlain Valley Hospital. Clergy were prohibited from proselytizing, for the sixteenth rule stated that "they are . . . to confine their conversation to persons of their own creed or denomination and to refrain from addressing or distributing books or pamphlets to other patients, unless by special invitation of the same and with the sanction of the superintendent."[38]

Records maintained by the sisters reveal that they did not neglect the spiritual dimension of their work at the hospital, particularly in treating Catholic patients. During the hospital's first month of operation, an elderly man suffering from heart trouble arrived at the institution. "As this man had not made his Easter duty for twenty-five years, the Srs. called a priest who heard his confession," they noted in their handwritten historical account. He later received the last sacraments before his passing. In November 1910, after an ill man arrived for care, they wrote: "The Sisters learning that he had neglected his religious duties for the last forty years persuaded him by kindness and entreaty to see the priest . . . [and] he went to confession and received Holy Communion." In January 1911, a man surnamed Varno, "(doubtless, more correctly Veroneau, for he was of Fr. Canadian origin)," recorded the sisters, arrived at the hospital after having been shot, and he died there two weeks later, "long enough to prepare for death by being baptized conditionally, and by going to confession and communion." In May 1911, the sisters recorded that a forty-five-year-old man taken to the hospital "had been living a disreputable life; probably through ignorance, for he seemed devoid of religious ideas and certainly had no religious knowledge." Suspecting the man, surnamed Miller, was of French-Canadian descent (possibly Meunier originally), the sisters questioned him and confirmed their intuition. They also learned that he had been raised by strangers and had not received religious instruction. "The Sisters seeing that he was about to die were anxious about his soul," they noted, but the man refused to see a priest until the day of his death, when he agreed to receive the sacraments of baptism, penance, and extreme unction, "dying in excellent and happy Christian dispositions," they claimed.[39] Evidence from the sisters' own accounts suggests, then, that while they did not proselytize, they also did not shy away from performing ministerial duties while treating the patients at their health-care institution.

Besides establishing a hospital, the Grey Nuns also created a school to train young women in the nursing profession. German sisters of the order of Hospital Sisters of the Third Order of St. Francis opened the first Catholic nursing school in the United States in 1886. By 1915, more than 30 communities of women religious administered about 220 nursing schools at their hospitals throughout the country. The Grey Nuns were part of this movement. Like the Sisters of Charity of Québec, the Sisters of Charity of Ottawa serving in Ogdensburg and Plattsburgh promoted the professionalization of nursing in the early twentieth century by developing nursing schools that they directed. In Ogdensburg, the Grey Nuns established in 1902 a School of Nursing that graduated its first class three years later. In Plattsburgh, the sisters designated part of one hospital floor as the training school for nurses, opening the school in July 1910, just two weeks after the hospital's opening, but they waited until February 1911 to hold a formal opening ceremony.[40] By establishing nursing schools in upstate New York, the Sisters of Charity of Ottawa contributed to a growing movement among women religious to found Catholic training schools around the turn of the twentieth century.

About eight women pursued nursing studies with the Grey Nuns at Champlain Valley Hospital in 1911. Their school was nonsectarian, "open to all young women meeting its requirements, irrespective of religious affiliations." Those requirements included being at least eighteen years of age, a high school graduate, in good health, and of good moral character. Nursing students attended classes offered by physicians and the head nurse, Sister Mary Alice, who had served in the same capacity at the Ottawa Training School. The school followed the curriculum prescribed by the New York State Board of Regents. The seven doctors who made up the initial faculty lectured on such topics as hygiene, physiology, bacteriology, anatomy, surgery, and dietetics. Nursing students had to study and train as assistant nurses for three years before receiving their diplomas.[41]

Dr. E. E. Lakin, the chairman of Champlain Valley Hospital's medical staff, described in 1916 the hard work nursing students had to complete in their program of study: "She enters the institution of her choice as a probationist generally for a period of six months, during which time she is employed as a scrub-woman, a waitress and chambermaid, duties which may seem rather hard and unnecessary, but which form the foundation for cleanliness and order." Lakin noted the fortitude required to persist in nursing school: "It is also a test of her determination to continue in a vocation which she early discovers is not all cakes and ale." After the probationary period, the nursing student wore a uniform and had a combination of practical work and studies to complete. Her day began at 7:00 a.m. and ended at 7:00 p.m., with breaks for meals in between. Over the three-year program of study, nursing students had only one or two weeks of vacation each year. Lakin contrasted the rigor of nursing school with the four-year undergraduate programs of colleges and universities and contended that medical professionals "feel that a trained nurse should have the same standing and consideration shown her that a graduate of any institution in this country has."[42]

Among the eight graduates in 1913, when Champlain Valley Hospital was three years old and held its first graduation for the School of Nursing, were three nuns: Sr. St. Antoine de Padoue (née Lynott), Sr. Ste. Christine (née Madden), and Sr. St. Majoric (née Paquin). Both Sr. Antoine de Padoue and Sr. Christine were Canadian-born nuns, while Sr. Majoric was born in the United States.[43] The Champlain Valley Hospital School of Nursing served, then, as a training ground not only for laywomen but also for women religious from the United States and Canada who joined the order of the Sisters of Charity of Ottawa.

The 1915 New York State census provides us with a snapshot of the student nurses at Champlain Valley Hospital. All twenty nursing students in that year were white women who had been born in the United States and were, as a result, US citizens. They ranged in age from eighteen to twenty-six. None had a French surname; most had Irish or Anglo-American family names.[44] Data from the census suggests, then, that Champlain Valley Hospital's School of Nursing, like the hospital, was not a francophone institution.

The training accorded women at Champlain Valley Hospital's School of Nursing gave them access to professional employment and good earnings in the early twentieth century. Mayme Kavanaugh graduated from the school in 1915 and worked at the hospital during the Great War. She also made home visits to expectant mothers, enabling her to earn $25 a week for her nursing work. "Not a bad salary. It was as much as some men were taking home," Kavanaugh stated during a 1992 interview. While her earnings were competitive with those of men in that period, gendered expectations required her to stop working when she married in 1917. "You didn't work after getting married," Kavanaugh stated. "You just didn't in those days," she emphasized. But when her husband died in 1948, she returned to nursing and continued this line of work until 1972, when she retired at age seventy-nine.[45]

Kavanaugh's training at the Champlain Valley Hospital School of Nursing thus opened to her a professional path that was important at different points in her life. The Grey Nuns, like other sister nurses, created professional opportunities for many other young women over the years. As Nelson explains, vowed Catholic women "spent their lives establishing the social institutions that were to become critical to nineteenth- and twentieth-century society. In so doing, they pioneered the professional paths that eventually opened to all women."[46]

It was common for religious personnel at Catholic hospitals at the turn of the twentieth century to live on the top floor of the facility. Two nuns lived in the nurses' residence on the third floor of Champlain Valley Hospital, while the other sisters had their quarters on the top (fourth) floor of the building.[47] The continuous presence of Catholic nuns in the building and their administration of it made it hard for some to understand that the hospital was a secular institution.

Even after one year of operation, the board of directors still had to work to dispel the notion that Champlain Valley Hospital was not a sectarian institution, because "much misrepresentation has been indulged in, chiefly, of course, because the people at large have not understood the matter," they noted in the hospital's first report in 1911. In that report, the directors underscored that Article II of the hospital constitution stated: "The object of this corporation is the establishment of an institution for the purpose of affording medical and surgical aid to sick or disabled persons of every creed, nationality, and color; and shall be *a non-sectarian* institution." The directors commented that, during the hospital's first year, "There has been some misunderstanding with regard to this matter, therefore we feel that this statement may not be amiss." They went on to elaborate: "Although we have in our employ Sister-nurses, and a Sister of the Order of the Gray [sic] Nuns, as Superintendent, still the Hospital is not a Roman Catholic institution, for it is held in trust by a board of Directors, who individually represent every shade of religious belief, and is truly representative." The directors noted in their report that

Champlain Valley Hospital would not have been founded without the work of the Sisters of Charity who had prepared at the Ottawa Training School for nurses. "The Champlain Valley Hospital is catholic in just one particular, viz:—that it is for all men of all religions, and all races," they emphasized.[48]

Yet the vowed women who ran the hospital understood clearly the spiritual dimension of their medical work. In a handwritten account found in their archives, likely written in 1917, the author comments "that such an Institution should prove a special boon to heal the soul as well as the body of many, the annals of the hospital affirm." The author also writes: "The great work of restoring spiritual life, as well as corporal strength to many, is the history of the hospital." As evidence, the author discusses people repenting and confessing, as well as receiving sacraments before dying, and in some cases converting to Catholicism while at Champlain Valley Hospital.[49] In essence, then, it was a Catholic institution that served people of all faith traditions.

The 1915 New York State census reveals that the patients at Champlain Valley Hospital came not only from Plattsburgh, but also from twenty-three nearby towns in upstate New York, as well as from Vermont and Montréal, making evident that the public did not view the institution as Plattsburgh's city hospital. Five of the forty-three patients enumerated in the state census had been born abroad in Canada (3), Spain (1), and Poland (1) and were not US citizens at the time of their hospitalization. Only eight of the forty-three of the enumerated had French surnames, providing impressionistic evidence that this was not a French-Canadian ethnic institution.[50]

In their 1911 report, the board of directors noted that Champlain Valley Hospital served people of all classes: "Needy poor are always admitted without question as to ability to pay." During the hospital's first year of operation, there were 305 paying patients and 102 "free patients," according to Sister Anne. During its second year, the hospital admitted 584 paying and 85 free patients. There were, apparently, limits to the amount of care the hospital could provide at no charge. After a woman from the town of Churubusco had stayed at the hospital for over two years, the board of directors decided in August 1914 to instruct the superintendent to contact her family and to give them a week to make alternative arrangements for her; otherwise, they would ask the county Superintendent of the Poor to take charge of her care.[51] Despite having received funding for those unable to pay for hospital stays, Champlain

Valley Hospital did not have unlimited funds, nor did it want to evolve into a nursing home for the elderly and the infirm.

One of the ways Catholic nuns from various religious orders throughout the United States raised money for their hospitals in the late nineteenth and early twentieth centuries was by selling insurance tickets. At Champlain Valley Hospital, the board of directors agreed in January 1912 to sell $5 certificates as a fundraising activity, whereby the purchaser would receive free medical treatment at the hospital for up to two weeks during the next year, if needed. The advent of mandatory workers' compensation legislation, a progressive reform measure adopted by state governments, eventually ended the need for worker groups to buy such insurance tickets in New York and other states.[52]

Donations continued to be an important source of support for Champlain Valley Hospital after it opened. Sr. Anne de Jésus indicated in her second report that the hospital had received donations in-kind of fruit, vegetables, jelly, and preserves over the past year. A young girl from the city, Catherine Delaney, raised $25 to help furnish the children's ward by selling flowers during the summer in 1912. Local employers whose workers the hospital treated also contributed funds to the institution. In 1920, for example, the Underwood Paper Mills and the Plattsburgh Wall Paper Company jointly sent a check for $100 to the hospital in recognition of the care and treatment provided their employees.[53]

The Women's Auxiliary of Champlain Valley Hospital continued actively to raise funds for the institution after it opened its doors to the public. By 1911, the Women's Auxiliary had contributed a women's ward, furnished rooms, and provided linens at the hospital. They also gave the patients baskets of goods containing such items as coffee, tea, jelly, fruits, vegetables, and household supplies. In 1912, the auxiliary had 500 members and furnished the hospital's maternity ward, something it hoped might later garner contributions to its organization, if a future industrialist or financier were born there. "Who knows, but in time, there may be a [J. P.] Morgan or [John D.] Rockefeller among them and realizing that the Champlain Valley Hospital was their natal place, will endow the Woman's Auxiliary with a sufficient sum to broaden our field of humanity," they wrote in their second annual report. The auxiliary also contributed to filling the icehouse and to supplying gray linens for dresses for the nuns. In addition, the auxiliary furnished and maintained for their members a hospital room at a cost of $350 so that there would be no charge to them if they required hospitalization. Just as it did prior to the hospital's opening, the Women's Auxiliary raised its funds largely through membership dues, donations, card and tea parties, and suppers and dances during the second decade of the twentieth century.[54]

The auxiliary occasionally found other means to raise funds. When the Clinton County fair was underway in September 1913, members of the Women's Auxiliary held a tag sale to benefit the hospital. Supporting their efforts, the *Daily Press* noted: "Hundreds of poor people have been treated at this hospital since its opening three years ago, and the bulk of the expense in connection with the treatment of these patients has been provided for by the Auxiliary." In 1917, members of the women's organization were working to raise money for a wing in the original hospital design that had not yet been built.[55]

The Women's Auxiliary also advocated for Champlain Valley Hospital in other ways. In 1914, a delegation of the organization appeared before the Plattsburgh Board of Public Works to ask that it improve one of the streets leading to the hospital so that the ambulance could more easily reach the building. Reflecting the gendered norms of the period, the *Daily Press* reported: "The ladies said they had no preference as to which of the two streets leading to the institution was improved, but that one of them should receive the attention of the city fathers." The board assured the women it would attend to the matter when weather conditions permitted.[56]

The hospital that doctors founded in Plattsburgh also relied heavily upon the work of women to get its start. In mid-June 1910, women gathered at the home of Mrs. George Kellogg to form an auxiliary for the hospital and reportedly had 150 charter members in their organization. Article II of the bylaws of the Women's League indicated that the broad objective of the organization was "to aid the Hospital in whatever ways its help is needed."[57]

Three months later, the press announced that physicians would constitute the entire board of directors of the new hospital, which would bear the name Physicians' Hospital of Plattsburgh—"the Plattsburgh part of the name merely applying to the location, as physicians from every town in the county are affiliated with it and it is intended for the use of the entire county," the *Sentinel* explained. Forming half of the four-member executive committee of the board of directors were doctors Cassius Silver and J. H. LaRocque. Several years later, in 1914, the board of directors elected LaRocque as its president. To raise the startup funds for their institution, 27 doctors, constituting the founding board of directors, formed a corporation with $10,000 in capital stock, whereby 1,000 shares were offered at $10 each. In this way, Silver and other area doctors pooled their resources to generate the capital needed to launch the new hospital.[58]

Physicians' Hospital sprang up during a phase of US hospital development, from 1890 to 1920, during which for-profit institutions run by doctors became common.[59] Physicians' Hospital directors therefore had to disabuse members of the community that theirs was a profit-seeking venture. Article XIII of the organization's bylaws governed the use of the institution's funds, and it stipulated that income from all sources would be used to treat the ill, to maintain the facilities, and to pay the salaries of employees, but that none would "be used to pay dividends upon stock or profits" and that the board of directors would serve without pay. As the new hospital prepared to open with thirty beds in a mansion on Court Street in January 1911, the institution cited this article from its bylaws to dispel in the press any misconceptions that the hospital was a profit-making venture. Those connected with the institution will not receive dividends nor the directors a salary, the board explained to the public.[60]

Sixteen white women made up the nursing staff of the hospital in 1915, and all but one lived at the mansion on Court Street that also functioned as the Nurses' Home. The staff ranged in age from seventeen to thirty-five. Fifteen of the women had been born in the United States, were citizens, and had Anglo-American or Irish surnames. Only one of them was an immigrant: she had been born in French Canada and had lived in the United States for only three years and was thus still not a naturalized citizen in 1915. The patients these women served came from Plattsburgh and thirteen nearby communities, as well as the state of Vermont. Of the twenty-three patients enumerated in the 1915 census, all were US citizens and four had French surnames, a proportion slightly lower than those of French-Canadian descent who convalesced at Champlain Valley Hospital.[61]

Facing economic challenges, including a low patient population, Physicians' Hospital became a nonprofit corporation in 1917, placing it under the supervision of the New York State Board of Charities, eliminating its tax burden, and making it a public institution. The legislation allowing the change to nonprofit status shifted the hospital from a stock (business) corporation to a membership corporation and allowed the existing stockholders to gain a life membership in the new corporation. The 1917 law allowed for a maximum of 17 trustees, a measure that a 1926 amendment enlarged to 100 trustees. Section 7 of the new act of incorporation made explicit that the institution was a nonprofit entity: "The hospital was not established and shall not be maintained or conducted for the pecuniary profit of its members, and no member of the corporation shall be entitled to or shall receive any such profit." The 1917 incorporation papers also stipulated that "the hospital shall be strictly non-sectarian, and no more than one-third of its trustees shall belong to any one religious denomination." Given its secular nature, Physicians' Hospital did not exclude Catholic priests from ministering on its premises. In 1911, for example, the board of directors passed a resolution thanking the Oblate priests for a "Communion set" for the hospital, a gift that allowed Catholic patients to receive the sacrament of Communion from Roman Catholic priests.[62]

One source of income for the hospital was the Common Council of the City of Plattsburgh, which authorized payments for charity patients from the city. In 1918, for example, representatives from both Physicians' and Champlain Valley Hospitals asked the Common Council to raise their reimbursement rates from $1 to $1.50 per day for those unable to cover the cost of their medical care, and the council complied. This increase only partially subsidized hospital care for the indigent, for actual costs ranged from $2.65 daily at Physicians' Hospital to $2.88 per day at Champlain Valley Hospital. Physicians' Hospital did not maintain any free beds but followed the practice of not turning away the indigent "as far as its capacity will permit," noted the *Daily Press*. In fact, the Women's League of Physicians' Hospital took charge of assisting the indigent, stating in its 1911 incorporation papers that one of its purposes was "to extend help and relief to any persons who are in need of medical or surgical treatment, and are unable to pay for the same." In 1918, Champlain Valley Hospital still maintained several free beds and did not turn away patients unable to afford medical treatment.[63]

Champlain Valley Hospital did receive requests at different points to assist those in need. Just prior to US entry into the Great War, federal government officials from Washington, DC, contacted the hospital to ask how it might contribute to the war effort. The board of directors decided in March 1917 to offer care for fifty war patients at cost, putting the hospital "at the disposal of the Government." The board then authorized Sr. St. Anthony, a member of the nursing school's first graduating class who succeeded Sr. Anne as the superintendent, to complete and send the form to Washington. In its reporting of this action, the *Daily Press* commended the hospital, acknowledging in its subheadline: "The C. V. Hospital Proves Its Loyalty to Country."[64]

But the institution clearly had expenses to cover. When the United States entered World War I, the salary of each Grey Nun working at Champlain Valley Hospital was $200 annually. The following year, the board of directors increased the salary of each sister to $300 annually, which they did at the intervention of the Mother House in Ottawa. Because nurses at Champlain Valley Hospital had worked for at least six years at low wages, the Council of the Mother House requested an augmentation of their salary, and the Superior General traveled from Ottawa in April 1917 to make the request formally to the board of directors in Plattsburgh. Besides the modest salaries of the sisters, and the hospital maintenance costs, the board also had to cover the cost of enlarging the hospital grounds, for in 1917 the board purchased for $2,500 an additional 3.34 acres for the hospital property.[65] Thus, fundraising by groups such as the Women's Auxiliary proved essential to the operation of both Physicians' and Champlain Valley Hospitals in Plattsburgh.

In conclusion, this chapter has highlighted the community effort involved in creating Plattsburgh's first civilian hospital. That effort, orchestrated by the enterprising Sisters of Charity of Ottawa, and challenged by a large group of local physicians, demonstrates the historical agency of the Catholic nuns who founded and managed the medical facility and its nurse-training program. In nineteenth-century Québec, religious vocations served as an avenue to upward mobility for women, allowing them to gain access to typically male occupations. Vowed women in their own institutions in the United States, according to Margaret Susan Thompson, "enjoyed tremendous authority and autonomy from men—more, perhaps, prior to the present day, than virtually all of their female contemporaries." At Champlain Valley Hospital and its nursing school, the Grey Nuns worked alongside male doctors and with a male board of trustees. But they created and managed the institutions and had enormous influence over their evolution and success. Like nuns in Québec, they worked to improve educational opportunities for women in the United States.[66] They provided lay and religious women access to careers in the medical profession. Moreover, the Grey Nuns provided all women with excellent models of how to overcome obstacles and how to push the social boundaries of their era.

Chapter Six

The Visibility of the Canada–US Border
Separating Nuns and Nations, 1910–1920

In *Histoire des Franco-Américains*, published in 1958, Robert Rumilly assesses in chapter 32 the state of French-Canadian lifeways in the United States around the year 1911. He writes that francophone elites worried about the preference of young Franco-Americans to speak English. In some regions, ethnic societies did not have a strong presence, and Rumilly points to upstate New York, specifically mentioning towns near Plattsburgh, such as Champlain, Chazy, and Cooperville. "Certain descendants of the exiles of [18]37 have forgotten the language of [Ludger] Duvernay, and sometimes modified [anglicized] their name," comments Rumilly.[1] Available evidence suggests that Americanizing forces continued to have an impact on French-Canadian descendants in Plattsburgh during the 1910s, but that bilingualism in French and English persisted through the decade, even though the city had few ethnic societies. During the 1910s, the Canada–US border became more visible, particularly during the Great War, and so did differences between priests and nuns over language issues. By the end of the decade, the border tended to separate people from the two countries and from within the order of the Grey Nuns.

Because English was part of the curriculum that the Brothers of Christian Instruction had to teach in Canada, it was essential for members of the order to study the language. The brothers also hoped to expand their numbers in the United States. Consequently, they opened a juvenate in Plattsburgh in 1911 to prepare English-Canadian and American young men to become brothers. In 1915, there were twenty-five male boarding students ranging in age from ten to sixteen at the juvenate; while one was from England, seven in that year were native of French Canada, and the large majority were born in the United States. Of the twenty-five students, three-quarters had French surnames. The juvenists produced an English-language publication, the *Assumption Gazette, Revue de la semaine au Juvénat des Frères de l'Instruction Chrétienne à Plattsburg*, in which "all is written in English, well understood, except the motto *God Alone*," the brothers noted in French in their periodical, *Écho des Missions*. The expense of maintaining the juvenate at Mount Assumption led the Brothers of Christian Instruction, who were strapped for cash, to close it in 1919, after which candidates to the order received their training in La Prairie, Québec.[2] In short, the francophone Brothers of Christian Instruction crossed the Canada–US border during the 1910s to offer English-language instruction to their recruits. The international border thus represented a linguistic divide for this order. As we will see, the border also fostered a linguistic divide among the Grey Nuns.

The opening of the juvenate in Plattsburgh coincided with a reduction in the number of Brothers of Christian Instruction employed by St. Peter's parish and with the suspension of its secondary school program. In 1910, twelve brothers taught at St. Peter's Academy. Saddled with a large school debt of around $30,000, the parish could no longer afford to pay the salaries of all the brothers by 1911. In that year, only eight brothers taught at the parish school, and from 1912 to 1917, St. Peter's employed only five brothers. At least one, Brother Cléonique-Joseph, was reassigned from the parochial school to teach at the juvenate in 1911, joining a staff of five religious who taught at or administered the institution.[3]

When Brother Cyprius-Celestine Tregret arrived in the United States in 1911 to become the assistant director of the juvenate, he made some interesting observations about Plattsburgh's economy. Tregret discovered that sandy soils made it difficult for farmers to eke out a living, and that the high rates charged by the only railroad company, the Delaware and Hudson, discouraged industry. While he found that local electric power and lumber plants provided work to some residents, local commerce was particularly prosperous: "Plattsburgh was the shopping center for the people for miles around and for the summer and winter tourists who came to the mountain resorts up country."[4] As a commercial center in upstate New York, Plattsburgh offered opportunity to French-Canadian immigrants who settled there. Moving into retail sales often provides an ethnic population with a means to climb from the working class to the middle class in society, and doing so often necessitates some facility in the language of the host society. Bilingualism in French and English, then, served to facilitate the socioeconomic climb of French-Canadian descendants in US communities like Plattsburgh.

One means to identify the predominant language or languages of an ethnic group is to note the ones used in important events. Plattsburgh's proximity to the Canadian border, and particularly to the city of Montréal, made easier cross-border exchanges with francophone societies. In 1911, the *Plattsburgh Daily Press* reported that the French-speaking people of Plattsburgh organized a convention of semi-military groups, welcoming them with signage in French and English, and local businesses hung American, French, and Canadian-British flags on their establishments.[5] The St. John Baptist Society, Les Chasseurs de Salisbury Guard, the Malone Military Band, and the Ville Marie (Montréal) Zouave Guard paraded from downtown to the fairgrounds off Montcalm Avenue, with Dr. J. H. LaRocque serving as the marshal. An estimated 5,000 men, women, and children attended an outdoor mass celebrated by Rev. Paul LaRocque, Bishop of Sherbrooke, Québec, and uncle of Dr. LaRocque. Clergymen from Québec and Montréal assisted LaRocque, as did Rev. J. H. Driscoll, the Irish pastor of St. John's Church. Rev. Dr. J. E. Emery, an Oblate priest from St. Peter's parish, addressed the group in French after the gospel reading.[6]

The language(s) used in religious celebrations shed considerable light on the evolution of an immigrant community in a society of adoption. The ceremony of Confirmation, by which young people are admitted to full membership in the Catholic Church, provides us a window into the community of St. Peter's parish. In 1912, Rev. J. H. Conroy, the auxiliary bishop of Ogdensburg, preached in French at Confirmation. In 1914, Conroy confirmed nearly 100 youth at St. Peter's Church and gave them a short address in French after the ceremonial laying of the hands. Two years later, in 1916, Bishop Henry Gabriels himself confirmed sixty-four children and addressed them afterward in French. The following year, Conroy administered Confirmation to eighty-two children at St. Peter's Church, where he preached a sermon in English and French.[7] Thus, Confirmation ceremonies at St. Peter's parish in the 1910s reveal that French was still being used by its youth; they also reveal evidence of the population's bilingualism.

So do the school ceremonies of the parish. In 1918, while the Great War was still underway, the program for the end-of-year exercises at St.

Peter's School included songs in French. Third graders, for example, sang "Restons Toujours Américains-Français" ("Let Us Forever Remain French Americans"). Boys and girls from the parish school who made the best progress in their study of French received gold medals presented by the president of the St. John Baptist Society. The following year, in 1919, when five young men graduated from St. Peter's Academy, Dr. LaRocque addressed them in French and Arthur Hogue in English. Hogue told the young men that their knowledge of French and English would allow them "access to the literary, scientific and commercial interests of both those great races," reported the *Plattsburgh Daily Republican*.[8]

Activities at Notre-Dame des Victoires reveal that it was also a bilingual parish. In 1912, clergy from St. Peter and St. John parishes in Plattsburgh, along with clergy from the nearby communities of Redford and Treadwell's Mills, gathered at Our Lady to dedicate the 500-pound church bell that had been imported from France. Rev. M. J. Sweeney of St. John's preached his sermon in English, while Rev. J. H. A. Bachand, the pastor of Notre-Dame, gave his sermon in French. In 1918, when area clergy gathered at Our Lady of Victory Church to bless the statue of the church's patron saint, Rev. Walter Plaisance of St. Peter's gave a sermon in French and Rev. J. J. Kelly of Cadyville preached a sermon in English. But it was not only the consecrations of bells and statues at Our Lady that were bilingual—so were the weekly masses. Roman Catholic clergy sang masses in Latin to the 1960s but preached their sermons in the vernacular. Published reports of the mass schedule of Our Lady during the 1910s indicate that it held two masses every Sunday, one with a sermon in English and the other with a sermon in French.[9]

The evolution of Our Lady of Victory Academy during the 1910s not only reflects the bilingual nature of the parish community but also the significant challenges of forming a Catholic institution. The Sisters of Charity of St. Louis developed their school with modest means. When they arrived in Plattsburgh in 1910, the only revenue source they had at their immediate disposal was the 50-cents monthly tuition each student paid to attend the parochial school. One parishioner suggested that Mother Stéphanie ask for donations from the men at the nearby Plattsburgh barracks, and some soldiers made monthly contributions after receiving their pay. The $178.00 the Sisters of Charity collected in 1911–1912 from the soldiers constituted over one-fifth (22.7 percent) of their receipts in that school year. The sisters continued to receive donations from soldiers stationed in Plattsburgh at least through the 1915–1916 fiscal year. The wives of the soldiers also assisted by paying the sisters for French lessons, and the sisters increased their revenues during their first decade in Plattsburgh by offering piano and other music lessons as well.[10]

By 1915, Notre-Dame des Victoires had erected a new church, leaving the sisters full use of the convent/school building. They converted the top floor of the structure into two large dormitories, created more classrooms, established dining rooms for students and sisters, and set up a chapel. When the renovations to the physical plant were complete, the Sisters of Charity opened a boarding school in Plattsburgh "to provide daily bread." Indeed, revenue from boarding students was substantial, peaking during the 1910s at $4,263 in the 1919–1920 school year, representing the large majority (nearly 82 percent) of the receipts of the sisters during that year.[11]

The building renovations also secured Plattsburgh as the site of an English-language juvenate for the Sisters of Charity of St. Louis. The congregation printed from its Mother House in Vannes, France, a newsletter titled *L'Hirondelle d'Arvor*, beginning in 1913. In the following year, the newsletter explained to all sisters in the order the purpose of the Plattsburgh juvenate, "where the Congregation will draw English-language subjects to sustain already existing houses and to form others in a semi-Protestant country, where Catholic schools are so necessary to maintain and increase the faith." The juvenate also brought income to the Plattsburgh convent. The Provincial House of the Sisters of Charity in Canada, for example, paid the sisters in Plattsburgh $125 in the 1912–1913 school year for their work in training the postulants.[12]

Our Lady of Victory Academy educated boarding and day students by following the New York State curriculum, and it received its charter from the Regents of the University of the State of New York in 1913. From that date, the school offered its students Regents exams twice yearly in January and June. French-language instruction was, of course, part of the Regents curriculum, and the Sisters of Charity of St. Louis taught the subject in Plattsburgh.[13]

Beyond the school day, the sisters supervised various extracurricular activities at their boarding school. The student leaders of the study, literary, musical, and athletic clubs had the responsibility of organizing an evening program on a regular rotation. The first two clubs helped students develop their language skills. The study club's purpose was to stimulate English-language study through poetry, compositions, and other works. For its part, the literary club examined classic works and read essays its members wrote in English and French, offering advice and encouragement.¹⁴

Our Lady of Victory Academy displayed its bilingual and bicultural nature in other ways as well. When the Mother General from France visited Plattsburgh in 1920, following a rough transatlantic voyage, students from Our Lady of Victory made recitations in English and French in her honor. During the trip to New York, the Mother General also visited the order's house in Keeseville, where she was as warmly received as in Plattsburgh. "Our sisters have well remained French despite their long years of exile," *L'Hirondelle d'Arvor* commented, adding, "everywhere we caught sight of our tricolor flag and, so far from our homeland, it made [our] hearts beat."¹⁵ The French roots of the women religious at Our Lady of Victory Academy thus were still evident a decade after their arrival in Plattsburgh.

This bilingualism and biculturalism displayed during the Mother General's visit, of course, was not new to the Plattsburgh community, and previous chapters have documented its existence since the mid-1800s. They have also documented the participation of French-Canadian descendants in clubs that were not based on a shared ethnic heritage. This trend, of course, continued in the 1910s. From 1912 through 1914, Victor Boire, a prominent Franco-American attorney who had been elected Judge of the Clinton County Surrogate's Court in 1912, served as Grand Knight of the Knights of Columbus. In 1919, when the Knights of Columbus initiated 120 men from Plattsburgh into its organization, St. Peter's Church hosted the ceremony, and its pastor gave the benediction. Seven hundred members of the Knights of Columbus from northern New York, Vermont, and Canada participated in the celebration. The surnames of the clergy (e.g., McCarty, Kenny, and Gallagher) and of the Grand Knights (e.g., Hackett, Kennedy, and Dwyer) who attended make clear that this was not exclusively a Franco-American affair.¹⁶ For French-Canadian descendants of St. Peter's to join the Knights of Columbus suggests that the organization functioned as a space for intercultural mixing.

Impressionistic evidence also suggests that Plattsburgh Franco-Americans intermixed with different cultural groups in other organizations as well. In October 1915, the Plattsburgh Elks asked its members to meet one morning and to attend as a group "the funeral of their late brother, B. St. Louis," at St. Peter's Church. Among the business papers of Filmore Columbe was a four-page flyer containing information about the fourth annual convention of the New York State Association of Elks, sent to all of the society's members in New York.¹⁷ By joining societies like the Elks Club and the Knights of Columbus during the second decade of the twentieth century, Plattsburgh Franco-Americans showed evidence—besides their bilingualism—of their continued acculturation in US society.

That process was not without conflict. Controversies over instruction, particularly French-language teaching, led to disharmony between the women and men religious of St. Peter's parish in the 1910s. Earlier chapters have documented occasional tensions between the Oblate priests who administered the parish and the Grey Nuns who had charge of younger children in the parish school and who conducted D'Youville Academy, their school for girls. An extract of an agreement between the Oblates and the Grey Nuns, which was to take effect in September 1910 and to continue for three years, reveals that the parish planned to pay nine sisters "capable of teaching English and French" each $200 per year.¹⁸ This agreement naturally highlights the importance of bilingual instruction in the parish school, a priority of the Oblates.

The backgrounds of the Oblate priests serving St. Peter's parish had changed by the late nineteenth and early twentieth centuries. Census records reveal that a majority of the priests serving the parish from the 1860s to the 1880s were born in France, while from the 1890s to 1910 a majority were born in French Canada (see Table 1). In the northeastern United States, priests of French-Canadian birth and background tended to be more assertive than those from France about issues of survivance—the preservation of the French language, Roman Catholic faith, and French-Canadian lifeways. In 1910, all six Oblate priests who resided at St. Peter's rectory had been born in French Canada, as had all of their parents. Each could speak English, and three of the six Oblates were naturalized US citizens. By 1915, half of the Oblates in residence at St. Peter's were from French Canada and the other half from the United States.¹⁹ The Oblates, then, surely recognized the importance of English-language instruction, yet it is clear from their agreement with the Grey Nuns that they did not want parish children to lose the ability to speak French. As we will see, this led to a significant clash between the superiors of the Oblates and of the Grey Nuns in Plattsburgh.

The agreement between the Oblate priests and the Grey Nuns indicated that the latter would have to forego the salary of one teacher for the Oblates to provide them with a chaplain, daily mass, monthly religious instruction, and annual retreats. The sisters accepted this condition during their negotiations, but there existed continual sources of tension between the men and women religious. On the first day of September 1911, the Grey Nuns noted in their chronicle that unspecified difficulties between them and the Oblates resulted in the sisters having to teach all of their classes in the convent "or else we would lose the children from the better families." They recorded that the parish school had not yet opened and that no arrangements had been made with the sisters about teaching there. In late April 1912, the superior of D'Youville Convent, Sr. Marie McMillan, and the hospital superior, Sr. Anne, traveled to Ogdensburg for the installation of the auxiliary bishop, Conroy. A few days later, Sr. McMillan took the opportunity to speak to Conroy about the situation with the Oblates in Plattsburgh, and when she ran into the Oblate Provincial in Ogdensburg, the question of schools "came back up again for discussion."[20]

Less than one month after his installation as the auxiliary bishop, Conroy traveled to Plattsburgh to preside over the Confirmation ceremony at St. Peter's Church. While in Plattsburgh, he convened a meeting of the Mother General of the Grey Nuns, the Oblate Provincial, Sr. McMillan, and Rev. J. A. Sirois, who was the Oblate pastor and superior. The chronicle of the sisters makes clear that the conflict between them and the Oblates centered on language instruction. The sisters recorded that Sirois brought up again "the question of French that we do not teach in our classes, and some other small grievances, more or less insignificant." During the meeting, Conroy stated that the academy conducted by the sisters was an entity separate from the parish and from its pastor, who had jurisdiction over the parish school.[21] That the sisters recorded this point suggests that the issue between them and the Oblates was one where the men religious might have overreached their authority in trying to influence the curriculum of the convent school.

Two days later, Sr. McMillan was summoned to Champlain Valley Hospital, where she found Sirois, the Oblate Provincial, the Mother General, and Sr. Marie de la Victoire were assembled. The one terse line the sisters recorded about the meeting made clear their exasperation: "Always the same question, the same old story—For the grace of God." The Mother General and the sister who accompanied her returned to Ottawa, while the Oblate Provincial called on the local superior later in the day to encourage her patience, intimating that the differences between the sisters and the priests would resolve themselves in due course.[22]

In early June, Regents inspectors visited the school of the sisters. A Mr. Cobb took statistics on their academy and left "content and satisfied." A Mr. Price, who inspected French classes, "approves the methods of Sr. Marie de l'Enfant Jésus," noted the sisters.[23] The complimentary comments from the inspectors probably provided some consolation to the sisters about their work at the convent school.

When D'Youville Academy held its end-of-year exercises in 1912, Conroy returned to Plattsburgh to preside over them. Although several priests were invited, none responded, and none accompanied the auxiliary bishop to the ceremonies. The sisters recorded their disappointment: "We expect members of the clergy at least to demonstrate a little exemplary conduct—This is not what we see these days."[24]

Friction with the Oblates continued for the rest of 1912. One strategy male clerical leaders used to assert control over communities of women religious, notes Margaret Susan Thompson, was to depose nuns with whom they came into conflict. In July, the Oblate superior in Plattsburgh traveled to the Mother House of the sisters in Ottawa to ask that Sr. McMillan be replaced with another superior "more sympathetic to the works of the parish." He also complained to Bishop Gabriels in December about the role of the sisters at the bazaar held the previous month, to which they contributed by selling tickets and making costumes for the performances. The sisters acknowledged that the bishop and his auxiliary were aware of the real issue: "This Father [Sirois] and another from the same house [rectory] would like to see the Academy closed." In March 1913, Sr. McMillan was reassigned by the Grey Nuns to serve as the superior in Pembroke, Ontario, and Sr. Marie de la Victoire (née Marie Duquemin) replaced her as the superior in Plattsburgh.[25]

Ethnic differences may have undergirded the clash between the local superiors of the Grey Nuns and the Oblate priests. Census records indicate that Sr. Marie McMillan was born in English Canada of mixed parentage (her father was a Canadian immigrant from Scotland and her mother was a native of French Canada), while Rev. J. A. Sirois was born in French Canada.[26] The dispute between the two Canadian-born superiors may have even reflected on a small scale an ethnolinguistic conflict that was being played out in Canada during the late nineteenth and early twentieth centuries. During that period, provinces with English-speaking majorities, such as Ontario, New Brunswick, Manitoba, Alberta, and Saskatchewan, enacted legislation to curb or to eliminate bilingual instruction for French-speaking minorities that had previously obtained public financial assistance for their Catholic schools. French descendants in Canada consequently became more strident regarding issues of language and culture, something witnessed in Plattsburgh in the actions of the French-Canadian Oblates at St. Peter's parish.[27]

But ethnolinguistic differences may not have been the only sources of tension. In Plattsburgh, the Grey Nuns acted independently of the Oblate priests in conducting their convent school. The autonomy of the women religious in running their own academy, acknowledged by the auxiliary bishop, must have chafed the Oblates.

During the 1910s, the Grey Nuns continued to recruit students from Lowell, Massachusetts, to attend D'Youville Academy in Plattsburgh. As in the past, two sisters escorted the students to and from Plattsburgh at, respectively, the beginning and end of each school year. This sometimes involved two different modes of transportation. In June 1917, for example, the superior and the accompanying sister traveled with the boarders by boat to Burlington, Vermont, and then by train to Lowell on the line that connected Burlington and Boston.[28]

The Grey Nuns generated money for their order by accepting boarding as well as day students to their academy. In 1915, for example, they had 106 day students from the local area attending their convent school. In that year, they also had thirty-four boarders, but not all of the boarders were enrolled at their school. Several boarders in 1915, for example, were women who attended the Plattsburgh Normal School. The room and board charges they paid the sisters provided some income for the order. In 1915, the Grey Nuns also taught 215 students in their parish-school classes, a task for which they were remunerated by the parish.[29]

Bazaars and various performances the sisters oversaw also generated revenue, both for their order and for the church. In 1914, the sisters organized their students to participate in some of the programming for a bazaar to benefit St. Peter's Church that raised $60 in ticket sales. Besides making the arrangements for musical and dramatic performances, the sisters and their boarding students made items they would sell at the bazaars to raise money for the convent. To do so required the permission of the bishop, which the sisters secured in December 1914. Because there was considerable unemployment in the local community and money was generally tight in 1914, the end-of-year bazaar ran for only a few days, and admission was set at 15 cents so that parents could watch their children perform and more people might purchase the objects on sale. Children performed in the two operettas, one in French and the other in English, at the bazaar, which netted $203 for the sisters—an amount surpassing their expectations given the large number of people out of work that winter. A year later, in December 1915, the sisters organized their academy students for a concert, during which they performed two operettas, one in French ("La Charité") and the other in English ("The Night before Christmas"). Performed primarily for the benefit of the parents of students, the sisters charged only 25 cents admission and took in $55.[30] The concerts and bazaars the Grey Nuns oversaw not only served to generate needed revenue but also reflected the bilingualism of their work and of their student population.

Continuing a tradition the Grey Nuns had practiced since their arrival in Plattsburgh in the mid-1800s, they and their academy students celebrated St. Patrick's Day in the 1910s. State and federal census data reveals that at least one Irish nun resided at D'Youville Convent in most census years from 1870 to 1910 (see Table 2). St. Patrick's Day generally was a vacation day for their convent-school students, and the sisters prepared them for a concert that generated revenue for the convent. In 1912, in addition to the St. Patrick's Day concert, students put on the play *An Irish Evening*. In 1914, tickets for the St. Patrick's Day concert sold for 50 cents each and generated $160. There was music, pantomime, singing, and the play *Mollie Brown, an Irish Loyalty*. The concert revenues were sometimes matched by the objects sold; in 1917, the St. Patrick's Day concert raised $66.55 and the objects sold at the event generated another $65.10.[31] The Irish-themed activities and concerts also highlighted the non-French dimension of their convent school.

Other concerts served to cultivate their ties with the Oblate priests, particularly the pastor. To celebrate the birthday of Rev. Sirois, the parochial school students put on a concert in October 1914. The following year, the sisters invited Sirois to say mass and have breakfast with them on his birthday, during which "he was very pleasant at his breakfast," and he conversed "for quite a while and most agreeably," they noted. The sisters also guided their students to put on a concert on his behalf.[32]

These diplomatic gestures on the part of the Grey Nuns did not inhibit the Oblate superior from making additional demands upon them and their teaching, however. The sisters had been taking over the classes that the brothers were not able to teach because of parish budget cuts. After a five-year hiatus caused by significant financial challenges, the parish decided to reopen its secondary program in 1916. To pull this off required some reorganization of teaching assignments and classrooms. Sirois went through the Bishop of Ogdensburg and the Superior General of the Grey Nuns to request that the sisters in Plattsburgh take over the second-grade boys. Two Grey Nuns, the former Superior General and the bursar, traveled from the Mother House in Ottawa to the convent in Plattsburgh in late August to meet with Sirois, who proposed sending the sisters who teach at "our school"—that is, their academy—to the sacristy and to the school of the Brothers of Christian Instruction, where there were four vacant classrooms. According to Brother Cléonique-Joseph, who returned to Plattsburgh in 1916 to teach at St. Peter's Academy, the brothers employed by the parish had a private house on Cornelia Street across from the Grey Nuns, and the sisters and brothers were to swap teaching stations. This would necessitate the sisters leaving their school "that we built at our expense for the parish, unoccupied for not paying rent," they complained. The sisters found the proposal of the Oblates "unreasonable and unacceptable." After several meetings with the Oblate superior, the visiting sisters from the Mother House tentatively agreed that the Grey Nuns would continue teaching at their school but would pay rent of $50 per class and take charge of the second-grade class of boys. This would result in the Grey Nuns teaching all of the young boys and girls, while the Brothers of Christian Instruction would teach the boys from grade eight and up. The Grey Nuns' Council in Ottawa had to ratify the agreement before it could take effect.[33]

On the first Sunday in September 1916, the Oblate priests announced at masses that the parish schools would not reopen until the eleventh day of the month. Upon hearing this news, the sisters interpreted the announcement as a sign that their Mother House had not yet given the Oblate superior a final answer about the assignments of the sisters. But city schools also delayed the start of the new school year to the eleventh of September because an exposition was underway in the city, and they undoubtedly anticipated poor school attendance as a result. Two years earlier, when the school year opened on September 8, 1914, few students attended the classes of the sisters because many participated in the one-hundredth anniversary celebration and reenactment of the Battle of Plattsburgh that had taken place during the War of 1812–1814 with the British. When the Mother House agreed to the demand of the Oblate superior that the Grey Nuns take charge of the second-grade boys, classes resumed in 1916.[34]

The Oblate pastor quietly started searching for another order of women religious to replace the Grey Nuns at St. Peter's parish. The archives of the Dominican Sisters reveal that the process of soliciting their order to teach in Plattsburgh began in October 1916 through the conduit of a

Dominican priest from upstate New York. Rev. Henry Cormerais, a member of the Dominican order and a native of France who had fled during religious persecutions around 1880, arrived in the Diocese of Ogdensburg in 1902 and, after serving in various North Country churches, became the pastor of St. Patrick's Church in Rouses Point in 1915. In October 1916, he wrote the Dominican Sisters of Fall River, Massachusetts, to let them know that the Oblate superior and pastor at St. Pierre Church in Plattsburgh had asked for his help in finding a community of six to eight women religious to take over the parish school. Cormerais informed the Dominican Sisters that the Grey Nuns currently in charge of the school no longer wanted to teach boys, and he inquired if the Dominicans might be interested in establishing themselves in Plattsburgh in a French-Canadian parish. Cormerais suggested that the superior contact Sirois, and she promptly did. When Sirois acknowledged receipt of the superior's letter, he indicated he would either visit or write her again after obtaining direction from the bishop.[35]

The following year, in early September 1917, the new Oblate superior in Plattsburgh, Rev. Walter Plaisance, called the local superior, Sr. Marie de la Victoire, to inform her that he had secured the approval of the bishop and of the Superior General for the Grey Nuns to teach the elementary classes of boys and girls to grade eight at St. Peter's Academy. The Brothers of Christian Instruction had been teaching at that school for the past decade. Still saddled with a large debt for the new school building they had constructed, the Oblates decided to economize by assigning the elementary-school grades to the Grey Nuns whom the parish paid less than the brothers, writes Brother Cyprius-Celestine Tregret. The leaders of the order in Québec had pressured the parish in 1914 for a raise in salary to $350 for each teaching brother, due to rising living expenses during the Great War and because the brothers earned that much in the rural parishes of Québec where expenses were less than in the United States. In 1917, the Brothers of Christian Instruction asked the Oblates for $400 in salary for each brother teaching high school, plus $120 to cover the room and board of each. The Oblate Superior balked and appealed to the bishop, who sided with the brothers in this dispute. Under protest, Plaisance ultimately agreed to pay the brothers each $360 in salary and $80 for such expenses as lodging and heat, but he cut the number of brothers on the parish payroll to three and assigned them to teach high school classes. The parish continued to employ only three brothers to 1919. Plaisance further informed the sister superior that the three brothers would teach high school classes at the sisters' school for girls, "built on our own land by our Community [Grey Nuns]," they noted. The news shared in this phone call completely surprised the superior, who opposed the sisters' teaching of boys beyond the second grade. To explain the change, Plaisance indicated simply that the Brother Provincial had asked for a salary increase that exceeded the means of the parish. When the new school year began, the brothers took over the first floor of "our convent school," recorded the sisters, where they taught their high school classes plus grade eight, which the sisters could not staff that school year. The sisters also recorded that one result of the change in personnel was that boys in the upper elementary grades opted to attend public school rather than the classes of the sisters.[36]

The biggest challenge the following school year proved to be the worldwide influenza epidemic that also affected the Plattsburgh community and led to the closing of its schools. In October 1918, local officials closed Plattsburgh's meeting places and schools to prevent the flu from spreading. Several of the boarding students of the sisters acquired the flu by mid-October, and the Grey Nuns transformed a nearby former school building into a hospital that two sisters staffed as nurses. Local doctors, including J. H. LaRocque, also attended to the sick students, as did some of the mothers who chose to assist in the care of their children at the makeshift hospital. The improvised hospital allowed the sisters to isolate sick residential students from the others.[37]

As Sisters of Charity, the Grey Nuns who taught in Plattsburgh continued to visit the sick and poor in the Plattsburgh community even after the opening of Champlain Valley Hospital in 1910. The register of the sisters reveals that they made as few as three visits to as many as forty-eight visits annually to the homes of the sick during the decade from 1910 to 1919. In 1918, the year of the influenza epidemic, they made thirty-three sick visits. Besides assisting individuals suffering from the flu, the other maladies they treated at the homes of community members during the 1910s included pneumonia, anemia, cancer, paralysis, indigestion, sore throats, and even old age, according to their register.[38] Given this charitable work, it is unsurprising that the teaching sisters would create a temporary hospital for their students and continue ministering to the needs of the larger community during the flu epidemic.

Among the Sisters of Charity of Ottawa serving the Plattsburgh community, the teaching sisters functioned independently of the hospital sisters. Yet they were part of the same religious family, and both groups of Grey Nuns intermixed on occasion. The teaching and hospital sisters periodically gathered together to dine and socialize with each other, typically on religious occasions such as New Year's Day and the feast of the Blessed Virgin. Sometimes the sisters intermixed during their retreats. In 1918, while the Great War was underway, four sisters from Champlain Valley Hospital and three Grey Nuns from Ogdensburg joined eighteen sisters from D'Youville Convent for a retreat preached by a priest from Lowell. The retreat was not an occasion to socialize, however, for the sisters had to observe silence, noting: "The observed silence directs the soul to reflection and raises it to the supernatural." Gatherings had special meaning beyond the religious dimensions for the sisters. When the hospital sisters joined the teaching sisters, some arriving for lunch and others for dinner, one Sunday in October 1915, the chronicler noted that "it is a true family celebration." This type of "familial" gathering was important to the sisters who had left their own families of origin to join their religious community. When, in May 1917, Sr. Marie du Sacré-Coeur graduated from the Champlain Valley Hospital's School of Nursing, and Sr. Anne de Jésus came to Plattsburgh to visit from the Pembroke, Ontario, hospital where she now served as the superior, the hospital sisters put on a luncheon attended by some of the teaching Grey Nuns. The chronicler at D'Youville Convent noted that the sisters participating in the luncheon expressed their pleasure at being able to share such a nice occasion "as a religious family."[39] While their spirituality was important, so too was the sense of family ties among members of their community of women religious.

In late October 1918, the teaching sisters closed their makeshift hospital, noting, "Everybody is cured." Most of their boarding students had returned home until the quarantine was lifted. Classes reopened in mid-November, but officials closed the local schools again in mid-December because more children fell ill. There were no sick students at the convent school at the time, so the sisters decided to send their students home early for vacation. The school closings not only adversely affected the education of their students but also an important source of their income, causing "great damage to the receipts."[40]

One casualty of the 1918 influenza epidemic was the Oblate pastor and superior, Rev. Plaisance, who succumbed. Plaisance's successor, Rev. Julien Racette, had been born and educated in Lowell, Massachusetts, before training for the priesthood. When the sisters welcomed Racette to St. Peter's parish, he told them he was pleased to work with them and that he had been educated by Grey Nuns. This comment gave the sisters hope that relations between themselves and the Oblates might improve. "Let us hope that harmony will cross [make a religious sign over] our priests and that all ill feeling will disappear—To do good works, with the children particularly, requires the union of hearts and intentions!!"[41]

What transpired over the next few years, however, was the local conflict between nuns and priests playing itself out on a larger platform in the Roman Catholic Church. Men religious had long exerted their paternalism over women religious like the Grey Nuns, including by ignoring the preference of some orders not to teach boys. In January 1872, for example, the Oblate Provincial in Canada had acknowledged in a letter to his superior in France that Mother Élisabeth Bruyère, the foundress of the Sisters of Charity of Ottawa, had often expressed to him her desire that Grey Nuns no longer be required to teach boys. Nearly half a century later, the Grey Nuns took a strong stand. In early January 1919, the Sisters of Charity of Ottawa let the Bishop of Ogdensburg know of an important change in their Rule (the principles under which they conduct themselves). The Superior General informed Monsignor Conroy that the Grey Nuns had decided at a general chapter not to teach boys over the age of twelve; with some exceptions, they could work with boys to age fourteen, but no older.[42]

Racette worried about the implications for St. Peter's parish. He wrote Conroy in English on stationery headed with the French words "Eglise St. Pierre" ("St. Peter's Church") that the Grey Nuns taught the classes from kindergarten through grade seven in the parish schools, and that they were needed to teach boys through grammar school, for boys represented 177 of the 379 children enrolled. Racette compiled figures to demonstrate that fifty-five of the boys from grades three through seven were age twelve or older. Accommodating the change in teaching would create financial problems for the parish, Racette insisted, and would adversely affect "the efficiency of our school." Racette asked the bishop for help at least in holding off implementation of the change until such time that "no harm will be done."[43]

As the Vicar General and Auxiliary Bishop of Ogdensburg, Conroy appealed the decision of the Grey Nuns to the Pope's representative in Canada. He informed him that the diocese could not replace the Grey Nuns and would have to close Catholic schools. Conroy also attacked the logic of the Grey Nuns, arguing that if their teaching of boys was harmful, then no women religious should do it, and in his experience it was not harmful. Conroy went on the offensive against the Grey Nuns, stating of Catholic schools: "Their stability and permanence should not be dependent upon the whims of the good nuns whom the latest election has placed in office." Using language he surely would not have used with the Superior General, Conroy continued: "Various administrations which inaugurated and approved co-educational high school work were presumably as intelligent and zealous as the present incumbents." Conroy requested of the Apostolic General that if the Grey Nuns were allowed to withdraw from high school teaching, the decision be delayed until he could line up other teachers for different parishes of the diocese, something that would take two or three years—particularly to train replacements to teach the advanced subjects.[44]

Conroy also appealed to the Apostolic Delegate in the United States. "Although the community involved is a Canadian one and the question is therefore to be referred to the Delegate to Canada," Conroy wrote, "the point at issue is such a serious [one] and so international in its scope, that I take the liberty of referring the entire matter to Your Excellency, inasmuch as you are more familiar with conditions existing here in the United States." Conroy implored the delegate's help in obtaining "a happy solution."[45]

On the same day that he penned letters to the Apostolic Delegates to Canada and the United States, Conroy wrote the Superior General of the Grey Nuns. The prelate began his letter diplomatically, asking the Grey Nuns to reconsider their decision not to teach boys twelve and over. He pointed out their history, noting that they had taught in Ogdensburg's Cathedral High School for over thirty years, and he appealed to their Catholic devotion, alleging that many boys would have to attend public schools if the sisters carried out their decision.[46]

But Conroy did not stop there. In other parts of his letter, the auxiliary bishop intimated that following through on their decision would lead to questions about the fitness and competence of the Grey Nuns, and it would give fuel to anti-Catholic forces then prevalent. His strategy, then, turned to intimidation. "It would also cause grave scandal by making people wonder why nuns should not teach boys," Conroy suggested. "Thousands of women are doing this work in public grade and high schools and our enemies will doubtlessly charge that nuns are either mentally incompetent to teach advanced pupils or have not sufficient strength of moral character required for the teaching of the opposite sex," he alleged. "Cruelly false as such assertions would be," Conroy continued, "they would certainly gain currency and credence among those who hate everything Catholic, especially Catholic nuns and Catholic schools."[47] The auxiliary bishop undoubtedly was aware of the rise of the Second Ku Klux Klan throughout the United States, a group that especially targeted Catholics.

In his dispute with the Sisters of Charity of Ottawa, Conroy capitalized upon some tensions within the order over language to create division between the US- and Canadian-based Grey Nuns. Conroy contacted Sister Verecunda (née Quinn), an Irish nun who had previously been stationed in Plattsburgh but who now served at Sacred Heart Convent in Ogdensburg. Sr. Verecunda reported that, at the General Chapter held in Ottawa in March 1918, the Grey Nuns enacted a statute about French-language use. The ninth of nine statutes explicitly stated: "The custom of using the French language for our religious exercises must be maintained in all our houses." That this order of women religious, which had showed evidence of bilingualism from its origins, felt compelled to codify the use of the French language suggests that it had concerns over the loss of French in its ranks. Each house in the community received a copy of the statute, Sr. Verecunda informed Conroy, noting that it was viewed as a recommendation until the Superior General stated at their annual retreat "in a most forcible manner, that the statutes of the recent Chapter . . . must be enforced." She told Conroy that sixteen English-speaking sisters and one half-French, who conversed better in English, lived in their community in Ogdensburg and that she had enforced the rule at their convent "solely through a motive of obedience." Sr. Verecunda continued, "About one[-]half our number understand practically nothing of French readings, subjects of meditation or particular examen." Moreover, she reported, "the few who understand French fairly well, claim that they are too tired after teaching all day, to concentrate their attention to a degree, sufficient to derive any benefit from spiritual reading."[48]

The next day, Conroy conveyed this information by letter to Rev. Dennis Dougherty, formerly the Bishop of Buffalo and now the Archbishop of Philadelphia. Conroy reported that the Mother General of the Grey Nuns at a retreat of the Community Superiors in Ottawa had held up the order's amended Book of Rules and insisted that the nine statutes enacted in 1918 be followed "and that no priest or bishop could dispense from their observance." Those attending the retreat, Conroy noted, especially believed that she referred to the ninth statute: "The custom of using the French language for our religious exercises must be maintained in all our houses." Conroy pointed out that the Grey Nuns were also required to use French "in recreation." By this, Conroy referred to the limited block of free time sisters enjoyed as part of their structured daily routines. The rule about language use was causing distress and damage, he asserted: "From what the Sisters tell me, this insistence upon a foreign language in the United States is causing much discontent." The nuns who cannot follow French "are consequently suffering spiritual damage from the statute," Conroy contended. Appealing to the notion of patriarchy within the Roman Catholic Church, Conroy asserted: "Inasmuch as it is our duty to safeguard the religious interests of the nuns working in this Diocese, I am writing Your Grace to voice, before the proper authorities, our emphatic protest against this harmful enactment."[49]

Besides giving voice to his religious paternalism, Conroy further advocated separating the American from the Canadian provinces of the Grey Nuns. He argued that the order's internal tensions over language use aided the cause of division: "It serves to emphasize the need of a separate Province in the United States for the nuns who are working here and in other American Dioceses." To support his case, Conroy pointed to differences in the Canadian and US educational systems, arguing that requirements for teachers in Canada did not necessarily meet those for certification in New York State. Conroy's comment, of course, ignored the longstanding practice of Grey Nuns in communities like Plattsburgh to study for and take New York exams to become certified to teach in the state. Conroy nonetheless carried his argument further, asserting that the differences between Canadian and New York teacher-training requirements might result in state directives to supply qualified teachers or to close Catholic schools, thus making "it imperative that a Province should be established in the United States at a very early date." Conroy concluded his letter by asking the archbishop to take up this matter with the Apostolic Delegate before he left for Rome and to provide him with the documents he sent to support forming an American province of the Grey Nuns.[50]

Two months later, Conroy expanded his argument for a separate administrative province. He wrote the Archbishop of Philadelphia that the Superior General of the Grey Nuns had showed a pastor in Ogdensburg some documents to suggest that the nuns were in demand in Canada and could earn higher salaries there. "To my mind this is but another weighty argument for the establishment of a separate community in the States," Conroy asserted. Because there is no separation of church and state in Canada, religious schools received public funding, something that posed a challenge for the bishop: "We cannot compete with a Canadian schedule where they receive State aid and Catholic taxes are allowed to be applied to their own schools."[51]

Conroy also tried to enlist the support of another prelate, Rev. William Turner, the Bishop of Buffalo, to the cause of creating a US province of Grey Nuns. In November 1919, Conroy wrote the bishop that "a very large number of the Grey Nuns now doing work in the United States" believe as he does that the decision not to teach boys fourteen and over "will work disaster to the schools and institutions which the Grey Nuns have successfully opened and conducted during the past fifty years."[52] In arguing for an American branch of Grey Nuns, Conroy wrote: "The Grey Nuns of Ottawa asked and obtained separation from their parent community in Montréal for reasons less cogent, I think, than those which are urged in the present case." He also pointed to the lack of reciprocity in accepting teaching credentials across the border, whereby US teaching certificates were not accepted in Canada and Canadian teaching certificates were not accepted in the United States, as "a strong practical reason in favor of a division." Conroy, it appears, had encouraged the Grey Nuns in his diocese to draft a formal petition. Conroy then asked Turner to support the petition of Grey Nuns to separate from the Mother House in Ottawa by advocating "the case to the proper Church Authorities with a view to a decision that will save our schools from disruption and possible extinction."[53]

Conroy had apparently written the Bishop of Buffalo several times, for the prelate wrote in December 1919 to acknowledge receipt of Conroy's letters regarding the Grey Nuns. Turner informed Conroy that he had discussed the matter recently with the Apostolic Delegate, who advised that they approach authorities in the Catholic Church of Ottawa and, if they responded unfavorably, they should appeal to Rome. The Apostolic Delegate recommended enlisting the support of the Archbishop of Boston, and Turner indicated he would write him to that end. Turner also asked Conroy to inform Sister Vincent de Paul of Turner's meeting with the Apostolic Delegate. A US-born nun of Irish descent, Sr. Vincent de Paul served as the superior of the Ogdensburg City Orphanage and Home for the Aged. "I thought that, in case we should fail, it would be better not to have her figure in the petition, although her cooperation is valuable," Turner wrote.[54]

The five key religious advocating the Canada–US border as the dividing line to separate the American- from the Canadian-based Grey

Nuns had much in common. Each was of Irish descent. Sr. Verecunda was a first-generation Irish immigrant who had come to the United States as a minor, and she had become a naturalized US citizen by age eighteen. Bishop Turner, who was also born in Ireland, migrated to the United States as a young adult and became a naturalized citizen in his mid-twenties. While Sr. Vincent de Paul, Conroy, and Dougherty had each been born in the northeastern United States, the parents of each one had been born in Ireland. Thus, all were Americans of Irish descent by the time they collaborated to pursue the administrative division of the Grey Nuns. The five were also close in age. By the end of the second decade of the twentieth century, each was middle-aged, ranging in age from forty-eight to fifty-four, except for Conroy, who was in his early sixties.[55] Moreover, each had devoted their career to serving the Roman Catholic Church in the United States and had risen to a position of authority in the US Catholic hierarchy. As a result, Sr. Verecunda, Sr. Vincent de Paul, Conroy, Turner, and Dougherty undoubtedly shared a worldview that put them at odds with the Canadian-based francophone leaders of the Sisters of Charity of Ottawa.

In October 1919, the Superior General of the Grey Nuns wrote Conroy to indicate that the Grey Nuns of the Cross in Ottawa had received word from Rome that they could for ten years teach boys up to fourteen years of age. She took the opportunity to inform Conroy that, after the close of the school year in June 1920, "we cannot take charge of classes in which are boys beginning their fifteenth year, or who, in the course of the same year, will attain this age." The Superior General continued: "We even hope to rid ourselves of those thirteen and fourteen, since at that age, the greater number are in the same grades as those of fifteen years."[56]

The bishop's office apparently did not comply with the wishes of the Grey Nuns. Exercising their agency, the Sisters of Charity of Ottawa took matters into their own hands. In October 1920, the Superior General informed Conroy that since he considered it impossible to remove the older boys from the classes of the sisters, they would remove themselves. She therefore announced that the 1920–1921 school year would be the last year that the Grey Nuns would teach "in your schools."[57] With this terse communication, the Grey Nuns indicated in French their withdrawal from all of the schools of the Diocese of Ogdensburg, which of course included St. Peter's parish school in Plattsburgh.

In November 1920, the sisters celebrated sixty years of service to the Plattsburgh community. D'Youville Academy had opened in

November 1860 and had received its charter from the Board of Regents of the University of the State of New York in October 1896. A 1920 promotional booklet, written entirely in English, featured eight pages of information about the college and normal school preparatory programs of their academy. Graduation standards, the brochure informed readers, allowed students to enter normal schools and colleges for women without having to take exams beyond the Regents exams provided each January and June by the New York Education Department in Albany. The four-year program included instruction in reading, composition, and math, as well as such practical skills as letter-writing, plain sewing, mending, and darning. "Neatness and order receive special attention," the promotional literature emphasized. The sisters welcomed students of all religious traditions, indicating in their brochure that "no undue influence is exerted over the conscientious conviction of non-catholics [sic]." But young women of other faith traditions were not exempt from devotional exercises, for they added: "Nevertheless[,] for the sake of order, they must be present at the religious exercises," though they could bring their own devotional books to chapel.[58] The Grey Nuns may not have anticipated having to close D'Youville Academy as they withdrew from the parish schools of the Diocese of Ogdensburg.

Census data reflects the changing composition of D'Youville Convent over time. While the Grey Nuns serving Plattsburgh were ethnically mixed from their arrival in the community, the majority in the census years during the period from 1870 to 1920 were born in Canada (see Table 2). But the proportion who were born in Canada declined in the second decade of the twentieth century, as a larger proportion of the Grey Nuns serving in Plattsburgh were born in the United States. As that change took place from 1910 to 1920, so did another dramatic shift: according to census data, two-thirds of the Grey Nuns at D'Youville Convent in 1910 were born in French Canada, whereas, a decade later, just over half of those at the convent in 1920 were born in English Canada (see Table 2). Thus, by the year 1920, all Grey Nuns at Plattsburgh's D'Youville Convent had been born in either the United States or an English-language province of Canada.[59] While there likely were French-Canadian descendants among them, the shift in the convent's ethnic composition points to the anglicization of the order in the United States by 1920.

Census data also reflects that a majority of the Grey Nuns serving at Champlain Valley Hospital in Plattsburgh during the hospital's first decade of operation were born in Canada (see Table 3). Data from the

1920 federal census reveals that over half of the nuns working at the hospital were Anglo- or Irish Canadian in origin, while under one-fourth were of French-Canadian heritage and less than one-fourth were born in the United States.[60] Like D'Youville Convent, the ethnic composition of the staff at Champlain Valley Hospital suggests that it was largely an anglophone institution by 1920. In short, by that year, the border appeared to divide the Sisters of Charity of Ottawa into separate ethnic and linguistic groups that no longer intermixed as easily as in the past.

Incidentally, a parallel development took place among the Brothers of Christian Instruction in Plattsburgh during the 1910s. In 1915, the five teaching brothers who resided in the city were all unnaturalized, with two having been born in France and three in French Canada. In 1920, however, of the eight brothers stationed in Plattsburgh, five were native of the United States, one of France, and two of Canada (see Table 4).[61] It is possible that the Americanization movement underway in the United States during and after the Great War, and the challenges of crossing the border during wartime, may have precipitated a shift in the composition and citizenship status of men and women religious serving in Plattsburgh by 1920.

In late November 1920, Turner wrote Conroy that he had seen the petition of the Grey Nuns who wished to separate from the Mother House in Ottawa, and he suggested that the prohibition against their teaching boys not be emphasized since it would not carry as much weight in Rome as it would in the United States. Turner recommended that the petition highlight instead that the Grey Nuns would attract more candidates to their order if they had a separate jurisdiction, stating: "I should mention the fact that American young women are deterred from entering by the dominant Canadian-French character which the Community has." In addition, Turner recommended that the petition focus on "the national, not the linguistic, line of boundary."[62]

In June of the following year, 1921, Mother St. Albert, the Superior General of the Sisters of Charity of Ottawa, received a letter from Rev. Dennis Dougherty, the Archbishop of Philadelphia who had recently been elevated to the rank of Cardinal, informing her that Rome had authorized the separation of the order's houses in the United States from those in Canada. The decree indicated that the sisters who wished to remain with the Ottawa congregation could do so, even if they were anglophone. Mother St. Albert then sent a circular letter to the Grey Nuns at their different missions to inform them of the separation and the reasons for it. "The Sisters, supported by or hired by their Excellencies, the Bishops, pointed out reasons which Rome, in its wisdom, deemed good," summarizes Sr. Paul-Emile in her historical account of the Grey Nuns. Those reasons included: "loss for the Community of many young girls who did not want to come to Ottawa in spite of their wish to become Grey Nuns, and consequently, the lack of subjects; difficulty in obtaining qualified Sisters for the United States; the needs peculiar to the houses they were directing and to which Ottawa could not respond."[63]

Sr. Paul-Emile writes that the division of the Grey Nuns incurred some opposition. There were Franco-American parishes in the United States that did not favor the division because it would mean a transfer of convents and schools to an English-speaking community of sisters. Oblate priests in Lowell and Marist priests in Haverhill, both in Massachusetts, along with Monsignor P. S. Garand, the pastor of Notre-Dame parish in Ogdensburg, all opposed the division.[64] Their institutions remained under the charge of the Ottawa community, "to the great relief of the Sisters constituting the personnel, all of whom were French-speaking," notes Sr. Paul-Emile.[65]

At Cardinal Dougherty's request, Mother St. Albert traveled in July 1921 to Buffalo, Ogdensburg, and Plattsburgh, New York, and to Lowell, Massachusetts, to identify the sisters who wanted to form the new community in the United States. The 139 sisters who signed on became known as Grey Nuns of the Sacred Heart in August 1921. The Sisters of Charity of Ottawa, known as Grey Nuns of the Cross, relinquished seven institutions to the new order: D'Youville College in Buffalo; Sacred Heart Academy, Hepburn Hospital, and the orphanage in Ogdensburg; D'Youville Academy boarding school and Champlain Valley Hospital in Plattsburgh; and Immaculate Conception convent in Lowell. Thirty-eight French-speaking nuns from those institutions moved to Ottawa.[66]

Plattsburgh's English-language newspapers informed the local community of the division of the Grey Nuns. The *Daily Republican* told readers in July 1921 that separate administrations in Canada and the United States, each with its own superior general, would oversee the work of the nuns in each respective country. Local Grey Nuns were involved in forming the leadership team of the newly formed Grey Nuns of the Sacred Heart. In September 1921, the *Plattsburgh Sentinel* informed readers that Sister Margaret Mary, the superintendent of Champlain Valley Hospital, had been elected councilor to the new organization. D'Youville Academy closed, and the English-speaking sisters who had remained in Plattsburgh to wrap up business following its closure moved on to larger cities, the newspapers reported. With the formation of the American branch of the Grey Nuns, the US property of the order went to the American branch, the *Republican* informed readers, but it had to compensate the parent institution for such real-estate holdings as D'Youville Academy in Plattsburgh, Sacred Heart Convent in Ogdensburg, and D'Youville College in Buffalo. The Grey Nuns in the United States temporarily made their headquarters in Buffalo, and in 1922 they established their Mother House in Philadelphia, Pennsylvania, at the invitation of Cardinal Dougherty. Some of the nuns who taught in the parish school remained in Plattsburgh until 1923. The *Sentinel* reported that Mother St. Albert had had the French-speaking sisters move into the convent at St. Peter's parish, which was under the jurisdiction of the Mother House in Ottawa, while the decree of separation went into effect.[67]

While the division of the Grey Nuns was underway, the Dominican Sisters contacted them at their Mother House in Ottawa to inquire about their experience in Plattsburgh. The Grey Nuns informed the Dominicans that the mission was "most advantageous," noting particularly that "the Franco-Americans are good [people], filled with lots of faith, like their schools and regret sincerely the departure of the Grey Nuns." The Grey Nuns of the Cross explained that their "American Sisters" had taken over the Plattsburgh mission after the order's division the previous year. But since the American Grey Nuns had no French-speaking sisters to send to Plattsburgh, the pastor had to look for another community of women religious. To encourage the Dominicans to take charge of St. Pierre School, the Grey Nuns pointed out that they would have no regrets, for a good number of girls who had attended the parish school and the academy of the Grey Nuns had joined their order, thus suggesting the possibility that the Dominican Sisters could cultivate recruits to their own community.[68]

The Dominican Sisters were aware of the serious clashes that had taken place within the Roman Catholic Church in the late nineteenth and early twentieth centuries in Fall River and throughout New England (discussed in chapter 3 of this volume). Those ethnic controversies had pitted Irish bishops against French-Canadian clergy and their flocks. The Dominican Sisters apparently asked the Grey Nuns whether similar controversies had taken place in upstate New York, for the Grey Nuns revealed in their letter that they did not get caught between any conflicts that might have existed between the priests of Plattsburgh and the bishop: "We absolutely never suffered from any problems that might have existed between the priests and the Bishop of Ogdensburg," they wrote. The Grey Nuns even put in a good word about the Oblates, noting that they showed great interest in their schools.[69] The Grey Nuns remained silent, however, about the conflicts they had themselves experienced with the Oblates in Plattsburgh and with the Irish bishop of Ogdensburg.

The division of the Sisters of Charity between Canada and the United States perhaps more aptly represented a divorce rather than a separation. Like a divorce, the proceedings were not quickly resolved and occasionally became contentious. What evolved was an international struggle to gain the services of the Grey Nuns. In April 1923, Rev. P. S. Garand, the Vicar General of the Diocese of Ogdensburg, wrote Rev. J. H. Conroy, who had ascended to the rank of bishop, of his meeting in Philadelphia with Cardinal Dougherty and Mother St. Vincent de Paul, who had become the Superior General of the new order of Grey Nuns. Word came "from Rome last week allowing all the English[-]speaking nuns (i.e., of Irish or Scotch descent) (but not English[-]speaking nuns of French extraction) who have already applied to Rome or will in the future, to pass over on this side [of the border] and become members of the Grey Nuns of the Sacred Heart," Garand wrote. Rome, according to Cardinal Dougherty, "has made it a language question." Dougherty followed up with a letter of his own to Conroy, indicating that he had received a decree from the Sacred Congregation for Religious "by which I was empowered to grant to certain English-speaking Grey Nuns in Canada permission, sought by them, to join the American Community of Grey Nuns." He also informed Conroy that if other anglophone Grey Nuns of Canada sought permission from the Holy See to join the American Grey Nuns, they would receive it.[70]

A little more than a month later, Dougherty wrote Conroy that some anglophone Grey Nuns in Canada had been pressured to remain where they were: "Influence has been brought, particularly in one diocese of Canada, upon English-speaking Grey Nuns not to join the American Congregation, in spite of the fact that they were granted permission to do so." Dougherty decided, however, not to get involved in this matter or in the circumstance of French-Canadian nuns getting pulled from the French-Canadian schools of Monsignor Garand by Mother St. Albert. Conroy responded by asking the cardinal to intervene. "Mother St. Albert should not be allowed by Rome to take her Sisters away from our schools unless Mother St. Vincent has a right to withdraw the English-speaking Nuns from Canada," Conroy protested. "Someone in position to do so should make this fact known to Rome and I believe Your Eminence is the influence on which we can rely to bring the matter to a head." In August 1923, in response to Conroy's request for more sisters to staff Garand's schools in Ogdensburg, Sister Ann of Jesus, now the Mother Assistant to the Grey Nuns of the Sacred Heart in Philadelphia, told Conroy that the Archbishop of Ottawa had asked for an intervention from Rome in this matter and was denied, "which means we suppose that the sisters are still free to come over if they choose."[71]

Thus, within the Roman Catholic Church, the international border between Canada and the United States became more salient during the early twentieth century. This was also true, of course, outside of Catholic Church wranglings. From June 1906, migrants had to pay an immigration, or head, tax and had to obtain a certificate of arrival before entering the United States. US immigration officials denied entry to Canadians who did not meet these requirements, and they deported those who had managed to enter the country without first obtaining the necessary documentation. In 1917, the United States imposed a head tax of $8 on immigrants. In that year, two Grey Nuns traveling from Canada to Plattsburgh had to pay $8 each at the border "to come to the United States, because they were born in Canada," they recorded.[72]

During the Great War, the international boundary between Canada and the United States became an obstacle, for "the national boundary line . . . could not be crossed, especially during the war, without sharp questioning from immigration officers," writes Tregret. "The war-time laws had become stricter." Because the Brothers of Christian Instruction did not get many vocations from St. Peter's in Plattsburgh, they needed to recruit from outside of the parish. The tightening of the Canada–US border during World War I "made it difficult to do recruiting in Canada," notes Tregret. The Brothers of Christian Instruction also "found out it would be hard for the Brothers to go to Canada for the retreat. Exit and re-entry caused serious problems." Tregret nonetheless chose to travel to Canada for his retreat, which necessitated obtaining a permit from the superintendent at the Rouses Point immigration office in upstate New York to leave and reenter the United States. The borderlands region, Tregret discovered, had become militarized. In Canada, he observed that military policemen rode the trains "controlling travel by male passengers" because "Canada was on the lookout for deserters and slackers."[73] Canada had not yet gained autonomy as a country when it entered the world conflict alongside England in August 1914, despite the strenuous objections of French Canadians, who felt anglophones were forcing them to take part in an imperial struggle that did not concern them; this led to a conscription crisis during which some French speakers evaded the draft.

Unlike in Canada, there was no conscription crisis among individuals of French-Canadian birth and background in the United States during World War I. In the early twentieth century, the Great War provided French-Canadian descendants an opportunity to prove their loyalty to their adopted country.[74] One week after the United States joined the war in April 1917, Franco-American organizations like the St. John Baptist Association of Plattsburgh declared their loyalty to the United States and pledged support to different levels of government. "There is no class of American citizens more loyal to the Stars and Stripes than are the French-Americans," wrote the *Sentinel*, "and the people of that race in this city who are members of the St. John Baptist society proved this fact last evening by unanimously voting to offer their services to the city, state or nation, as they may be required." The newspaper continued: "The history of the French in America is one of which every Frenchman can justly feel proud. They helped to fight our battles in the past and they now stand ready to perform similar duty in the present trouble with Germany." During a period of time when hyphenated Americanism was scorned, and the loyalty of immigrant groups was questioned, the *Sentinel* contended: "Plattsburgh has reason to feel proud of her French-American citizens. They have proven themselves loyal to the country in the past and there is not a shadow of a doubt but that they are equally as loyal in the present crisis."[75]

The next month, St. Peter's Church hosted the annual Memorial Day service of Plattsburgh. The Guard of Honor of the St. John Baptist Society escorted approximately sixteen veterans from the Walter Benedict Post of the Grand Army of the Republic to and from the church service, which the Spanish War veterans and the Women's Relief Corps also attended. The United States was at war, and during the sermon "Rev. Father Ouellette exhorted the young men of today to perpetuate the memory of those who fell in the Civil War and to rally to their country's standard as did the heroes of yesterday," reported the *Daily Republican*.[76]

In September 1917, Plattsburgh organized a large gathering to send off 156 men to fight in the Great War. "Not since the Champlain Tercentenary Celebration in 1909 have the streets of Plattsburgh been so thronged as they were on Saturday morning," commented the *Daily Republican*, "by the crowds that came to witness and take part in the send-off to the men of the second allotment of the drafted men for the National Army from Clinton County." The Guard of Honor of the St. John Baptist Society joined the Maccabee Rifles in escorting the men. Wearing the uniform of the Guard of Honor, Dr. J. H. LaRocque briefly addressed the men before their departure.[77]

Church organizations worked to raise money for the war effort. The Children of Mary, a religious organization for young women of St. Peter's, held a card party in 1917 to benefit the Junior Red Cross. Like other groups in the United States, St. Peter's parish supported the purchase of Liberty bonds to help finance US participation in the world conflict. In April 1918, 500 people attended a meeting at St. Peter's Academy to discuss the local drive for Liberty Loans. Rev. Walter Plaisance, St. Peter's pastor, presided over the meeting, explained the purpose of the third Liberty Loan, described the bonds, and encouraged subscriptions. Edward Gallant then sang the French national anthem, "La Marseillaise." The county chairman of the third Liberty Loan, John O'Brien, spoke about the drive and encouraged subscriptions to bonds to fight Prussianism and oppression. Judge Victor Boire discussed current threats to democracy and how individuals could help preserve liberty by subscribing to bonds. The event, which included music, motion pictures of war scenes, and cartoons, concluded with Gallant's leading the singing of one verse of the "Star Spangled Banner" at the program's end. A couple of days later, when the St. John Baptist Association voted to invest $100 of its funds in Liberty bonds, the *Daily Press* remarked that its actions served as "another illustration of the loyalty of the French people of this community."[78]

In May 1918, St. Peter's Church dedicated a service flag to honor the men of the parish who were serving in the armed forces. The parish invited the Liberty Loan Committee, the Plattsburgh Chapter of the American Red Cross, the Daughters of the American Revolution, the Grand Army of the Republic, and the St. John Baptist Society Guard of Honor to participate. Young girls, dressed to represent each of the allies in the war, had the responsibility of carrying out to the street the flag of ninety-two stars denoting the young men of the parish serving in the army and the navy; the Plattsburgh mayor was asked to receive the flag and to raise it in front of the church as children sang the "Star Spangled Banner."[79] Such ceremonies provided visual representations of the assertion of loyalty by French-Canadian descendants to their host society.

Later in May at the Memorial Day observance, which featured speeches and a parade, Judge Boire, "the orator of the day," spoke of the contributions of men who fought in the Civil and Spanish-American Wars to preserve the United States and its institutions just as young men today are doing the same abroad "to stamp out the tyranny of Germany and for the preservation of the manhood of the world," reported the *Sentinel*.[80] These words by a prominent Franco-American in Plattsburgh highlighted the theme of patriotism.

So did participation in Independence Day parades during the 1910s. In 1911, the St. John Baptist Society marched along with the fire companies, local unions, and Knights of the Maccabees. The society also gained recognition at the event for having the largest participating organization in the 1911 parade. In 1918, the Guard of Honor of the St. John Baptist Society joined Civil and Spanish-American War veterans, the American Red Cross, and Knights of Columbus in the July Fourth parade, carrying the Tricolor of France to cheers from the parade-watchers.[81] While demonstrating their loyalty to the United States, the members of the St. John Baptist Society continued to provide visual representations of their French heritage in their adopted country.

After the Great War concluded, Plattsburgh offered a multiethnic and interfaith service at the Plattsburgh Theatre to commemorate the war dead. The stage, according to the *Sentinel*, was "handsomely decorated in the colors of America and France." Members of the Grand Army of the Republic and local post of the United Spanish War Veterans shared the stage with Plattsburgh Mayor C. A. Barnard, local clergy, and invited guests. The rector of Trinity Church gave the invocation, and an assistant pastor at St. Peter's offered the benediction. During the ceremony, representatives of the Government of France presented French Memorial Certificates to the next of kin of deceased war heroes from Plattsburgh. Edward Gallant sang "La Marseillaise" and the event concluded with the singing of the "Star Spangled Banner."[82] The decorations, the songs, and the interethnic participation evident at this tribute to the war dead all were reminiscent of the public nineteenth-century celebrations organized by Plattsburgh's French-Canadian descendants. Those celebrations had demonstrated French and American themes and had underscored the intertwined identity of French speakers in the United States.

During the 1910s, then, Franco-Americans provided evidence of their patriotism while maintaining some of the traits that made them distinctive. They continued during this decade to build their ethnic institutions, including Our Lady of Victory Academy and a new church for Notre-Dame des Victoires parish. They also established St. Pierre

Cemetery, expanded the St. John Baptist Association, and created a new French-language organization by the end of the decade.

When St. Peter's parish opened its own cemetery in 1911, the Guard of Honor of the St. John Baptist Society and the St. Peter's Academy band escorted Bishop Gabriels and parish priests to the cemetery in carriages and automobiles for the consecration ceremony, witnessed by an estimated 1,500 to 2,000 people. Rev. Joseph Desjardins of Our Lady of Victory Church participated, but there is no mention of priests from St. John's attending. Property transactions recorded at the county courthouse reveal that the sale of cemetery plots functioned in effect as a fundraiser for the parish in the 1910s. The plots each sold for between $50 and $100, depending on the square footage, and an additional $50 for perpetual care. Terms of the conveyances ensured that the plots would not be used by non-Catholics. To take one example, the 1914 deed from the St. Peter's Church Corporation to B. A. Bessette for a plot in Cimitière St. Pierre stipulated: "This conveyance is made upon the Express Condition that no body of a deceased person, not entitled to Christian burial, according to the laws of the Roman Catholic Church, as interpreted by the Bishop of the Diocese, in case of doubt, shall be interred in same." As might be expected, the large majority (three-fourths) of those purchasing cemetery plots from St. Pierre during the 1910s had French surnames; most of the others had names that likely had been anglicized from the French, such as Carpenter (Carpentier) and Allen (Allain). Data found in city directories suggests that while some of the individuals purchasing cemetery plots during the first decade of operation were carpenters and laborers, most were engaged in sales, particularly of tobacco products, medicines, alcohol (before Prohibition), coal, and real estate, and thus they had joined the ranks of the middle class by the early twentieth century.[83] In short, Cimitière St. Pierre was a French Catholic burial place, and its initial financial support came largely from Franco-American parishioners who had risen to middle-class ranks in the United States.

The establishment of the French cemetery, of course, was not the only evidence of a growing French Catholic presence in Plattsburgh. By January 1911, the St. John Baptist Society had 360 members and had $3,000 in the bank. During the previous year, the society had paid out $1,460 in sickness benefits to its members and $987 to the widows and orphans of its male membership. Like other mutual-aid societies of its era, the St. John Baptist Society decided to organize a women's auxiliary to expand membership. The organization had sufficient assets to purchase a property in Plattsburgh in 1914, and it grew to about 400 members by 1916.[84]

While the St. John Baptist Association was one of the few French-Catholic societies of Plattsburgh, it was not the only one. Clergy from both French-language parishes of Plattsburgh made efforts to help their flocks retain their French-Canadian lifeways, and they helped new Franco-American organizations to form. In January 1920, for example, Rev. Bachand, the pastor of Our Lady of Victory, spoke at the initial gathering at St. Peter's Hall of an unnamed club for American citizens of French birth or descent. Bachand was a French-speaking immigrant of Canada who had moved to the United States in 1904 and was still not a US citizen in 1920. Bachand emphasized in his talk to 175 Clinton County Franco-Americans that members of the new club should not forget their French heritage but should understand that they were Americans and follow the laws of the country.[85] The formation of this new French club suggests that Plattsburgh-area residents had not embarked on a trajectory that moved unidirectionally toward assimilation in the host society.

To conclude, as the Canada–US border became more conspicuous in the second decade of the twentieth century, it served to separate nuns and nations, but the Franco identity in Plattsburgh did not fade. The events leading to the division of the Grey Nuns represent an interesting twist in the Irish-French controversies that existed in the Catholic Church of the northeastern United States from the late nineteenth to the early twentieth centuries. Many of those controversies centered on Irish bishops assigning Irish pastors to parishes with large francophone populations. While the separation of the Grey Nuns had a clear linguistic dimension, the dividing line was not parish boundaries but the international border between Canada and the United States. That boundary became more visible during this conflict within the hierarchy of the Roman Catholic Church. It also became more visible during the Great War, a war that accentuated differences between French speakers on both sides of the border. Francophones in Canada generally opposed conscription, whereas those in the United States supported it and the war effort. In demonstrating their loyalty to their adopted country and in the modest expansion of their ethnic institutions, Franco-Americans of Plattsburgh (like those in the northeastern United States) in the 1910s did not relinquish their French identity or heritage.

Chapter Seven

The Era of the Second Ku Klux Klan
Pursuing Interfaith Collaboration while
Expanding Catholic Institutions, 1920–1930

In the early morning hours on Thanksgiving Day 1926, the police were summoned to investigate four different cross burnings in Plattsburgh. During the 1920s, a revived Ku Klux Klan (KKK) spread to every corner of the United States. In the Northeast, the Second Klan especially targeted French-speaking Catholic communities as religious tensions between Protestants and Catholics increased all throughout the country.[1] While some of those religious tensions found expression in Plattsburgh during the so-called Roaring Twenties, Plattsburgh's experience reflects greater tolerance, acceptance, and interfaith collaboration than was found in other French-Canadian population centers.

By 1920, Plattsburgh's population had dropped by a couple of hundred people to 10,909 residents. The overwhelming majority (91.6 percent) were native-born and white, while a small proportion (8.2 percent) consisted of foreign-born white residents, and a tiny fraction (0.2 percent) was nonwhite. These figures only reflect one generation. If one adds to the total of the foreign-born the number of individuals who had one or both parents born abroad, it becomes evident that about one-third (31.8 percent) of Plattsburgh's residents in 1920 were first- or second-generation immigrants. Just as in past decades, most of the immigrant families in Plattsburgh in 1920 had come from Canada.[2]

During the 1920s, Plattsburgh's population grew, reaching 13,349 residents by 1930, a 22.4 percent increase over the course of the decade.

About one-fourth (26.0 percent) of the city's residents by the end of the twenties were foreign-born or had parents who were. After Canada, the countries sending the most migrants to Plattsburgh were (in descending order) Italy, Germany, England, the Irish Free State, Poland, and Russia. Among the Canadian immigrants, 54.6 percent were from French Canada and 45.4 percent from "Canada-Other," signifying that a sizeable proportion of the immigrants from the North were English-speaking Canadians. Consistent with past enumerations, only a tiny proportion (0.2 percent) of Plattsburgh's population was nonwhite, or African American, in 1930.[3]

Because of their small numbers outside of the South, African Americans were not the Ku Klux Klan's central targets in northeastern communities during the 1920s. Mass migration during the industrial era had changed the ethnic and religious composition of the Northeast, particularly diversifying it with people of Jewish and Catholic faith traditions, and they were the Klan's primary targets. During the twenties, the Klan expanded far beyond the South, as white, native-born, Anglo-Saxon Protestants joined the organization in an attempt to reassert control over their rapidly changing communities. The 1920s Klan attracted between three and six million ordinary Americans, thus becoming one of the largest social movements the United States has ever experienced.[4]

The hooded society was present all around Plattsburgh. Sixty miles to the north, the Ku Klux Klan migrated to Montréal in 1921 and allegedly burned Catholic buildings in the Province of Québec in the following year. To the east across Lake Champlain, the KKK took root in Burlington, Vermont, where several armed Klan associates broke into the Cathedral of the Immaculate Conception in August 1924. About ninety miles west of Plattsburgh, assisted by state troopers who directed traffic, an estimated 5,000 people attended a Ku Klux Klan meeting in Potsdam one Saturday evening in June 1927.[5]

A mere twenty miles from Plattsburgh, a dynamite bomb exploded, and crosses were burned at midnight in July 1926 in Champlain and Rouses Point, villages located on the Canadian border. A placard inked in red, signed "K.K.K.," featuring a skull and crossbones, explicitly warned Champlain resident Alex Bodette and other "Bootleggers and Lawbreakers of Champlain" to desist. "Where the Law Fails We Begin," the placard threatened, suggesting that the Klan would function as a vigilante group to support Prohibition. Similar signs were found at crossroads from Rouses Point all the way to Plattsburgh. Although Rouses Point police dismissed the burning crosses and KKK signs as a hoax, these surreptitious activities were consistent with those of reported Klan actions in other northeastern communities during the 1920s.[6]

Given the Ku Klux Klan's proximity to Plattsburgh, it is quite plausible that it was responsible for the cross burnings that took place in the city on Thanksgiving Day in 1926. On that morning, a woman called police to report seeing a fiery cross in a field on the corner of Cornelia and Broad Streets. This location away from the city center was not far from Champlain Valley Hospital, managed by the Grey Nuns of the Sacred Heart. Police arrived to find a cross 20 feet high and 15 feet wide, wrapped in rags and doused in kerosene. The police also received calls about sightings of cross burnings in other areas of Plattsburgh that same morning: one on Boynton Avenue at the stone quarry, another at Cumberland Head, and yet another in a field on Broad Street. The latter cross burning took place near the home of former lieutenant governor Thomas Conway, an Irish Catholic communicant of St. John's Church, who lived not far from the church, the parochial school it established in 1920, and the Sisters of Mercy who arrived in Plattsburgh in that same year to staff the school.[7] Despite the four burning crosses, no one spotted Klan members in regalia. These reports, published in the *Plattsburgh Daily Press* two months after the Ku Klux Klan marched for a second time on Washington, DC, constitute the best available evidence of possible Klan activity in Plattsburgh during the 1920s.[8]

Other northeastern communities with sizeable French-Canadian populations witnessed much more Klan activity during the 1920s. Klan parades, cross burnings, the explosion of dynamite bombs, and violent clashes between Klan and anti-Klan forces took place throughout New England.[9] The lack of more sustained Klan activity in Plattsburgh serves as another example of how it differed from other French-Canadian population clusters in the US Northeast. As we will see, Catholics of Plattsburgh maintained cordial ties with non-Catholics during the 1920s, even intermixing with Protestants and Jews in ways that were quite uncommon for that period of time.

After the United States entered the Great War, it promoted the Americanization of its ethnically diverse population in an effort to unite the country; in the postwar era, the Ku Klux Klan pushed the Americanization movement throughout the 1920s. That movement also found expression during and after World War I within the Roman Catholic

Church, which also worked to Americanize immigrant populations in the country. In the Northeast, for example, Irish bishops pushed French-Canadian descendants to shed their language and culture.[10]

There is no evidence to suggest that the Bishop of Ogdensburg pressured French speakers of Plattsburgh to abandon the French language or their French-Canadian heritage. When St. Peter's Church celebrated the seventy-fifth anniversary of its founding in 1929, Bishop Joseph Conroy "urged that the French people be diligent in continuing in their children a love of the parent language, that two languages never failed to be of value to all people," recorded the *Plattsburgh Daily Republican*. The festivities, like so many of the ethnic celebrations of years past, began with a solemn high mass in the morning, continued with field activities in the afternoon, and concluded with an evening concert and speeches. When Victor Boire took his turn on the dais, he "spoke eloquently for the preservation of the French tongue among the people of this community as an important contribution to an appreciation of culture and as a valuable asset," reported the *Daily Republican*.[11]

Such encouragement to preserve the French language may have gone against the tide. In 1926, Rev. Léo Deschâtelets, a recently ordained Oblate priest and an instructor at St. Joseph Scholasticate in Ottawa, visited the Oblates at St. Peter's parish in Plattsburgh. From them he learned that some older parishioners still spoke French, but younger generations did not. Yet many parishioners still understood French, so the Oblates continued making their announcements from the pulpit in French. They informed Deschâtelets that they believed the French language would soon disappear from Plattsburgh. Deschâtelets further noted, in the historical notes he compiled, that many French surnames in the community had become anglicized, for example, from Bélanger to Baker and Benoit to Bennet.[12]

Reports in the press also illustrate that a sizeable proportion of communicants of St. Peter's and Our Lady of Victory had anglicized by the 1920s. Commenting on the Christmas Eve services in 1922, the *Plattsburgh Sentinel* noted that "Rev. G. Sanche, assistant pastor of Our Lady of Victory Church, for the first time, delivered a sermon in English." This may have proven a challenge for Father Gédéon Sanche, who had recently migrated to New York from French Canada. In February 1924, children from St. Peter's parish participated in a weeklong retreat that the Oblate priest, Rev. L. Victor Lewis, preached in English. In November 1925, the *Daily Press* announced that an Oblate priest would preach a weeklong mission at St. Peter's "for the English[-]speaking people of the parish who cannot understand the sermons delivered in French during the mission which is held in the first part of Lent." At the end of the Lenten season the following year, the St. Peter's Church choir planned to sing "The Seven Last Words of Christ" in Latin, with an explanation of the song's words provided in English. The event, which in the previous year drew 1,500 people to the church, was open to the public regardless of their religious affiliation. In November 1926, St. Peter's Church announced that the upcoming retreat would be preached in English: "The services are in English and are especially for those of the congregation who do not understand French and for all others who desire to attend." In 1927 and 1928, the weeklong missions also offered the sermons in English.[13]

It is not that Plattsburgh's two Franco-American churches were without francophone priests. The *US Census, 1920*, listed French as the mother tongue for all four Oblate priests serving St. Peter's Church, including the two who had been born in the United States. The two priests serving Our Lady of Victory Church in 1920, both born in French Canada, also had French listed as their mother tongue (see Table 6). While the *US Census, 1930*, only provides the mother tongue of immigrants, both rectories were replete with French speakers. Three of the five Oblates in that year were native of France or French Canada and spoke French as their mother tongue; the two US-born Oblates, both of whom had French surnames, surely were French speakers as well. The one priest living at the rectory of Our Lady in 1930 was originally from French Canada and was a native French speaker.[14]

French-language or bilingual activities in both French and English in Plattsburgh became increasingly rare in the 1920s—but there were some. The commencement exercises at Mount Assumption Institute in 1922 consisted of fourteen parts, two of them in French. Paul Charlebois gave his graduation speech on "Réflexions sur la paix" ("Reflections on Peace"), while Noe Telmosse gave his on "Sur le succès" ("On Success"). The program concluded with the "Star Spangled Banner." Two of the sixteen parts of the 1924 commencement program at the Mount consisted of graduation speeches in French, and the program similarly ended with the "Star Spangled Banner." The catalog of that year noted that French was one of the four languages (besides English, Spanish, and Latin) taught in the high school curriculum of Mount Assumption Institute, and that French was optional for the seventh- and eighth-grade boys: "French is taught in the primary grades if the parents of the students desire it."[15]

Some activities at St. Peter's School and parish also took place in French in the 1920s. In June 1926, students of St. Peter's School entertained parents and friends with songs, skits, and gymnastic drills at the end of the academic year. While most of the programming was in English, one performance, likely a skit, was titled "Georgette est si nerveuse" ("Georgette is so nervous"). The program concluded with the singing of the "Star Spangled Banner." In February 1928, Oblate priests from Québec City and Trois-Rivières, Québec, preached a weeklong mission for women and girls in French at St. Peter's. In April 1929, a séance by fourth-year high school students taught by the Dominican Sisters included a performance in French of *Pauvre Sylvie* (*Poor Sylvie*) followed by the English play *Three Pegs*. Organizing the younger students to perform in French proved a greater challenge. In December 1929, the Dominican Sisters, who had taken charge of the parish school, noted that Sr. M. Jourdain had a hard time putting on a French play because of "the difficulty she encountered in practicing with young children unable to understand the French language."[16]

Newspaper announcements and the records of nuns and brothers of the parish activities noted above suggest several themes. First, communicants of St. Peter's Church were losing their facility in French, and English was becoming their dominant language. It appears that the same was true at Our Lady of Victory Church. Second, the anglicization of the parishes was being driven from within the church communities and not from outside pressures, such as an assimilationist Irish bishop or the nefarious Americanizers, the Ku Klux Klan. Third, St. Peter's continued to show its openness to people of other faith traditions, inviting them, for example, to the choir performance during Lent in 1926. Finally, St. Peter's also continued to provide evidence of its Americanness, such as by concluding commencement exercises with the US national anthem.

Providing evidence of American loyalties was quite important to Franco-American communities throughout the Northeast during and after World War I.[17] Pictures of Franco-American societies from the 1920s typically feature the members holding US flags as they pose for photographers. Singing the "Star Spangled Banner" or "America" at their events was another way to demonstrate their affinity with their country of adoption. At the same time, however, Franco-American communities largely did not abandon their traditions in the face of such nativist groups as the Ku Klux Klan. This was true in Plattsburgh. One month after the four cross burnings took place in the city, the two French Catholic parishes filled their churches to capacity during Christmas Eve midnight masses.[18]

For its part, the St. John Baptist Association did not modify its French character during the Americanization movement of the 1920s. Its membership rituals make that clear. A member would propose or nominate another man to join the mutual-benefit society, and he could become a candidate for admission after a doctor examined him to ensure that he did not have a malady that would potentially lead to an immediate payout and thereby reduce the association's coffers. Once candidates passed their physical exams, they were asked in French during the initiation ceremonies in the 1920s (and surely in previous decades) if they were practicing Catholics. The president would read them a script prepared in French indicating, among other things, that the St. John Baptist Association "is a Catholic society," that members should practice their religion, and that they were responsible "to demonstrate that Franco-Americans are proud of their origins, and it's up to you all, members of the St. Jean-Baptiste Society to speak your beautiful French language. Be proud of it, for it is the most beautiful language in the world."[19] The initiation ritual, preserved in print, especially demonstrates the continued importance to the society of the French language and the Roman Catholic faith, two pillars of survivance.

At the same time, it hints at the importance of good citizenship in the United States. During Prohibition, Plattsburgh residents participated in the illegal smuggling, trade, and consumption of liquor and beer from Canada, so the president of the St. John Baptist Association also counseled new members during the initiation ceremony to avoid intoxicating liquors. Following this advice may also have served to avoid the ire of the Ku Klux Klan, which supported Prohibition and functioned as a vigilante society to support law enforcement at the local level. People of Plattsburgh had a clear example just across Lake Champlain in Vermont. In September 1924, Klan organizer E. L. Rash testified at Burlington Municipal Court that he had given Deputy Sheriff Ferris Brown information that led to the seizure of liquor in the Agel family rum-running case, a case in which Max Agel was found guilty of possessing illegal alcohol, sentenced to prison for eleven to twelve months, and fined $1,000.[20] Through its initiation ritual, the St. John Baptist Association subtly acknowledged the importance of being a good citizen and of observing the law.

Other activities of the St. John Baptist Association illustrate particularly the importance of language, religion, and heritage. In February 1921, the society organized its first annual banquet, attended also by the wives and friends of its members. Dr. J. H. LaRocque, the president of the society, served as the toastmaster and made the opening remarks in

French. Rev. Victor Viaud of St. Peter's spoke in French of the French race and of following the example of their ancestors in the region. "The Champlain Valley in which we live is rich with the traditions of those intrepid Frenchmen who followed the cross into a savage wilderness and planted the seed from which all enjoy the fruits to-day as a common heritage," translated the *Sentinel* for its readers. Making his remarks in English, and echoing a similar theme, Victor Boire argued that joining the St. John Baptist Association "more than any other agency was helping to keep alive the traditions of the French pathfinders in the New World." Rev. J. H. A. Bachand, the pastor of Our Lady of Victory Church, "spoke of the French language and how it behooved all to keep it alive among the Babel of tongues which were now heard on every side in the United States." This comment, presumably made in French, acknowledged the growing diversity of Plattsburgh and the country as the result of mass immigration. Knowing French and passing it to offspring was a duty, Bachand charged, before giving the blessing at the end of the banquet.[21]

During the 1920s, then, the St. John Baptist Association remained a confessional organization as well as a French-Canadian ethnic society. When the organization celebrated its fiftieth anniversary in June 1921, it paraded to St. Peter's Church in the morning to attend a high mass, and it held an evening banquet, at which numerous clergy with French surnames from Plattsburgh and nearby communities spoke.[22] Such activities highlighted the society's religious and ethnic dimensions.

The association also had its business side. Treasurer Moses Bourdon reported at the February 1921 banquet that the society had spent about $6,000 to care for sick members and had paid out nearly $6,000 in death benefits during the last two-year period, along with distributing $275 to widowers following the deaths of their wives. Business meetings of the association would begin with a doctor's report of the names of ill members, how long they had been sick, and whether vouchers had been made out to cover the cost of their benefits.[23] The problem with mutual-aid societies like this one was that they did not follow sound actuarial principles, and their assets could be wiped out during a medical or financial crisis, such as an epidemic or a downturn in the economy.

There are various signs that the St. John Baptist Association faced financial challenges during the 1920s. In 1923, for example, it sold its property on Oak Street with the intention of purchasing another that could generate greater income from tenants. To that end, the society bought in the same year the Filmore Coulombe Block on River Street and used the second floor for its meeting space. It rented out its meeting hall to various groups, and it leased several large apartments in the building to bring in revenue. The Women's Auxiliary continued to enlarge the association in the 1920s and to bring in additional membership dues to help keep the society afloat. By the end of the decade, the St. John Baptist Association had 350 men and its auxiliary had 150 women as members. But the society could not balance its books. In 1929, the report of the Auditing Committee of the St. John Baptist Association Building Fund stated that the society had taken out a $500 loan in 1925 that Judge Boire had endorsed and that was still outstanding. Furthermore, it reported: "At various times during the period covered [1923–1929], Mr. V. F. Boire, Treasurer of the Building Fund, has made advances from his personal account to cover taxes, etc., and at the close of the audit he has $906.30 due him from such advances."[24] The association, then, faced pecuniary challenges in the 1920s that threatened its viability as an ethnic mutual-aid society.

The efforts of another mutual-benefit association highlight the challenge of ethnic preservation. Union Saint-Jean-Baptiste d'Amérique (USJBA), headquartered in Woonsocket, Rhode Island, had two councils in Plattsburgh. Those two councils, Montcalm and Sainte-Cécile, along with the St. John Baptist Guard of Honor and St. Peter's Church choir, attended a convention in Malone, New York, in June 1927 that the USJBA organized for its seventeen northern New York councils. The convention included a high mass at Notre-Dame Church, at which the St. Peter's choir sang. The following year, 1928, the USJBA held its convention in Plattsburgh, drawing 1,000 people to the city from northern New York and Vermont. A solemn high mass in the morning at St. Peter's Church preceded the afternoon parade and military drills. "A striking part of the parade was the the [sic] colorful arrangement of the two Vermont drill teams and the local St. John the Baptiste [sic] Guard of Honor," noted the *Daily Republican*. "Their uniforms formed the red, white and blue of the National colors," the newspaper added.[25] The "national" colors, of course, represented the colors of the US flag, but there was no indication that the press recognized that those same colors also represented the Tricolor of France. In short, the USJBA conventions in northern New York featured elements reminiscent of past conventions of French speakers: a religious component, a parade, and the display of the colors of the United States and France. But the conventions in the 1920s did not attract as much local interest or press attention as conventions from the late 1800s.

The problem, at least in part, was that ethnic societies like the USJBA had an aging membership base by the 1920s. The organization recognized that its future, and the survival of the French language in the United States, depended upon recruiting younger members. "The best way to assure this precious heritage of the language and traditions of ancestors is to have our children become young members of Union St-Jean Baptiste d'Amérique," stated an advertisement. Although a USJBA membership drive in 1929 added 200 members to the Montcalm and Sainte-Cécile councils in Plattsburgh and 600 members to the northern New York councils, bringing total membership in the region to about 2,000, the historian Robert Rumilly has noted that the mutual-aid society had found it increasingly difficult during the twenties to recruit new members from upstate New York. The younger generation, despite being so near the Province of Québec, was speaking less and less French, states Rumilly.[26] So they, naturally, were less inclined to join Franco-American mutual-aid societies, and an aging membership base of course diminished the vitality of these associations over time.

As French-language use declined and French-Canadian ethnic ties loosened, Plattsburgh youth in the 1920s were more likely to join an English-speaking Catholic society like the Knights of Columbus. The patron saint of French Canadians, St. John the Baptist, and his feast day no longer resonated with younger Franco-Americans. Annual celebrations of Saint-Jean-Baptiste Day no longer took place in Plattsburgh in the 1920s, although they continued with masses, parades, and banquets in francophone population centers of New England, such as Lowell, Massachusetts, and Lewiston, Maine, at least until the middle of the twentieth century. Perhaps no better example illustrates the changeover in Plattsburgh than what took place on June 22, 1924, two days before the feast day of St. John. On that Sunday, 125 men were conferred the third degree of the Knights of Columbus, with a benediction taking place at St. Peter's Church, followed by exercises and a banquet at St. Peter's Hall.[27] The 1924 celebration stood in sharp contrast to what would have taken place in previous years on the Sunday closest to the feast day of the French-Canadian patron saint. This ceremony of a society that was not a Franco-American organization symbolizes how much St. Peter's Church and its Franco-American population were changing.

Not only was the parish community of St. Peter's changing, but so was St. John's. In each of the state and federal census years from 1910 to 1930, the two priests serving the parish of St. John's were US-born (see

Table 7), making the clergy second- or third-generation Irish descendants. During the 1920s, the ethnic composition of the parish no longer consisted solely of people of Irish descent and of French-Canadians who intermixed with them. A 1975 parish publication revealed that it included Italians and other Catholics who had migrated to Plattsburgh from Europe.[28]

In 1920, St. John's founded its own parochial school on an estate it had purchased the previous year on Broad Street.[29] The opening-day activities highlight both Roman Catholic themes and the Americanism of the parish community. The academic year began with a mass at St. John's Church, followed by a procession up Broad Street to the school, led by someone carrying a cross and altar boys holding US flags, followed by the city band, students, and their parents. Outside the school building, Rev. J. H. Driscoll, the pastor of St. John's Church, raised the American flag and proposed three cheers for the stars and stripes, "and they were given with vigor which made the air ring," stated the *Daily Republican*. Inside the school, on the ground floor, was a "statue of Christ blessing the world," noted the newspaper, "directly opposite which are Old Glory, with a picture of [George] Washington and [Abraham] Lincoln on either side, under which is a lithographed copy of the Declaration of Independence."[30] During the post–World War I Americanization movement, Catholic groups in the United States found it important to display such American symbols alongside their Roman Catholic ones.

Founded by Catherine McAuley in Dublin, Ireland, in 1831, the Sisters of Mercy conducted St. John's School. This order of women religious came to North America in 1842 when it established itself at St. John's in Newfoundland, and in the following year in Pittsburgh, Pennsylvania. The Sisters of Mercy arrived in the Diocese of Ogdensburg in 1874 when the order took charge of a school in Malone, and in 1885 the sisters established a mission at Rouses Point, a town with a customhouse that functioned as a transportation center for travel between Canada and the United States. Rev. Driscoll had served as the pastor of St. Patrick's parish in Rouses Point, where he worked for eleven years with the Sisters of Mercy who took charge of its school, prior to his assignment as the pastor of St. John's in Plattsburgh in 1908.[31]

In Plattsburgh, the Sisters of Mercy founded their own residential school. In 1920, they opened a boarding school for young women in a large home in front of the parish school, and they operated it for nearly a quarter-century, closing it in 1944. Prior to the arrival of the Sisters of Mercy, many parish girls had attended D'Youville Academy, conducted by the Grey Nuns. The *US Census, 1930*, reveals that twenty-one girls and young women ranging from nine to twenty-two years of age participated in the residential program of St. John's Academy; while the large majority were born in the United States, four were native of French Canada, one of English Canada, and one of the Hawaiian Islands. Many of the US students who attended the academy came from communities near Plattsburgh, including Cadyville, Saranac Lake, Keeseville, Dannemora, Chazy, and Morrisonville.[32]

The Sisters of Mercy who taught the boarding and day students were predominantly US-born. Of the thirteen sisters teaching at St. John's in 1925, nine were native of the United States, while one each were from Canada and Newfoundland, and two were native of Ireland (see Table 8).[33] In 1930, ten of the twelve teaching sisters were US-born, with one each from Canada and Newfoundland; three of the twelve sisters had one parent who had been born in Ireland, making each a second-generation Irish descendant.[34] If one can judge from the snapshots provided by census records, the sisters teaching at the parish school, like the priests serving St. John's, were becoming more removed from their Irish ancestry with the passing of time.

This does not mean, however, that the Irish identity of the parish or school had faded. The visit of a prominent spokesperson from Ireland attests to that. In 1920, Éamon de Valera, leader of the Sinn Féin political party in Ireland that had won the 1918 general election, came to Plattsburgh. De Valera had participated in the Easter Rising of 1916 that called for an Irish republic and, by 1918, had become the president of an independent parliament governing Ireland. De Valera was in the United States on a one-and-a-half-year tour to raise money and support for the Irish cause among Catholic and Protestant Irish nationalists in the country. In Plattsburgh, de Valera gave a talk at the Catholic Summer School, and Rev. Driscoll invited him to do the same at his church. De Valera attended Sunday-morning mass at St. John's Church and afterward addressed communicants in English and Gaelic, sharing his vision for an Irish nation. He went on to have a long career in politics, eventually serving as the prime minister and the president of the Irish Republic until the early 1970s.[35]

Irish traditions did not vanish from St. John's in the 1920s. In 1924, 800 people gathered at the gymnasium of St. John's Academy to celebrate St. Patrick's Day. Large shamrocks and green crepe-paper streamers decorated the gym, and on the wall behind the rostrum were the words

"Erin Go Braugh" ("Ireland Forever"). The evening program consisted of Irish folk dances and songs, with children singing "How Ireland Got Its Name" and "The Dear Little Shamrock" and a woman singing solo "The Wearing of the Green."[36] This event of course highlighted the Irish heritage of St. John's parish and St. John's Academy.

The Sisters of Mercy also founded another Catholic institution in Plattsburgh in the early 1920s. With the assistance of Rev. Driscoll, who negotiated with the owner from Montréal on their behalf, the order purchased an estate in 1921 near Mount Assumption Institute that became known simply as the Loretta. The Sisters of Mercy managed the Loretta Residence from the 1920s through the 1950s. During the 1920s, the Loretta functioned as a novitiate to train young women of their community to teach in the order's schools in northern New York. Prior to purchasing the Loretta, postulants were trained in Gabriels, New York, where the Sisters of Mercy had located their Mother House since 1899 and where they had founded a sanitorium for patients with tuberculosis. "But the association of a novitiate with a tubercular sanitorium was not desirable and was considered detrimental to the increase of vocations," the sisters noted in their historical account. Financed by "taxing" other houses of the Sisters of Mercy in the diocese, the Loretta became a novitiate after the completion of renovations in 1924. According to the *NY Census, 1925*, seven young women between the ages of eighteen and twenty-five were being trained there for religious vocations by six nuns ranging in age from twenty-six to forty-three. While the 1925 census did not record the nativity of these thirteen women religious, it is clear that each was US-born, for the census noted that everyone was a US citizen who had lived in the United States the same number of years as her age. Just five years later, the *US Census, 1930*, reveals that the sisters at the Loretta were more ethnically diverse. There were eighteen sisters in residence, and they came from both the United States and English Canada; moreover, many of the US- or Canadian-born among them were the descendants of parents born in English Canada or the Irish Free State. The Loretta's function as a novitiate ended with the start of the Great Depression, however, for the novitiate moved downstate to Tarrytown in 1930.[37]

During the 1920s, then, Plattsburgh witnessed the growth of its Catholic institutions, particularly within the parish of St. John's. In 1922, St. John the Baptist parish had 450 families and 290 parochial school students. St. Peter's, the largest Catholic parish, had 672 families and 417 parochial school students in the same year, while Our Lady of Victory, the smallest parish, had approximately 200 families and between 156 and 175 students attending its academy. Until 1920, St. Peter's and Our Lady of Victory had administered the city's only Catholic schools. While the opening of St. John's School suggests a possible division within Plattsburgh's Catholic community, the historical evidence reveals that the city's Catholic churches collaborated in different activities during the 1920s. For instance, when St. John's installed seventeen bells, area priests, including the pastors of St. Peter and Our Lady of Victory, assisted with their blessing in 1927.[38]

Plattsburgh's three Catholic churches collaborated not only with each other but also with the community's Protestant churches and its Jewish synagogue to form the Interchurch Baseball League in summer 1920. St. Peter's won the league's first game in June when it faced off against the Methodist team at the local fairgrounds. After St. Peter's beat the First Presbyterian Church team by a score of nine to one, the *Daily Republican* downplayed the results, noting: "There was a number of excellent plays during the game, but on the whole the players showed the necessity of more practice." The newspaper pointedly added: "This was particularly true of the representatives of the Presbyterian church." Also participating in the Interchurch Baseball League were Episcopalians from Trinity Church, as well as Baptists and Jews who combined forces to form the Baptist-Beth Israel team. "All of the churches in the city have taken hold of the league in an enthusiastic way," reported the *Daily Republican* in midsummer. The St. Peter's Church team emerged as the league's champion in October.[39] While the baseball league appears only to have lasted one season, it afforded an opportunity for people of different faith and cultural traditions to intermix.

Music festivals in the late 1920s provided a similar opportunity. In 1928, the State Normal School in Plattsburgh served as the location of National Music Week, which featured performances by the choirs of St. Peter's Church, the Jewish Synagogue, and the Methodist Episcopal Church. The following year, the Presbyterian Church hosted a concert for National Music Week, and the St. John Baptist Association sponsored it. Among the participants were the St. Peter's Church choir, the Methodist Church choir, the Jewish Temple Quartet, and the Presbyterian Mixed Quartet, all of Plattsburgh, plus a choir from the Methodist Church of AuSable Forks.[40] The interchurch baseball games and music festivals in Plattsburgh brought together people of different faith traditions during a decade when nativist forces like the Ku Klux Klan strove to foment religious discord throughout the country.

As noted in previous chapters, religious tensions in France in the early twentieth century had led to the migration of women and men religious to the United States and ultimately to communities like Plattsburgh. Expelled from France in July 1903, on account of anticlericalism in the aftermath of the Dreyfus Affair, Dominican sisters migrated to the United States to teach in French Catholic schools, such as Saint-Pierre School of Lewiston, Maine. Given the imminent departure of the teaching Grey Nuns from Plattsburgh, St. Peter's Church purchased the former D'Youville Convent and adjacent property from them in 1922 and made it part of the parochial school of St. Peter's. When the Oblate priests set out to find another order of women religious to teach in the parish school, Bishop J. H. Conroy directed Pastor Julien Racette to the Dominican Sisters of Fall River, Massachusetts.[41]

The departure of most of the Grey Nuns in 1921 had left St. Peter's parish in desperate straits. "The result was the almost complete disorganization of the parish's educational system; the oldest pupils scattered to the different schools of the city, the majority going to the public schools," noted a parish publication in 1931. "For the two ensuing years the little children remained under the jurisdiction of eight Grey Nuns from Ottawa in the small brick building behind the convent. The academy had been closed indefinitely." In early February 1923, Racette wrote the Dominican superior that the remaining Grey Nuns were leaving that year, and he exerted pressure on the Dominicans to conduct the parish school. "If you do not agree to come, I will be obliged to close our parish school," Racette wrote, underscoring that he had not sought other communities of women religious to administer the school. "That is to say that all of our hopes rest on your community." By late February, the Prioress General of the Dominican Sisters of Fall River let Racette know that the General Council (governing body) of her order had decided to take charge of St. Peter's School, and she asked permission for the sisters to take in five or six boarders, undoubtedly to supplement the salaries of the sisters.[42]

After the Dominican Sisters agreed to administer St. Peter's School, Conroy wrote them for a copy of the order's constitution because, he explained to Racette, "they might have some rule against teaching real young children and boys over twelve." After reviewing the constitution of the Dominican Sisters, Conroy informed the Prioress General that he found it "to be perfectly satisfactory." As he stated, "My only concern was that perhaps you were not allowed to teach boys over twelve years of age—as was the case of the Grey Nuns of Ottawa who were obliged to withdraw from Plattsburgh on that account." Conroy wrote that he shared Racette's delight that the sisters were coming to Plattsburgh, commenting, "I am sure that your associations there will be most pleasant and I am confident that that section of the State will be rich in vocations for your Order."[43]

In response, the Dominican Sisters informed the bishop that they in fact had teaching preferences. The Prioress General wrote Conroy: "You will see that in parochial schools we take boys without specifying the age; only we would much rather not have the boys above the fourth grade as we find it difficult to have sisters who manage well a class of boys; besides, it is very tiresome." The Prioress General also pointed out to the bishop that Racette had told the sisters that brothers taught boys beyond grade four in another building.[44]

The terms of the contract, written in English and signed in July 1923, specified the precise terms the sisters required. Each teaching sister would be paid $300 over a period of ten months, and the parish would have to supply housing and utilities: "in short, everything except the Sisters' food and clothing." The Dominican Sisters agreed to teach both boys and girls, but boys only to the age of twelve.[45]

These arrangements apparently satisfied the bishop, pastor, and nuns, for four Dominican Sisters, and a young woman who aspired to become one, arrived in Plattsburgh in mid-August 1923. During their first year, the Dominican Sisters used a section of an old school building as their convent. When they reached the city initially, they found the furnishings sparse. So did the Bishop of Ogdensburg, who welcomed them a couple of weeks later. As Conroy blessed the sisters, he commented tongue in cheek on their austerity, teasing, "Your poverty is most edifying." To assist the Dominican Sisters, as they had the Grey Nuns more than half a century earlier, the women of the parish mobilized, organizing parties to raise money. Women in the parish Holy Rosary Society held a card party that generated $115 for the convent. Women who belonged to the Saint Cecile Council organized a "shower" during which a delegation of sixty women came bearing gifts to assist the nuns.[46]

The sisters also received assistance from men religious. In the Brothers of Christian Instruction they found "some powerful and charitable aides," for the brothers helped them with manual labor and counsel from the time of their arrival in the city. An Oblate brother, Alphonse Gagnon, went into the countryside in late August 1923 to purchase fifteen chickens for their coop, providing them with seven eggs on the first day. The sisters also maintained a garden to grow some of their own food.[47]

Racette formally welcomed the Dominican Sisters at all Sunday masses in early September, announcing to parishioners that their Mother House was in Fall River, that they were well regarded for their schools, and that they were among the best teachers in New England. Miss Maximilienne Bourret, the aspirant from St. Hyacinthe, Québec, taught grades one and two; Sr. Osanna Champagne, the superior born in St. Georges de Windsor, Québec, taught grade three; Sr. M. Ignatius Brown, originally of Venosta, Québec, taught grades four and five; Sr. M. Benoit Bouthillier, a native of Fall River, taught grades six and seven, while Sr. André Laferriere served as the cook. With a total of 221 pupils, consisting of 191 girls and 30 boys, the sisters were assisted by a lay teacher, Miss Eugenie Lynch, who taught the kindergarten class that alone had 65 students.[48]

The Dominican convent almost surely was a French-speaking institution. Just under half of the teaching sisters listed in the 1925 and 1930 censuses were born in French Canada; one in each census year was a nun of Irish descent from Canada, and the rest were from the United States (see Table 10). Significantly, six of the seven teaching sisters in 1925, and thirteen of the fourteen teaching sisters in 1930, had French surnames; the only one who did not in each year was the nun of Irish descent.[49] Given the preponderance of French-Canadian and Franco-American nuns in the convent, it would most likely have functioned as a French-speaking environment through at least the 1920s.

Like the Grey Nuns before them, the Dominican Sisters had to prepare the parish children for annual Regents exams. In June 1924, a Mr. Mooney, representing the Board of Regents, came to the parish school to examine the program of study and the students. Children in grades six and seven took Regents exams in that month in geography, math, history, and spelling. Mooney let the sisters know he was satisfied with their work, and he told one of the parish priests how impressed he was with the quality of their instruction. The inspector also commented on the quality of their English-language instruction, indicating that he had no complaints.[50]

Like the Grey Nuns before them, the Dominican Sisters all took the necessary steps to obtain New York State certification. In August 1924, seven sisters took exams for a week at the Normal School toward earning

State Life Certificates. This was followed by another week of exams in August 1925 and the completion of their final exams for the State Life Certificates in August 1926. At least two sisters took written and oral exams required for the teaching of French and earned their permanent certificates to do so. Some Dominican Sisters continued their education during summers by taking courses at the Catholic Summer School at Cliff Haven, as two did in July 1928.[51]

The Dominican Sisters apparently were in compliance with directives of the Bishop of Ogdensburg, who kept tabs on the education of women religious throughout the diocese. In June 1927, alarmed that few nuns had enrolled in the Diocesan Summer School, Conroy sent a memorandum to all of the communities of women religious teaching in the diocese, inquiring whether they had temporary or life certificates, how many were attending summer schools to obtain certification, and whether those schools were authorized by New York to grant credentials. Because of his concerns that uncredentialed teachers might result in the closing of Catholic schools, he demanded that the sisters who were not yet qualified for certification had to obtain it promptly: "In the interests of religion I must insist, therefore, that these credentials be obtained and without delay."[52]

Besides teaching elementary classes in the parish school of St. Peter's, the Dominican Sisters managed a high school program, beginning in 1925, in the D'Youville Academy building that St. Peter's reopened. Fourteen girls took their high school classes with the sisters in the first year. By 1925, the Sisters used the second floor of the building as their residence. Although it does not appear that the Dominican Sisters ran as large a residential school as the Grey Nuns before them, they did have some boarding students. In 1929, for example, the sisters had four boarders from Montréal who joined them to work on their English-language skills.[53]

Boarding schools for young women also generated income for the other orders of women religious in Plattsburgh. At Our Lady of Victory convent, the residential program served female students ranging in age from eight to twenty, with twenty-one of them in 1925 and twenty-nine in 1930. While the large majority came from the United States, there were a number from French Canada recorded at the convent school in both census years. Though only about one-fifth of the residential students in 1925 had French surnames, more than one-half did in 1930.[54] Thus, the Sisters of Charity of St. Louis, an order that had been expelled from France, conducted what in essence was a Franco-American boarding school.

The origins of the sisters who taught at Our Lady of Victory help explain this. The order had nuns in its Plattsburgh convent in the 1920s who were born in France, French Canada, Ireland, England, and the United States. The Sisters of Charity of St. Louis had houses in England, and from 1903 to 1924, twelve English and Irish nuns made the transatlantic voyage to serve in English-speaking missions in western Canada and the United States, including Plattsburgh. At least half of the sisters at Our Lady of Victory in the 1920, 1925, and 1930 census years had come to the United States from a French-speaking country (see Table 9). In 1925, New York census-takers even noted that the three sisters in the convent who had been born in England were of French descent. That the superior in each census year was a native of France also suggests that the Plattsburgh convent of Our Lady of Victory was a francophone institution. In fact, 87 percent of the 137 Sisters of Charity of St. Louis who migrated from France to Canada between 1902 and 1924 were originally from Brittany. This gave the order in Canada a strong Breton character, underscored by the Provincial at Pont-Rouge, Québec, who wrote in a circular letter to the sisters after returning from a trip to France in 1912: "It is necessary to *remain French and Breton women religious always*! I wish it upon all of us." According to Guy Laperrière, this strong sentiment helps account for why superiors of the Sisters of Charity of St. Louis in Canada were natives of France to 1948.[55] It similarly helps explain why superiors of the order in Plattsburgh during the census years spanning the twenties were also natives of France and why they conducted a Franco-American institution.

Another order that had been expelled from France, the Brothers of Christian Instruction continued to teach in the parish school of Plattsburgh and at their own academy for boys. While the ethnic composition of the brothers changed with time, anywhere from one to five in residence in Plattsburgh during each census year from 1905 to 1940 were originally from France (see Table 4). After the Brothers of Christian Instruction closed their juniorate in Plattsburgh, they founded in 1919 Mount Assumption Boarding Institute for Boys for grades seven through twelve in the former Vilas mansion. The building had been used continuously since the brothers purchased it in 1903: from 1903 to 1905, the French scholastics who attended Plattsburgh Normal School resided there; when they departed, the brothers taught St. Peter's High School classes in that building from 1906 to 1911; and from 1911 to 1919, the brothers housed their juniorate there. In 1919, the Oblate priests made an arrangement with the Brothers of Christian Instruction to pay the order $1,000 annually to provide a middle and high school education (grades seven through twelve) to boys from St. Peter's parish who would attend Mount Assumption Institute (MAI) as day students alongside the residential students. The brothers point out in their historical account that this oral agreement between the Oblates and themselves included a provision for an increase in payment if numbers warranted, but the priests and the brother who made it subsequently left Plattsburgh, and the remuneration remained the same for about twenty-five years. The parish would also pay the three brothers who taught in grades one through six at the parish school $450 each.[56] Mount Assumption Institute became accredited by the New York State Board of Regents in 1925. Its principal also served initially as the principal of St. Peter's Academy, and from the 1920s to the mid-1940s the acting principal of St. Peter's served under the direction of the principal of Mount Assumption Institute.[57]

Just as D'Youville Academy had brought income to the Sisters of Charity of Ottawa to support their order's works, Mount Assumption Institute similarly served as "the financial bulwark on which the province depended," notes Brother Patrick Menard. To ensure an adequate clientele for their educational institution, like the Grey Nuns had done at D'Youville Academy, the Brothers of Christian Instruction worked to attract students to Mount Assumption. One or two brothers traveled every September to New York City and brought to Plattsburgh by train the students they recruited there.[58]

Resident students outnumbered local students for much of Mount Assumption's history. The boarding students who attended the institute initially came from parishes near Plattsburgh, as well as from the New York City region, Vermont, and Québec. According to the US census, 31 male boarding students from eight to nineteen years of age attended Mount Assumption Institute in 1920, a majority (16) of them from Canada, while 14 came from the United States and 1 from Spain. The 1926 yearbook of the institute had a full page in French that served as a recruiting tool for francophone students of Canada, suggesting that they could learn English at Mount Assumption and become "better equipped than others who know only one of the two official languages of Canada."[59]

Despite the dramatic shift in the ethnic composition of the brothers in Plattsburgh, such that the majority serving in the city in 1920 were born in the United States and seven out of eight were US citizens (all except the bursar, who had migrated from Canada the previous year), this was a francophone order. The French page in the 1926 yearbook proclaimed that "the employed teachers know perfectly French and English," and it made clear that "English is the official language at Mount Assumption Institute and courses are given exclusively in this language." Besides subscribing to Plattsburgh's English-language newspapers, in the 1910s and 1920s the brothers maintained a subscription to *Le Devoir*, a French-language newspaper from Montréal. In 1920, all eight brothers in Plattsburgh reported French as their mother tongue. It is not surprising then that of the thirty-one residential students at Mount Assumption in 1920, nearly two-thirds had French surnames. It was at its core a Franco-American school. But, of course, not all of its students understood French. When the Superior General Brother John Joseph visited Plattsburgh in 1929, he addressed the students of Mount Assumption Institute in French, but another brother had to translate his remarks into English "for the benefit of the many students who do not understand the language," reported the *Sentinel*.[60]

During the 1920s, the Brothers of Christian Instruction acquired additional properties to expand their physical plant in order to meet the needs of their residential school. They bought in 1925 a property on Court Street near MAI, thus enlarging the institute's terrain. In 1927, the brothers bought from St. Peter's parish a parcel near the church that the Grey Nuns had once owned. Out of the 400-foot by 215-foot field the brothers created a football gridiron.[61]

Besides promoting physical training and sports, MAI also sponsored clubs that organized musical and dramatic productions. The MAI Glee Club, for example, donned blackface and put on minstrel shows during the 1920s. Minstrels were rooted in the singing and dancing of enslaved people on southern plantations during the antebellum period. While it is not known when white actors started performing in blackface, the practice of white actors impersonating Black people dates back to the pre–Revolutionary War period, and blackface minstrelsy came to be considered "the first and most popular form of American mass entertainment," according to the political scientist Michael Rogin. Following another war with Great Britain, the War of 1812, someone wearing blackface played the role of a Black sailor, singing the song "The Battle of Plattsburgh" around 1814 or 1815 in New York. In upstate New York, service organizations put on minstrel shows to raise money for their causes. Given the very small proportion of people who were nonwhite in the region, minstrel shows provided the means by which people of northern New York learned about

African Americans and their culture—but in ways that demeaned them, making them look inferior and less capable than whites, states independent scholar Amy Godine. Because of the efforts of service clubs that performed the minstrel shows, contends Godine, racism in the region became associated with community service.[62]

Catholic institutions in Plattsburgh similarly brought minstrel shows to North Country audiences. As mentioned in chapter four of this volume, Our Lady of Victory organized minstrels, performing them during the parish fair and at the Plattsburgh Theatre, to raise money for the new parish in 1909. In the 1920s, the decade in which the Ku Klux Klan permeated all corners of the United States, Mount Assumption Institute organized its own minstrel shows. A flyer from 1925 announced that the MAI Glee Club would perform at the Dannemora prison, publicizing the event as "a group of colored merry makers in a dazzling musical minstrel." The Glee Club, which had thirty-seven members, fifteen of them with French surnames, performed a minstrel show at St. Peter's Academy auditorium in mid-March 1925. Stanley Brunell, a graduate of the MAI class of 1923, described the performance as "one of the most deliciously fresh and amusing shows offered in this city during the spring season." After summarizing the first three acts, Brunell states: "But the moment of real pathos was the representation of a picturesque plantation scene." As he describes the fourth act, "A colored group sat lounging before a cabin door, little characteristic incidents sprang up and the music of this race with its haunting strains of plaintive melodies and riotous vivacity brought a fitting close to the admirable entertainment."[63] Brunell's depiction of the minstrel show suggests that it offered Plattsburgh residents stereotypical behaviors by which to learn about the lives of nonwhites.

One might wonder if the Klan's presence in the Northeast in the 1920s spurred the production of minstrel shows by Catholic groups. Perhaps the racism embodied in those musical and dramatic productions served to distinguish Catholics from the Klan's nonwhite targets during that decade. As the result of pressure from nativists, Catholic and Jewish immigrants after the turn of the twentieth century, following practices dating back to the colonial period, highlighted racial differences in the process of Americanizing themselves, contends Rogin. Wearing blackface moves ethnic groups from an exotic to a white category, he argues. "Put more exactly, racial masquerade moves white ethnics from a racially liminal to a white identity."[64] Plattsburgh's experience does not provide enough historical evidence from the 1920s to evaluate these suppositions, but they might suggest areas for further research.

The Klan's visible presence in the vicinity of Plattsburgh may have encouraged institutions like Champlain Valley Hospital to continue emphasizing their nonsectarian nature. When the hospital published its annual report in 1925, the year that the Klan peaked in the Northeast and in much of the United States, it quoted from its constitution: "The object of this Corporation is the establishment of an institution for the purpose of affording Medical and Surgical aid to sick or disabled persons of every Creed, Nationality and Color and shall be a Non-Sectarian Institution." The 1925 report also emphasized that the nursing school "is strictly non-sectarian."[65] Thus, in the 1920s the hospital and nursing school of the Grey Nuns continued to admit patients, and to train women, of all faith traditions.

But, as an institution run by Catholic women religious, the Champlain Valley Hospital Nursing School wanted to promote the spirituality of its students, and it added in its 1925 annual report: "Nurses are expected to assist at the Services held in their respective churches." The response of nursing student Myra Eileen Slattery to an examination question in a course titled "History of Nursing," taught by one of the nuns, suggests that religious teaching was infused in the curriculum. "At the opening of the Christian era, the Roman Empire extended over a greater part of Europe. The independent and dignified position thus held by the Roman women had a great influence on the 'development of nursing,'" Slattery wrote in response to the second question on her March 1926 exam. "'Christ's teachings' of brotherhood and love and many of his parables and miracles had dealt much with disease and death," Slattery continued. She concluded: "The Golden Rule left us by Christ was 'to minister unto, not to be ministered to.' He told His followers that when they were ministering to the poor and sick that they were ministering to him [sic]."[66] This response, which contributed to Slattery's achieving a score of 100 percent on this nursing exam, points to some of the Christian teachings in the Nurse Training School curriculum.

Although the nursing school and the hospital officially were nonsectarian institutions, Bishop Conroy addressed the graduates in 1923. Unsurprisingly, the school showed its patriotism when the orchestra opened the commencement exercises held in Plattsburgh Normal Hall by playing "America."[67] Having the bishop speak to graduates at a time when the anti-Catholic Ku Klux Klan was still gaining ground throughout the country demonstrates that the sisters—and for that matter the Plattsburgh community—were unfazed by the growth of this nativist organization.

In fact, one of the rare acknowledgements by the nursing school of US society in the Roaring Twenties had to do with women's fashions of that decade. The admission requirements for 1926 included a list of the clothing the nursing students needed to bring to the training school. Near the bottom of the list was the instruction: "Applicants having bobbed hair are to wear a hair net."[68] Though not opposed to the fashion trend sweeping the country, the sisters of course wanted to maintain hygienic practices in their hospital.

Through the 1920s, the large majority of sister nurses working at Champlain Valley Hospital were natives of Canada, despite the fact that their Mother House had shifted from Canada to the United States after the division of the Grey Nuns in 1921. In 1925, the New York census recorded that four-fifths of the hospital sisters were born in Canada and the remaining one-fifth in the United States (see Table 3). By 1930, the proportions had changed slightly: nearly three-fourths were born in Canada, while the others came in equal numbers from the United States and Ireland. The 1930 census specifically notes that the Canadian-born nuns were from English Canada; they, along with the sisters born in the United States and Ireland, helped make Champlain Valley Hospital an anglophone institution.[69]

Censuses for 1925 and 1930 reveal both continuities and changes in the population of student nurses trained by the Grey Nuns.[70] Just as in 1915, all students of the training school for nurses in 1925 and 1930 were white women ranging in age from eighteen to twenty-nine, and they largely came from the United States. In 1915, all twenty student nurses were US-born and none had French surnames; thereafter, more student nurses at Champlain Valley Hospital were foreign-born, and more had French surnames. Of the twenty-nine student nurses in 1925, for example, six were native of Canada, and four—all US-born—had French surnames. Of the thirty-nine student nurses in 1930, four were from English Canada, and nine—all US-born—had French surnames. During the era of the Ku Klux Klan, then, the Grey Nuns were admitting foreign-born (i.e., Canadian) students to the Champlain Valley Hospital School of Nursing. In addition, the proportion of Franco-American nursing students climbed from zero in 1915 to about one-seventh in 1925 and to approximately one-fourth in 1930.⁷¹ Thus, the ethnic composition of the training school for nurses became more diversified in the Roaring Twenties.

In that decade, women of different religious backgrounds continued to join the Women's Auxiliary to support Champlain Valley Hospital. The society's numbers grew steadily over the course of the twenties, climbing from 969 in 1922 to 1,165 in 1925, and from 1,173 in 1927 to 1,216 in 1929. The *Sentinel* extolled the work of the Women's Auxiliary, wondering in 1926 "how much would be accomplished along humanitarian lines were it not for the influence and work of women." The newspaper acknowledged that men made their contributions but noted that women attended to the "'small details' of movements which have for their object the betterment of humanity. That is probably the reason," the newspaper suggested, "for so many women's auxiliaries to societies and other organizations." The editorial went on to compliment the Champlain Valley Hospital Women's Auxiliary for its work in raising money for the hospital, as well as for furnishing textiles, dietary items, and even rooms at the institution.⁷²

When Champlain Valley Hospital opened in 1910, the building was not fully complete, but by the early 1920s all five levels from the basement to the fourth floor were finished. After a decade of operation, the hospital found itself overcrowded, and the board of directors decided to build a separate nurses' residence to free up the third floor for private and semiprivate rooms for patients. By May 1921, the hospital carried nearly $102,000 in debt. The board of directors decided therefore to launch a $150,000 fundraising campaign to eliminate the debt and to finance the Nurses' Home, a children's ward, a pathological laboratory, and new X-ray equipment.⁷³

The glossy fundraising brochure put out by the hospital emphasized that clergy representing each of Plattsburgh's religious denominations spent time at the institution: "The clergymen of St. John's, St. Peter's and Our Lady of Victory (Catholic), Trinity (Episcopalian), First Methodist, Presbyterian, Baptist and Congregation Beth Israel [Jewish] [*sic*] have been regular and welcome visitors at the Hospital." It also pointed out to potential contributors that sizeable endowments publicized in the press could not be used to finance construction. Among those endowments was a gift of $10,000 from the estate of Francis Lynde Stetson "for a free bed in perpetuity." G. F. Underwood and his wife, both of New York City, in 1921 gave the hospital $10,000 to endow two beds for their employees at the Plattsburgh Wall Paper Company and Underwood

Paper Mills. After Underwood died in 1923, his widow donated in his memory another $10,000 for the care of their workers. These donations by the Underwoods, of course, served as an example of welfare capitalism common in the early twentieth century, where some large employers provided for the medical and other needs of their workers. When William Kufler of Plattsburgh suffered an accident at Underwood Paper Mills in 1929, causing him to lose two fingers from his left hand and crushing a third, it was Champlain Valley Hospital that treated him.[74]

Another significant contribution came from David Merkel, who established the Merkel Memorial Laboratory at Champlain Valley Hospital in honor of his parents in 1922. David's father, Isaac, had migrated to the United States from Germany and used to peddle goods by horse and buggy from New York City to Plattsburgh before founding Merkel's Department Store in the city in 1910. Designed to analyze specimens of contagious diseases and to examine milk and water for bacteria, the Merkel lab made it unnecessary to send specimens to Albany, which had to be done in the past, taking time and risking spoilage en route. After the Merkel Laboratory gained approval from the State Board of Health, Clinton County provided it with an annual appropriation of $2,000 to assist with its public-health work. Dr. Leo Schiff, who had joined other area physicians in declining an appointment to the medical staff of Champlain Valley Hospital in 1910, oversaw the new laboratory from 1922.[75]

Champlain Valley Hospital also benefited from other funding sources in the 1920s. In 1923, the *Sentinel* commented that friends of the hospital "are legion" and that it represents "the ideal of unselfish, cheerful, efficient service"; the newspaper also encouraged readers to support the institution by attending performances at the Plattsburgh Theatre on two designated days in August. In 1929, the Plattsburgh Glee Club oversaw the production of *The Pirates of Penzance* at the Strand Theater, a fundraiser for Champlain Valley Hospital that netted the institution nearly $1,100. Each fall, there would appear an announcement in local newspapers to alert readers that Donation Week was underway at the hospital, and the Women's Auxiliary collected, or area residents dropped off at the hospital, donations of produce preserved from their gardens such as jams, jellies, and pickles. As part of its fundraising efforts, Champlain Valley Hospital included in its 1925 annual report the language that potential benefactors should use to make a bequest to the institution in their wills. Readers of the report found the page hole-punched to facilitate its removal from the rest of the report.[76]

In 1926, a group of men organized the Samaritan League of Plattsburgh that raised the funds to establish the children's ward at the hospital. The men, who were from the Plattsburgh area, each paid $10 yearly in dues to the Samaritan League, and the organization in turn contributed $1,000 annually to Champlain Valley Hospital for its child welfare and charitable work. The organization continued to make a substantial annual contribution to the hospital at least through the early years of the Great Depression.[77]

The hospital had to tap all possible means to raise funds to meet its objectives. In September 1923, the board of directors had a special meeting during which it decided to put off for at least a year the building of the nurses' home because of high construction costs. In June 1925, the board decided to contact the Mother General of the Grey Nuns to meet "to consider ways and means of financing the construction of the nurses' home and paying the interest on the loan for this purpose." Two Grey Nuns traveled from the Mother House in Philadelphia to meet with the board and an architect at a Plattsburgh bank. During the meeting, board members accepted a bid to build the nurses' home and, to finance it, agreed to a bond issue of $150,000, secured by a mortgage on the hospital property. At the meeting, the sisters were made aware that $3,000 per year plus interest had to be paid on the bonds, and they promised their cooperation and agreed to make the arrangements for the groundbreaking ceremony.[78]

These were significant expenses for a nonprofit institution. Despite them, the hospital continued its charitable activity. For example, when forty-three families from AuSable Forks lost their homes and possessions to fire, the hospital's board of directors decided at its May 1925 meeting to offer medical care at no cost to those who needed treatment.[79]

In August, the assistant general of the Grey Nuns of the Sacred Heart, who was the chief fundraiser for Champlain Valley Hospital, traveled to Plattsburgh to break ground for the nurses' home. Because the hospital still needed to raise a significant amount of money to finance the home's construction, the *Sentinel* beseeched readers when it reported on the ceremony. "If there are any wealthy residents of Clinton County who need to dispose of surplus funds in order to avoid paying a large income tax," the newspaper stated, "the nurses say they will be glad of the money toward their new home, as the funds in hand are not sufficient to entirely pay for the cost of construction."[80]

To raise additional funds, the hospital's board of directors sold thirty-year, first-mortgage bonds that yielded 6 percent interest paid twice a year on the first of January and on the first of July at Plattsburgh National Bank. The bond sales generated $25,000 in capital by June 1926 and $80,000 by February 1927. Following the opening of the new nurses' home in January 1927, the board announced plans to retire about $3,000 in bonds every year. As it did so, the board continued making improvements to the hospital's physical plant. By early August 1927, the former quarters of the nurses on the third floor were remodeled and opened for patient use (fig. 7.1).[81]

The board also came up with creative ways to work with community vendors who aided the institution. In May 1928, for example, the board agreed to allow Thomas Carlisle, a florist, "to use a part of the grounds belonging to the hospital for the purpose of growing flowers, in return for which he is to aid in beautifying the hospital grounds to whatever extent he feels able."[82]

The board had to cover other significant expenses, such as the installation of a sprinkler system in every room of the hospital to improve safety in 1929. Although the hospital board did not have the funds at the time to pay for this safety measure, it proceeded anyway and planned to do some fundraising to cover the expense. The sister nurses worked

Figure 7.1. Champlain Valley Hospital (right) and School of Nursing / student residence (left), c. 1920s, founded by the Sisters of Charity of Ottawa. Courtesy of Archives des Soeurs de la Charité d'Ottawa, accession P-M 57/1.

for modest rates, but they too needed to be paid, and they occasionally received salary increases, such as the $10 per month augmentation approved by the board in November 1929.[83]

Like Champlain Valley Hospital, Physicians' Hospital organized a School of Nursing of its own in 1910, but it opened the school in the following year. Each institution had a similar organizational management in that the superintendent of the hospital served as the superintendent of the nursing school in the 1920s. Both nursing schools had comparable curricula, for they each followed the curriculum of the New York State Department of Education for nurse-training schools. Similar to Champlain Valley Hospital, nurses in training at Physicians' Hospital initially had their living quarters in one wing of the hospital. There is another significant way in which both schools were similar: the issue of religion and religious services, an important consideration in the 1920s. Not unlike the School of Nursing of Champlain Valley Hospital, that of Physicians' Hospital noted in a brochure in 1928 that "the school is nonsectarian and students are afforded an opportunity for attending church services at least once on Sunday." Although not affiliated with a religious institution, the nursing school of Physicians' Hospital had its religious expectations. It also had a religious character: the brochure opened and concluded with quotations invoking God.[84]

Censuses from 1925 and 1930 shed additional light on the nursing students of Physicians' Hospital.[85] In 1925, with only seventeen students, the nursing program was smaller than Champlain Valley Hospital's, but in 1930, with sixty students, the Physicians' Hospital Nursing School was much larger than that of the other program. In both census years, at each school, all student nurses were white women of the same general age range, though a few at Champlain Valley were slightly older. All seventeen Physicians' Hospital student nurses in 1925 were US-born, and two of the sixty in 1930 were born in Canada; consequently, it had significantly fewer foreign-born student nurses, both numerically and proportionately, than did the Champlain Valley School of Nursing. Physicians' Hospital did attract some nursing students with French surnames—up to three of them in both 1925 and 1930.[86] Its nursing school, however, was not quite as ethnically diverse as was Champlain Valley Hospital's in the same period.

Another way in which Plattsburgh's two hospitals differed in the 1920s was in the charitable contributions they received from William Miner. Born in Wisconsin, Miner moved to Chazy, New York, to live with relatives following the deaths of his parents. He became wealthy by inventing a better shock absorber for railway cars that reduced the damage to them and by building a company in Chicago that produced railroad parts. In 1921, one of the directors of Champlain Valley Hospital noted that Miner had contributed $2,400 to the institution over the years. In contrast, Miner and the foundation he established contributed substantially more money to Physicians' Hospital over time. Dr. Cassius Silver, the chief of staff at Physicians' Hospital, was a friend of Miner and secured his support for the hospital. Miner paid to build and equip a new Physicians' Hospital in Plattsburgh in the 1920s, and he subsequently became the president of the hospital's board. When Miner died in 1930, the foundation he established continued to have a controlling interest in the institution. Newspaper reports from the middle and late twentieth century reveal that the Miner Foundation provided large cash infusions to the hospital long after the 1920s. By 1952, when the Miner Foundation contributed $840,000 for a nurse's residence, the Miners and their foundation had contributed a total of $7,765,000 to Physicians' Hospital, and other large donations followed: $100,000 in 1953 and $80,000 in 1990, to take two examples.[87] In short, unlike Champlain Valley Hospital that had to cobble together funds from a wide variety of sources to manage its expenses, Physicans' Hospital in the 1920s had one main benefactor that made it possible for it to build a new facility and to cover a large share of its operating expenses.

Both hospitals later shared a physician who brought his innovations to the practice of medicine. Born in Willsboro, New York, Lyman Barton studied mechanical engineering before attending medical school. After completing his medical studies in 1891, Barton took over his father's practice. F. C. Dossert has written of the conditions facing physicians like Barton in northeastern New York in that period: "All operations were performed in private houses and were done on the kitchen table, as this was usually the most suitable one found in any home." Barton accepted an appointment at Champlain Valley Hospital when it opened in 1910. Because the surgical equipment Barton's father had passed on to him proved inadequate, he purchased additional instruments and made some himself with the help of a blacksmith. In 1925, while on the staff of Champlain Valley Hospital, Barton officially introduced the new obstetric forceps he had designed. The Barton forceps, for which he became famous, addressed what the physician viewed as a mechanical problem in the positioning of some fetuses, using the forceps to facilitate childbirth "with less danger to the child and less damage to the mother," writes Archibald Donald Campbell. Over time, Barton designed at least fifteen different instruments and appliances for hospitals, including an ether dropper, various types of forceps, a metal fracture frame, and rib shears. A medical practitioner for fifty-three years, Barton also served on the staff of Physicians' Hospital, where he oversaw at one time the X-ray department before his death in 1944.[88]

One physician the two hospitals apparently never shared, however, was Dr. J. H. LaRocque. In 1910, when both Champlain Valley and Physicians' hospitals were founded, area physicians elected LaRocque the president of the Clinton County Medical Society. LaRocque joined the staff of Physicians' Hospital and served in the early 1920s as the president of its board of directors.[89]

When LaRocque died in 1924, the bell of St. Peter's Church tolled to announce his passing. Many businesses closed, as did city hall, on the day of his funeral. All municipal officials and large delegations from the St. John Baptist Association and the Knights of Columbus gathered at St. Peter's Church to mourn LaRocque's death, noted the *Sentinel*. Consistent with LaRocque's wishes, his remains were interred at the family plot at Saint-Jean-sur-Richelieu, Québec.[90] A French-Canadian immigrant who became a naturalized US citizen, LaRocque preferred his country of birth as his final resting place.

LaRocque's version of Americanism, which combined a respect for host institutions while preserving the language and traditions of the sending society, was not one that nativists of the 1920s would have understood. But an English-language newpaper of Plattsburgh apparently did. "Although born in an alien land, Dr. LaRocque possessed the spirit and understanding of true Americanism to the highest degree," stated the *Daily Press*. LaRocque's contribution, the newspaper underscored, lay in being a physician, citizen, and humanitarian. "Withal, he never forgot the land of his birth nor failed to revere its best traditions which are as much akin to our own as though no imaginary line divides it from those with whom he spent the best years of his life."[91] Thus, the *Daily Press* comprehended what members of the Ku Klux Klan in the 1920s did not, namely that foreign-born Catholics could be productive members of US society, even while retaining some of the traits that made them distinctive.

That is the story of growth and development of Plattsburgh's Catholic institutions during the era of the Second Ku Klux Klan. New orders of women religious, the Dominicans and the Sisters of Mercy, arrived in the city during the twenties to conduct Catholic schools. St. John's parish founded its own parochial school, and the Sisters of Mercy who staffed it founded their own boarding school for girls and a novitiate for their order in the city. At the same time, the Grey Nuns at Champlain Valley Hospital erected a residence hall for their student nurses and expanded the capacity of their hospital. Concurrently, the Brothers of Christian Instruction enlarged the physical plant of Mount Assumption Institute. As the analyses of state and federal census data reveals, each of Plattsburgh's religious orders included Catholic immigrants from abroad, a group that especially worried the Klan of the 1920s. But other than the cross burnings near Catholic people and institutions on Thanksgiving Day 1926, there is little evidence to suggest that religious divisions plagued the city of Plattsburgh during the twenties. The community support of Catholic institutions and the interchurch collaboration fostered by sports and musical events promoted tolerance and acceptance. So did the welcoming disposition of those Catholic institutions, which displayed their Americanness and, when possible, a nonsectarian nature. Like Dr. LaRocque, Catholics of Plattsburgh in the 1920s did not feel the need to hide their ethnic roots while becoming a part of larger US society.

Chapter Eight

The Depression Years

Collecting Nickels, Dimes, and Quarters, 1930–1940

As the Great Depression permeated all corners of the United States during the 1930s, church communities such as St. Peter's of Plattsburgh struggled to survive. The 1931–1932 parish yearbook made known the material needs of the church, and it implored communicants to do more. One notable line states: "The church gets some of the people's nickels and dimes, but how few as compared to the movies!" The chiding did not stop there. "The world has no nickel resorts, few theatres have nickel seats, refreshment parlors no longer have nickel glasses, even the street cars have abolished nickel fares," the publication continued. "But the nickel is still big enough, people think, to buy religion, despite the advance in cost of building material, labor, repair, work, fuel, light, insurance, and every other item of current or extraordinary expenditure."[1] These words in the yearbook of Plattsburgh's largest Franco-American parish suggest the emotional and economic challenges the community faced in confronting the Great Depression during the early 1930s.

One of the ways in which St. Peter's continued to raise money during the Depression was through the sale of burial plots at its cemetery. Wealthier parishioners paid handsome sums for large family plots as well as the right to erect monuments and slabs on their gravesites. In October 1930, for example, Plattsburgh dentist Isidore Boulé and his neighbor, real-estate agent Solomon Kelley, each paid the church $900 for a 180-square-foot plot at the cemetery. Boulé's deed indicated that the purchase price included perpetual care and the "privilege in conjunction with Solomon Kelley of use of Pieta group as a family monument, and the placing of one slab at foot of same, if found convenient." Kelley's deed contained similar language.[2]

Borrowing money from wealthier parishioners was another means to generate capital or to reduce obligations. In January 1934, Rev. Arthur Lemire informed the Chancery Office that a parishioner had lent the church $500 at 5 percent interest. The church used the loan to replace another it had out at 5.5 percent interest.[3]

Various organizations also contributed to the needs of the parish. The Tuesday Club, which had formed before the start of the depression, consisted of a group of women who met on Tuesday afternoons to play cards. In the early 1930s, they raised nearly $1,000 for St. Peter's Church.[4]

Organized in 1929, the St. Vincent de Paul Society of St. Peter's parish showed particular interest in welfare work and parochial schools. Rev. Joseph Pelletier invited members of the parish to form a local chapter of this worldwide society that had originated in Paris, France, in 1833. The society set up free dental and health clinics in Plattsburgh's parochial schools. In 1930, the society envisioned helping "perhaps, to some extent at least, the population of Plattsburgh as a whole," reported the *Sentinel*. In 1931, the society organized a lawn social at St. Peter's, where over 2,000 people enjoyed such activities as a candy booth, fishpond, bingo games, linen sales, and open-air card parties. Advertised as "Welfare Day," a second annual lawn social attracted 1,800 people to the booths and activities on the grounds of St. Peter's parish in August 1932. The proceeds, the *Daily Press* reported, would benefit "the unfortunate families of Plattsburgh and vicinity." The advertisement for the fourth annual lawn social in 1934 noted: "All proceeds of party for Welfare Work in Plattsburg."[5] These lawn socials served as an example of how members of Plattsburgh's Franco-American community assisted each other and the larger community before the advent of social-assistance programs in the Franklin D. Roosevelt administration's New Deal.

Other groups also contributed to the St. Vincent de Paul Society's efforts. In 1931, for example, the Little Theatre of Plattsburgh scheduled a performance of the Broadway comedy *The Torch Bearers* to benefit the charitable work of the society. As a women's auxiliary to the St. Vincent de Paul Society, the Sewing Circle gathered for a couple of hours one afternoon each week to make or mend clothing to assist the poor, and they also supplied milk to schoolchildren.[6]

A parish of modest means, Our Lady of Victory organized its own fundraising events. In 1931, it held a boxing exhibition and smoker at the Plattsburgh Athletic Club, attended by nearly 300 people, to raise money for the church. The following year, the pastor of Our Lady canceled the smoker, which had apparently been an annual event according to the *Daily Press*, to opt instead for a card party and social. The newspaper reported that Rev. J. H. A. Bachand felt a smoker would not be appropriate, though his specific reasons went unrecorded, and no other smokers were sponsored by the parish. When Bachand celebrated the twenty-fifth anniversary of his pastorate in 1936, the *Daily Republican* complimented him on his stewardship of a parish that was far from wealthy, indicating that "to build the church was not easy as most of us can appreciate, realizing that the parishioners were not blessed abundantly with funds." In 1937, Bachand made the arrangements for a St. Patrick's social during Lent at the Our Lady of Victory church hall. According to the *Daily Republican*, the event's purpose was "to honor the memory of Good Saint Patrick who unwittingly has made it possible for the faithful to break their fast and to make merry on at least one night during the Lenten season."[7] This tribute to the patron saint of Ireland also served to raise funds in a Franco-American parish struggling to meet the financial challenges of the Great Depression.

Plattsburgh's Catholic churches continued to organize minstrel shows in the 1930s to generate cash for their institutions. In November 1931, St. John's put on a minstrel show to benefit the parish, and youth from its school contributed to the performance. The St. John Minstrels then repeated their performance the following night for the benefit of the St. Vincent de Paul Society of St. Peter's parish. The following year, the St. John Baptist Association sponsored a minstrel show of its own at St. Peter's School auditorium that it dubbed its first annual minstrel show, designed to benefit both the society and St. Peter's Church (see fig. 8.1). The program announced that it would reverse minstrel routine by opening with "An Evening in Kentucky." Next on the program was "Little Pickaninny," a song composed by Plattsburgh resident Roswell Sharron; other performances carried such titles as "My Trixie" and "Carry Me Back to Old Virginia." The minstrel show was well received. "Playing to a capacity house each of the three nights, the minstrel show[,] comprising local talent of [the] St. Jean Baptiste Association and St. Peter's church," commented the *Daily Republican*, "closed its run last

210 | Catholics across Borders

MON., APRIL 18, 1932

> **OPENING PERFORMANCE**
> of the Big Plattsburgh
> **MINSTRELS**   **TONIGHT!**
>
> People going to this show, desiring to have a suit, coat or a dress, cleaned for this evening,
>
> **SPIEGELS**
>
> will give special service all day today. Any garment cleaned in
>
> **Three Hours!**
>
> Please do not miss this show. Remember, we are giving special reduced prices all this month, on every article that is brought in for cleaning.
>
> Join the crowd and go to the St. Peter's Auditorium this evening. See an old time minstrel show, featuring Plattsburgh home town stars, who will entertain you and keep you laughing every minute. Another performance also tomorrow night. Do not miss these two big events--for the benefit of the St. John the Baptist Society.
>
> Just Give
> **SPIEGELS**
> a Phone Call
>
> Ask for number "TWO"
>
> Twenty years of practical experience is your assurance of master service - - -
> OR LOOK FOR
> *"The Little Place with the Big Reputation"*

Figure 8.1. Community Advertisement for Minstrel Show, 1932. *Plattsburgh Daily Press*, April 18, 1932, 10.

night with an exhibition that will long be remembered as one of the best local productions ever staged in this city." St. Joseph's Church in nearby Coopersville subsequently engaged the group to share its songs, dances, and jokes there.[8]

When the St. Peter's Dramatic Club put on a minstrel show in 1936 at the school hall to benefit the church, the cast had more than seventy people, including children. Lemire spoke from the pulpit to invite parishioners to this minstrel show, characterizing the production as "wholesome amusement." He also suggested that revenues from the production would help keep the parish schools open.[9]

The Sisters of Mercy at St. John's Academy also organized their students to perform minstrels. Their 1938 program, "Swanee Strutters," included singing, dancing, comedy and monologues and dialogues, all "built around an old-fashioned minstrel circle," reported the *Daily Republican*. The newspaper announcement of the variety show indicated that two girls would represent two "mammies" and several boys from the school would do "blackface varieties that should add to the spirit of the program." Following the closing night, the newspaper let readers know that the performances had gone well.[10]

The minstrel shows organized by Plattsburgh's Catholic churches and societies may have been one means to lift the spirits of people faced with the significant financial and emotional challenges of the Great Depression. At the same time, they promoted the idea of white superiority among Franco-American and Irish ethnic groups in the city. In "Constructing Race, Creating White Privilege," Pem Davidson Buck argues that blackface minstrel shows were part of a strategy in the mid-1800s whereby white intellectuals in the United States promoted white superiority. "This sense of superiority allowed struggling northern Whites to look down their noses at free Blacks and at recent immigrants, particularly the Irish," Buck writes. In addition, in blackface minstrel shows, "white superiority was phrased as if whiteness in and of itself was naturally a benefit despite its lack of material advantage."[11]

Applying Buck's arguments to a different historical period, Kathryn Vaggalis suggests that changing notions of whiteness appealed to economically disenfranchised poor whites and immigrants in the early twentieth century. This may have been true of Plattsburgh's ethnic Catholics during the 1920s and especially during the economic crisis of the 1930s. As the immigration restrictions of the 1920s were applied to continental migrants by 1930, the number of new immigrants who arrived in Plattsburgh from Canada and other parts of the world became quite limited during the Great Depression. Without new immigrants against whom to contrast themselves, Irish and French-Canadian descendants in Plattsburgh may have fostered a notion of whiteness based on their exposure to minstrelsy. It was through such mechanisms as the minstrel shows, Vaggalis has argued, that white supremacy moved into lay culture.[12]

Outside the minstrel troupes, associational life remained fairly strong during the Depression, providing social outlets to the community. More than 300 Franco-Americans were members of the Montcalm and Sainte-Cécile councils of Union Saint-Jean-Baptiste d'Amérique (USJBA) in the early 1930s. Such mutual-aid societies continued to provide sickness and death benefits to members of the Franco-American population of Plattsburgh during the Depression. In the early 1930s, the sick benefit fund paid out between $5 and $15 for up to fifteen weeks, providing its members a safety net against prolonged illness. To draw attention to the organization in order to increase membership, the two local councils sponsored a series of monthly talks. Demonstrating ongoing ties to the church, the councils invited Rev. Eugene Noury to speak in May 1939 on his foreign travels.[13]

During the 1930s, as in previous decades, the St. John Baptist Association made news by its participation in parades and military exercises in Plattsburgh and beyond. In September 1933, the city organized a half-day holiday to celebrate the work of the National Recovery Administration (NRA), a New Deal agency created during the Great Depression. The parade featured carpenters, plumbers, painters, barbers, veterans, boy scouts, girl scouts, the fire department, and students from the city's public and parochial schools, as well as the St. John Baptist Guard of Honor. The guard executed a number of drills during the afternoon activities on the field of Plattsburgh High School, drawing the accolades of the *Daily Republican*: "We were impressed by the skill and precision with which the members of the guard executed the various military evolutions or exercises, which must have required years of training in order to become so highly proficient."[14]

Founded during the planning process for the Lake Champlain Tercentenary celebration, the St. John Baptist Guard of Honor performed periodically with other guards in Plattsburgh and in Montréal. Affiliated with the Federation of Canadian Guards, the St. John Baptist Guard of Honor organized conventions with them. In 1934, 15 units from the federation brought 700 members to Plattsburgh for a convention and parade that took place on a Sunday in August. "Sunday was indeed 'Canada Day' in this city," proclaimed the *Daily Republican*, which went on to suggest that one day each year be so designated to cultivate ties between Canadians and Americans. "It is sound policy to cultivate the friendship of those people, get them accustomed to coming here in large numbers, even as we Americans used to flock to Montreal and other Canadian cities during the 'dry' era," the newspaper stated. In 1938, units of the Union of Catholic Guards of Canada and the United States assembled in Plattsburgh over Labor Day weekend for their first annual convention. That convention, which brought units from Montréal and St. Hyacinthe in the Province of Québec and from New Hampshire and Massachusetts in New England, opened with a military mass at St. Peter's Church on Sunday morning and continued with drill exhibitions on the athletic field of Plattsburgh High School in the afternoon. St. Peter's Hall served as the venue for the convention's meetings, at which 382 men appeared in uniform, with family and friends swelling the number of attendees to 1,000. An editorial in the *Daily Press* heaped high praise on the convention that the local St. John Baptist Guard of Honor had organized: "Every person, whether of French-Canadian extraction, or one of the hundreds who still reside in the home of their fathers, but who were with us for the celebration, has a right to feel proud at the showing made by his compatriots on those two days."[15]

In 1931, Plattsburgh celebrated the Fourth of July with two days of festivities that included Canadian visitors and the St. John Baptist Guard of Honor. On Saturday, a parade with floats traveled to the city beach, where swimming and other contests took place. So many Canadian cars were observed in the parking lot the next day that the *Daily Press* commented: "Sunday seemed to be Canada's day at the beach." That afternoon, uniformed societies marched down the boardwalks to the beach. The newspaper gave special thanks to the St. John Baptist Guard of Honor and to the Girls' Guard of the Saint Cecile Council for making "the celebration the unqualified success it was." The women's council had performed a drill in uniform that had drawn great applause.[16]

The military exercises of Franco-American organizations like the St. John Baptist Guard of Honor, executed as part of local celebrations, often attracted the attention of the larger community. So did the carnivals the association brought to Plattsburgh during the Depression years. In 1936, the St. John Baptist Association organized a five-day engagement of the World of Mirth Shows, which arrived in Plattsburgh with its own thirty-car train directly from Ottawa, to showcase a mentalist, individuals with dwarfism, and Florida Seminole Indians who subdued alligators in the Everglades, among other acts.[17]

Male parishioners of St. Peter and Our Lady of Victory also remained active in non-French societies like the Knights of Columbus during the Depression decade. Roughly 120 to 200 members of the Knights of Columbus marched from their hall on a Sunday morning each May or June to attend an early mass at St. Peter or Our Lady, celebrating to honor the departed members of the organization. After the annual church service, the Knights marched to a local hotel or to their hall for an annual communion breakfast.[18] The participation of Franco-Americans in such nonfrancophone organizations gave evidence of the group's ongoing cultural integration in the host society.

Another sign of cultural adaptation was the growing use of English by the Franco-American community during the Great Depression. The 1931 promotional materials of Our Lady of Victory Academy appeared entirely in English. Although a Catholic institution, the academy welcomed prospective students of all faith traditions and made clear it did not impose Catholicism on non-Catholics. This, too, serves as an example of cultural adaptation. Yet this Catholic institution maintained its bilingual character. After noting that the academy was chartered by the New York State Board of Regents, the brochure made clear it "offers to young ladies all the advantages of a thorough English and French education."[19]

Except for one advertisement, the St. Peter's yearbook of 1931–1932 also appears entirely in English. At the end-of-year séance of boys and girls from the third to the sixth grades that took place at St. Peter's Hall in 1931, the pastor exhorted parents "to speak French to the children," presumably because they were not doing it. This is not to suggest, of course, that the parish had anglicized completely. Despite the growing use of the English language in St. Peter's parish in the 1930s, the French language still had its place. End-of-year séances in 1932 and 1936, and likely in other years, included a song in French and one in English. When salutarian Nathalia St. Denis made the welcoming remarks at the St. Peter's High School graduation ceremony in 1939, she did so in French.[20]

In 1934, St. Peter's offered communicants the choice of five different masses to attend on Sunday mornings. While the 6:00 a.m. mass had no sermon, the four other masses had sermons evenly divided in number between English and French. It is clear that younger members of the parish community were not being raised in French, for the 8:30 a.m. children's mass had an English sermon.[21]

Thus, the parish incorporated English into a variety of activities, including the retreats for children and adults. Parish missions throughout the 1930s were conducted in both French and English, but from the middle of the decade, the three one-week Lenten retreats generally featured only one preached in French for all parishioners while two others, one for women and girls and the other for men and boys, were preached in English.[22] Thus the language of religious services, of retreats, and of parish publications also suggests greater emphasis on English-language use at St. Peter's during the Depression years.

The St. John Baptist Association similarly showed some signs of anglicization in the 1930s. When the society had its sixtieth anniversary in 1931, ribbons for the event all appeared in English. But other evidence suggests that it remained an ethnic society. To celebrate the sixtieth anniversary, members paraded through Plattsburgh's streets alongside some Canadian organizations, and they participated in a high mass at St. Peter's Church, during which the Oblate preacher from Lowell, Massachusetts, "stressed the great benefits of the Union and the perpetretion [sic] of the French language among Franco-Americans," noted the *Daily Republican*. The priest "also mentioned the necessity of reverence of God as the mainstay of all organizations." Thus, members of the organization continued to hear the familiar refrain of the importance of maintaining their language, faith, and traditions. An afternoon review of the uniformed ranks took place at St. Peter's athletic field, followed by an evening banquet at a local hotel. The association at the time of its anniversary had 250 male members, and 200 women formed an auxiliary. The society organized social activities for members and their wives that they opened to other French-Canadian descendants in an attempt to increase membership. In December 1933, for example, the association held an event at its hall, announcing through the press that "any Franco-American man in Plattsburgh between the ages of 15 and 45 are [sic] especially invited to attend this affair, so that new members can be taken in to swell the ranks of the society."[23] Efforts to recruit new members to maintain the vitality of such ethnic associations demonstrate a desire to retain some distinctive traits in the host society.

The regular participation of Franco-American societies in local events functioned to demonstrate ethnic pride. So did the accession of the group to important professions and city posts. One of the bright spots of the Great Depression for Franco-Americans, and particularly for St. Peter's parish, was that another one of their own became the mayor of Plattsburgh. The 1931–1932 yearbook of St. Peter's points out with obvious pride that Leander Bouyea (which it spelled Boyer) was the third mayor the parish had furnished the city, following on the heels of Albert Sharron and Dr. Andrew Senecal. "The City Hall is not, however, the only theatre, where the Franco-Americans of our congregation have distinguished themselves, and held premier honors," the yearbook interjected. "All along they have been met with [distinction] in every walk of life: on the Judicial Bench, in the medical as well as in the legal profession, amidst the financial and business world."[24]

Campaigning against wasteful spending that had allegedly benefited the incumbent mayor and his family rather than taxpayers, Bouyea won the mayoralty of Plattsburgh in 1931. A native of Morrisonville, New York, Bouyea worked as a baker for different establishments for a decade before starting his own baking company in 1913, which became one of the largest in Plattsburgh. Bouyea served as mayor of the city for six consecutive terms from 1932 to 1944.[25]

Like other prominent Franco-American leaders in the early twentieth century, Bouyea participated in a mixture of ethnic and nonethnic organizations. He was a member of the Franco-American organizations of the St. John Baptist Association and the USJBA. He was also a member of such non-French societies as the Knights of Columbus, the Loyal Order of Moose, and the Plattsburgh Lodge of Elks.[26] Membership in these associations likely led him to form the kinds of social, financial, and professional connections that helped him succeed in business and in politics.

Although described by the *Press-Republican* as "a staunch Democrat," Bouyea mustered Republican support during his long tenure as mayor. In 1937 he secured the Democratic Party's nomination, and because Republicans had no candidate in that year, he also received the endorsement of Republican voters as a write-in candidate during the primary. He therefore ran unopposed for reelection in 1937.[27]

Bouyea's correspondence as mayor sheds some light on how the Great Depression affected Plattsburgh. When a man from South Dakota wrote him to ask for assistance in securing a job, Bouyea advised him that employment prospects in the city were not good and that he could not help him. "This section of the country, while not highly industrial, still feels the results of depression and recession," Bouyea wrote. He went on to describe the reduction in employment of some of the city's businesses: "At the present time one mill, usually employing 700, has reduced its force to 350. Another factory generally employing 150 is now giving employment to about 25 people." Bouyea noted that retail establishments were also hurting: "What little business there is is not of a gainful nature, inasmuch as most of our merchants are operating on a small margin of profit, due to chain store activity." In addition, Bouyea pointed out that the city's tourist industry was suffering, and he advised his correspondent in 1938 that it was not a good time to seek work in Plattsburgh.[28]

Bouyea observed that Canadian traffic to northern New York continued during the Great Depression. When a man from Montréal wrote Bouyea to complain about a problem he experienced with state police as the result of an accident near Plattsburgh, Bouyea took the occasion to tell him "that many Canadian people visit our Municipal Beach, and as a whole are exceedingly proud that they select Plattsburgh as a rendezvous for holiday or week-end meetings." Bouyea concluded with a note of consolation, stating: "I can truthfully say that we appreciate having you with us, if for nothing more than a mutual friendship."[29]

While the mayor may have touted cross-border traffic to Plattsburgh, the Brothers of Christian Instruction found that the Canada–US border became a clear line of demarcation, particularly during the Depression. In June 1931, the order purchased property from Shakers in Alfred, Maine, to serve as their American juvenate and scholasticate. "Our Canadian province could with difficulty continue training subjects for our establishments in the United States," the brothers noted in their chronicle. "Differences of nationality, of language, of programs, without mentioning stricter immigration regulations, necessitated the foundation of a house of formation in the United States," they added.[30]

Despite the challenges the border posed in obtaining personnel to staff their institutions, the Brothers of Christian Instruction (see fig. 8.2) continued to draw students from Canadian families for Mount Assumption

Figure 8.2. Brothers of Christian Instruction, Plattsburgh, NY, 1935. Courtesy of Archives des Frères de l'Instruction Chrétienne, La Prairie, Québec.

218 | Catholics across Borders

Institute (MAI) in Plattsburgh. Their boarding students in the early 1930s came not only from Canada but also from the eastern United States, Cuba, Puerto Rico, and Mexico. But the Great Depression negatively affected enrollments at MAI. While resident student numbers had peaked at 175 in the mid-1920s, they dropped to 120 in 1930, 85 in 1931, and 55 in 1933. Not until the mid-1930s did the declining numbers reverse, with 90 boarders at Mount Assumption in 1936.[31]

The Dominican Sisters (fig. 8.3) also noted the effects of the Depression. Fewer students appeared at the parish school on the first day of classes in September 1932, they observed, and they had ten boarding students in that year. By 1939 the situation had changed: the sisters

Figure 8.3. Dominican Sisters, St. Peter's Parish, Plattsburgh, NY, 1936. Courtesy of Dominican Sisters of Hope Archives, Ossining, New York, accession F623.01.

recorded that they had their highest registrations at the parish school (427) and among their boarders (16).[32]

But the intervening years were difficult, and the pastor of St. Peter's, Rev. Auriemma Veronneau, wrote the Mother General of the Dominican Sisters in 1933 that parish revenues had declined significantly during the economic crisis and asked the order to accept a salary reduction from $350 to $300 a year for the teaching sisters. The pastor put considerable pressure on the order, intimating that the sisters would lose their jobs if they did not accept a salary reduction: "If you refuse to share our sacrifices, we will soon see ourselves forced to abandon our children to the public schools." Mother General M. Madeleine offered to accept $41 less per month during "la dépression," an amount absorbed by reducing each sister's monthly salary by $2 and deducting $15 monthly from the parish allotment for maintenance.[33]

The Dominican Sisters came up with a number of strategies to raise money to meet their and the parish's needs during the Great Depression. One strategy was to prevail upon the well-to-do in the community for contributions. In 1933, when the sister who managed the convent's laundry asked for an electric ironing machine, the sisters noted that "Mother Dominique proposes asking our richest and most fortunate friends to offer us something." Through direct solicitation, the sisters raised $153, most of it from prominent men in the community. The men, some with French surnames and some without, each contributed $15 to $50; this group included the mayor (Bouyea), the former lieutenant governor (Conway), an attorney (Cotter), the president of the St. Vincent de Paul Society (Tremblay), and a businessman (Brown). A few women each contributed from $1 to $2 each, and the girls attending the first year of the sisters' high school contributed $10 together.[34]

The Dominican Sisters also organized card parties, bingo games, and drives to raise money for their order and the parish. The proceeds of a card party at St. Peter's Hall, for which players bought 25-cent tickets, benefited the sisters in January 1931. A bingo game at the convent in mid-December 1935 raised $48 for parish projects. After another bingo game and fundraising drive generated $325, of which the efforts of the brothers contributed $132, schoolchildren presented the funds to the pastor at the parish hall with a song in French and "a nice, short compliment in English" that one of the sisters had written. Bingo games the sisters organized in 1936 and 1937 raised $190 and $481, respectively, for the church.[35]

Séances contributed to the parish coffers as well. In March 1937, third- and fourth-grade students put on a play at St. Peter's Hall; the sale of tickets and ads for the program raised nearly $266, which the sisters handed over to the pastor. A Christmas playlet put on by the students of the sisters in December 1937, for which attendees each paid 25 cents admission, raised $75, and the sisters added this sum to the bingo monies generated that month before offering them to the pastor. Seniors put on a show in the parish hall in February 1938, raising $240, an amount "which permits the Father Comptroller to pay his debts," the sisters recorded. The following year, seniors raised nearly the same amount ($231) to benefit the church.[36] The quarters and other proceeds obtained from the student performances, games, and drives organized by the Dominican Sisters all helped ease the financial burdens of the church and the school.

Taking the veil in the Dominican order was not generally a means of avoiding the difficult circumstances of the Great Depression. Women who wanted to join the order in the 1930s received no remuneration for their time in community, and they were expected to cover their personal expenses and clothing costs during their novitiate. In addition, candidates were expected to bring a dowry of $100 to defray the expenses of their training and education. The order did make provisions, however, for deserving women whose families could not provide a dowry or who could not meet all of their expenses.[37]

In 1930, the Plattsburgh convent of the Dominican Sisters had fifteen resident nuns and was elevated to a priory, which was named St. Dominique Convent. A priory functioned like a Mother House, had a prioress as administrator, and maintained certain rules like perpetual silence in the dining room. As with other orders of women religious, a class division existed in the priory of the Dominican Sisters. The *US Census, 1940*, which recorded the highest grade each individual had achieved, reveals that the sisters with only a grade-school education did the work of the "household," whereas those with college educations taught school. Education conferred certain benefits within the priory. One day in March 1939, all Dominican Sisters enjoyed a day of recreation, except the lay sisters, that is, those responsible for the manual labor, who spent the day washing and ironing. "Obedience is worth more than sacrifice," recorded the chronicler. Not until 1947 did the Dominican Sisters modify their constitution to eliminate the class system in their order, stating: "Hereafter, there will be only one category of Sisters, all having the same privileges and obligations, although some will be employed chiefly in teaching and others in manual work, according to the judgment of the Superior."[38]

Reports of St. Dominique Priory to the General Council shed additional light on the functioning—and the finances—of the Dominican Sisters in Plattsburgh during the Great Depression. They began taking boarding students in September 1928, and by 1930 the convent had generated enough money to send $7,150 to the Mother House. The sisters benefited from federal-relief aid when Works Progress Administration workers renovated two large rooms in their convent at no charge. Beginning with the 1936–1937 school year, the Dominican Sisters offered business courses to third- and fourth-year high school students and to some postgraduates. They did so because they realized they were losing students who wanted to pursue classes in typing, shorthand, and bookkeeping. Rev. Lemire raised the initial funds to purchase typewriters for the day and evening business classes, noted the sisters. Beyond that, the bingo games, raffles, and séances the sisters organized generated funds not only for the parish, but also for the typewriters, an adding machine, and other supplies the commercial school program required. From September 1934 to May 1937, the sisters generated by their various activities $15,923 in revenue, and they sent more than half ($8,152) of it to the Caisse Générale, the general fund of the Mother House.[39]

Registers of the Dominican Sisters serving in Plattsburgh for the 1930–1931 and 1935–1936 academic years reveal that while about half were born in the United States and half in Canada, all but one or two of the teaching sisters had French family names. Thus, most of the Dominican Sisters likely had a facility with French-language expression, and the sources reveal that they worked to maintain their French-language skills so they could continue teaching French in their schools. Four Dominican Sisters received certificates to teach French in New York State in October 1934, for instance, and a Mr. Mosher of the State Board of Education came to Plattsburgh the following year to administer oral exams in French to several others.[40]

The students of the Dominican Sisters were part of a large cohort who attended Catholic schools in Plattsburgh. Mayor Bouyea noted in 1939 that "at least two-thirds of the students in this City attend the Parochial Schools."[41] Given that those Catholic schools did not receive public assistance, the Dominican Sisters, the Brothers of Christian Instruction, and the Sisters of Charity of St. Louis faced significant obstacles during the Great Depression to keep their schools functioning.

The Sisters of Mercy who administered St. John's Academy faced their own financial challenges and also came up with creative solutions to address them. To generate income following the closure of the novitiate in Plattsburgh, the Sisters of Mercy made the Loretta Residence in September 1931 the site of a nonsectarian commercial school to train stenographers and secretaries. From the 1930s through the 1950s, the Loretta simultaneously served as a residence for successive groups. From 1929 to 1936, students attending Plattsburgh Normal School could live there in what the sisters promoted as a nonsectarian residence for young women. In 1931, eight Normal School students resided at the Loretta, along with the students taking secretarial and business courses from the sisters. From 1936 to 1959, the Loretta served as a retirement home for women; when census-takers came around in 1940, four women between the ages of sixty and eighty-seven resided there. Some of the sisters who taught at St. John's Academy also lived at the Loretta Residence.[42]

Others lived at the convent on Broad Street attached to St. John's Academy. In August 1931, a group of thirty-five Sisters of Mercy from northern New York gathered at that convent to participate over nine days in an annual retreat led by Jesuit priests from Montréal. Despite the tightening of the international border, it appears that the Sisters of Mercy continued to maintain cross-border ties with religious personnel during the early years of the Depression.[43]

One of the creative ways women religious of Plattsburgh met financial obligations was through an exchange of services. When several Dominican Sisters required medical attention in 1937, they recorded in their chronicle: "In return we continue to give to the good hospital sisters [Grey Nuns] lessons in French, accounting, etc."[44] In this way, women religious participated in a barter economy with other nuns in the city.

That the hospital sisters accepted French lessons suggests they had no or few French speakers among them. Although there had been Grey Nuns of French-Canadian birth serving at Champlain Valley Hospital in the 1920 and 1925 census years, during the 1930 and 1940 censuses, all Canadian-born religious personnel at the institution were from English Canada. In fact, Anglo-Canadian nuns made up a majority of the staff in each of the latter two census years.[45] This demographic data suggests that the hospital continued to function in the 1930s as an anglophone institution. The language of the annals the hospital sisters maintained adds further weight to this impression: they begin with an entry in January 1937, and all entries in the volume appear in English.[46]

The work of these anglophone nuns attracted significant attention in Plattsburgh. In the early 1930s, the Plattsburgh community honored the Champlain Valley Hospital's founding Grey Nun, Sr. Ann Whelan, who had served in the city from 1902 to 1916. On the occasion of Sr. Ann's diamond jubilee as a woman religious, Plattsburgh Chamber of Commerce President C. Fuller Austin thanked her in a public letter for her contributions to the community: "Plattsburgh and northern New York are always indebted to you for your vision and tireless efforts in the establishment in Plattsburgh of the Champlain Valley Hospital." Two years later, when Sr. Ann succumbed to pneumonia and influenza, her obituary in the *Daily Republican* concluded: "The community will ever connect her name with the fine institution that the C. V. Hospital is and proclaim it as a monument to her memory." An editorial in the *Daily Press* similarly extolled her work and repeated what the newspaper had said at the time of her diamond jubilee: "It has been said that 'by their works you shall know them,' and thus through the work of one noble woman now gone shall the Champlain Valley Hospital ever be known as a monument to work well done."[47] These tributes to the hospital's founder suggest that Sr. Ann's efforts in Plattsburgh, first as a teaching sister at St. Peter's School and then as the administrator of the city's first hospital, provided opportunities for non-Catholics to get to know Catholics in the community.

In the following year, 1934, the *Daily Press* had more complimentary things to say about the Grey Nuns who served at Champlain Valley Hospital. The occasion was the graduation of student nurses from the Hospital Training School. The editor stated: "In the years of their training they have been in the hands of the good sisters who have so serenely surrendered all personal ambition for the one purpose of assuaging the suffering of humanity." In saying this, the editor probably did not consider that women religious like the Grey Nuns had access to professional positions at their institution somewhat unlike those that women in the larger community could enjoy. "The aid they may give—and that alone—is the recompense for their great sacrifice," continued the editor.[48] As Catholic women religious, the Grey Nuns of Champlain Valley Hospital and Training School surely would have appreciated the ethereal dimensions of their work, but they likely also enjoyed the achievement of gaining access to professional positions not available to most laywomen of their historical period.

Although Champlain Valley Hospital from its founding professed to be a nonsectarian institution, church officials regarded it as a Catholic hospital. The Bishop of Ogdensburg appointed Catholic chaplains to the institution, and they were expected to say masses and to administer the sacrament of Communion regularly. In 1939, Rev. Lemire informed Bishop F. J. Monaghan that the nurses who worked evenings at Champlain Valley Hospital had to go without Holy Communion for five to seven weeks at a time on account of their schedules and could not observe the required fasting period prior to Communion. Lemire asked the bishop for permission to give the nurses Communion during the week while they were at work. The bishop flatly denied the request to administer Communion "outside of chapel except when confined due to illness." Monaghan asked Lemire to show the letter to the Sister Superior at the hospital, and he directed her to organize the hospital schedule so that Catholic nurses could receive Communion on Sundays and Holy Day mornings if they had fasted since midnight. The bishop stated emphatically: "This is one of the reasons for the existence of Catholic Hospitals, the promotion of religion and piety and virtue. If Champlain Valley Hospital cannot afford this convenience to Catholic nurses[,] it has ceased to serve the purpose of its existence." Monaghan went on to describe his plans to overhaul Catholic hospitals in the Diocese of Ogdensburg, noting that some in New Jersey had been closed "because they had ceased to serve Catholic purposes," and he expressed his hope that none in his diocese would meet a similar fate. "We will insist that all Catholic hospitals conform constantly and consistently with the Catholic ends for which they were primarily instituted and permitted to exist in this diocese; after that has been effected We [*sic*] will then and only then be concerned about their saecular [*sic*] standing." The bishop punctuated his message with the remark: "They exist for religion, not religion for them."[49]

Like the Catholic institutions in Plattsburgh, Champlain Valley Hospital benefited from fundraising activities to help meet its financial needs during the Great Depression. In 1932, the Plattsburgh Little Theatre presented three one-act plays at the Junior High School auditorium to raise money for the hospital. The Women's Auxiliary of Champlain Valley Hospital in the 1930s continued to take a leadership role in fundraising, and between 900 and 950 women served in the organization during the Depression. Pledges, card parties, gifts, magazine subscriptions, and dances helped the women's organization to raise $1,284 for the hospital in the 1935 fiscal year alone.[50]

Dances during the Depression appeared to have been one of the more popular fundraising activities. Annual Christmas dances, sponsored by the Women's Auxiliary, raised money for medical and other supplies Champlain Valley Hospital needed. In 1934, around 200 couples attended the Christmas evening dance at the Witherill Hotel. Dances were held to benefit the hospital in other seasons as well. An Easter dance in 1935, also sponsored by the Women's Auxiliary, drew 150 couples, largely representing the "elite of Plattsburgh and the surrounding community," reported the *Daily Republican*. A dinner dance the auxiliary organized at Hotel Champlain in August 1935 drew 600 couples and raised $392.[51]

According to the *Daily Republican*, due to unemployment during the Depression, many in the community could not pay their own hospital bills, and dinner dances like the one in August 1935 helped to cover the medical expenses of the needy. "Unfortunately, there are no large corporations in our area and few rich citizens from whom the hospital can expect to receive substantial sums," wrote the newspaper's editor. The journalist undoubtedly alluded to the significant financial support that the Miner Foundation provided Physicans' Hospital. The editor applauded the Women's Auxiliary of Champlain Valley Hospital for its role in organizing dances to raise the funds needed to meet the health-care needs of destitute members of the community: "The public appreciates that the Ways and Means committee [of the Women's Auxiliary] has had a problem on its hands in securing funds in these years of depression when few persons in the community have had much of it to spare."[52]

After a group of young women formed the Junior League of Champlain Valley Hospital in 1936, they, too, organized dances to support the institution, particularly the nursery and the children's ward. Some of the dances the Junior League organized in the mid-1930s also attracted as many as 600 couples. In addition to hosting dances, the young women of the Junior League met weekly to sew clothing for needy children at the hospital.[53]

Throughout the United States, as many Catholic hospitals served the indigent during the Great Depression and refused to turn them away, they accumulated significant debt and could not satisfy their creditors. In contrast to them, as the direct result of the fundraising activities of multiple groups, and of the substantial contributions of the Grey Nuns, Champlain Valley Hospital weathered the Depression quite well. The hospital's board of directors noted at an August 1937 meeting that the institution's debts were decreasing and that the hospital anticipated being debt free by year's end. The directors made it a point to give credit in their January 1940 report to the efforts of the Grey Nuns in contributing to the success of the hospital in the preceding year: "Without the work of these Sisters, which is given for almost nominal sums, this record could not have been made, and it is proper that recognition of the work of these faithful and devoted women be noted in this report and placed in the records of the hospital."⁵⁴

In contrast to Champlain Valley Hospital, Physicians' Hospital struggled financially during the 1930s. While it also relied on donations from citizens, such as the canned goods, pickles, preserves, fruits, and vegetables it gathered on Donation Day in the fall season, and while it also generated income from paying patients, its main benefactor was the Miner Foundation. In July 1931, the foundation informed the hospital's board of directors that the Depression had had such a negative effect on its income that it might no longer be able to provide the institution with financial assistance. Physicians' Hospital ran a deficit during the Depression, and the Miner Foundation's trustees notified the hospital board that it could no longer cover the monthly hospital deficit after December 1931. Consequently, the Physicians' Hospital board took measures in 1932 to reduce expenses, including laying off forty employees and raising its rates on hospital rooms.⁵⁵

The minutes of the Champlain Valley Hospital board from April 1935 reveal that "there was also some discussion about the possibility of merging the Champlain Valley and Physicians Hospital[s] because of the financial difficulties encountered by the Physicians Hospital due to the size of the plant, and the necessity of enlarging the Champlain Valley Hospital in the near future because of lack of sufficient space." In fact, the Grey Nuns of the Sacred Heart noted in their annals in 1937 that their hospital had "been obliged to borrow beds from the Physicians' Hospital. They were most gracious about lending them," they added. The two institutions worked cooperatively on other matters as well, combining forces in 1939, for example, to seek from Clinton County and individual towns an increase in the daily rate for welfare patients, raising it from $2.50 to $3.00.⁵⁶

Physicians' Hospital board members questioned in 1932 how Champlain Valley Hospital could operate at a small profit when Physicians' Hospital was running a $40,000 deficit despite its cost-reduction efforts. By comparing the expenses of the two institutions, the treasurer discovered that the biggest difference lay in the amount paid for salaries and wages—an annual difference of about $33,000. Treasurer Leif Norstrand wrote: "This single item accounts for very nearly the entire present operating deficit of this hospital. It is, of course, impossible for this hospital to cut its annual cost in salaries and wages to anything like that of our neighbor due to their nursing order." Norstrand, of course, referred to the significant contribution of the Grey Nuns of the Sacred Heart at Champlain Valley Hospital. To survive, Physicians' Hospital cut the wages of its staff and required them to do additional work without pay. Although the Miner Foundation was able to offer Physicians' Hospital about $10,000 to $12,000 in 1935 to meet its deficit, the hospital had a low patient population, and it continued to struggle financially until the early 1950s.[57]

In conclusion, the nickels and dimes that Plattsburgh's Catholic parishes found in their collection baskets on Sundays during the Great Depression were not enough to sustain their churches or their schools. The quarters that the women religious collected from attendees of the student musical and dramatic productions they organized, which they shared generously with the men religious along with the other funds they raised, helped the parishes meet their financial obligations. So did the fundraising activities of the Franco-American societies. Similarly, the women's auxiliaries helped Champlain Valley Hospital meet its financial needs. Most significantly, the low salaries of the women religious who conducted Plattsburgh's Catholic schools and hospital made it possible for those institutions to weather the economic crisis of the 1930s. Their sacrifices, indeed what laypeople might call "self-exploitation," allowed Plattsburgh's Catholic institutions and heritage to persevere beyond the Depression years.

Chapter Nine

Plattsburgh during World War II and the Early Cold War

Retaining a Catholic Heritage, 1940–1950

United States immigration restrictions that were applied to continental migrants by 1930 of course slowed the flow of immigrants from the North. Consequently, data on the nativity of the religious personnel serving the Catholic institutions of Plattsburgh demonstrates that increasing proportions of women and men religious in the city were US-born by midcentury. Yet religious personnel of Canadian birth could still be found in Plattsburgh in the 1940s, and they—as well as their colleagues of Canadian descent—continued to exert some influence on the ethnic character of the city's institutions in the middle of the twentieth century. They particularly helped Plattsburgh to preserve its Catholic heritage during World War II and the early Cold War years.

By 1940, Plattsburgh had a total population of 16,351. As in previous periods, only a tiny proportion (0.07 percent) of Plattsburgh's residents was nonwhite. A larger proportion (5 percent) was foreign-born. Just like in previous decades, a majority of the city's immigrant population had come from Canada, with somewhat greater numbers in 1940 having arrived from "Canada-Other" rather than "Canada-French," signaling that English-speaking Canadian migrants slightly outnumbered their francophone counterparts.[1]

Plattsburgh's population grew during the 1940s not so much from immigration, which was restricted, but from natural increase or migrations from elsewhere in New York or the United States. By 1950, Plattsburgh had 17,738 residents. The foreign-born white people who lived in Plattsburgh in that year made up 4.7 percent of the city's population. As with the 1940 census, the largest numbers of foreign-born people in the city had come from Canada, with the immigrants from English Canada again outnumbering those from French Canada. The number of Plattsburgh residents who were nonwhite increased during the forties, but people of color still constituted a very small proportion (0.2 percent) of the city's overall population in 1950.[2]

One woman of color who lived in Plattsburgh in the 1940s was Dr. Vashti Curlin, a Brooklyn native who had earned her medical degree from the Boston College of Physicians and Surgeons in 1946 and who held a yearlong internship at Champlain Valley Hospital. "Immediately, Dr. Curlin entered upon her duties with a devotion that was an inspiration to those about her and won the immediate esteem of staff members and hundreds of patients with whom she came in contact during her year at the hospital," stated the *Plattsburgh Press-Republican* in announcing her departure from the city. Curlin planned to practice in metropolitan New York. Julian Reiss of Lake Placid, a member of the New York State Anti-Discrimination Commission, held Dr. Curlin up as an example of a courageous, high-achieving African American woman. Paraphrasing an article Reiss had written in *Opportunity*, "a magazine devoted to Negro life," the *Press-Republican* reported that Reiss "writes that[,] admittedly, America has a long distance to travel in providing equal opportunity for its Negro citizens, but stresses that it is an amazing paradox of history that American Negroes, despite these adverse conditions, have made and continue to make significant advances in all fields of human endeavor."[3] This kind of reporting in the *Press-Republican* reflects, on the one hand, how unusual it was for people in the North Country to have contact with a person of color. On the other hand, it also suggests the role journalists could play in conveying positive images of individuals who were different from the larger population or who differed from their common perceptions.

Curlin's migration to Plattsburgh served as an example of an internal migration within the state and the country. Religious personnel serving in Plattsburgh in the 1940s also moved from other parts of the United States to Plattsburgh and, to a lesser extent than in the past, from outside of the country to the city. By the middle of the twentieth century, a large majority of the Oblate priests serving at St. Peter's Church were native of the United States (see Table 1); most had French surnames.[4] Census data suggests, therefore, that the Oblate priests of St. Peter's largely remained a Franco-American order during the 1940s.

One of the US-born, Franco-American priests, Rev. Arthur Lemire, initially appointed to St. Peter's Church as an assistant in 1933 and as its pastor in 1945 and again in 1948, gave a sermon on Mother's Day in 1949 that highlighted themes in French-Canadian history. A bus transported parishioners to Notre-Dame de Lourdes in Jericho, Vermont, where Lemire's sermon brought up the 1837–1838 Rebellion in Canada as well as the past connections of Louis Riel to the local area and to the Oblate order.[5] While information on the sermons of the Oblates is scarce, this content culled from the annals of the Dominican Sisters reveals that themes of French-Canadian history had not disappeared from the sermons of the priests of St. Peter's parish by midcentury.

While St. Peter's continued to offer weeklong missions preached in English during the Lenten season, it also offered missions in French during the 1940s. Sometimes, as in July 1947, St. Peter's parish organized a retreat in Montréal for French-speaking women of the Plattsburgh area.[6] Newspaper announcements of these French-language retreats and missions suggest that sufficient numbers of communicants of St. Peter's Church retained the language skills to warrant these religious services in French.

The ethnic composition of the women religious serving St. Peter's parish helped it to continue its French-language traditions to midcentury. According to the *US Census, 1940*, and snapshots of the personnel records of the Dominican Sisters from the 1940–1941 and 1945–1946 school years, about one-fourth of the Dominican Sisters teaching in the city had been born in French Canada, while the rest had birthplaces in different northeastern states. But the order was changing. By 1950, the proportion of US-born Dominican Sisters at St. Peter's parish rose and the proportion of Canadian-born sisters dropped (see Table 10).[7]

Although a Franco-American order, the Dominican Sisters had among them by the late 1940s an English-speaking contingent. The preacher of the April 1949 retreat surprised these anglophone nuns by giving a talk in English, apparently his first in the English language, on the last day of their retreat, inspiring the chronicler to write: "This thoughtfulness was quite appreciated and we were eager to offer him our congratulations." Despite the anglicization and Americanization of the order in Plattsburgh, the Dominican Sisters had not forgotten their Canadian heritage. They opened in 1942 a new convent in Mooers

Forks, a community north of Plattsburgh on the Canadian border, and in December 1948 the sisters of Plattsburgh visited Mooers Forks in a bus driven by the Brothers of Christian Instruction. During the downpour on their trip home, the Dominican Sisters sang "our most beautiful Canadian songs, French and English."[8] This episode, of course, underscores that the Canadian heritage of the Dominican Sisters of Plattsburgh was not at midcentury simply a faded memory.

They celebrated other heritages as well. The Dominican Sisters, like the Grey Nuns, continued in the early 1940s to celebrate St. Patrick's Day. On March 17, 1941, the chronicler penned a note: "St. Patrick's Day which warranted a day off for us." In 1942, the Dominican Sisters had St. Patrick's Day off again, and several went to Champlain Valley Hospital to watch movies and to enjoy a light lunch with the Grey Nuns, who decorated their chapel and sang hymns to St. Patrick as part of their celebration.[9]

One of the Grey Nuns of Irish descent brought cheer to patients at Champlain Valley Hospital during the 1930s and early 1940s. Born in Ireland, Sr. St. Cyprian migrated to the United States in 1888 at age twenty, and she served in missions of the Grey Nuns in Canada and Ogdensburg, New York, before arriving in Plattsburgh. A registered nurse, Sr. St. Cyprian served as a librarian at Champlain Valley Hospital, according to the *US Census, 1930*, by which year she had reached the age of sixty-two. Newspaper accounts of her death in 1942 reported on her colorful and genial nature, commenting that she had a pet canary "from which she seemed inseparable" and with which, perched on her forefinger, she visited patients. "She had in her eye that kindly Irish twinkle that was of the kind to win confidence," reported the *Plattsburgh Daily Press*. The Grey Nuns of the Sacred Heart were surprised by how many individuals turned out for Sr. St. Cyprian's funeral services at St. John's Church, including about ten priests, the graduate nurses who formed a guard of honor, women from the hospital auxiliary, members of the hospital's board of trustees, different communities of women religious from the area, and Protestants who knew her. "This spontaneous and sincere tribute paid to Sister by all classes and creeds, especially, by the Clergy, and members of different Communities [of women religious], was a tangible proof of the high regard in which our beloved Sister St. Cyprian was held," recorded the Grey Nuns. After the funeral mass at St. John's Church, Sr. St. Cyprian's remains were interred at Mount Carmel Cemetery, where the Grey Nuns of the Sacred Heart had a plot.[10] That

Sr. St. Cyprian was buried from the Irish church and at the Irish cemetery of Plattsburgh was a fitting denouement for this woman religious, one of Erin's daughters.

Living among the Dominican Sisters, who were largely bilingual, were young women from Canada who came to Plattsburgh to learn English. The Dominican Sisters had between sixteen and nineteen boarding students to the mid-1940s, depending on space. Just as in the previous decades, these students provided an important source of revenue for the order: "For their part they will be a large financial help," noted the chronicler at the start of the 1943–1944 school year.[11]

In an action reminiscent of the one the Oblate priests had taken several decades earlier with the Grey Nuns of the Cross, the pastor of St. Peter's wanted to close the boarding school of the Dominican Sisters in the mid-1940s. He planned to make more room for classes and ostensibly for the sisters in their convent. "He therefore let leave our dear boarders who were practically our living," noted the Dominican Sisters of Plattsburgh in their 1948 report to the General Council in Fall River, as they lamented the loss of income and hence the size of their financial contributions to the Mother House.[12]

The Prioress General took up the matter with the parish trustees in July 1948. "I am sure you will readily understand that the salary we receive in the parish is not sufficient to support the Community even with the strictest economy we can practice," she wrote. "It has always been necessary to supplement that salary by other means of income, and the principal one available to us has been the boarders." The Prioress General pointed out that the rising cost of living in the postwar period compounded the financial challenges of the sisters. If they could no longer have boarding students, an alternative the Prioress General suggested was to allow the sisters to organize "a play or some other organization to raise money, permitting the proceeds to go to the Community."[13]

The pastor, Rev. Lemire, found working with the Dominican hierarchy a bit confusing as he tried to reach an agreement with the sisters in the following year. He summarized his understanding, asking for corrections if inaccurate, that the principal handled school matters, the local superior oversaw local community matters, and the Mother House managed the contract with the parish. Lemire pointed out to the Prioress General that he found the Oblate hierarchy easier to navigate: "Among us it is simpler, for the pastor is also the superior of the community." As alternatives to the revenue of boarding students, Lemire discussed with the Prioress General a fee of 10 cents per grammar-school pupil and possibly the same amount for students in the high school, proceeds from a séance each year, and asking the St. Vincent de Paul Society to cover the cost of books for poor students. In the past, the sisters had to raise funds themselves for those unable to afford textbooks.[14]

In October 1949, when the Prioress General was in Plattsburgh, Lemire drafted in his own handwriting on parish stationery a note he alone signed specifying the terms of the parish agreement with the Dominican Sisters. St. Peter's agreed to pay each teaching sister an annual salary of $300; to allow one dramatic production each year to benefit the sisters; to allow them to charge 10 cents per pupil, except from the destitute families, decided on a case-by-case basis by the pastor; to cover the cost of heat, lighting, and "repairs, as possible"; and to provide $15 monthly to maintain the convent.[15]

Though these terms were relatively austere, the Dominican Sisters made more sacrifices. In late October, the Prioress General wrote Lemire to indicate that the General Council had approved using the 10-cent monthly fee from pupils to make repairs to the D'Youville yard rather than having it go to the sisters' community for a period of two years; after that time, those revenues would revert to the sisters. In addition, she informed Lemire that the General Council had voted to spend $300 for a new stove or washing machine "in case the expense for these is too great for the parish, or to make it easier for the parish to undertake the repairs that are so urgent in the refectory and other parts of the basement."[16]

Lemire greatly appreciated the sacrifices of the Dominican Sisters. In the mid-1950s, when he was no longer at St. Peter's, after not noticing any mention of the accomplishments of the Dominican Sisters in celebratory parish publications, he wrote them to express his personal annoyance about that silence. Lemire commented that St. Peter's had amassed a debt of $45,000 when the Grey Nuns left the parish in the early 1920s and subsequently "the Dominicans came, lived in unacceptable conditions for years, and then sacrificed money, raised money and did more than any parish group to pull us out of debt."[17]

Séances organized by the Dominican Sisters generated funds for their order and the parish throughout the 1940s. In April 1941, the séance that high school girls put on raised $500 for the parish coffers. The $450 that the February 1944 séance generated went to the pastor to repair old parish buildings in decline. The February 1945 séance put on by the high school girls featured the play *Brave Little Holland* and the dance "Le Tournoi des Tulipes" ("Tulip Tournament") with Dutch costumes, raising over $580 that also went to the pastor. The following year, "The Lady in Gray," a comedy in three acts, brought in $794 that the sisters handed over to the pastor. The sisters did reserve some of the funds raised by student performances for renovations to their convent, as they did in 1944, and for their Mother House in Fall River, Massachusetts, to which they sent $1,100 in February 1950.[18]

Minstrel shows also raised funds for the school of the Dominicans and for the parish. One day in May 1944, high school juniors put on a minstrel show in the morning and afternoon for, respectively, elementary and high school students. The proceeds were to be used for their senior banquet after the completion of their studies. The minstrels went well, commented the Dominican chronicler, noting: "These children generated laughs and brightened several worried faces. Come back again." After the Peru Junior Minstrels performed at the Peru Central School, several of the religious societies of St. Peter's brought them to Plattsburgh to perform at the parish hall to benefit the church in 1949.[19]

Previous chapters have suggested that minstrelsy brought Black culture into the predominantly white North Country. They have also suggested that minstrel shows performed by or for the Catholic institutions of Plattsburgh may have helped foster a sense of white privilege or superiority among the city's Catholic population. An anecdote from the Dominican Sisters gives us a sense of the kind of racial climate that appeared to exist in Plattsburgh in 1950 when few people of color lived in the city. In October, the biological mother of one of the Dominican Sisters flew to Plattsburgh to surprise her daughter with a visit. The woman had cleared her travel plans with the superior of the convent, who shared the information with another sister. That woman religious had a hard time keeping the secret. "During the recreation she made us laugh by repeating from time to time this famous refrain: 'I know something, I won't tell. Two little niggers in a peanut shell.'"[20] That Roman Catholic nuns would be aware of and use such a phrase—which in contemporary society would be denounced as racist language—suggests the extent to which subtle forms of racism had permeated North Country Catholic communities by the middle of the twentieth century.

This is all the more important because the Catholic parishes contributed substantially to the education of North Country residents. When the new school year began in September 1940, the *Daily Press* revealed that St. John's School, Mount Assumption Institute, Our Lady of Victory

Academy, St. Peter's Parochial School, and D'Youville Academy together enrolled 3,981 students. The communicants of each Catholic parish supported these schools and saved local taxpayers a great deal of money, underscored the editor of the newspaper.[21]

By the mid-1940s, the Dominican Sisters taught all of the elementary and high school girls at St. Peter's parish and boys only in grade one. After the Second World War concluded, the Brothers of Christian Instruction asked for a large salary increase, and the pastor had to consider replacing them. The pastor naturally turned to the Dominican Sisters, but they did not have enough teaching sisters to take over the classes of the brothers. The pastor subsequently approached other orders of men and women religious but, finding none, had to rehire the brothers, doing so initially with a one-year contract for five Brothers of Christian Instruction to teach at St. Peter's in 1947.[22]

As an organization, the Brothers of Christian Instruction had grown during World War II. From 1939 to 1945, sixteen establishments opened in the region of Montréal and twelve in the region of Québec City. In 1946, the order decided to form four administrative districts out of the La Prairie province, districts based in La Prairie, Oka, New Brunswick, and the United States. The Notre-Dame district, centered in Alfred, Maine, oversaw the eight houses and eighty-three brothers in the United States, including Plattsburgh. As part of the reorganization, the mother district of La Prairie agreed to accept the debts and liabilities of Mount Assumption and to transfer its properties in Plattsburgh to the Notre-Dame district.[23]

Archival sources suggest that the creation of an American district of the Brothers of Christian Instruction took place for administrative reasons unrelated to linguistic divisions or internal tensions within the order, as had been the situation with the Grey Nuns following World War I. After the English-speaking Grey Nuns formed an American province, they could no longer supply French-language teachers to St. Peter's parish school. This was not the case with the Brothers of Christian Instruction, as portrayed by their ethnic composition in the US censuses for 1940 and 1950 (see Table 4).

One of the trustees of St. Peter's Church, Wilfrid Tremblay, reminded Brother Cyprius-Celestine Tregret in 1940 that the Brothers of Christian Instruction had been brought to Plattsburgh initially to stem the decline of the French language among parish youth. Tremblay alleged that the brothers had not succeeded. Tregret responded: "The school has enabled the people to pass from a French-speaking to an English-speaking community without the faith suffering in anyway." When Tregret added, "There is more piety in the parish than there was before," Tremblay conceded the point.[24] In the middle of the twentieth century, Tregret—and apparently many in the Franco-American community—no longer subscribed to the adage, "Qui perd sa langue perd sa foi" ("Whoever loses his language loses his faith").

Other evidence suggests that the brothers continued to some degree their linguistic and sports heritage from French Canada. At Mount Assumption Institute, "French is taught in the Elementary grades; this gives a decided advantage to the pupils entering High School," the brothers noted in their 1948 admissions brochure. They also promoted a cherished French-Canadian pastime as an extracurricular activity in Plattsburgh: "HOCKEY, the favorite game of the Canadian students, has become a popular sport among the Americans also, and several of these are now worthily occupying positions on the varsity team," proclaims the admissions brochure. About half of the thirty-seven international boarding students documented in the *US Census, 1950*, were from Canada, while the others mostly came to Plattsburgh from Central and South America.[25]

Census data also provides a window onto the ethnic composition of the other Catholic institutions in Plattsburgh. As a small parish, Our Lady of Victory had only two priests in 1940, both immigrants: one had been born in French Canada and the other in Holland. By the time census-takers came around in 1950, both priests at Our Lady were US-born, representing a significant departure from past census years when all were immigrant priests (see Table 6). Moreover, in 1950, only one of the priests at Our Lady had a French surname.[26]

Half of the fourteen teaching Sisters of Charity of St. Louis in 1940 had been born in French Canada, while the other half were native of the United States; most notably, none was native of France in that census year. Nor were there any sisters of French birth when census-takers came around in 1950, when equal numbers of Sisters of Charity (fig. 9.1) were US- and Canadian-born (see Table 9). Despite the sizeable proportion of sisters of Canadian birth or background, Our Lady of Victory Academy functioned as an English-language institution during the 1940s. Its yearbooks from that decade, for example, all appear entirely in English. Yet, in following the Regents curriculum, the Sisters of Charity of St. Louis continued to offer French-language instruction in the 1940s.[27] Given the ethnic composition of their order, they certainly had the personnel to do so.

Figure 9.1. Faculty of Our Lady of Victory Academy, conducted by the Sisters of Charity of St. Louis, 1949. Courtesy of Archives des Soeurs de la Charité de Saint-Louis du Québec, accession 24,022–003–003.

When New York State Education officials visited Our Lady of Victory Academy in 1940, they cited its inadequate physical plant as a negative element in the institution's rating. Consequently, the Sisters of Charity began making plans for a new school, but US involvement in the Second World War interrupted those plans. The sisters may also have lacked the necessary resources to proceed. Two terse lines from the bishop to the superior suggest that Rev. Joseph Bachand, the pastor of Our Lady of Victory parish since 1911, may not have been paying the salaries of the teaching sisters. Bishop Francis Monaghan informed the superior: "I have written Father Bachand to pay his debt to you. If this is not done by the end of this year, I direct that you notify me." State inspectors in 1947 indicated that Our Lady of Victory's classroom building was too small and that it lacked a gymnasium, auditorium, and library. So, the Sisters of Charity proceeded in spring 1948 to build a new high school, despite the scarcity of resources and materials in the aftermath of World War II.[28]

In the middle of the twentieth century, this type of undertaking required the sisters to jump through all sorts of financial, legal, and religious hoops. For example, they had to secure permission from church authorities, not only in the Diocese of Ogdensburg but also at the Vatican in Rome, to borrow the $300,000 necessary to put up the new facility. When the sisters discovered some discrepancies in the legal work by which they had acquired the chapel/school building from the parish corporation in 1910, they had to clear their title in 1948 by filing new documents with the Clinton County clerk's office. Beyond that, the Sisters of Charity, like other Catholic orders before them, decided to pursue their incorporation in New York State. Introduced by Plattsburgh assemblyman James Fitzpatrick, Chapter 688, "An Act to Incorporate The Congregation of the Sisters of Charity of St. Louis," became law in New York in April 1949 with the signature of Governor Thomas Dewey. This incorporation allowed the sisters to train postulants to their order in conjunction with the provincial house in Bienville, Québec; to establish schools following the rules and guidelines of the Regents and education commissioner of New York State; to work with any charitable, religious, or educational corporations in the state; and, importantly for their goal of erecting a new school building, the ability to purchase and convey real and personal property and to enjoy tax-exempt status.[29]

To raise money for the new school, Our Lady of Victory organized bazaars in the late 1940s and early 1950s, something it had not done in several decades, according to the press. The June 1949 carnival featured games, music, and embroidery exhibits of the sisters, all intended to raise money for school equipment. The October 1950 bazaar, which lasted four days, featured a supper each night in addition to booths and various games. Although young men from Our Lady of Victory parish had put on a minstrel show at the church hall in 1940, there is no evidence to suggest that the sisters organized any minstrels to support their school during the forties. Instead, bingo games, various sales, dramatic plays, and film showings all contributed to funding the new school building.[30]

Benefactors assisted as well. A woman who was a friend of one of the nuns paid for a communication system and furnished drapes, rugs, and statues for the parlor. Another woman, who was the niece of another nun, donated a four-foot-high statue of the Sacred Heart made of white stone and with a white marble base. Other benefactors donated hospital beds, encyclopedias for the library, and a rug for the chapel.[31]

Although the new building could accommodate 125 boarding students, Our Lady of Victory did not attract enough students to reach those numbers. As Sisters of Charity, the order decided to take in aged, sick, and abandoned women to fill some of the vacant spaces in the new facility. This was the start of the Sacred Heart Home for the Aged.[32]

Opening a summer school served as another strategy to generate revenue. Students who failed their June exams could attend summer classes with the Sisters of Charity of St. Louis starting in July 1950, and thirty young women did. Some of the Sisters of Charity from the Redford house joined the Plattsburgh sisters in teaching at the summer school. Students who passed their exams at the end of the summer thus avoided delaying their graduation from Our Lady of Victory Academy.[33]

Between Our Lady and St. Peter parishes lay St. John's Church. The priests residing at St. John rectory in 1940 and 1950 were—with one exception—all native of the United States and, most likely, of Irish descent. The Sisters of Mercy in Plattsburgh had also Americanized. Of the eighteen teaching Sisters of Mercy living at St. John Convent or the Loretta Residence in 1940, fourteen were from states in the US Northeast, one was from the Irish Free State, one was native of French Canada, and two were from Newfoundland. In 1950, nearly three-fourths of the Sisters of Mercy teaching in Plattsburgh were US-born. Nonetheless, the school the order conducted, St. John's Academy, continued in the 1940s to be regarded by the community as an Irish school. In its reporting of a football game in October 1948, where Mount Assumption Institute defeated St. John's team, the *Press-Republican* referred to the latter as "the Irish eleven."[34]

It was not just the Catholic schools that competed against each other. Sponsors of the basketball teams in the Church League included St. Peter, St. John, and Our Lady of Victory, along with the Presbyterian, Methodist, Baptist, Trinity, and Salvation Army churches, as well as the YMCA. Many of those same church groups also participated in the interfaith music festivals that took place among high school students at the Plattsburgh Normal School in the 1940s.[35]

Near the Normal School were the Grey Nuns of the Sacred Heart (fig. 9.2) who administered Champlain Valley Hospital and its training school for nurses. These women religious constituted some of the Anglo-Canadian immigrants living in Plattsburgh. More than half of the Grey Nuns who served those institutions in 1940 had been born in English Canada, but this order was Americanizing as well. The sisters demonstrated their intention to remain in the United States, for six of the eight immigrant nuns in 1940 had become US citizens and the other two had taken out their first papers in the naturalization process. In 1950, exactly half of the Grey Nuns serving in Plattsburgh were native of Canada, and all of the Canadian-born sisters were naturalized US citizens. One unnaturalized sister in that year was native of England.[36]

Plattsburgh during World War II and the Early Cold War | 241

Figure 9.2. Grey Nuns of the Sacred Heart, nurses and administrators of Champlain Valley Hospital and instructors of the School of Nursing, 1962. Courtesy of Grey Nuns of the Sacred Heart Archives, Philadelphia, Pennsylvania, RG 900.

Three of the forty-six student nurses at Champlain Valley Hospital in 1940 had been born in French Canada, contributing to the growing proportion (nearly two-fifths) of the student nurses with French surnames. By 1950, the Champlain Valley Hospital School of Nursing had seventy-five students, all white women between the ages of seventeen and twenty-one who had been born in the United States. Thus, the 1950 cohort was larger and younger than in past census years, but the proportion that was Franco-American was smaller.[37] As we will see, the expansion of the nursing program in the 1940s took place to help address the shortage of nurses during World War II.

The chronicles of women religious shed some light on events in Plattsburgh during the war years. In March 1942, four months after the United States entered the Second World War, six Dominican Sisters participated in first-aid classes largely for religious personnel taught at Mount Assumption Institute by Dr. A. De Grandpré, a local physician. "These lessons are given in order that help can be given the wounded if the horrors of the war were experienced in our vicinity," recorded the

Dominican chronicler. The sisters enrolled their students, most of whom were girls, in the Junior Red Cross.[38]

The war, of course, disrupted routines, including religious routines. Because of the rationing and scarcity of gasoline during the war, the confessor of the Dominican Sisters, typically a priest from outside of the parish, could not travel to Plattsburgh. So, the sisters found themselves having to go to confession with laypeople in the church basement and wishing "each week waiting that things return to normal and that order is reestablished." After US entry into the war, their students collected scrap materials for recycling, gathered books for soldiers, and sold war bonds. To encourage the purchase of war bonds, the elementary and high school students participated in a parade in June 1944.[39]

The chronicles of the Grey Nuns of the Sacred Heart who administered Champlain Valley Hospital add further insight into how the war played out on the home front. At Christmastime in 1942, the sisters commented on the hospital's decorations: "Although, lights and other profuse decorations had to be restricted by reason of the war effort, still, the halls and rooms were not lacking in cheerfulness and decorative evergreens and reds, in which the V—for Victory was a characteristic and patriotic feature at the C. V. H." The sisters had hoped to expand their hospital by adding a maternity wing, plans the Great Depression had "shattered," but they noted in 1943 that Mrs. Lyman Barton had conceived of the idea of a "Birthday War Bond Fund" to attract donations from the parents of children born at the hospital. The monies raised during this campaign for the maternity wing went toward the purchase of war bonds so that construction could begin after the war's conclusion. The chronicler also noted in 1944 that both the Papal Flag and the Stars and Stripes hung at their sanctuary, serving as "reminders that we should re-double our prayers for the boys 'Over There.'"[40]

The *Press-Republican* informed readers in April 1943 that hospitals had to assist the Office of Price Administration with its wartime rationing program. Specifically, hospitals had to collect the ration books of patients who spent more than seven consecutive days and took eight or more meals a week there. Hospital staff then had to remove the stamps that expired during the hospital stays of the patients and turn them over to the local war price-and-rationing board. To ensure the compliance of patients, "hospitals are prohibited from serving food to any person who does not turn over all his ration books to the management when required to do so," warned the *Press-Republican*.[41]

Sources document the role of the Grey Nuns in training nurses during the Second World War. In September 1940, the *Daily Republican* reported that the Nurse Training School of Champlain Valley Hospital had admitted twenty women, its largest entering class, to help meet the nationwide demand for nurses. After the United States entered the war, the Training School participated in the statewide campaign of the New York State Nurses' Association to recruit more women to the nursing profession. As part of this effort, they admitted a special class in February 1942—"a class which has been inaugurated this year as a step to help alleviate the impending shortage of trained nurses," reported the *Daily Republican*. Articles published in the local newspapers in that month discussed the career opportunities available in the army, in hospitals, and in public and private welfare agencies to the women who undertook nurse training. "Getting ahead is an American tradition, and nursing offers [the] best chance for a young woman to get ahead, in the finest sense of the word," began one article, which ended by encouraging interested women to contact Sr. Mary Philip, the chair of Champlain Valley Hospital's Committee on the Recruitment of Student Nurses.[42]

During the Second World War, Champlain Valley Hospital conducted the only School of Nursing in the northeastern corner of the state, as Physicians' Hospital had discontinued its nursing school in 1934. In the early 1940s, Champlain Valley Hospital gained approval to participate in the US Cadet Nursing Corps and received a federal government allotment to train students in the program. To encourage women to join the corps, the federal Bolton Act covered their tuition and entrance fees, supplied a uniform, and provided a monthly allowance for personal expenses during the period of their training.[43]

Local newspapers promoted nurse-recruitment efforts. While the women participating in the US Cadet Nursing Corps had to serve for the duration of the war, publicity efforts sought to quell potential concerns of their elders. "Parents of prospective students are assured that membership in the corps does not mean that their daughters will be pressed into service against their will," concluded a *Press-Republican* article on the program. Nursing was one of the few professions open to women in war work, one recruiting article pointed out, as it encouraged high school "girls" and "older women" up to age thirty-five to consider joining the cadets. It also touted the field of nursing as excellent preparation for marriage and motherhood, claiming that "a higher percentage of nurses marry than do women in any other professional group. This is because the many qualities which nursing develops in a woman are those most admired and respected by men." The article extolled the virtues of the nursing profession: "It develops the ability to maintain successful human relationships and to keep confidences. It is a career in which a woman learns the art of human kindness which will stand her in good stead all the rest of her life."[44]

As the Grey Nuns accepted students who enrolled in the Cadet Nurse Corps, they had to consider ways to expand their teaching facilities to accommodate their growing numbers. By June 1944, sixty-nine of the seventy-three nurses enrolled at their Training School were Cadet Nurses. Initially, the board of directors renovated the basement rooms of the nursing-school building before approving an addition to the structure. In July 1944, Representative Clarence Kilburn announced that the Federal Works Agency would cover half of the estimated $43,600 cost of the three-story addition to the Champlain Valley Hospital nurses' residence, an offer the hospital's board of directors formally voted to accept in the following month. Ultimately, it cost $80,000 to construct the annex, which was completed and fully paid by December 1946. From February 1943 to June 1946, the Grey Nuns trained 116 students in the Cadet Nurses program. After World War II concluded, Champlain Valley Hospital continued to admit large numbers of women into its Nurse Training School, with newspaper announcements touting the entering classes of 1947 and 1950 as the largest yet for the institution.[45]

While Physicians' Hospital no longer had a formal nurse training program in the 1940s, it did become involved in efforts to address nursing shortages during the war years. For example, Physicians' Hospital participated with Champlain Valley Hospital in training nurses' aides in the early 1940s, an effort sponsored by the Office of Civilian Defense and the American Red Cross. In 1943, the Plattsburgh State Teacher's College adopted the Cadet Nurse Corps Program, training forty-eight women in its first class; the women had nine months of pre-cadet training at the college, and then they completed twenty-one months of clinical work at Physicians' Hospital in Plattsburgh and could participate in specialized training in tuberculosis, pediatrics, or psychiatrics in one of three other cooperating hospitals elsewhere in New York State. After World War II ended, the college converted the program into a four-year nurse-teacher program leading to a bachelor's degree.[46]

Besides funding from the federal government to support the training of nurses and the expansion of the nurses' residence, Champlain Valley Hospital benefited from other sources of aid in the 1940s. The Benevolent and Protective Order of Elks donated a blood-bank storage unit to the hospital in July 1942, and several members of the organization made blood donations at that time. The Elks, the American Legion, and the Veterans of Foreign Wars teamed up in 1945 to donate a rare metal—radium—to the hospital. The American Legion offered scholarships covering a year's tuition for each of two nursing students at Champlain Valley Hospital School of Nursing, provided that they had a family connection to a veteran of either World War I or II. A women's Jewish society provided scholarships for two nurses in 1949, and yearly they brought toys for children being treated at the hospital.[47]

Religious personnel contributed services and sometimes monies to the institution. As of December 1940, the Grey Nuns of the Sacred Heart who worked at Champlain Valley Hospital each received a salary of $30 monthly. Even the hospital administrator earned this modest salary in the mid-1940s. The Grey Nuns apparently did not charge women and men religious for their hospital stays, but they sometimes received contributions anyway. In December 1943, the Dominican Sisters voted to send $25 to the hospital for having provided care at no cost to its women religious. In 1947, Bishop Bryan McEntegart sent the sisters a check for $250 for their care and treatment of a diocesan priest. In acknowledging—and accepting—the check, Sr. Annunciata wrote: "We are always happy to do what we can for God's priests without remuneration."[48]

In the 1940s, the Champlain Valley Hospital Women's Auxiliary continued to function as one of the biggest sources of support for the medical facility. The *Daily Press* summarized its various efforts for readers. It noted in 1940 that the society's 980 members, who each paid $1 in annual dues, bought and made materials to supply all of the hospital's linens; they collected jars of pickles, jellies, and jams; and they organized dances and card parties. In addition, they maintained and paid for one hospital room for their members, and they had a committee to visit the sick. When the Champlain Valley Hospital Nurse Training School enrolled students participating in the US Cadet Nurse Corps, the nurses' residence could not accommodate all of them, and the school had to rent a nearby house in 1944 to serve as a dormitory. The women's auxiliary stepped up and opened a fundraising campaign to supply the makeshift dormitory with sheets, bedding, and towels, noting that it was a "patriotic duty" to support nurse recruitment in the Cadet Corps during wartime.[49]

During World War II, the auxiliary replaced its social events with an annual fund drive, a measure the *Press-Republican* attributed to "wartime exigencies." In 1946, when the Women's Auxiliary conducted its third annual fundraising drive, in lieu of organizing various forms of entertainment to generate income, it called the measure "more appropriate and more practical." But the hospital women found that it was not an easy way to attract donations. Three weeks into the third campaign, they had raised only $1,000 toward their $2,500 goal, causing them to worry they would not have enough money to purchase the necessary materials to supply the hospital with pillowcases, bandages, and hospital gowns.[50]

Membership in the Women's Auxiliary apparently dropped and then rose again during the course of the war. The *Press-Republican* reported that there were 598 women in the auxiliary in 1943–1944, representing an increase of 101 over the previous year. In 1944–1945, there were 592 members whose dues were fully paid. By 1949, the auxiliary had 636 members, and that number grew to 650 in 1950, with 274 members from Plattsburgh and 376 from nearby communities.[51]

A related society, the Junior League, had 300 members by 1949, an increase of 100 over the previous year. While the Women's Auxiliary supplied linens and surgical bandages to Champlain Valley Hospital, the Junior League provided them for the nursery and the children's ward. By 1942, after six years of existence, the Junior League had furnished a formula room at the hospital, a sterilization unit for the delivery room, and beds and trays for the children's ward. The Junior League engaged in a variety of fundraising activities, including organizing luncheons and bridge parties. The Junior League suspended its benefit dances during the Second World War, but they resumed them after the war ended. Among other activities in the aftermath of the war, the Junior League organized a Mercy Mail drive, collecting clothing, canned goods, and cash to help underfed and underclothed young and aged people in Germany.[52]

Like the Women's Auxiliary, one of the Junior League's main activities was to sew articles for the hospital. The organization's sewing committee made mattress covers, blankets, shirts, gowns, diapers, diaper holders, and bottle holders for the nursery. For the children's ward, it made sheets, towels, face cloths, diapers, diaper holders, panties, pajamas, and shirts.[53]

Taken together, all of the public and private sources of assistance described above helped Champlain Valley Hospital to prosper at midcentury. Its board of directors was able to retire early the bonds the hospital had issued in 1926 and that were payable in 1956.[54] Aided by different charitable and religious organizations, Champlain Valley Hospital could retire much of its debt by 1950.

Available evidence suggests that the religious nature of Champlain Valley Hospital and its Nurse Training School became more salient during the 1940s. Annals of the Grey Nuns of the Sacred Heart reveal that two of them attended the conventions of the Catholic Hospital Association of the United States and Canada as well as the Montréal Convention of Catholic Hospitals, both taking place in June 1942, and they attended Catholic hospital conventions in other years as well. In 1943, a woman religious who served as the assistant inspector of the Catholic Hospital Association of the United States and Canada conducted a site visit at Champlain Valley Hospital.[55]

But it was more than the professional affiliations of the sister nurses that were religious in nature—so were the daily practices they required of their nursing students. The handbook from the forties stipulated that "all students must be present" for morning prayers that took place daily at 6:50 a.m. in the hospital chapel. Students in the nursing program were provided a small booklet of fifteen pages containing the Lord's Prayer, the Hail Mary, and many other prayers to recite.[56]

The ceremonies involving nursing students were similarly religious in nature. A capping ceremony took place at the hospital chapel in June 1942 for the class of 1945. "The ceremonies, religious in form, terminated with [the] Benediction of the Most Blessed Sacrament at which Rev. George A. Lemieux, O.M.I., who had received Holy Orders earlier in the day, was celebrant," reported the *Daily Press*. At the capping ceremony that took place at the hospital chapel in February 1947, Rev. Patrick Babin blessed the caps of the nursing students and emphasized in his remarks the importance of moral training and religion in their chosen profession.[57]

Graduation ceremonies had religious components and similarly conveyed religious themes. An 8:00 a.m. mass in the hospital chapel was scheduled to precede graduation in June 1946. In August 1947, a 6:00 a.m. mass at the chapel and a Communion breakfast at the hospital were scheduled in advance of graduation exercises held at the Plattsburgh State Teachers College. Men and women religious often served as graduation speakers, even on the college premises. In 1948, Sister St. Geraldine, a Grey Nun of the Sacred Heart from D'Youville College in Buffalo, told the graduates assembled at the college "that they had been so equipped through their training that they were dispensers of corporal and spiritual works of mercy," reported the *Press-Republican*. She also "termed the defense of Christianity 'your responsibility,'" according to the newspaper.[58]

This comment, of course, was typical of messaging in the postwar era. After the end of World War II, as the superpower competition between the United States and the Soviet Union escalated into the Cold War, the USA increasingly sought to portray itself as a Christian nation in opposition to the atheist Soviet Union. That geopolitical climate provided the space for Catholic institutions of Plattsburgh to assert their Christian foundations—even their Catholic heritage—in the late 1940s and beyond.

Lay graduation speakers also addressed Cold War themes in the post–World War II period. In June 1946, Supreme Court Justice Andrew Ryan addressed the graduates of the Champlain Valley Hospital School of Nursing, warning them to steer clear of socialized medicine. Ryan asserted, "You will be untrue to your goal [of service to mankind] if you permit your personalities to become submerged in movements which will bring about the curtailment of medical liberty and the negation of the best traditions of nursing." Ryan suggested that efforts underway in the forties to extend medical care to all Americans, however well intentioned, actually concealed an "insidious" objective in the advocacy of socialized medicine.[59]

Another sign of the increasing religiosity of Champlain Valley Hospital at midcentury is that it formed by 1946 a sodality of Our Lady of Peace. A local priest served as the spiritual director of the sodality, and one of the hospital nuns served as the assistant spiritual director. The Oblate chaplain of the hospital, Rev. Charles Dozois, became concerned in 1946 after some non-Catholic student nurses confided to him that they felt pressured to attend the religious services of the sodality "through fear of incurring further displeasure of the local authorities [nuns] and with the clear knowledge that they needed their good-will to continue their studies till graduation." As reported in the press, Dozois had taught at Rivier College in Nashua, New Hampshire, and at the Oblate seminary in Natick, Massachusetts, before assignment to "his first pastoral duties" at St. Peter's Church and Champlain Valley Hospital in Plattsburgh. Correspondence on file at the Chancery archives in Ogdensburg suggests that the eager new pastoral assistant may have been overzealous in addressing the concerns of the non-Catholic nursing students, as he took those concerns directly to the bishop and to the Superior General of the Grey Nuns rather than handle the matter locally and quietly. None of the superiors of the men or women religious disagreed with the basic point Dozois made that non-Catholic student nurses should be able to practice their own religious beliefs and not be forced to follow Catholic teachings or practice.[60] Those had been tenets of the Champlain Valley Hospital and Nurse Training School from their origins.

The parochial schools followed the same basic tenets. Each of Plattsburgh's Catholic schools accepted students of different races and faith traditions without seeking to convert them to Catholicism, reported the *Daily Press* in 1940. While Mount Assumption provided daily religious instruction, its admissions brochure noted that the school offered a secular curriculum that conformed to New York State guidelines for elementary and secondary schools. The Sisters of Charity of St. Louis offered all grades from elementary through high school at Our Lady of Victory Academy, where they also followed the Regents curriculum. Nonetheless, while following a secular curriculum, one of the objectives of the academy, stated its recruitment brochure, was "to encourage and evolve those traits of character that are basic and essential to a Christian personality." The brochure emphasized that all students had to pursue their religious obligations, noting, in particular: "All Catholic students are required to attend the classes in Christian doctrine, to be present at prescribed chapel exercises, and are urged to approach the Sacraments at least once a month."[61] These kinds of comments, of course, did not obscure the religious nature of Our Lady of Victory Academy.

It is important to note that undercurrrents of anti-Catholicism were still at play in the United States by the mid-twentieth century. Although the Ku Klux Klan of the 1920s did not survive as a social movement in the country, its philosophies and prejudices far outlived it. Anti-Catholicism constitutes one of the most prominent examples. An intellectual anti-Catholicism thrived during the 1930s and 1940s. Nurtured by such Protestant ministers and writers as Paul Blanshard and Norman Vincent Peale, who both attracted large followings, anti-Catholicism flourished in the middle of the twentieth century.[62]

Yet that did not diminish the resolve of Catholic orders like the Sisters of Charity of St. Louis from pursuing their religious ends. In the 1940s they continued to recruit young women to religious life. While Our Lady of Victory Academy did not serve as a novitiate in that period, its 1949 recruiting brochure suggested that it might open one in upstate New York if there were a sufficient number of young women interested in pursuing a religious vocation. Otherwise, those with French-language skills could train at the novitiate in Bienville, in Lévis, Québec, and those who wanted to train in English could do so in Moose Jaw, Saskatchewan.[63]

The 1949 recruiting brochure distributed by Our Lady of Victory sheds considerable light on what training for the sisterhood entailed. The Sisters of Charity of St. Louis recruited young women ages sixteen and older. Their postulancy of six months served as the period of time to help determine if they were fit for "royal life," according to the brochure, after which they would "advance slowly to the altar in bridal dress and veil." During this ceremony, women who joined the sisterhood became brides of Jesus, the King: "What an honor for your parents 'to have Jesus for their Son-in-Law' as an old general once said, and what a glory for a family to have one of its members espoused to a KING!" The recruitment brochure elaborated. During the formal religious ceremony, presided over by the bishop and in the presence of family and friends, "you publicly offer yourself to serve the KING of kings; then you are vested with His livery, and given a religious name." Postulants to the order took vows of poverty, chastity, obedience, and education for a one-year period on this "wedding" day, renewing those vows yearly for five consecutive years, after which they would spend two months at the order's Mother House to contemplate their perpetual vows.[64]

The recruitment brochure of the Sisters of Charity of St. Louis also sheds light on the daily and yearly lives of women religious. They had two hours of recreation each day, during which time they could sew, go for walks, play the piano, sing, visit companions, or play games. Once each month, and at Christmas, they could visit family and friends. The sisters whose relatives lived too far away would be given four days off every five years to visit their families.[65] While the women who joined the congregation of the Sisters of Charity had to make sacrifices, the brochure tried to convey that they would not be relegated to lives of drudgery. Given the reach of the Catholic institutions of Plattsburgh, the information in this brochure undoubtedly appealed to some women from the North Country, educated in the region's Catholic schools, who felt called to a religious vocation.

The scant information that exists on another Catholic organization, the St. John Baptist Society, suggests that it continued in the 1940s its religious character and that it also continued to engage the larger community. With the Second World War raging in Europe, the association asked its members to attend a mass for world peace at St. Peter's School in the early morning one day in September 1940. Its announcement in the local paper specifically requested that its Guard of Honor "report in full dress uniform without sidearms" to join the society for mass and Communion.⁶⁶

While these kinds of announcements in the press suggest that the St. John Baptist Society retained its religious character in the 1940s, others reveal that it also pursued nonethnic ends. The association continued in that decade to bring carnivals to Plattsburgh. An "annual turkey social," open to the public in November 1941, suggests that the society had adopted the US custom of Thanksgiving over time. Beyond the turkey socials, the association organized a public forum at its hall so that voters could meet candidates for city and county political offices, suggesting another means with which the society engaged the public at midcentury in ways not particular to its French-Canadian heritage.⁶⁷ Thus, available evidence suggests that the St. John Baptist Society had evolved by the middle of the twentieth century into one that maintained its religious ties but that contributed to larger purposes and activities than those strictly ethnic in character.

One theme of the 1940s, then, is that Franco-American ethnic traditions appear to have loosened and diminished somewhat while the Plattsburgh community became involved on the home front with activities to support US efforts in the Second World War. It is also possible, though somewhat difficult to document in the sources available, that Franco-Americans became more aware of subtle forms of disparagement and discrimination in the postwar years. This would have contributed to movement away from Franco-American ethnic traits and traditions.

A publication by a non–Franco-American intimates the kind of ethnic climate that may have existed in the North Country in the middle of the twentieth century. One of the patients of Champlain Valley Hospital started writing poetry while recuperating from an appendectomy, and he kept writing during his convalescence from two other major operations at the hospital. A native of Cadyville, a small village near Plattsburgh, Herbert Dewey assembled 111 poems and stories in a book titled *Ramblings of a Convalescent: Homespun Philosophy and Dialect Tales in Prose and Verse, Reflecting Fifty Years as a Farmer, Salesman and Country Storekeeper*. Dewey wrote close to one-third of the works in the dialect of the North Country. While Dewey expressly states that "no references to actual persons are intended or implied in the dialect pieces in this collection," it is clear that he was using French-Canadian speech patterns in those poems and stories, especially with characters bearing such French-sounding names as Joe La Boufe, Joe La Beau, Toussant Barbeau, Nevette Trulene, Misses La Chance, Gramma La Chance, and Pierre La Point. The *Press-Republican* stated: "His imaginary 'cronies' Joe La Beau, Toussant Barbeau, Grandma La Chance and many others are sure to please readers who are interested in this delightful old fashioned North Country dialect which has been popular for so many years."[68]

The poems and prose in Dewey's book address some serious circumstances, like poverty in rural communities, but most others represent an attempt at humor. In one poem, "When Babette Learned to Drive," Dewey pokes fun at women drivers, as Toussant tries to teach his wife to handle an automobile. The third stanza reads:

> Babette doan yet no reverse from hi,
> Dem crow better keep hi in de sky.
> If Babette start out wid dat Ford in reverse,
> Den I tink sum tornado aint be no worse.

While the poems in the collection do not say anything specific about social relations between French-Canadian descendants and other ethnic groups in the North Country, the use of French-Canadian dialect conveys volumes. In the opening stanza of a poem titled "Joe La Beau, My Bes Fran," Dewey writes:

> Joe La Beau, she my bes Fran,
> Dar's mans on who you can depan.
> He doan read da pape, nor rote sum lettair,
> She tink when you no les, you get long bettair.

Note that Dewey occasionally refers to his "fictitious" French-Canadian friend by using feminine pronouns, effectively emasculating him. Moreover, Dewey seeks to ridicule La Beau's lack of education and sophistication. Dewey continues in the same vein in another poem about La Beau, titled "Day-Lite Tam," in which it takes La Beau three decades to figure out that his eight-day clock only needs to be wound up once a week. Here are the first two stanzas:

> For t'irty year, each nite at nine,
> Joe La Beau, she woun her clock,
> An den he mak de dis-co-vair

'Twoud run 8 days an nevair stop.
A mader man I nevair see
Dan my Fran, Joe La Beau,
To tink she set up each nite till nine
When for a week 'twoud tick on t'rou.[69]

Here, again, Dewey derides La Beau's lack of awareness and intelligence.

The content of Dewey's poems and the use of broken speech patterns common to nonnative speakers of English serve to disparage the education and intelligence of Franco-Americans. They do so in ways not unlike the racial comment the Dominican Sister made to the other nuns (described earlier) when she could not keep news of a surprise to herself. Innocuous as the comment may have seemed to her and the other sisters present at the time, it represented a degrading of another racial group. In the same way, Dewey's use of a broken French-English dialect serves as an example of an action that diminishes another ethnic group, namely French-Canadian descendants in the North Country.

Dewey, of course, was not the first to do so in the northeastern United States. Chapter 3 of this volume referenced (see endnote 52) the unusual phenomenon known as the Jumping Frenchmen Syndrome that plagued French-Canadian lumbermen most notably in the Maine woods. By the early twentieth century, it had become part of the folklore of the state. Holman Day used the dialect of French-Canadian lumbermen in a 1902 poem titled "The Jumper," in which a French-Canadian man describes his condition and how others enjoy surprising him involuntarily. The sound of a passing train startles the jumper, and he unwittingly strikes his wife, who decides to sleep in another part of the house. When the jumper shares this with the railway boss, he finds himself the object of teasing:

"I'll tal yo' w'at," say he bam-by,
—He wap' hees eye off lak' he cry—
"I'll tol' yo' w'at dees ro'd weell do:
We'll send op our construckshong crew,
We'll beeld, to show dat we hain't mean,
Wan good, beeg cage an' pot yo' een."

Historian Stephen Whalen and sociologist Robert Bartholomew underscore the possible negative effects of Day's poem: "While Day probably used a local dialect to add a regional flavor to his description, this use of *patois* also reinforced the perception of the French Canadian as being different or peculiar, and certainly capable of exhibiting a strange behavior."[70] That is the effect of Dewey's book, published nearly half a century later, in upstate New York. Thus, in much the same way that minstrel shows demeaned people of color, poems like Day's and Dewey's made French-Canadian descendants appear inferior to their anglophone counterparts in northern communities.

This practice apparently was not confined to the northeastern United States. The poetry of an Irish physician of Montréal, William Henry Drummond, became popular following the 1897 publication of his first book, *The Habitant and Other French-Canadian Poems*, poems that used French-Canadian dialect. Day and Dewey probably were familiar with Drummond's poetry. Historian Jay Gitlin has found that the practice existed even earlier in the upper Midwest, roughly from the mid- to late nineteenth century. As Grosse Pointe, Michigan, strove to cultivate a reputation as an elite, white, Anglo-Saxon community, Gitlin argues, it relegated its French population to "local color" with stereotypes and patois: "The French are portrayed as peasants incapable of progress, and their language is reduced to gibberish." In one 1886 story that Gitlin recounts, the couple portrayed in the work "seem to be characters in a French habitant minstrel show."[71] The poetry of Day and Dewey had the same effect in the Northeast.

In conclusion, during the 1940s Catholic residents of Plattsburgh, assisted by other groups in the city, continued to develop their institutions. While those Catholic institutions appear to have become somewhat less ethnic in orientation during World War II and the early years of the Cold War, they did not show evidence of a decline in their religious orientation. The network of women and men religious who served those Catholic establishments in Plattsburgh were increasingly US-born by midcentury. In that period, they appear to have worked harder to help the community retain its Catholic traditions over its Franco-American heritage. Subtle forms of prejudice, reflected in Herbert Dewey's poetry, may have worked to promote a loosening of ethnic attachments at midcentury.

Conclusion

Nearly three and a half centuries after Samuel de Champlain made his excursion to what became upstate New York, pundits were still commenting about his journey and its aftereffects on the region. In July 1943, the *Plattsburgh Press-Republican* began an editorial commemorating the seventy-fifth anniversary of St. John the Baptist Church with a paragraph about Champlain's 1609 voyage to the North Country and his discovery of "a choice jewel for the crown of the beloved France," the lake that now bears his name. "Years later and not far from the spot where Champlain and his companions entered the lake," the editor continued, "the village of Plattsburgh was founded and the character of the immigrants who organized this community teaches us as a nation a much needed lesson." The editor went on to describe the contributions of immigrant Catholics to the village, emphasizing that "they carried with them into this vast wilderness the three great freedoms—the church, the school and the town meeting, each in its own right our precious heritage."[1] This community study of Plattsburgh, New York, has focused on the contributions of Catholic immigrants in creating churches, schools, and charitable or fraternal organizations over a century of historical time. The "lessons" of their migration and settlement are as instructive to contemporary society as they were when this writer penned their lines in 1943, for the United States today still strives to understand and appreciate the religious and cultural diversity that immigrant groups bring to the country.

Plattsburgh presents an interesting community study of the effects of transnationalism and of the evolution of the borderlands region over historical time. Twenty miles away from the Canada–US border, and just sixty miles south of Montréal, the largest French-speaking population center in North America, Plattsburgh lies geographically closer to the French-

Canadian cultural hearth than do many other francophone population centers of the US Northeast. Despite that proximity, it developed in a number of respects differently from other, more studied French-Canadian cities of New England.

One reason is that Plattsburgh had a smaller French-Canadian population base than did those other communities. They drew far larger numbers because they had industrial jobs in the textile mills and shoe factories to offer Canadian immigrants. Rural, upstate New York tended to offer work in farming, mining, and lumbering and therefore did not attract as many immigrants as the larger industrial cities did. Without a critical mass, Plattsburgh could not sustain a French-language newspaper, or French-Canadian ethnic societies of comparable size, or even the French language for the same duration as those more populated urban centers.

Another reason has to do with the composition of the religious congregations. This monograph has shared much about the role of the religious personnel who fled to Canada to avoid religious persecution in France and who then remigrated to US cities like Plattsburgh to serve Catholic institutions. It has also shed light on the critical role men and women religious born in Canada played in the development of Catholic institutions and history in the North Country. Besides exploring the immigration of people of French-Canadian birth, this work has examined the migration of English speakers from Canada to the United States, particularly in its consideration of the evolution of a group of English-speaking nuns in a francophone religious order. In sum, the ethnic composition of the religious orders that served in Plattsburgh contributed to its cultural diversity and to its different evolution from other francophone centers in the United States.

Among the first religious orders to serve Plattsburgh, the Order of Mary Immaculate and the Grey Nuns of the Cross were ethnically mixed. From their origins in the village, both congregations had Irish descendants in their convent or rectory. This had a profound impact on the community's ethnic relations, particularly between residents of Irish and French-Canadian descent, who showed more cooperation in Plattsburgh over time than could be found in many other northeastern cities.

Although they were a Catholic order of women religious, the Sisters of Charity of Ottawa taught in Plattsburgh's public school system for thirty-seven years, and they founded a nonsectarian hospital to serve the community's needs. Their schools and hospital came about as the direct result of the efforts of people of different faith traditions who assisted them. Those interdenominational efforts mitigated the kinds of religious tensions that existed in other cities of the Northeast, including those tensions fomented by anti-Catholic groups such as the Ku Klux Klan in the 1920s.

The collaboration of lay and veiled women in creating, financing, and supporting Catholic institutions in Plattsburgh underscores another important theme. Their foundational work created pathways that pushed social boundaries and expanded economic opportunities for women throughout the century from 1850 to 1950. The efforts of these women in establishing Catholic schools and a hospital in Plattsburgh gave younger women access to education and to professions like nursing. These opportunities, as the composition of their student bodies attest, were open to women of different faith traditions.

Yet even while reducing the possibilities for ethnic and religious conflict, in part by promoting the celebration of different cultural traditions and the acceptance of non-Catholics at their institutions, the Catholic orders that served Plattsburgh also sowed some seeds of intolerance. They did so through their promotion of minstrel shows in the twentieth century as a form of entertainment to raise funds to support their establishments. Perhaps unwittingly, they devalued people of color and embedded within Catholic institutions the grains of racism. Understanding this history helps us comprehend to some extent the persistence of racism among Catholic-affiliated groups in contemporary society.

Today we hear much in corporate America, higher education, and other parts of society about the themes of diversity, equity, and inclusion. What we observe in the migrations of Catholics across the northern border and their settlement in Plattsburgh is how they fashioned Catholic institutions from 1850 to 1950 that promoted similar themes. This book has focused on the religious and ethnic diversity the Catholic religious orders fostered in the United States, while not overlooking the seeds of racism they may have sowed, however inadvertently. The lessons learned from Catholic immigrants from the North, as the *Press-Republican* editor pointed out in 1943, were valuable for the country as a whole. This is still true today. As the United States contemplates contemporary migrations across the southern border and from other regions of the world, it would do well to recall the contributions and tolerance of the immigrants who crossed its northern border.

Afterword

The middle of the twentieth century marked the apex of Plattsburgh's Catholic institutions. Since then, nearly all of the religious orders have left the city, and most of the institutions these men and women religious conducted have either closed or merged with others in Plattsburgh. These developments in the city ran parallel to those taking place within the larger Roman Catholic Church. The next few pages will provide a brief description of what happened in Plattsburgh from the 1950s to the present time; a more detailed account of their history awaits another author.

By the middle of the twentieth century, Champlain Valley Hospital had an aging physical plant that had reached its capacity in number of patients, was not fireproof, and needed updating to meet the needs of patients and staff. An architectural firm from New York City inspected the building in 1946 and urged the hospital's board of directors to consider replacing the structure. Two years later, in 1948, the Clinton County Medical Association recommended that Champlain Valley Hospital merge with Physicians' Hospital—to eliminate the duplication of staff, equipment, and facilities—and the boards of the two hospitals began discussions about the idea as they considered the medical needs of the community.[1]

But the two hospitals did not pursue a merger until two decades later. The Champlain Valley Hospital Board of Directors instead embarked upon a $750,000 campaign to build a new hospital wing of three stories, but the capital campaign was not successful and achieved only about one-third of its goal. As a result, Champlain Valley Hospital had to mortgage its facility and carry a debt of over $400,000 into the early 1960s.[2]

This was not the only financial challenge Champlain Valley Hospital faced. By the late 1950s, enrollments dropped at the School of Nursing, in part because more young women chose to pursue nurse-training programs that led to a college degree, with which they could gain supervisory and nurse-teacher positions and higher salaries. Declining enrollments led to the School of Nursing running at a substantial deficit, because the costs of training students exceeded the revenues generated by tuition. To limit Champlain Valley Hospital's financial liability, the board of directors separated the nursing school from the hospital—a move approved in 1958 by the New York State Board of Regents.[3]

Another survey of the hospital, requested by the Grey Nuns of the Sacred Heart, concluded in 1961 that merging Plattsburgh's two hospitals served as the best plan of action for the community. The Grey Nuns subsequently announced their decision to withdraw from Champlain Valley Hospital and Nursing School, and they left Plattsburgh in 1963. Lay personnel replaced the sisters at both the hospital and the nursing school.[4]

With the support of the Clinton County Medical Society, the boards of Physicians' and Champlain Valley Hospitals finally agreed to a merger in 1965, forming Champlain Valley Physicians Hospital Medical Center in January 1967 on the Physicians' Hospital site. The State of New York purchased the property of Champlain Valley Hospital in that same year to support the expansion goals of the State University College at Plattsburgh. The following year, 1968, the women's auxiliaries of both hospitals also merged.[5]

The School of Nursing gave up its independent charter in 1969 when it relocated to the site of Physicians' Hospital and became again a hospital diploma school. But it did not survive. In 1976, the Champlain Valley Physicians Hospital School of Nursing began the transfer of its program to Clinton Community College.[6]

Closures and mergers also took place among Plattsburgh's other Catholic institutions, even while some new buildings sprang up. The grade school of St. John's burned in 1955, and the parish built a new elementary school that opened in 1958. Displaced from St. John's convent, on which site the new school was being built, the Sisters of Mercy moved to the Loretta Residence in 1955, in turn displacing the aged women who resided there. When the Sisters of Mercy moved back to St. John's, the order sold the Loretta.[7]

In 1958, Our Lady of Victory Secretarial School opened under the direction of Sr. Theresa Martel, picking up where the defunct Loretta Business School had left off. The Sisters of Charity of St. Louis had started offering business classes in Québec as early as 1918, but they developed most of their business programs in the province after World

War II. Their secretarial school in Plattsburgh, the last one they founded in North America, functioned until 1993 when Sr. Theresa retired and no sister from her congregation could take over the direction of the school. When the secretarial school closed, the students who had completed the first year of the two-year program continued their education at Clinton Community College.[8]

In the wake of the Second Vatican Council that met from 1962 to 1965, many men and women religious questioned their apostolic involvement and chose to leave religious life. To take one quantitative example, of the 141 women who made their first profession to join the congregation of the Sisters of Charity of St. Louis in North America, 83 (59 percent) left the order between 1965 and 1975, the decade following the conclusion of Vatican II. The significant drop in vocations affected not only hospital staffing but also Catholic school systems in Plattsburgh, throughout the United States, and even around the world.[9]

Along with the decline in vocations, Catholic schools faced the challenge of lower enrollments during the sixties. St. Peter's parish dedicated a new elementary-school building in 1960, but the Brothers of Christian Instruction withdrew from St. Peter's School in that year due to a shortage of personnel and to focus on secondary-level teaching, and the Dominican Sisters took charge of the boys.[10] Half a decade later, St. Peter's had to close its high school when the Dominican Sisters withdrew. The sisters had staffed St. Peter's High School for girls since 1925, but in 1966 they faced low enrollments and a shortage of personnel. A lack of professions and the need to hire lay teachers for their academy in Fall River, Massachusetts—"our principal source of income," they informed the bishop—required the order to reallocate personnel and resources. Some Dominican Sisters continued their association with the parish until 2002.[11]

Our Lady of Victory parish opened a new elementary school, Notre Dame, for students in grades one through eight in 1961. Initially staffed by the Sisters of Charity and one lay teacher, Notre Dame School replaced the grade school of Our Lady of Victory Academy. When the academy closed in 1969, it became the Our Lady of Victory Secretarial School.[12]

In 1965, in a joint venture with the Diocese of Ogdensburg and the New York State Health Department, the Sisters of Charity of St. Louis opened Sacred Heart Home in a new building. The seventy-four-bed nursing home replaced the twenty-nine-bed facility at Our Lady of Victory Academy. Several decades later, the administration passed from the sisters to private hands.[13]

Before the Oblate priests withdrew from Plattsburgh, one of its members made a singular contribution. In 1971, Rev. Roland St. Pierre, O.M.I., became the first Catholic priest in the country to become mayor of a US city. St. Pierre, who had formerly served as the pastor of St. Peter's Church, was a Democrat who switched to the Republican Party, helping the GOP to recapture the mayoralty after two decades of Democratic control.[14]

It is unlikely that the St. John Baptist Association aided in St. Pierre's victory, because the organization was by then on its way out. Declining membership resulted in a situation where, by November 1973, the St. John Baptist Association could no longer raise the funds necessary to maintain its property, and it faced foreclosure. Consequently, the society sold the River Street property it had owned since 1923, effectively bringing an end to a once-vibrant French Catholic society in the city.[15]

On the heels of the closures of St. Peter's High School and Our Lady of Victory Academy, St. John's became a Central High School in September 1969 for fourteen parishes from Plattsburgh and surrounding towns. In the mid-1970s, St. John's Academy and Mount Assumption Institute engaged in talks about merging their high schools. When parents of St. John's rejected the plan, to remain viable Mount Assumption opened its doors to young women and became a coeducational school, beginning with the 1976–1977 academic year. But it struggled, and its fundraising efforts yielded little return; a campaign for Mount Assumption Institute in 1979, for instance, generated $61,000 but cost $37,000 to conduct.[16]

By 1977, the Order of Mary Immaculate, which had in the past supplied a chaplain to Champlain Valley Physicians Hospital, experienced personnel shortages and had to limit its coverage to five days a week. In the next year, the Oblates could no longer provide a regular chaplain to the hospital. The Bishop of Ogdensburg acknowledged the order's limitations but expressed his hope that the Oblates could continue staffing "St. Peter's Church in Plattsburgh because this is one of our largest and most important parishes."[17]

But the Order of Mary Immaculate could only supply priests to Plattsburgh for another decade. In 1986, the Oblate order and the Diocese of Ogdensburg signed a three-year contract that effectively constituted a transition plan. Among other measures, the agreement stipulated that real and personal church property remain in the name of St. Peter's parish and that Oblate funds not be commingled with those of the parish. Over the next three years, the bishop and the Oblates finalized their agreements for the order to turn St. Peter's parish over to the diocese, a process that concluded when the Oblates departed in 1989.[18]

In that same year, St. John's Academy and Mount Assumption Institute, under directives from the diocese, resolved their differences and merged to form Seton Catholic Central, housed initially in the former Mount Assumption building. Resident students continued to contribute to the financial stability of the newly consolidated school. Today, the institution lives on as Seton Catholic in another building in Plattsburgh and still admits international students, hosted by members of the community, to assist it financially. The Brothers of Christian Instruction no longer teach at the school, the order dissolved its New York state incorporation in 2017, and the remaining brothers moved to the order's provincial house in Alfred, Maine.[19]

In 1992, Our Lady of Victory parish changed the French name of its elementary school from Notre Dame to Our Lady of Victory Academy. A decade later, the parish could no longer support the school, and its elementary students in the fall of 2002 had to attend either St. John's Academy or St. Peter's School to receive a Catholic education. Four years later, St. Peter's and St. John's elementary schools merged to form Seton Academy in the building of the former St. Peter School.[20] Today, the school is part of Seton Catholic and is housed in the same building.

In conclusion, not only the schools but also the parishes have now merged. In 2020, the three Catholic parishes of Our Lady of Victory, St. John, and St. Peter began consolidating to form Holy Cross parish under one pastor.[21] Similar mergers have taken place in other northeastern communities from the middle of the twentieth century to the present, reflecting the decline and consolidation of Catholic institutions founded and staffed, to a large degree, by Canadian immigrants and their descendants.

Appendix

Table 1. Nativity of the Oblate Priests of St. Peter's Parish

Year	Place of Birth	Number
1860	France	2
1870	France	2
	Canada	1
1880	France	2
1892	France	1
	Canada	2
1900	France	1
	French Canada	3
1905	French Canada	4
	United States	1
1910	French Canada	6
1915	French Canada	2
	United States	2
1920	France	2
	United States	2
1925	France	1
	Canada	1
	French Canada	1
	United States	2
1930	France	1
	French Canada	2
	United States	2
1940	French Canada	2
	United States	5
1950	French Canada	1
	United States	5

Sources: *US Census; 1860, 1870, 1880, 1900, 1910, 1920, 1930, 1940, 1950; NY Census, 1892, 1905, 1915, 1925.*

Table 2. Nativity of the Grey Nuns of the Cross at D'Youville Convent

Year	Place of Birth	Number
1870	Canada	9
	Ireland	1
	United States	2
1880	Canada	10
	Ireland	1
	United States	4
	Norway	1
1892	Canada	12
	United States	2
1900	French Canada	15
	Ireland	1
	United States	3
	England	1
1905	French Canada	16
	English Canada	1
	Prince Edward Island	1
	Ireland	1
	United States	4
1910	French Canada	13
	Canada (Irish)	1
	United States	5
1915	Canada	9
	United States	8
1920	English Canada	12
	United States	10

Sources: *US Census, 1870, 1880, 1900, 1910, 1920*; *NY Census, 1892, 1905, 1915*.

Table 3. Nativity of the Grey Nuns at Champlain Valley Hospital

Year	Place of Birth	Number
1911	Canada	6
	United States	3
1915	Canada	5
	United States	4
1920	English Canada	3
	Canada (Irish)	4
	French Canada	3
	United States	3
1925	Canada	12
	United States	3
1930	English Canada	11
	Ireland	2
	United States	2
1940	English Canada	8
	United States	7
1950	Canada	7
	United States	6
	England	1

Sources: Because the *NY Census, 1915*, indicates that all nine women religious had US citizenship, which was unlikely given that this was a Canadian order, the figures on their nativity were corrected with records generated by the ASCO. Figures for 1911 and 1915 come from: États de la Maison-Mère et des Autres Missions, 1897–1927, 247, 303, microfilm, COO; List, Soeurs de la Charité d'Ottawa Missioned in Plattsburgh, 1860–1921, and supplement, ASCO. Figures for other years come from: *US Census, 1920, 1930, 1940, 1950; NY Census, 1925.*

Table 4. Nativity of the Brothers of Christian Instruction

Year	Place of Birth	Number
1905	France	2
	French Canada	4
1910	France	5
	French Canada	7
1915	France	2
	French Canada	3
1920	France	1
	Canada	2
	United States	5
1925	France	3
	Canada	6
	United States	6
1930	France	4
	French Canada	9
	English Canada	3
	United States	3
1940	France	1
	French Canada	7
	English Canada	2
	United States	9
1950	France	1
	French Canada	6
	Canada (Irish)	2
	United States	13

Sources: *NY Census, 1905, 1915, 1925*; *US Census, 1910, 1920, 1930, 1940, 1950*.

Table 5. Nativity of the Boarding Students of the Grey Nuns at D'Youville Convent

Year	Place of Birth	Number	Surname	Number
1870	Canada	3	French	3
	United States	14	Non-French	14
1880	Canada	0	French	4
	United States	21	Non-French	17
1892	Canada	2	French	5
	United States	21	Non-French	18
1900	Canada	4	French	17
	French Canada	1	Non-French	38
	United States	46		
	Unknown	4		
1905	Bonaventure Island	1	French	43
	French Canada	3	Non-French	20
	United States	59		
1910	Canada	2	French	18
	United States	38	Non-French	22
1915	Canada	2	French	15
	United States	32	Non-French	19

Sources: *US Census, 1870, 1880, 1900, 1910; NY Census, 1892, 1905, 1915.*

Table 6. Nativity of the Diocesan Priests at Our Lady of Victory Parish

Year	Place of Birth	Number
1910	French Canada	1
	France	1
1915	n/a	
1920	French Canada	2
1925	French Canada	2
1930	French Canada	1
1940	French Canada	1
	Holland	1
1950	United States	2

Sources: *US Census, 1910, 1920, 1930, 1940, 1950; NY Census, 1925.*

Table 7. Nativity of the Diocesan Priests at St. John the Baptist Parish

Year	Place of Birth	Number
1860	Ireland	1
1870	Ireland	1
1880	Ireland	1
1892	Ireland	1
	United States	1
1900	Ireland	1
	United States	1
1905	Ireland	1
	United States	1
1910	United States	2
1915	United States	2
1920	United States	2
1925	United States	2
1930	United States	2
1940	United States	3
1950	United States	3
	Canada	1

Sources: *US Census, 1860, 1870, 1880, 1900, 1910, 1920, 1930, 1940, 1950; NY Census, 1892, 1905, 1915, 1925.*

Table 8. Nativity of the Sisters of Mercy

Year	Place of Birth	Number
1925	United States	9
	Canada	1
	Newfoundland	1
	Ireland	2
1930	United States	10
	English Canada	1
	Newfoundland	1
1940	United States	14
	French Canada	1
	Newfoundland	2
	Irish Free State	1
1950	United States	14
	Canada	3
	Newfoundland	2

Sources: *NY Census, 1925; US Census, 1930, 1940, 1950.* Data represents only the sisters engaged as teachers or administrators at St. John Academy or the Loretta Business School. The Sisters of Mercy who lived at the Loretta Residence in 1940 and 1950 are therefore included in this data, but those from the 1925 and 1930 censuses who were postulants or their trainers at the novitiate are not included.

Table 9. Nativity of the Sisters of Charity of St. Louis at Our Lady of Victory

Year	Place of Birth	Number
1915	n/a	
1920	France	3
	French Canada	1
	Ireland	1
	England	1
	United States	2
1925	France	3
	French Canada	4
	England	3
	United States	1
1930	France	1
	French Canada	5
	England	1
	United States	1
1940	French Canada	7
	United States	7
1950	Canada	7
	England	1
	United States	7

Sources: *US Census, 1920, 1930, 1940, 1950; NY Census, 1925.*

Table 10. Nativity of the Dominican Sisters at St. Peter's Parish

Year	Place of Birth	Number
1925	French Canada	3
	Canada	1
	United States	3
1930	French Canada	6
	English Canada	1
	United States	7
1940	French Canada	4
	United States	13
1950	Canada	3
	United States	16

Sources: *NY Census, 1925*; *US Census, 1930, 1940, 1950.*

NB: Data on the teaching orders of men and women religious in the tables above excludes the brothers or nuns identified in the censuses as cooks, housekeepers, seamstresses, janitors, or other occupations in which the person would likely not have had a significant role in the formation of students.

Abbreviations

AD-NDC: Archives Deschâtelets-NDC des Missionaires Oblats de Marie Immaculée, Province Notre-Dame-du-Cap, Richelieu, Québec

AG-OMI: Archivum Generale O.M.I., Romae, Italia

ASCO: Archives des Soeurs de la Charité d'Ottawa, Ottawa, Ontario

BCI: Archives of the Brothers of Christian Instruction, Notre Dame Province, Alfred, Maine

CCCO: County Clerk's Office, Clinton County Courthouse, Plattsburgh, New York

CCHA: Clinton County Historical Association, Plattsburgh, New York

CCHO: County Historian's Office, Clinton County Courthouse, Plattsburgh, New York

COO: City of Ottawa Archives, Ottawa, Ontario

CVPH: Champlain Valley Physicians Hospital Archives, University of Vermont Health Network, Plattsburgh, New York

DSH: Archives of the Dominican Sisters of Hope, Ossining, New York

FIC: Archives des Frères de l'Instruction Chrétienne, La Prairie, Québec

FLSC: Feinberg Library Special Collections, State University of New York, Plattsburgh, New York

GNSH: Archives of the Grey Nuns of the Sacred Heart, Philadelphia, Pennsylvania

NYS: New York State Archives, Albany, New York

OPL: Ottawa Public Library Ottawa Room, Ottawa, Ontario

PPL: Plattsburgh Public Library Local History Collection, Plattsburgh, New York

RCDO: Archives of the Roman Catholic Diocese of Ogdensburg, Ogdensburg, New York

SCSL: Archives des Soeurs de la Charité de Saint-Louis du Québec, Lévis, Québec

SPP: St. Peter's Parish, Plattsburgh, New York

Notes

Introduction

1. William G. Tyrrell, *Champlain and the French in New York* (Albany: University of the State of New York; State Education Department, 1959), 15; John Herd Thompson and Mark Paul Richard, "Canadian History in a North American Context," in Mark Kasoff and Patrick James, eds., *Canadian Studies in the New Milennium*, 2nd ed. (Toronto: University of Toronto Press, 2013), 40–41; *The Souvenir Industrial Edition of Plattsburgh, 1897* (1897; repr., Plattsburgh, NY: Corner-Stone Bookshop, 1978), 16; David Hackett Fischer, *Champlain's Dream* (New York: Simon and Schuster, 2008), 263; Allan S. Everest, *Briefly Told: Plattsburgh, New York, 1784–1984* (Plattsburgh, NY: Clinton County Historical Association, 1984), 1; Rev. John Talbot Smith, *A History of the Diocese of Ogdensburg* (New York: John W. Lovell [1884]), 54–55.

2. Yves Roby, *Les Franco-Américains de la Nouvelle-Angleterre (1776–1930)* (Sillery, Québec: Septentrion, 1990), 13; Armand Chartier, *Histoire des Franco-Américains de la Nouvelle-Angleterre, 1775–1990* (Sillery, Québec: Septentrion, 1991), 14; Smith, *A History of the Diocese of Ogdensburg*, 20–22; Patrick Lacroix, "Promises to Keep: French Canadians as Revolutionaries and Refugees, 1775–1800," *Journal of Early American History* 9 (2019): 71–72. While these francophones from British North America were migrating to northeastern New York, aristocrats fleeing the Reign of Terror in France attempted to create a utopian colony called Castorland in northwestern New York in the late eighteenth and early nineteenth centuries. On their efforts, see Edith Pilcher, *Castorland: French Refugees in the Western Adirondacks, 1793–1814* (Harrison, NY: Harbor Hill, 1985.)

3. Anastasia Pratt, *Plattsburgh through Time* (Charleston, SC: Arcadia, 2015), 3; Historical Sketches and Photographs of School Systems in Cities and Villages, ca. 1850–1920, Series A3042, Subseries 1: Historical Sketches, typescript, Box 2, Folder 11: Plattsburgh, 1, NYS; *The Souvenir Industrial Edition of Plattsburgh*, 25, 63.

4. Smith, *A History of the Diocese of Ogdensburg*, 26; Pratt, *Plattsburgh through Time*, 3; Yearbook and Church Directory of St. Peter's Church, Plattsburg,

N.Y. [1931–1932], PPL, Pam334. Older sources varied in the use of the letter "h" in spelling Plattsburgh.

5. Roby, *Les Franco-Américains de la Nouvelle-Angleterre*, 14; Chartier, *Histoire des Franco-Américains de la Nouvelle-Angleterre*, 16; Robert Rumilly, *Histoire des Franco-Américains* (Montréal: Chez l'auteur, 1958), 19–21; Allan Greer, *The Patriots and the People: The Rebellion of 1837 in Rural Lower Canada* (Toronto: University of Toronto Press, 1993), 341.

6. Rumilly, *Histoire des Franco-Américains*, 22; Roswell A. Hogue, *Centennial, 1853–1953: St. Peter's Roman Catholic Church, Plattsburgh, N.Y.* (Plattsburgh, NY: St. Peter's Church, 1953), 10.

7. See, for example, Guy Omeron Coolidge, *The French Occupation of the Champlain Valley from 1609 to 1759* (1938; Fleischmanns, NY: Purple Mountain Press, 1999), 172; Smith, *A History of the Diocese of Ogdensburg*, 29; Everest, *Briefly Told*, 16.

8. Yolande Lavoie, *L'émigration des Québécois aux États-Unis de 1840 à 1930* (Québec: Éditeur officiel du Québec, 1979), 45; Yves Roby, "L'évolution économique du Québec et l'émigrant (1850–1929)," in Claire Quintal, ed., *L'émigrant québécois vers les États-Unis (1850–1920)* (Québec: Le Conseil de la Vie française en Amérique, 1982), 8, 12–13, 17, 19; Roby, *Les Franco-Américains de la Nouvelle-Angleterre*, 33–45; Paul-André Linteau, René Durocher, and Jean-Claude Robert, *Histoire du Québec contemporain: De la Confédération à la crise (1867–1929)* (Montréal: Boréal, 1989), 168.

9. On migrations to the Midwest, see Jean Lamarre, *The French Canadians of Michigan: Their Contribution to the Development of the Saginaw Valley and the Keweenaw Peninsula, 1840–1914*, trans. Howard Keillor and Hermione Jack (Detroit: Wayne State University Press, 2003). Among the few accounts of migrations to New York, see Susan Ouellette on rural upstate New York and Daniel J. Walkowicz on urban-industrial Cohoes in the capital district: Ouellette, ed., *Conflict and Accommodation in North Country Communities, 1850–1930* (Lanham, Maryland: University Press of America, 2005); Walkowitz, *Worker City, Company Town: Iron and Cotton-Worker Protest in Troy and Cohoes, New York, 1855–84* (Urbana: University of Illinois Press, 1978). For an exploration of the French cultural heritage of northern New York, see Peter C. van Lent, *The Hidden Heritage / L'Héritage caché: The French Folk Culture of Northern New York* (Malone, NY: Malone Arts Council, 1988).

10. Susan Ouellette, "Mobility, Class, and Ethnicity: French Canadians in Plattsburgh, New York, 1850–1880," in Ouellette, ed., *Conflict and Accommodation in North Country Communities*, 38n5.

Chapter One

1. Yearbook and Church Directory of St. Peter's Church [1931–1932]; St. John's Church, Plattsburgh, New York, 1868–1943, PPL, Pam415; Peter S.

Palmer, *Historical Sketch of Plattsburgh, N.Y. from Its First Settlement to Jan. 1, 1893* (1871, supplemented 1893; repr., Elizabethtown, NY: Crown Point Press, 1968), 80–81; Ouellette, "Mobility, Class, and Ethnicity," 27; *The Souvenir Industrial Edition of Plattsburgh, 1897*, 31.

2. Hogue, *Centennial*, 18–19; Sister Mary Christine Taylor, *A History of Catholicism in the North Country* (Ogdensburg, NY: Roman Catholic Diocese of Ogdensburg, 1972), 21; *Plattsburgh Daily Republican*, 20 November 1916, 3; texte dactylographié, Gaston Carrière, O.M.I., "Un siècle d'apostolat à Plattsburgh" (1953), 1, AD-NDC, LE6401.L91R7; texte dactylographié, Leo Deschâtelets, O.M.I., "Notes historiques sur notre maison Saint[-]Pierre de Plattsburgh [et] sur les anciennes missions de Redford, N.Y., de Cadyville, de Morrisonville, de Dannemora [et] de Burlington" [1926], 28 juillet 1853, AD-NDC, LE6401.L91R1; Livre des Déliberations des Syndics de l'Église St. Pierre de Plattsburgh, 1853–1935, 1–3, SPP; Yearbook and Church Directory of St. Peter's Church [1931–1932]. All translations in this work from French to English are my own. The Bishop of Albany must have been concerned about the possibility of losing French-Canadian "souls" to Protestant churches. In 1856, just a few years after the bishop authorized the Oblates to organize a French-Canadian national parish in Plattsburgh, francophones met to organize the First Regular French Baptist Church and Society of Chazy, a village near Plattsburgh, and elected five men with French surnames as their trustees. Deed Book 28, p. 406, CCCO.

3. Livre des Déliberations des Syndics, 2.

4. Carrière, "Un siècle d'apostolat à Plattsburgh," 2; Deschâtelets, "Notes historiques sur notre maison," 12 octobre 1856.

5. Yearbook and Church Directory of St. Peter's Church [1931–1932]; Hogue, *Centennial*, 24; Ouellette, "Mobility, Class, and Ethnicity," 26; Carrière, "Un siècle d'apostolat à Plattsburgh," 3.

6. Mortgages Book X, pp. 359–61, CCCO; Livre des Déliberations des Syndics, 3; Hogue, *Centennial*, 21; Yearbook and Church Directory of St. Peter's Church [1931–1932]. French-Canadian women organized bazaars to raise money for the church in other years as well; in 1864, for example, the church netted $600 as a result of their efforts. *Plattsburgh Republican*, 1 March 1862, 3, 10 December 1864, 3; Chroniques de la Maison de Plattsburgh [hereafter SCO Chroniques], vol. 1, 19 décembre 1864, 86, 25 décembre 1864, 87, ASCO, M005,SA,SS2.

7. Hogue, *Centennial*, 24; Taylor, *A History of Catholicism in the North Country*, 22; Smith, *A History of the Diocese of Ogdensburg*, 203; Yearbook and Church Directory of St. Peter's Church [1931–1932]; Deschâtelets, "Notes historiques sur notre maison," December 1, 1854.

8. *Republican*, 8 July 1854, 2. English-language sources, such as newspapers and government documents, typically used the English name of the church. The names St. Pierre and St. Peter will be used interchangeably in the narrative.

9. *Republican*, 8 July 1854, 2; Livre des Déliberations des Syndics, 3–4. The form of this announcement in 1855 likely was to comply with existing New

York law, for the trustees of St. Pierre Church noted a decade later in their minutes that they had to announce the parish elections scheduled for 5 May 1864 for three consecutive Sundays prior to the election to conform to New York requirements for religious societies. The bishop occasionally would direct the parish to follow New York statutes. In 1869, for example, Rev. John Conroy, the Bishop of Albany, wrote the pastor of St. Pierre Church to have the parish become incorporated following legislation passed in 1863. The trustees voted to do so, and the transfer of church property from the old to the new corporation was recorded at the county clerk's office later in the year. Livre des Délibérations des Syndics, 28, 57–58; Deed Book 60, pp. 52–53, CCCO.

10. Pamphlet, "St. Peter's Parish 150th Anniversary" [2003], Phyllis Wells Collection, FLSC, 2011.1.

11. Carrière, "Un siècle d'apostolat à Plattsburgh," 4–5; Livre des Délibérations des Syndics, 6–7.

12. Émilien Lamirande, *Élisabeth Bruyère: Fondatrice des Soeurs de la Charité d'Ottawa* ([Saint-Laurent]: Bellarmin, 1993), 417; Eugène [Guigues, O.M.I.], Évêque de Bytown, à Monseigneur [d'Albany], 16 décembre 1857, AD-NDC, JM401.C21R4.

13. P. Duchaussois, O.M.I., *The Grey Nuns in the Far North (1867–1917)* (Toronto: McClelland and Stewart, 1919), 13–16, 28, 43.

14. Booklet, Sister Paul-Emile, s.c.o., "Mother Élisabeth Bruyère: A Pioneer of Bilingual Education in Eastern Ontario" [198?], 6–8, OPL; Peter Tremblay Business and Personal Papers, box 4, folder 61, FLSC, 69.9.

15. Sister Paul-Emile, s.c.o., *Mother Elisabeth Bruyere: Her Life and Her Work*, The Grey Nuns of the Cross, vol. 1: General Thrust, 1845–1876, trans. Sister Gabrielle L. Jean, s.c.o. ([Ottawa: Sisters of Charity of Ottawa, 1989]), 298, OPL; Soeur Élisabeth Bruyère, Supérieure, Ottawa, au Révérend Père Jean-Joseph Magnan, O.M.I., en France, 27 janvier 1860, dans Élisabeth Bruyère, *Lettres d'Élisabeth Bruyère*, vol. 3: 1857–1862, Jeanne d'Arc Lortie, s.c.o., comp. (Montréal: Médiaspaul et Ottawa: Soeurs de la Charité d'Ottawa, 1998), 269–70.

16. Lamirande, *Élisabeth Bruyère*, 417; SCO Chroniques, vol. 1, 13 août 1860, 1, 18 septembre 1860, 1, 10 octobre 1860, 1–2, 20 octobre 1860, 3; texte dactylographié, "Cadre historique et géographique," 5–6, D'Youville Convent, Plattsburgh, ASCO, M005,SA,SS1,D1; Everest, *Briefly Told*, 21; *Republican*, 17 December 1859, 3, 23 June 1860, 3.

17. SCO Chroniques, vol. 1, 31 octobre 1860, 5, 4 novembre 1860, 9–10; "Cadre historique et géographique," 6.

18. "Cadre historique et géographique," 7. The perception of the Grey Nuns was not accurate here, for St. Pierre had founded a school in 1856 near its church that it initially staffed with lay teachers. Taylor, *A History of Catholicism in the North Country*, 271; Everest, *Briefly Told*, 21.

19. "Cadre historique et géographique," 5, 7; Hogue, *Centennial*, 33; SCO Chroniques, vol. 1, 6 novembre 1860, 10, 15 novembre 1860, 16; *US Census, 1860, 1870*.

20. "Cadre historique et géographique," 7, 11; SCO Chroniques, vol. 1, 13 août 1860, 1, 6 novembre 1860, 10; Deed Book 56, p. 349, CCCO; *US Census, 1860*; *Republican*, 18 February 1893, 1; *The Souvenir Industrial Edition of Plattsburgh*, 31.

21. *US Census, 1860*; SCO Chroniques, vol. 1, 6 novembre 1860, 11. Listed in the 1860 federal census as a farmer, Bernard McKeever was by 1875 the co-owner of a company that sold coal. *Webb's Plattsburgh Directory, 1875–6–7* (New York: W. S. Webb, 1875), 30.

22. "Cadre historique et géographique," 7–8; SCO Chroniques, vol. 1, 9 novembre 1860, 12, 16 novembre 1860, 16.

23. "Cadre historique et géographique," 8; SCO Chroniques, vol. 1, 12 novembre 1860, 13, 15 novembre 1860, 15.

24. "Cadre historique et géographique," 5; Hogue, *Centennial*, 158. The regulations of the Sisters of Charity of Québec also allowed them to make home visits to the sick, and they themselves made 3,900 visits in the suburbs of Québec in 1869. Étienne Berthold, *Les Soeurs de la Charité de Québec: Histoire et patrimoine social* (Québec, Québec: Les Presses de l'Université Laval, 2019), 29.

25. SCO Chroniques, vol. 1, 5 novembre 1860, 10; Registre de la Visite des Malades à Domicile de la Maison de Plattsburg, Commencé le 7 novembre 1860, 1860–1919, 1–19, D'Youville Convent, Plattsburgh, ASCO, M005,SE; États de la Maison-Mère et des Autres Missions, 1845–1896, 47, microfilm, COO; email communication with the author from Dr. Marie Hoffmann, Archiviste en chef, ASCO, 8 July 2020.

26. SCO Chroniques, vol. 1, 8 novembre 1860, 11–12, 9 novembre 1860, 13, 22 novembre 1860, 17.

27. Soeur Élisabeth Bruyère, Ottawa, à Mère Julie Hainault-Deschamps, Supérieure, Montréal, 22 juin 1861, in Bruyère, *Lettres d'Élisabeth Bruyère*, vol. 3, 354–56; List, Soeurs de la Charité d'Ottawa Missioned in Plattsburgh, 1860–1921, ASCO.

28. SCO Chroniques, vol. 1, 16 décembre 1861, 40, 13 janvier 1862, 41, 29 février 1864, 72.

29. Bruyère à Sallaz, 11 novembre 1863, 423, AG-OMI, partagé par AD-NDC, GLPP3071; Carrière, "Un siècle d'apostolat à Plattsburgh," 14.

30. Bruyère à Sallaz, 11 novembre 1863.

31. *Republican*, 15 June 1867, 2; SCO Chroniques, vol. 1, 15 novembre 1860, 16.

32. Bruyère à la Mère St-Vincent de Paul, Supérieure des Soeurs du Bon-Pasteur, Québec, décembre 1860, in Bruyère, *Lettres d'Élisabeth Bruyère*, vol. 3, 314–17.

33. *Republican*, 23 June 1860, 3.
34. *Republican*, 22 June 1861, 3, 9 July 1864, 2; Livre des Déliberations des Syndics, 31 mai 1863, 24; SCO Chroniques, vol. 1, 4 juillet 1864, 80.
35. SCO Chroniques, vol. 1, 4 juillet 1865, 93; Livre des Déliberations des Syndics, 26 mai 1865, 34; *Republican*, 8 July 1865, 2.
36. Yves Roby, *The Franco-Americans of New England: Dreams and Realities*, trans. Mary Ricard (Sillery, Québec: Septentrion, 2004), 94; Félix Gatineau, *History of the Franco-Americans of Southbridge, Massachusetts* (1919; trans., Salem, MA: Elizabeth Blood, 2020), 94.
37. *Plattsburgh Sentinel*, 20 June 1867, 3.
38. "Cadre historique et géographique," 11; SCO Chroniques, vol. 1, 19 mars 1861, 28–29, 17 mars 1865, 89, 17 mars 1868, 109, 17 mars 1869, 121.
39. See Mark Paul Richard, *Loyal but French: The Negotiation of Identity by French-Canadian Descendants in the United States* (East Lansing: Michigan State University Press, 2008), 7–25.
40. SCO Chroniques, vol. 1, 28 décembre 1860, 24, 23 décembre 1863, 65–66, 24 décembre 1864, 87.
41. SCO Chroniques, vol. 1, 25 décembre 1865, 95, 25 décembre 1867, 108, 25 décembre 1869, 143.
42. Margaret Susan Thompson, "Women, Feminism and the New Religious History: Catholic Sisters as a Case Study," in Philip R. Vandermeer and Robert P. Swierenga, eds., *Belief and Behavior: Essays in the New Religious History* (New Brunswick, NJ: Rutgers University Press, 1991), 150, 153; Bruyère à Guigues, 27 décembre 1862, in Bruyère, *Lettres d'Élisabeth Bruyère*, vol. 3, 562–64.
43. SCO Chroniques, vol. 1, 2 février 1864, 71, 20 mars 1864, 74–75.
44. US Department of the Interior, Census Office, *Population of the United States in 1860; Compiled from the Original Returns of the Eighth Census, under the Direction of the Secretary of the Interior* (Washington, DC: Government Printing Office, 1864), 331; *Sentinel*, 7 June 1866, 3.
45. *Sentinel*, 6 December 1866, 3, 4 April 1867, 3, 16 July 1869, 3; *Republican*, 6 April 1867, 2, 17 July 1869, 3.
46. *Sentinel*, 6 December 1866, 3, 4 April 1867, 3, 11 April 1867, 3; Altina Waller, "The Perils of Capitalism: Smith Weed and Entrepreneurship in Northern New York, 1864–1902," *New York History* 75, no. 2 (April 1994): 179, 185; *Republican*, 16 February 1867, 2, 6 April 1867, 2.
47. *Sentinel*, 15 November 1867, 3, 6 December 1867, 3, 3 January 1868, 3; *Republican*, 21 December 1867, 3, 28 December 1867, 3.
48. *Sentinel*, 24 April 1868, 3; "*Republican*, 17 November 1866, 2, 25 April 1868, 3.
49. *Republican*, 25 April 1868, 3; *Le Messager* (Lewiston, Maine) 6 décembre 1892, 28 avril 1893. On the unsuccessful efforts of Québec and Canada to repatriate French-Canadian emigrants, see Robert G. LeBlanc, "Regional

Competition for Franco-American Repatriates, 1870–1930," *Québec Studies* 1 (Spring 1983): 110–29.

50. *Sentinel*, 30 July 1869, 3.

51. *Sentinel*, 20 June 1867, 3.

52. *Sentinel*, 16 July 1869, 3; *Republican*, 17 July 1869, 3; Carrière, "Un siècle d'apostolat à Plattsburgh," 5–6. Available sources shed no further light on this civil suit nor why it was filed in Schenectady. Possibly Carrière, who compiled the Oblate historical notes more than eighty years after these events took place, was referring to the case heard in the Platttsburgh Circuit Court in 1871.

53. Deschâtelets, "Notes historiques sur notre maison," 1 octobre 1869, le lundi de Paques 1870.

54. *Sentinel*, 20 May 1870, 3, 1 July 1870, 3; *US Census, 1870*.

55. *Republican*, 2 July 1870, 3; *Sentinel*, 24 June 1870, 3, 8 July 1870, 3.

56. *Sentinel*, 5 June 1868, 3, 8 July 1870, 3; SCO Chroniques, vol. 1, 24 juin 1870, 154, 4 juillet 1870, 156–57.

57. *Sentinel*, 8 July 1870, 3; *Republican*, 9 July 1870, 3; Hélène Plouffe, "Vive la Canadienne," 2013, canadianencyclopedia.ca.

58. Roby, *The Franco-Americans of New England*, 94–95.

59. *Sentinel*, 20 January 1871, 3, 27 January 1871, 3, 31 March 1871, 3; Supreme Court Judgments Book 5, 203, CCCO.

60. *Sentinel*, 24 March 1871, 3, 31 March 1871, 3; *Republican*, 25 March 1871, 3; Yearbook and Church Directory of St. Peter's Church [1931–1932]. Members of the new society called it the St. John Baptist Association, not the St. John the Baptist Association. *Sentinel*, 24 March 1871, 3; *Republican*, 4 September 1875, 4.

61. *Sentinel*, 31 March 1871, 3; *Republican*, 29 June 1872, 3.

62. Linteau, Durocher, and Robert, *Histoire du Québec contemporain*, 258–59, 265–66; Susan Mann Trofimenkoff, *The Dream of Nation: A Social and Intellectual History of Quebec* (Toronto: Gage, 1983), 93, 125.

63. *Sentinel*, 18 September 1868, 3, 31 March 1871, 3, 27 October 1871, 2; *Republican*, 1 April 1871, 3.

64. Ronald A. Petrin, *French Canadians in Massachusetts Politics, 1885–1915: Ethnicity and Political Pragmatism* (Philadelphia: Balch Institute, 1990), 164, 168; C. Stewart Doty, *The First Franco-Americans: New England Life Histories from the Federal Writers' Project, 1938–1939* (Orono: University of Maine Press, 1985), 156.

65. *Sentinel*, 27 October 1871, 2.

66. Historical Sketches and Photographs of School Systems, Subseries 1, 5; letter, inserted in SCO Chroniques, vol. 1, février 1869, between pp. 118 and 119, 2–3; Livre des Déliberations des Syndics, 45; "Cadre historique et géographique," 15.

67. Handwritten notes inserted into SCO Chroniques, 1, vol. 1, février 1869, between pp. 118 and 119.

68. Notes inserted into SCO Chroniques, vol. 1, février 1869, 3–4, 6; "Cadre historique et géographique," 16; SCO Chroniques, vol. 1, 10 février 1869, 119–20; Historical Sketches and Photographs of School Systems, Subseries 1, 26, and Subseries 2: Photographs, Box 7, Folder 1: Plattsburgh, NYS; James K. McGuire, ed., *The Democratic Party of the State of New York*, vol. 2 ([New York]: United States History Company, 1905), 264, PPL, 329.3974Dem.

69. *Sentinel*, 5 March 1869, 3.

70. Notes inserted into SCO Chroniques, vol. 1, février 1869, 7; Allan S. Everest, "The Grey Nuns in Plattsburgh," *Antiquarian* 7, no. 1 (Fall 1990): 2; "Cadre historique et géographique," 14. Another borderlands area made a similar transfer when the parish school of Frenchville, located in northern Maine's St. John Valley, became a public school in the early 1900s following a fire that destroyed the village's public school. William Leo Lucey, S.J., *The Catholic Church in Maine* (Francestown, NH: Marshall Jones, 1957), 308.

71. Historical Sketches and Photographs of School Systems, Subseries 1, 5; "Cadre historique et géographique," 16; SCO Chroniques, vol. 1, 15 mars 1869, 120, 12 septembre 1869, 132–33, 2 novembre 1869, 138.

72. SCO Chroniques, vol. 1, 3 février 1870, 145.

73. Notes inserted into SCO Chroniques, vol. 1, février 1869, 5; *Sentinel*, 5 March 1869, 3, 11 June 1920, 5; Historical Sketches and Photographs of School Systems, Subseries 1, 5; SCO Chroniques, vol. 1, 4 juillet 1885, 350.

Chapter Two

1. Chapter 324, *Laws of the State of New York Passed at the Ninety-Fourth Session of the Legislature*, vol. 1 (Albany: Argus, 1871), 633–34.

2. Thompson, "Women, Feminism and the New Religious History," 147; Deed Books 56, p. 349, 71, p. 343, 71, p. 345, 72, pp. 611–13, 88, pp. 640–41, CCCO.

3. Chapter 324, *Laws of the State of New York* (1871), 634.

4. [Florent] VandenBerghe, O.M.I., Montréal, au [Père Pierre Aubert, O.M.I., Paris], 26 janvier 1872, 425, AG-OMI, partagé par AD-NDC, GLPP3072.

5. Chapter 528, *Laws of the State of New York, Passed at the Ninety-Fifth Session of the Legislature*, vol. 2 (Albany: V. W. M. Brown, 1872), 1219–20; Lamirande, *Élisabeth Bruyère*, 420.

6. Hogue, *Centennial*, 43; Chapter 418, *Laws of the State of New York* (1871), 827.

7. Mortgage books MM, pp. 307–8, TT, p. 303, CCCO; Deed Books 29, p. 122, 29, pp. 349–50, 39, pp. 42–43, 56, pp. 347–48, 62, pp. 737–38, 62, p. 742, 62, p. 755, 62, p. 767, 62, pp. 786–87, CCCO.

8. Roman Catholic Diocese of Albany, "Past Bishops," 2020, cathedralic.com; Lamirande, *Élisabeth Bruyère*, 419–20; SCO Chroniques, vol. 1, 13 février 1872, 185, 14 février 1872, 185, 17 février 1872, 185, ASCO.

9. Yvon Beaudoin and Gaston Carrière, O.M.I., "Florent Vandenberghe," 2017, omiworld.org; Gaston Carrière, O.M.I., "Joseph Pierre Blaise Aubert," 2017, omiworld.org; VandenBerghe à Aubert, 26 janvier 1872, 424–25.

10. VandenBerghe à Aubert, 23 février 1872, 435–36, AG-OMI, partagé par AD-NDC, GLPP3074; VandenBerghe au Père [Joseph] Fabre, Supérieur Générale, 1 mars 1872, 438, AG-OMI, partagé par AD-NDC, GLPP3180; VandenBerghe à Aubert, 4 mars 1872, 440, AG-OMI, partagé par AD-NDC, GLPP3076.

11. Roby, *Les Franco-Américains de la Nouvelle-Angleterre*, 146; Deschâtelets, "Notes historiques sur notre maison," 1871. On characterizations of French Canadians as clergy-dominated, see, for example, Rev. Alexandre-Louis Mothon, cited in J. Antonin Plourde, *Dominicains au Canada: Livre des documents*, vol. 2: Les cinq fondations avant l'autonomie (1881–1911) (1975), 48; and Robert Cloutman Dexter, "Fifty-Fifty Americans," *World's Work* 48 (August 1924): 369–70.

12. Lamirande, *Élisabeth Bruyère*, 420–23, 427; VandenBerghe à Aubert, 19 janvier 1872, 421–22, underscoring in original, AG-OMI, partagé par AD-NDC, GLPP3071; VandenBerghe à Aubert, 17 octobre 1872, 536, AG-OMI, partagé par AD-NDC, GLPP3095; Deschâtelets, "Notes historiques sur notre maison," 20 octobre 1873.

13. *Plattsburgh Sentinel*, 21 February 1873, 3; Yearbook and Church Directory of St. Peter's Church [1931–1932]; Lamirande, *Élisabeth Bruyère*, 420–21; Deed Books 70, pp. 959–61, 71, p. 342, CCCO; SCO Chroniques, vol. 1, 1 novembre 1888, 388.

14. Lamirande, *Élisabeth Bruyère*, 420; Taylor, *A History of Catholicism in the North Country*, 2; *The Catholic Church in the United States of America*, vol. 3 (New York: Catholic Editing, 1914), 620.

15. *Plattsburgh Republican*, 6 July 1872, 3; SCO Chroniques, vol. 1, 30 juin 1872, 191–92; *Sentinel*, 5 July 1872, 3; Scrapbook, Bishop Edgar P. Wadhams, 1872–1874, RCDO.

16. *Republican*, 3 June 1871, 3.

17. *Republican*, 20 May 1871, 3; SCO Chroniques, vol. 1, 24 juin 1871, 177; *Sentinel*, 30 June 1871, 3.

18. *Sentinel*, 30 June 1871, 3.

19. *Sentinel*, 30 June 1871, 3.

20. *Sentinel*, 21 July 1871, 2, 20 February 1874, 3; Brouillard des Séances de L'Association St-Jean Baptiste, Plattsburgh, NY, 17 juillet 1872—7 juillet [1875], Association St. Jean Baptiste Collection, CCHA, 74.656.0001; *Republican*, 14 February 1874, 1.

21. *Republican*, 30 June 1877, 1. The Oblates and Grey Nuns regularly moved members of their orders among their various missions in Canada and the United States, sometimes reassigning them to places they had previously served, which would explain why Bournigalle was back in Plattsburgh by the late 1870s. Men and women religious were periodically given "obediences" by their superiors that precipitated their reassignments. As Rev. Alexander Trudeau explained to well-wishers before leaving Plattsburgh in 1876, "they were soldiers of Christ, and had no particular home, and were obliged to obey the command of their superiors." *Sentinel*, 22 September 1876, 3.

22. *Sentinel*, 21 June 1878, 3.

23. SCO Chroniques, vol. 1, 6 décembre 1870, 165.

24. SCO Chroniques, vol. 1, 17 mars 1870, 147, 17 mars 1875, 213, 17 mars 1876, 224, 17 mars 1879, 255, 17 mars 1882, 308; *Republican*, 21 March 1874, 1; St. John's Church, Plattsburgh, New York, 1868–1943; Deschâtelets, "Notes historiques sur notre maison," octobre 1879; *US Census, 1880, 1900*; *NY Census, 1892*; *Sentinel*, 27 January 1882, 3, 14 July 1882, 1.

25. SCO Chroniques, vol. 1, 4 juillet 1876, 231.

26. Registre de la Visite des Malades, 1860–1919; SCO Chroniques, vol. 1, 7 janvier 1874, 204, 11 janvier 1874, 204–5, 19 janvier 1874, 205.

27. *Republican*, 4 September 1875, 1; SCO Chroniques, vol. 1, 22 juin 1871, 177, 19 novembre 1873, 202, 5 septembre 1874, 210, 11 octobre 1875, 221, 21 novembre 1875, 222, 12 janvier 1876, 223, 29 août 1876, 233; *Sadliers' Catholic Directory, Almanac, and Ordo, for the Year of Our Lord 1875* (New York: D. & J. Sadlier, 1875), babel.hathitrust.org., 271.

28. SCO Chroniques, vol. 1, 24 décembre 1873, 203.

29. SCO Chroniques, vol. 1, 9 mai 1871, 173.

30. Chapter 353, *Laws of the State of New York Passed at the Ninety-Eighth Session of the Legislature* (Albany: Hugh J. Hastings, 1875), 338; *Sentinel*, 24 December 1875, 1; *Republican*, 25 December 1875, 4.

31. *Sentinel*, 31 December 1875, 2. On the June 1875 legislation, see Chapter 567, *Laws of the State of New York*.

32. *Sentinel*, 7 January 1876, 2, 21 January 1876, 2, 11 February 1876, 3.

33. William C. Fellows, "A Study of the Franco-American Community and the Plattsburgh State Normal School from Its Founding to World War II, 1890–1939" (Honors 125 paper, 14 May 1988), 2–4, FLSC, PAM189/3; *Republican*, 29 January 1876, 1.

34. Yves Frenette, "Macroscopie et microscopie d'un mouvement migratoire: les Canadiens français à Lewiston au XIXe siècle," dans Yves Landry, John A. Dickinson, Suzy Pasleau et Claude Desama, dirs., *Les chemins de la migration en Belgique et au Québec: XVIIe–XXe siècles* (Beauport, Québec: MNH, 1995), 228; Yves Frenette, "Understanding the French Canadians of Lewiston, 1860–1900: An Alternate Framework," *Maine Historical Society Quarterly* 25 (Spring 1986),

205, 213, 222; Yves Frenette, "La genèse d'une communauté canadienne-française en Nouvelle-Angleterre: Lewiston, Maine, 1800–1880" (Thèse de PhD, Université Laval, Québec, 1988), 162.

35. Ouellette, "Mobility, Class, and Ethnicity," 27, 32, 37.

36. Alexandre Belisle, *Histoire de la Presse Franco-Américaine* (Worcester, MA: L'Opinion Publique, 1911), 255–56. Specific details about *Le National*'s founding are not known, but the newspaper in its first edition gave thanks to Paul Girard, E. Erno, and Dr. J. H. LaRocque of Plattsburgh for their valuable support in enabling its publication. *Le National*, 7 juin 1883, 3. Girard and Erno, identified in the previous chapter, were among the early leaders of Plattsburgh's French-Canadian mutual-aid and political societies; like them, as we will see, LaRocque was active in local ethnic and political organizations.

37. Belisle, *Histoire de la Presse Franco-Américaine*, 31; *Le National*, 7 juin 1883, 1, 9 avril 1885, 3.

38. Rumilly, *Histoire des Franco-Américains*, 122, 129; *Le National*, 7 juin 1883, 1; Roby, *Les Franco-Américains de la Nouvelle-Angleterre*, 187; François Weil, *Les Franco-Américains, 1860–1980* (Paris: Belin, 1989), 122; Stuart Bruce Kaufman, "Birth of a Federation: Mr. Gompers Endeavors 'not to build a bubble,'" *Monthly Labor Review* (November 1981): 26; *New York Times*, 13 February 1883, 3.

39. *Le National*, 7 juin 1883, 2.

40. *Le National*, 7 juin 1883, 1; *Sentinel*, 10 August 1883, 8.

41. *Sentinel*, 10 August 1883, 8. French Canadians undoubtedly staffed these fire-hose companies. *Le National*, for example, referred to the Lafayette fire-hose company as "our [French-] Canadian company, the Lafayettes." *Le National*, 7 juillet 1887, 3.

42. *Sentinel*, 10 August 1883, 8.

43. *Sentinel*, 10 August 1883, 8. Referring to Native peoples as "wild" or as "savages" of course dehumanizes them and marks them as an inferior and unequal group. Erika Lee, *America for Americans: A History of Xenophobia in the United States* (New York: Basic Books, 2019), 8. This kind of reporting was not uncommon in the Plattsburgh press in the late nineteenth and early twentieth centuries.

44. *Sentinel*, 18 March 1881, 3, 10 August 1883, 8; *Le National*, 11 novembre 1886, 1; McGuire, *The Democratic Party of the State of New York*, 372; *Le National* (Lowell, MA), 26 février 1892, 1, CCHA, 2013.079.0097; *The Souvenir Industrial Edition of Plattsburgh, 1897*, 79.

45. *Le National*, 23 juillet 1885, 2, 13 août 1885, 3, 20 août 1885, 3.

46. *Sentinel*, 20 June 1884, 1, 24 June 1887, 1, 21 June 1889, 1, 16 June 1893, 1; *Plattsburgh Daily Press*, 21 May 1895, 3.

47. *Sentinel*, 28 June 1889, 1; SCO Chroniques, vol. 1, 25 septembre 1881, 296–97, 26 septembre 1881, 297; *Le National*, 27 juin 1889, 2, 3.

48. *Sentinel*, 28 June 1889, 1; *Le National*, 27 juin 1889, 3; *Republican*, 29 June 1889, 1.

288 | Notes to Chapter Two

49. *Republican*, 29 June 1889, 1; *Sentinel*, 28 June 1889, 1.

50. *Republican*, 29 June 1889, 1; *NY Census, 1892*; *Sentinel*, 28 June 1889, 1; *Le National*, 27 juin 1889, 3.

51. *Daily Press*, 15 June 1899, 1. In 1899, Plattsburgh held its Saint-Jean-Baptiste celebration in mid-June to accommodate excursionists from Montréal and Burlington who otherwise would not have been able to attend because of planned celebrations in their communities closer to the feast day of the French-Canadian patron saint. *Daily Press*, 28 April 1899, 6.

52. *Daily Press*, 16 June 1899, 1–2.

53. Decoration Day became more commonly known as Memorial Day in the 1880s, but Plattsburgh's newspapers often used the terms interchangeably through the end of the century. *Republican*, 31 May 1884, 1, 5 June 1897, 1; *Le National*, 2 juin 1887, 3; *Sentinel*, 3 June 1887, 1, 31 May 1889, 1, 3 June 1892, 1.

54. *Sentinel*, 1 June 1883, 1, 3 June 1887, 1.

55. *Le National*, 25 juin 1885, 3, 1 juillet 1886, 1, 27 juin 1889, 2; *Republican*, 4 July 1885, 1; *Sentinel*, 10 July 1885, 1.

56. SCO Chroniques, vol. 1, 15 mars 1881, 289; Deschâtelets, "Notes historiques sur notre maison," 15 mai 1881.

57. Roby, *Les Franco-Américains de la Nouvelle-Angleterre*, 266; Corporations Book 1, pp. 59–60, CCCO. Because previous papers may not have met legal requirements in New York State, St. Peter's Church filed a new set of incorporation papers in August 1922, signed by the bishop, the vicar general, the pastor, and two lay trustees. Corporations Book 2, pp. 391–92, CCCO. This five-trustee model was still in effect a century later. See *The Roman Catholic Church of Saint John the Baptist, 1827–2012* (Plattsburgh, NY: broadstreetcatholics.org [2012]), 11, FLSC.

58. Roby, *Les Franco-Américains de la Nouvelle-Angleterre*, 266–267; Greer, *The Patriots and the People*, 68. On the Corporation Sole Controversy in Maine, see Michael Guignard, "Maine's Corporation Sole Controversy," *Maine Historical Society Newsletter* 12 (Winter 1973): 111–30.

59. Bancs, 1870–1877, SPP; Roby, *Les Franco-Américains de la Nouvelle-Angleterre*, 146.

60. *Sentinel*, 21 July 1882, 1, 28 July 1882, 1, 8.

61. Smith, *A History of the Diocese of Ogdensburg*, 204; *Le National*, 20 août 1885, 3, 29 octobre 1885, 3, 11 novembre 1886, 2, 9 décembre 1886, 3, 20 janvier 1887, 3; *Sentinel*, 20 October 1882, 1, 27 October 1882, 1, 30 October 1885, 1; Livre des Déliberations des Syndics, 63.

62. *Le National*, 20 janvier 1887, 3, 27 janvier 1887, 3, 20 décembre 1888, 3.

63. *Republican*, 14 January 1893, 1, 23 December 1893, 1; Palmer, *Historical Sketch of Plattsburgh*, 94; *Sentinel*, 8 April 1892, 1; note dated 24 July [18]91

to Rev. Fournier, O.M.I., Plattsburgh, from Edw. V. Murphy, Chancellor and Secretary, Correspondence, Bishop Edgar P. Wadhams' Secretary & Chancellor, 1880–1891, 46, RCDO; *Daily Press*, 11 October 1898, 7, 12 October 1898, 5.

64. Clergy List, 1883, 3, in Scrapbook, Bishop Edgar P. Wadhams, 1860s–1880s, RCDO. The diocese provides a figure of 60 girls at the convent school in 1883, but government census figures indicate that enrollments, at least in other years, were much lower: 17 in 1870, 21 in 1880, and 23 in 1892. *US Census, 1870, 1880*; *NY Census, 1892*.

65. *Le National*, 7 juin 1883, 3; SCO Chroniques, vol. 1, 10 juillet 1882, 313, 11 avril 1883, 321, 12 juin 1883, 324, 14 juillet 1883, 325, 17 septembre 1883, 329, 19 octobre 1883, 330; Allan S. Everest, "The Grey Nuns in Plattsburgh," 5; *US Census, 1880*; États de la Maison-Mère et des Autres Missions, 1845–1896, 310, 375, microfilm, COO; email from Hoffmann to author, 8 July 2020.

66. SCO Chroniques, vol. 1, 8 juin 1883, 323, 27 août 1883, 328. The Sisters also borrowed money from a third source but did not provide the details in their chronicle, vol. 1, 27 août 1883, 328.

67. *Sentinel*, 28 December 1883, 1, 20 February 1885, 1, 20 March 1885, 1; *Le National*, 5 mars 1885, 3, 19 mars 1885, 3; *The Souvenir Industrial Edition of Plattsburgh, 1897*, 79; SCO Chroniques, vol. 1, 22 juillet 1883, 327.

68. Sister Paul-Emile, s.c.o., *The Grey Nuns of the Cross: Sisters of Charity, Ottawa, Ontario*, vol. 2: Evolution of the Institute, 1876–1967, trans. Sister Gabrielle L. Jean, s.c.o. ([Ottawa: Sisters of Charity of Ottawa, 1989]), 42–44, OPL; SCO Chroniques, vol. 2: 5 septembre 1893, 31 décembre 1917, 20 octobre 1893, 3, 7 novembre 1893, 3, 26 juin 1896, 20–21, 4 septembre 1896, 4, 25 juin 1897, 33, 6 septembre 1897, 35, 5 septembre 1899, 52.

69. Armand Chartier, *The Franco-Americans of New England: A History*, trans. Robert J. Lemieux and Claire Quintal (Manchester, NH: ACA Assurance; Worcester, MA: Institut Français of Assumption College, 1999), 119; *Le National*, 10 septembre 1885, 2, 6 mai 1886, 2.

70. *Le National*, 17 février 1887, 2, 24 février 1887, 2, 3; *Republican*, 14 January 1893, 1.

71. SCO Chroniques, vol. 1, 26 juillet 1887, 373–74, 2 août 1887, 374, 25 mars 1889, 396.

72. *Le National*, 14 juin 1888, 2, 5 juillet 1888, 3, 14 février 1889, 2, 27 juin 1889, 3.

73. SCO Chroniques, vol. 1, 4 novembre 1885, 353, 28 juin 1888, 385, 17 janvier 1889, 392, 25 janvier 1889, 392–93; *NY Census, 1892*; *Republican*, 3 December 1881, 1, 22 November 1884, 1; *Le National*, 5 juillet 1888, 2; untitled typescripts, D'Youville Convent Célébrations, 4 November 1885, ASCO, M005,SG,SS4,D01; Registre de la Visite des Malades; Oeuvres de Charité au dehors, Compte-Rendu de la Maison de Plattsburgh pour le Chapitre Général de 1884, D'Youville Convent file, ASCO, M005,SB,D2.

74. SCO Chroniques, vol. 1, 25 janvier 1889, 392–93; *Republican*, 11 May 1889, 1. A Democrat in a Republican bastion, Weed had won election six times to the state assembly from the mid-1860s to the mid-1870s and had been nominated by Democratic lawmakers for a US Senate seat in 1887. Plattsburgh's French-language newspaper pointed out in that year that Weed was considered the head of New York's Democratic Party. Weed also had interests in railroads and local mines. While in the state assembly, he worked to get the railroad link connecting New York City to Plattsburgh and hence to Montréal. A businessman, Weed formed the Chateaugay Ore and Chateaugay Iron companies in 1874, merged them in 1881, and served as the president until 1903. McGuire, *The Democratic Party of the State of New York*, vol. 2, 264, 267; Mark L. Barie, *The President of Plattsburgh: The Story of Smith Weed* (Rouses Point, NY: Crossborder, 2014), 107; Elise Miller St. Pierre, "Smith Weed and the Political Economy of Northern New York," *Antiquarian* 7, no. 1 (Fall 1990): 10–14; *Le National*, 27 janvier 1887, 3; *Sentinel*, 8 June 1920, 5.

75. SCO Chroniques, vol. 1, 25 janvier 1889, 392–93, 28 janvier 1889, 393, 30 janvier 1889, 393, 12 août 1889, 399.

76. *The Past and Present of Plattsburgh* (Troy, NY: Troy Times, 1891), 11; Cahier de compositions [de] Laura Lareau, D'Youville Convent, 1891–1892, Dr. LaRocque Collection, CCHA, 2013.079.0012; *Daily Press*, 4 September 1896, 3. Census records reveal that the large majority of the students attending the academy of the sisters were native of the United States in 1870, 1880, and 1892 (see Table 5). *US Census, 1870, 1880*; *NY Census, 1892*.

77. SCO Chroniques, vol. 2, 15 janvier 1894, 5, 12–14 mars 1894, 6, 11–16 juin 1894, 8, 29 mai 1896, 19, 13–14 août 1896, 22; *The Souvenir Industrial Edition of Plattsburgh, 1897*, 42; *Republican*, 5 September 1896, 1.

78. SCO Chroniques, vol. 2, 9 août 1897, 34, 7 août 1899, 51; *Sentinel*, 24 June 1892, 1, 24 February 1893, 1; *Daily Press*, 9 August 1899, 2.

Chapter Three

1. For a fuller treatment of this issue, see Mark Paul Richard, "'Riel . . . vivra dans notre histoire': The Response of French Canadians in the United States to Louis Riel's Execution," *Journal of Canadian Studies / Revue d'études canadiennes* 51, no. 3 (Fall 2017): 697–724.

2. Lavoie, *L'émigration des Québécois aux États-Unis*, 45; Thompson and Richard, "Canadian History in a North American Context," 49; Bob Beal and Rod Macleod, *Prairie Fire: The 1885 North-West Rebellion* (Toronto: McClelland and Stewart, 1994), 24; Jennifer Reid, *Louis Riel and the Creation of Modern Canada: Mythic Discourse and the Postcolonial State* (Albuquerque: University of

New Mexico Press, 2008), 10; Maggie Siggins, *Riel: A Life of Revolution* (Toronto: HarperCollins, 1994), 159; Gilles Martel, *Le messianisme de Louis Riel* (Waterloo, Ontario: Wilfrid Laurier University Press, 1984), 132; J. M. Bumsted, "Louis Riel and the United States," *American Review of Canadian Studies* 29 (Spring 1999): 23; Pierre Anctil, "L'exil américain de Louis Riel, 1874–1884," *Recherches Amérindiennes au Québec* 11, no. 3 (1981): 241; Louis Riel, *The Collected Writings of Louis Riel / Les Ecrits complets de Louis Riel*, vol. 5: Reference / Référence, ed. George F. G. Stanley, Thomas Flanagan, and Claude Rocan (Edmonton: University of Alberta Press, 1985), 82.

3. A. I. Silver, *The French-Canadian Idea of Confederation, 1864–1900* (Toronto: University of Toronto Press, 1982; 2nd ed., 1997), 52–55, 74–76, 78; *Foyer Canadien*, 2 juin 1874, 2; Roby, *Les Franco-Américains de la Nouvelle-Angleterre*, 51, 56; Armand Chartier, *Histoire des Franco-Américains de la Nouvelle-Angleterre*, 39–40; Thomas Flanagan, *Louis 'David' Riel: 'Prophet of the New World'* (Toronto: University of Toronto Press, 1979), 43; Rumilly, *Histoire des Franco-Américains*, 72.

4. Riel, *Collected Writings*, vol. 5, 83; Chartier, *Histoire des Franco-Américains de la Nouvelle-Angleterre*, 40; Anctil, "L'exil américain de Louis Riel," 241; Rosaire Dion-Lévesque, *Silhouettes Franco-Américaines* (Manchester, NH: L'Association Canado-Américaine, 1957), 604–6; *Le National*, 1 juillet 1886, 1; Rumilly, *Histoire des Franco-Américains*, 76–77.

5. Bumsted, "Louis Riel and the United States," 23; Mason Wade, *The French Canadians, 1760–1967*, vol. 1: 1760–1911 (Toronto: Macmillan, 1968), 405; Riel, *Collected Writings*, vol. 5, 84; Louis Riel, Keeseville, NY, à Major E. Mallet, 10 mai 1875, 2 juillet 1875, Correspondence, Major Edmond Mallet Collection, Emmanuel d'Alzon Library Manuscript Collection, Assumption University, Worcester, Massachusetts.

6. Riel, *Collected Writings*, vol. 5, 84; Bumsted, "Louis Riel and the United States," 25; Anctil, "L'exil américain de Louis Riel," 241; Riel à Mallet, 10 mai 1875, 2 juillet 1875, Correspondence, Mallet Collection; F. Barnabé, Keeseville, NY, au Major Edmond Mallet, 29 novembre 1874, Correspondence, Mallet Collection. Riel followed up on his meeting with Grant by sending him a letter detailing his plans. See Hartwell Bowsfield, ed., "Louis Riel's Letter to President Grant, 1875," *Saskatchewan History* 21, no. 2 (1968): 67–75.

7. Joseph Howard, *Strange Empire: Louis Riel and the Métis People* (1952; Toronto: James Lewis and Samuel, 1974), 321–22, 326; Notes on Riel Furnished Judge Bryant, 9, Research Notes, Mallet Collection; Edmond Mallet to Rev. J. E. Marcoux, Rector of Laval University, Montréal, 30 December 1885, Correspondence, Mallet Collection; Riel, *Collected Writings*, vol. 5, 84–85; *Guide Franco-Américain, 1921: Les Franco-Américains et la Guerre Mondiale* (Fall River, MA: Albert A. Bélanger [1921]), 101, 154; Chartier, *Histoire des Franco-Américains de la Nouvelle-Angleterre*, 40; *Foyer Canadien*, 21 juillet 1874, 2; J. B. Primeau

à Mallet, 31 décembre 1875, Correspondence, Mallet Collection; Anctil, "L'exil américain de Louis Riel," 245; Wade, *The French Canadians*, 405; Flanagan, *Louis 'David' Riel*, 65–66; Bumsted, "Louis Riel and the United States," 26.

8. Barnabé à Mallet, 12 octobre 1878, Correspondence, Mallet Collection; Wade, *The French Canadians*, 405, 443n67; Riel, *The Collected Writings of Louis Riel*, vol. 2: 8 décembre 1875–4 juin 1884, ed. Gilles Martel (Edmonton: University of Alberta Press, 1985), 220–21, 266–77, vol. 5, 85; Howard, *Strange Empire*, 349.

9. Beal and Macleod, *Prairie Fire*, 107; Thompson and Richard, "Canadian History in a North American Context," 49; Riel, *Collected Writings*, vol. 5, 94–95; Siggins, *Riel*, 418, 422.

10. Thompson and Richard, "Canadian History in a North American Context," 50; Beal and Macleod, *Prairie Fire*, 305; undated newspaper article attributed to *L'Étendard National* (Montréal), scrapbook 1, 65, Mallet Collection; Silver, *The French-Canadian Idea of Confederation*, 102–3; Reid, *Louis Riel and the Creation of Modern Canada*, 155–56.

11. See, for example, *Le Messager* (Lewiston, Maine), *L'Indépendant* (Fall River, MA), *Le National* (Plattsburgh, NY), and *Le Castor* (Fall River, MA).

12. *Le Messager*, 13 août 1885, 2, 27 août 1885, 2; *Le National*, 13 août 1885, 2, 20 août 1885, 2.

13. *Le National*, 3 septembre 1885, 2; Ambrose Choquet, Counselor at Law, Rochester, NY, to T. F. Bayard, Secretary of State, 15 October 1885, and Bayard to Choquet, 27 October 1885, and copy of the naturalization certificate of Louis David Riel, all in Benjamin Harrison, "Message from the President of the United States, Transmitting, In response to Senate resolution of February 11, 1889, a report upon the case of Louis Riel," Ex. Doc. No. 1 of the Special Session, 51st Congress, 1889, *Congressional Serial Set* 2613, 10–12. Choquet subsequently moved to Plattsburgh, where he practiced law and became an assistant editor of *Le National* in 1886–1887. From Plattsburgh, Choquet relocated to Worcester, Massachusetts, to become the editor in chief of *Le Travailleur*. *Le National*, 6 mai 1886, 3, 22 septembre 1886, 2, 25 novembre 1886, 3, 28 avril 1887, 3.

14. Beal and Macleod, *Prairie Fire*, 296; Bumsted, "Louis Riel and the United States," 33.

15. *Essex County Republican* (Keeseville, NY), 19 November 1885, 4; *Le Messager*, 3 décembre 1885, 1; *La Presse* (Montréal), reproduit dans *Le Messager*, 14 janvier 1886, 1; La Chronique du couvent de Saint-Pierre et Saint-Paul de l'ordre des Frères Prêcheurs, Lewiston, Maine, dans la série couvents et paroisses, la sous-série couvent des Apôtres Pierre et Paul de Lewiston, Maine, vol. 2, 2 décembre 1885, 12^1[sic], Archives des Dominicans, Montréal, Québec; Paul V. Labonté et C. A. Lacroix, *Le Messager*, 17 décembre 1885, 2; *Courrier des États-Unis*, reproduit dans *Le Messager*, 24 décembre 1885, 2; *Le Messager*, 31 décembre 1885, 2; *Le National*, 26 novembre 1885, 3, 3 décembre 1885, 3,

17 décembre 1885, 2, 31 décembre 1885, 2; F. P. G., *L'Indépendant*, 4 décembre 1885, 2; *L'Indépendant*, 11 décembre 1885, 2; Flanagan, *Louis 'David' Riel*, 98.

16. *Le National*, 3 décembre 1885, 2.

17. *Le National*, 3 décembre 1885, 2; *L'Indépendant*, 11 décembre 1885, 2; Ferd. Gagnon, *Le Travailleur*, 1 décembre 1885, 2; *Le Messager*, 28 octobre 1886, 2.

18. *Le Messager*, 24 juin 1886, 2, 1 juillet 1886, 2, 5 août 1886, 1.

19. Richard, *Loyal but French*, 40; *L'Indépendant*, 27 juillet 1888, 2, 17 août 1888, 2, 31 août 1888, 2, 14 septembre 1888, 2, 2 novembre 1888, 2.

20. *Le National*, 25 février 1886, 2, 9 août 1888, 2, 6 septembre 1888, 2, 1 novembre 1888, 2; Patrick Lacroix, *"Tout nous serait possible": Une histoire politique des Franco-Américains, 1874–1945* ([Québec, Québec]: Les Presses de l'Université Laval, 2021), 5, 47. By 1892, *Le National*'s owner, Benjamin Lenthier, had bought or founded between fifteen and nineteen newspapers (the sources vary on the actual number) in French-Canadian population centers of the northeastern United States to support the presidential campaigns of Grover Cleveland. Lenthier acquired the newspapers with the financial support of Josiah Quincy, the secretary of the national Democratic Party. Most of Lenthier's newspapers disappeared by the mid-1890s, following Cleveland's election in 1892 to a second, nonconsecutive term as president. Back in the Oval Office, Cleveland subsequently appointed Lenthier to the post of US consul, stationed in Sherbrooke, Québec. Chartier, *Histoire des Franco-Américains de la Nouvelle-Angleterre*, 56; Brault, *The French-Canadian Heritage in New England*, 80–81; Rumilly, *Histoire des Franco-Américains*, 140; Belisle, *Histoire de la Presse Franco-Américaine*, 256.

21. Lauren L. Basson, "Savage Half-Breed, French Canadian or White US Citizen? Louis Riel and US Perceptions of Nation and Civilisation," *National Identities* 7 (December 2005): 370.

22. See, for example, Altina Waller, "The Tabor-Chapleau Murder," *The Antiquarian* 3, no. 1 (Fall 1986): 12–18; and Waller, "The Chapleau-Tabor Murder: Class, Ethnicity, and Accommodation in Plattsburgh, New York," 5–23, in Ouellette, *Conflict and Accommodation in North Country Communities*.

23. *Le National*, 31 janvier 1889, 3. Local newspaper accounts give Tabor's first name as Irvin, but government records, such as the court transcript of the murder trial and Tabor's death certificate, all use Irwin. *The People of the State of New York vs. Joseph Chapleau*, copy of transcript of Court of Oyer and Terminer, Clinton County, 2, 14, and elsewhere, CCHO; New York, Death Index, 1852–1956, ancestrylibrary.com.

24. *Le National*, 21 février 1890, 3.

25. *Le National*, 4 juin 1885, 2.

26. *Le Castor*, 13 mars 1885, 2; J. Antonin Plourde, O.P., *Dominicains au Canada: album historique* (S.é., 1973), 72–75; Chartier, *Histoire des Franco-Américains*

de la Nouvelle-Angleterre, 46–47; Rumilly, *Histoire des Franco-Américains*, 110; *Le National*, 26 mars 1885, 2.

27. *Le National*, 18 mars 1886, 2, 22 septembre 1886, 2.

28. *Le National*, 15 octobre 1885, 2, 4 février 1886, 2.

29. *Le National*, 27 janvier 1886, 2, 25 février 1886, 2, 18 mars 1886, 3, 3 juin 1886, 2.

30. *Le National*, 3 mars 1887, 3, 18 avril 1889, 3, 24 décembre 1889, 2, 21 janvier 1890, 3, 7 mars 1890, 3.

31. *Le National*, 9 août 1888, 2, 23 août 1888, 2. Dr. LaRocque provided a good example for French-Canadian immigrants in the host society. In 1879, the year following his arrival in Plattsburgh, LaRocque declared his intention to become a US citizen, and he became a naturalized citizen in 1883. Certificate of Record of Citizenship, Dr. LaRocque collection, CCHA, 2013.079.0029.

32. *Le National*, 30 août 1888, 3, 6 septembre 1888, 3.

33. *Le National*, 25 avril 1889, 2, 25 avril 1889, 2 (reproduced from *L'Avenir Canadien*), 4 octobre 1889, 2, 11 octobre 1889, 2, 15 octobre 1889, 2.

34. *Le National*, 1 novembre 1889, 3.

35. *Plattsburgh Sentinel*, 1 February 1889, 1; *US Census, 1900*; Deed Books 68, p. 458, 82, p. 142, 83, p. 17, CCCO; *Plattsburgh Morning Telegram*, 29 January 1889, 4; *Plattsburgh Republican*, 2 February 1889, 1; Waller, "The Tabor-Chapleau Murder" (1986), 13.

36. *Morning Telegram*, 29 January 1889, 4; *Sentinel*, 18 January 1889, 1; *US Census, 1900*. Service in the US armed forces had created a pathway since 1862 for immigrants to naturalize. *Naturalization Records of New York State* (Hilton, NY: Leaded Pane, 1996), 2. Possibly that is how Chapleau gained his US citizenship.

37. *Sentinel*, 1 February 1889, *Republican*, 2 February 1889, 1.

38. *People vs. Chapleau*, 93–96; *Sentinel*, 1 February 1889, 1.

39. *US Census, 1880, 1900*; *People vs. Chapleau*, 103–4; *Republican*, 2 February 1889, 1; *Sentinel*, 1 February 1889, 1.

40. *People vs. Chapleau*, 116; *US Census, 1880, 1900*.

41. *Sentinel*, 1 February 1889, 1.

42. *Morning Telegram*, 30 January 1889, 4; *Sentinel*, 1 February 1889, 1.

43. *People vs. Chapleau*, 144–45, 148–49, index; *Sentinel*, 1 February 1889, 1.

44. *US Census, 1880*; *People vs. Chapleau*, 116.

45. *Republican*, 13 April 1889, 1. Chapleau evidently did not expect to be exonerated. He deeded to his wife in March 1889 his share of the forty-acre property they owned together. But Eliza Chapleau apparently could not maintain the farm on her own, and she sold it two years later subject to a mortgage plus back interest for one year, and she sold off the cows, horses, farm supplies, and some household goods at public auction. Deed Books 85, p. 225, 87, p. 369, CCCO; *Sentinel*, 13 February 1891, 4.

46. *People vs. Chapleau*, 1, 35–36, index; *Sentinel*, 24 January 1890, 1; *Republican*, 29 June 1889, 1.

47. *People vs. Chapleau*, 181–82; Waller, "The Chapleau-Tabor Murder" (2005), 5; *New York Times*, 17 July 1890, 2. Altina Waller has suggested that the governor's and the community's support of leniency for Chapleau may have sprung from the suspicion that Tabor had molested domestic servants and possibly even Chapleau's wife. Hill decided that justice would be better served with life imprisonment. After Chapleau had served 14 years behind bars, more than 100 people petitioned Republican Governor Benjamin Odell to pardon him, arguing that he had been punished sufficiently for his crime. Despite this public support for leniency, Chapleau nonetheless lived the rest of his life behind bars, dying in 1911, after twenty-one years in jail. Waller, "The Chapleau-Tabor Murder" (2005), 18–19; *New York Times*, 17 July 1890, 2; *Plattsburgh Sentinel and Clinton County Farmer*, 23 October 1903, 1; *Sentinel*, 5 May 1911, 8.

48. SCO Chroniques, vol. 1, 31 janvier 1889, 393, 2 février 1889, 393, 10 février 1889, 394, 14 février 1889, 394–95, 17 février 1889, 395, ASCO; List, Soeurs de la Charité d'Ottawa; États de la Maison-Mère et des Autres Missions, 1845–1896, 451; email from Hoffmann to author, 8 July 2020.

49. SCO Chroniques, vol. 1, 31 janvier 1889, 393. The misconception about Chapleau's educational level arises from the reporting of local English-language newspapers and is reproduced in Waller. The *Sentinel* reported (31 January 1890, 1) that, at his sentencing, Chapleau told the court he could read and write and was a college graduate. The *Essex County Republican* shared the same information when it published the *Sentinel*'s article one day earlier (30 January 1890, 8.) Waller cites information about Chapleau's education and literacy skills from the former's article to make the argument that his college education and middle-class family background made him different enough from his French-Canadian peers, most of whom she contends were impoverished and illiterate, that he could be expected to rise above their ranks and to mix more easily with Plattsburgh's Anglo population. Waller, "The Chapleau-Tabor Murder" (2005), 8–9, 21n12. There is little evidence to support this class analysis.

50. Claude Galarneau, *Les Collèges classiques au Canada français (1620–1970)* (Montréal: Éditions Fides, 1978), 46; Robert G. LeBlanc, "A French-Canadian Education and the Persistence of La Franco-Américanie," *Journal of Cultural Geography* 8 (Spring/Summer 1988): 50–52, 54.

51. Waller, "The Tabor-Chapleau Murder" (1986), 13, 16; Waller, "The Chapleau-Tabor Murder" (2005), 5–6; *Morning Telegram*, 29 January 1889, 4.

52. *New York Times*, 5 July 1889, 4. Newspaper accounts in New York, reproduced around the country, even exoticized French speakers of upstate New York during this period in their reporting of an odd condition they exhibited of presumed neurological origin. By the mid-1890s, the *New York Journal* pro-

claimed the Jumping Frenchmen Syndrome an "epidemic in New York" State. Those afflicted with this "peculiar disease" might laugh insanely and obey sudden commands, even those causing self-injury, it informed readers. *New York Journal*, reprinted in *Oakes (Dakota Territory) Weekly Republican*, 25 September 1894 and 28 September 1894; *Turner County Herald* (Hurley, Dakota), 27 September 1894; *Bottineau (ND) Pioneer*, 27 October 1894; *Cook County Herald* (Grand Marais, Minn.), 22 December 1894. For a historical account of the jumping syndrome among French descendants in North America, see Mark Paul Richard, "A Peculiar Condition: A History of the Jumping Frenchmen Syndrome in Scientific and Popular Accounts," *Journal of the History of the Neurosciences* 27, no. 4 (2018): 355–74.

    53. *New York Times*, 5 July 1889, 4.

    54. *New York Times*, 5 July 1889, 4.

    55. John Higham, *Strangers in the Land: Patterns of American Nativism, 1860–1925* (1955; New Brunswick, NJ: Rutgers University Press, 1992), 62; Richard, *Loyal but French*, 69–70; *Press-Republican*, 16 August 1972, 22; SCO Chroniques, vol. 2, 1 juin 1894, 7–8.

    56. *Daily Press*, 22 March 1897, 3, 8 April 1897, 3, 17 January 1898, 4; *Republican*, 10 February 1894, 1, 13 March 1897, 1.

    57. *Daily Press*, 22 March 1897, 3. As a result of the investigation, Justice Kellogg found that the village trustees had improperly expended funds. Among other actions, they paid debts in one tax year that were incurred in another, something the General Municipal Law did not allow, and for which the village charter could make them personally liable. Kellogg also found that some trustees, including Crete, had benefited personally from the expenditure of village funds to construct a road. Kellogg therefore sided with the plaintiffs in this case and ordered the village trustees to pay the costs of the investigation. The trustees appealed the decision and succeeded in a court suit to recover close to $2,800 in costs from the village of Plattsburgh. *Daily Press*, 8 April 1897, 3; Circuit Court Records, vol. 5, pp. 304, 423, CCCO; Judgment Book in Supreme Court, No. 14, Defaults, p. 156, CCCO.

Chapter Four

    1. US Department of the Interior, Census Office, *Twelfth Census of the United States, Taken in the Year 1900*, vol. 1, part 1 (Washington, DC: United States Census Office, 1901), 277; proportions calculated from *Twelfth Census of the United States* (1901), 670; Hogue, *Centennial*, 63–64.

    2. Bélanger, dir., *Guide Franco-Américain* [1921], 208; Richard B. Frost, *Plattsburgh, New York: A City's First Century* (Virginia Beach, VA: Donning, 2002), 15; *Plattsburgh Press-Republican*, 10 March 1943, 3; Hogue, *Centennial*, 63–64.

3. *Plattsburgh Daily Press*, 7 May 1902, 2.

4. *Daily Press*, 2 December 1908, 5; *Plattsburgh Sentinel*, 17 May 1901, 5.

5. *Daily Press*, 18 July 1904, 3.

6. SCO Chroniques, vol. 2, 24 juin 1905, 107–8, ASCO; *Sentinel*, 6 December 1907, 5; *Daily Press*, 2 December 1908, 5.

7. *Daily Press*, 4 July 1903, 4, 31 May 1905, 3, 6 July 1905, 3, 3 September 1907, 1; *Plattsburgh Republican*, 7 July 1906, 1, 27 July 1907, 1; *Sentinel*, 6 June 1902, 6.

8. Knights of Columbus, "Knights of Columbus Founded," 2023, kofc.org.; Knights of Columbus 60th anniversary booklet, 15, Our Lady of Victory, Plattsburgh, file, RCDO; Arthur Preuss, comp., "Maccabees," *A Dictionary of Secret and Other Societies* (St. Louis, MO: B. Herder, 1924; repr. Detroit: Gale, 1966), 262; Alan Axelrod, "Maccabees" *The International Encyclopedia of Secret Societies and Fraternal Orders* (New York: Facts on File, 1997), 166; *Sentinel*, 16 February 1894, 1, 27 April 1894, 8, 11 January 1895, 1.

9. *Daily Press*, 11 February 1901, 3; *Sentinel*, 7 December 1900, 1, 14 December 1900, 1, 10 December 1909, 1.

10. *Sentinel*, 28 December 1900, 7, 27 December 1907, 5, 31 December 1909, 8; *Le National*, 15 juillet 1886, 2; *Daily Press*, 14 July 1903, 4; Linteau, Durocher, and Robert, *Histoire du Québec contemporain*, 265.

11. *Republican*, 3 August 1907, 5; *Daily Press*, 29 July 1907, 5, 30 August 1909, 3.

12. Pamphlet, "French and English Books of the St. Peter's Church Library, Catalogue 1903, Plattsburgh, N.Y.," PPL, Pam339, front and inside covers, 1–19, 21–32.

13. SCO Chroniques, vol. 2, 25 décembre 1905, 120; *NY Census, 1905*; *Sentinel*, 30 April 1909, 5; *Daily Press*, 3 May 1909, 3; Association St. Jean Baptiste membership booklet, 19[00s], Association St. Jean Baptiste Collection, CCHA.

14. SCO Chroniques, vol. 2, 14 février 1905, 100, 21 novembre 1905, 116–17.

15. SCO Chroniques, vol. 2, septembre 1903, 67, 22 juin 1905, 107, 6 septembre 1905, 111, 5 septembre 1906, 134, 4 septembre 1907, 147–48, 1 novembre 1907, 149, 23 juin 1908, 159, 14 septembre 1908, 162, 26 janvier 1909, 165, 27 janvier 1909, 165; *US Census, 1900, 1910*; *NY Census, 1905*.

16. *US Census, 1900, 1910*; *NY Census, 1905*.

17. SCO Chroniques, vol. 2, 17 mars 1904, 77, 17 mars 1905, 102, 16 mars 1906, 128.

18. SCO Chroniques, vol. 2, 14 janvier 1904, 74, 21 juin 1905, 106–7, 21 juin 1909, 168.

19. SCO Chroniques, vol. 2, 6 septembre 1904, 89; *US Census, 1910*; *Daily Press*, 23 June 1908, 3; *Sentinel*, 30 September 1910, 5.

20. *NY Census, 1905*. State and federal census-takers in the early twentieth century often listed the nativity of French-Canadian immigrants as "Canada French" or "French Canada" in their enumerations.

21. Taylor, *A History of Catholicism in the North Country*, 66; Everest, *Briefly Told*, 21; typescript, Br. Patrick Menard, "The Brothers of Christian Instruction in the United States (1903–1981)" [1981], 9–10, 12, 15, 19, BCI; Edmond G. Drouin, *The Brothers of Christian Instruction*, adapted from Paul Cueff, *Deux congrégations mennaisiennes* (Rome: Brothers of Christian Instruction, 1982), 14–15, 20, 27–28, 30, 39, 43, 51; pamphlet, Br. Marcel Sylvestre and Br. Andrew Paquin, eds., "150 Years of Missionary Service by the Brothers of Christian Instruction" (1988), 5–29, 43, BCI; Jean Laprotte, F.I.C., *De la Bretagne au Québec: Comment 108 Frères de l'Instruction chrétienne ont refusé la laïcisation votée en 1903 par les chambres françaises* (La Prairie, PQ: Archives des Frères de l'Instruction Chrétienne, 2002), 8; Guy Laperrière, *Les congrégations religieuses: De la France au Québec, 1880–1914*, tome 2: *Au plus fort de la tourmente, 1901–1904* (Sainte-Foy, Québec: Les Presses de l'Université Laval, 1999), 187; typescript, Brother Cyprius-Celestine Tregret, F.I.C, "The Brothers of Christian Instruction, Plattsburgh, New York, 1903–1919" [1971], 3, BCI. In all, 614 brothers from different congregations migrated from France to Québec in the period from 1900 to 1904. Laperrière, *Les congrégations religieuses*, 499.

22. Menard, "The Brothers of Christian Instruction in the United States (1903–1981)," 16; Julien Bablée, F.I.C. (Frère Cléonique-Joseph), *Autobiographie*, 2e éd. (La Prairie, PQ: Archives des Frères de l'Instruction Chrétienne, 1992), 27; Tregret, "The Brothers of Christian Instruction," 3–4; Frère Anastasius, Assistant du Supérieur Général, Frères de l'Instruction Chrétienne, Laprairie, PQ, au Monsieur le Curé, 10 juin 1903, Scrapbook, Mount Assumption Institute, 1903–1934, BCI, 49004; Livre des Délibérations des Syndics, 74.

23. *Daily Press*, 17 August 1903, 3; warranty deed and indenture between S. Hudson Vilas and Emily C. Vilas, Burlington, Vermont, to Rev. Joseph N. Pelletier, Plattsburgh, New York, 14 August 1903, and indenture between Pelletier and the Brothers of Christian Instruction, 30 April 1904, dossier Plattsburgh Mount Assumption Institute, Communauté, Titres de propriété, box 5203, FIC; Deed Book 104, pp. 82, 265, 266, 594–96, 753–55, and Book 105, pp. 569–71, CCCO; scrapbook "Clippings, Champlain Valley Hospital from 1902 to 1927, 1938 to [1955]," 1, Champlain Valley Hospital and School of Nursing, Record Group 600, box 3, GNSH; *Écho des Missions*, Janvier 1908, 100, Juillet 1918, 459–60, BCI; Tregret, "The Brothers of Christian Instruction," 5.

24. Bablée, *Autobiographie*, 35, italics in original.

25. *Un Cinquantenaire, 1886–1936: La Branche Canadienne des Frères de l'Instruction Chrétienne* (La Prairie, PQ: Frères de l'Instruction Chrétienne, 1937), 381, 531; Fr. Urbain-Marie Delisle, Fr. Patrice Ménard et Fr. Gaston Roy," Frère Denis-Antoine Gélinas," *Ménologe des Frères de l'Instruction Chrétienne de Ploërmel*, tome 5 (Bannalec [Brittany]: Imprimerie régionale, 1991), 1918–1919, FIC; email communication with the author from François Boutin, Archivist, FIC, 11 January 2022; Menard, "The Brothers of Christian Instruction in the

United States (1903–1981)," 110; *Écho des Missions*, Janvier 1908, 101; Tregret, "The Brothers of Christian Instruction," 7.

26. *Écho des Missions*, Septembre 1905, 20–22; *Un Cinquantenaire, 1886–1936*, 382.

27. Tregret, "The Brothers of Christian Instruction," 6, 10; *Écho des Missions*, septembre 1905, 21.

28. Menard, "The Brothers of Christian Instruction in the United States (1903–1981)," 16; Hogue, *Centennial*, 167; *NY Census, 1905*. The term "alien," viewed pejoratively today, was used on census forms in earlier periods of time to refer to immigrants who had not become naturalized US citizens.

29. Tregret, "The Brothers of Christian Instruction," 7; Douglas R. Skopp, *Bright with Promise: From the Normal and Training School to SUNY Plattsburgh, 1889–1989* (Norfolk, VA: Donning, 1989), 36. The Brother Provincial had also secured the permission of the Apostolic delegate in Canada for the brothers to attend classes at Plattsburgh Normal School. Bablée, *Autobiographie*, 28; Laperrière, *Les congrégations religieuses*, 354.

30. Fellows, "A Study of the Franco-American Community and the Plattsburgh State Normal School," 12–16.

31. Laperrière, *Les congrégations religieuses*, 187; Ulysse [Brother Provincial] à Abel [Superior General], 10 novembre 1903 et 1 décembre 1903, et Abel à Ulysse, 30 mars 1905 et 27 avril 1905, dans Laprotte, *De la Bretagne au Québec*, 16, 50–51, 54, 56–58; Menard, "The Brothers of Christian Instruction in the United States (1903–1981)," 19.

32. Liste du personnel au 8 décembre 1904, Institut des Frères de l'Instruction chrétienne, 8, FIC; Bablée, *Autobiographie*, 24, 26, 35–36, annexe IV.

33. Tregret, "The Brothers of Christian Instruction," 8; Menard, "The Brothers of Christian Instruction in the United States (1903–1981)," 110; *Plattsburgh Sentinel and Clinton County Farmer*, 12 February 1904, 4; *Daily Press*, 23 March 1904, 4; *Republican*, 21 May 1904, 2; Chapter 150, *Laws of the State of New York Passed at the One Hundred and Twenty-Seventh Session of the Legislature*, vol. 1 (Albany: J. B. Lyon, 1904), 269–270; Corporations Book 1, pp. 462–64, CCCO.

34. *NY Census, 1905*; *US Census, 1910*.

35. *Republican*, 9 September 1905, 1.

36. *Republican*, 12 October 1907, 1; *Écho des Missions*, Juin 1910, 78, 80–81.

37. SCO Chroniques, vol. 2, 2 janvier 1906, 121–22, and newspaper clipping from *The Evening News* inserted onto p. 122. Roman Catholic nuns in religious habits also taught in tax-supported schools in other parts of the United States, such as in northern Maine's St. John Valley and in Oregon, something that drew the ire of the Ku Klux Klan during the 1920s. See Mark Paul Richard, *Not a Catholic Nation: The Ku Klux Klan Confronts New England in the 1920s* (Amherst: University of Massachusetts Press, 2015), 38.

38. SCO Chroniques, vol. 2, 3 janvier 1906, 122, 5 janvier 1906, 122, 7 janvier 1906, 123.

39. Letter to Hon. A. S. Draper, Commissioner of Education, Albany, NY, minutes, Board of Education, Plattsburgh, NY, 19 January 1906, 461–63, FLSC, MM52.

40. SCO Chroniques, vol. 2, 25 janvier 1906, 124, 27 janvier 1906, 125; Plattsburgh Board of Education, 6 March 1906, 466, 468; report of the education committee, inserted into SCO Chroniques, vol. 2, 27 janvier 1906, 125.

41. SCO Chroniques, vol. 2, 17 avril 1906, 128–29, 4 juin 1906, 129; *O'Connor v. Hendrick*, 77 N.E. 612, 184 N.Y. 421, New York Court of Appeals, 1906, www.CourtListener.com; minutes, Plattsburgh Board of Education, 8 June 1906, 471.

42. Frost, *Plattsburgh, New York*, 77; Everest, "The Grey Nuns in Plattsburgh," 3; SCO Chroniques, vol. 2, 21 juin 1906, 131, 18 septembre 1906, 135.

43. *Republican*, 12 October 1907, 1; *Daily Press*, 3 September 1907, 1, 6; *US Census, 1910*.

44. *Daily Press*, 14 November 1907, 5; *Sentinel*, 15 November 1907, 8; *Republican*, 16 November 1907, 1.

45. *Daily Press*, 14 November 1907, 5.

46. *Sentinel*, 24 September 1909, 2; *Daily Press*, 27 January 1910, 3.

47. Yearbook and Church Directory of St. Peter's Church [1931–1932].

48. Yearbook and Church Directory of St. Peter's Church [1931–1932]; Hogue, *Centennial*, 175; *Daily Republican*, 10 August 1933, 4; *Daily Press*, 27 April 1900, 3; *Republican*, 18 June 1910, 4. Later purchases in the 1910s and 1920s expanded the size of St. Pierre cemetery. Deed Books 114, pp. 656–57, 143, p. 99, 147, pp. 450–51, CCCO; *Sentinel*, 5 September 1924, 4.

49. *Republican*, 14 December 1912, 7; *The Catholic Church in the United States of America*, 654.

50. *NY Census, 1892, 1905*; *US Census, 1900, 1910*. The parents of the US-born assistant pastor in 1900 were both native of Ireland. Although the New York censuses for 1892 and 1905 do not reveal the birthplace of the parents of the US-born priests in those years, they were likely of Irish descent as well.

51. A St. John's Parishioner, *Daily Press*, 23 August 1907, 2.

52. Corporations Book 1, pp. 590–91, CCCO; *Daily Press*, 29 September 1941, 3; *Plattsburgh City Directory for 1908* (Newburgh, NY: L. P. Waite, 1908), 69; *Plattsburgh City Directory for 1912*, vol. 16 (Newburgh, NY: L. P. Waite, 1912), 68; Deed Book 110, pp. 443, 444, CCCO. The parish expanded its real-estate holdings in the following decade with another purchase from Israel Crete in 1915. Deed Book 122, pp. 418–19, CCCO.

53. *Daily Press*, 23 October 1909, 5, 9 November 1909, 4; *Sentinel*, 31 July 1908, 12, 17 December 1909, 1.

54. Émilie Guilbeault-Cayer, *Les Soeurs de la Charité de Saint-Louis en Amérique, 1902–2018* (Québec, Québec: Septentrion, 2018), 13, 20–21, 24–26, 28–29, 38, 48, 50–51, 273–75; Laperrière, *Les congrégations religieuses*, 402, 500.

55. Alphonse Desilets, *Sous le signe de Charité: Les Soeurs de la Charité de Saint-Louis et leurs missions en Amérique* (Québec: s.n., 1950), 80, 82, SCSL; Guilbeault-Cayer, *Les Soeurs de la Charité de Saint-Louis en Amérique*, 80–83, 89–90; Soeurs de la Charité de St-Louis, *45 ans de dévouement sur le sol d'Amérique, 1902–1947* (Québec: Soeurs de la Charité de St-Louis, 1948), 179, SCSL, 1120.01-256.

56. Registre du Conseil de la Congrégation des Soeurs de la Charité de Saint-Louis, Maison-Mère Vannes, 1887 à 1927, Conseil du 26 Avril 1910, 107, SCSL Generalate, Montréal, Québec, F4-1/1887, courtesy of Sr. Lise Barbeau, SCSL; Deed Books 113, p. 438, 259, pp. 447–48, CCCO; Everest, *Briefly Told*, 22.

57. Soeurs de la Charité de St-Louis, *45 ans de dévouement sur le sol d'Amérique*, 178–79; Taylor, *A History of Catholicism in the North Country*, 262; Les Soeurs de la Charité de St-Louis, "Soeur Saint Michel (1874–1950)," *Souvenir à nos chères soeurs pieusement endormies dans le Seigneur* (Bienville, Lévis, Québec: Les Soeurs de la Charité de St-Louis, 1958), 560, SCSL, 19,121-002; "Mère Marie-Stéphanie (1878–1959)," Congrégation de la Charité de St-Louis, "A la Mémoire de nos soeurs, 1958–1967," vol. II, 1988, 60, 62–63, SCSL, 19,121-004; Congrégation de la Charité de St-Louis, "Soeur Marie-Véronique," *A la Mémoire de nos soeurs, 1968–1973*, vol. III (s.p.: Congrégation de la Charité de St-Louis, 1988), 45–47, SCSL, 19,121-005; email communication with the author from Sr. Lise Barbeau, s.c.s.l., 23 June 2022.

58. Congrégation de la Charité de St-Louis, "Soeur Saint-Clément," dans "A la Mémoire de nos soeurs, 1958–1967," 170–71; Guilbeault-Cayer, *Les Soeurs de la Charité de Saint-Louis en Amérique*, 33. In the name of Our Lady of Victory Academy, the Sisters of Charity of St. Louis purchased in March 1919 a parcel of land on South Catherine Street of about fourteen acres, providing them space for a small farm. Deed Books 132, pp. 27–28, 28–29, and 374, pp. 221–23, CCCO.

59. Soeurs de la Charité de St-Louis, *45 ans de dévouement sur le sol d'Amérique*, 179; Congrégation de la Charité de St-Louis, "Soeur Célanire Larochelle," *A la Mémoire de nos soeurs, 1979–1982*, vol. V (Maison Généralice, Rome: Congrégation de la Charité de St-Louis, 1982), 25, SCSL, 19,121-007; S. Annette Pepin, c.s.l., "Soeur Emilienne-Marie," dans Congrégation de la Charité de St-Louis, *A la Mémoire de nos soeurs, 1983–1987*, volume VI (Maison Généralice, Rome: Congrégation de la Charité de St-Louis, 1987), 169–71, SCSL, 19,121-008; Guilbeault-Cayer, *Les Soeurs de la Charité de Saint-Louis en Amérique*, 90; Donald Garrant, "History of Our Lady of Victory Academy," in the pamphlet, Golden Jubilee, April 18, 1960: Sisters of Charity of St. Louis, Our Lady of Victory Academy, Plattsburgh, New York, 1910–1960, SCSL, 3303-01-07.

60. *Daily Press*, 6 July 1907, 3; *Republican*, 8 May 1909, 1, 7 August 1909, 2; *US Census, 1910*; Kimberly Lamay Licursi and Celine Racine Paquette, *Images of America: Franco-Americans in the Champlain Valley* (Charleston, SC: Arcadia, 2018), 15.

61. Sylvie Beaudreau, "Commemorating a Transnational Hero: The 1909 Celebration of the Tercentenary of the Discovery of Lake Champlain," *Vermont History* 77, no. 2 (Summer/Fall 2009): 99; *Daily Press*, 5 July 1909, 7, 24 June 1937, 3; Yearbook and Church Directory of St. Peter's Church [1931–1932]; *Sentinel*, 2 April 1909, 5; *Press-Republican*, 20 August 1958, 3.

62. *Republican*, 10 July 1909, 1; *Daily Press*, 6 July 1909, 5; SCO Chroniques, vol. 2, 5 juillet 1909, 169.

63. Frost, *Plattsburgh, New York*, 122; *Sentinel*, 9 July 1909, 2; Marcel Lajeunesse, "Zotique Racicot," *Dictionary of Canadian Biography* online, vol. 14 (University of Toronto/Université Laval, 1998), www.biographi.ca; Hogue, *Centennial*, 76–77; *Republican*, 10 July 1909, 1.

64. SCO Chroniques, vol. 2, 7 juillet 1909, 169–70; *Republican*, 10 July 1909, 1; *Sentinel*, 8 June 1920, 5. Weed had become Plattsburgh's most prominent political figure in the late nineteenth century. His political associations had included former Democratic New York governor and 1876 presidential aspirant Samuel Tilden, and former Democratic New York governor Grover Cleveland, who won the US presidency for two nonconsecutive terms in 1884 and 1892. When President Cleveland passed through the Adirondacks in August 1885, he stopped for lunch at Weed's home. Weed's political career effectively ended when he did not gain the Democratic nomination for the Senate in 1891. When Weed died in 1920, the *Sentinel* described him as a local institution, asserting that "he was as much a part of this city as the Champlain monument." Barie, *The President of Plattsburgh*; *Le National*, 13 août 1885, 3; Waller, "The Perils of Capitalism, 203; *Sentinel*, 8 June 1920, 5.

65. *Press-Republican*, 20 August 1958, 3; postcard of Champlain Tercentenary Parade, Plattsburgh, 7 July 1909, CCHA, 84.17.10.

66. *Republican*, 7 May 1910, 3; J. W. Harkness, *Republican*, 25 June 1910, 4; *Sentinel*, 11 February 1910, 2.

67. *Sentinel*, 5 November 1909, 2, 3 September 1912, 2; Hogue, *Centennial*, 78; *Daily Republican*, 29 July 1927, 3; *Republican*, 18 February 1911, 2; *Daily Press*, 28 June 1911, 5. Incidentally, between the terms of Sharron and Senecal, the Common Council of Plattsburgh selected Montréal-born Joseph Payette to serve as mayor of the city in 1907 after Dr. A. E. Hyde resigned the post; although nominated by the Republican Party to run in the general election that fall, Payette had to decline when he discovered he was not yet a US citizen because his father had become naturalized only after Payette had turned twenty-one. *Daily Press*, 23 April 1907, 5, 23 September 1907, 5; *Evening Enterprise* (Pokeepsie, NY), 17 October 1907, 5; *Republican*, 19 October 1907, 1; *New York Evening Post*, 17 October 1907, 11; *Sentinel*, 11 January 1927, 5.

68. *Sentinel*, 9 July 1912, 5.
69. *Daily Press*, 8 July 1912, 4–5; *Sentinel*, 9 July 1912, 5.
70. *Daily Press*, 8 July 1912, 4–5, 22 July 1912, 2; *Sentinel*, 9 July 1912, 5, 7 December 1920, 3; *Republican*, 13 July 1912, 8.
71. For an account that considers the emergence of Champlain as an American hero in 1909, see Beaudreau, "Commemorating a Transnational Hero," 99–118.

Chapter Five

1. Carlan Kraman, OSF, "Women Religious in Health Care: The Early Years," in Ursula Stepsis, CSA, and Dolores Liptak, RSM, eds., *Pioneer Healers: The History of Women Religious in American Health Care* (New York: Crossroad, 1989), 21, 23, 37–38; Sioban Nelson, *Say Little, Do Much: Nurses, Nuns, and Hospitals in the Nineteenth Century* (Philadelphia: University of Pennsylvania Press, 2001), 1, 4, 6, 13, 15, 32; Christopher J. Kauffman, *Ministry and Meaning: A Religious History of Catholic Health Care in the United States* (New York: Crossroad, 1995), 64.

2. SCO Chroniques, vol. 2, 3 décembre 1901, 59, ASCO; Registre de la Visite des Malades, 1860–1919; Compte-Rendu de la Maison de Plattsburgh pour le Chapitre Général de 1884, 1888, 1893, 1898, 1903, 1908, 1913, 1918, D'Youville Convent file, ASCO, M005,SB,D2.

3. *Plattsburgh Daily Press*, 24 January 1895, 3, 31 December 1897, 27; *The Souvenir Industrial Edition of Plattsburgh, 1897*, 30.

4. Frost, *Plattsburgh, New York*, 61; brochure, "For Health Security: A Greater Champlain Valley Hospital, Plattsburg, New York" (1952), 3, Champlain Valley Hospital documents, box 6, CVPH.

5. Typescript, "History of the Grey Nuns in Diocese of Ogdensburg" (n.d.), Grey Nuns of the Sacred Heart file, RCDO, 1–3, 5; Katherine Briggs, "The Grey Sisters of Canada Come to Ogdensburg," *The Quarterly* 34, no. 3 (July 1989): 15; Kraman, "Women Religious in Health Care," 37.

6. *Daily Press*," 19 October 1900, 4.

7. Martin H. O'Brien, Attorney and Counsellor at Law, Plattsburgh, NY, to Rev. Mother Kirby, Ottawa, Ontario, 11 June 1901, and Kirby to Right Reverend H. Gabriels, D.D., Bishop of Ogdensburg, 16 June 1901, Grey Nuns of the Sacred Heart file, RCDO; "The Roman Catholic Church of Saint John the Baptist, 1827–2012," broadstreetcatholics.org.

8. "Clippings, Champlain Valley Hospital," 2–3; SCO Chroniques, vol. 2, 22 août 1902, 60, septembre 1903, 67; List, Soeurs de la Charité d'Ottawa; *NY Census, 1905*; *Daily Press*, 28 August 1902, 3; *Sentinel*, 29 August 1902, 1.

9. Berthold, *Les Soeurs de la Charité de Québec*, 57–58; Deed Books 102, p. 290, 102, p. 298, 106, p. 336, CCCO; *Sentinel*, 27 June 1902, 1; *Plattsburgh Republican*, 28 June 1902, 1; SCO Chroniques, vol. 2, 18 novembre 1909, 172;

Resolution by trustees, 30 June 1902, D'Youville Convent, Plattsburgh, files, ASCO, M005,SA,SS3.D1. Patrick Hanlon later bequeathed $1,000 to the Grey Nuns of Plattsburgh to aid in their work. SCO Chroniques, vol. 2, 18 novembre 1909, 172; Wills Book 3, p. 124, CCCO.

10. Annals, 15 July 1916, in "Clippings, Champlain Valley Hospital," 39–40; *Sentinel*, 26 September 1902, 1, 18 July 1916, 1; *Plattsburgh City Directory for 1902–'03* (Newburgh, NY: L. P. Waite, 1902), 9, 10, 61, 83, 85, 92, 110, 111, 112, 117, 122, 130, 142, 150; Hogue, *Centennial*, 63–64; Taylor, *A History of Catholicism in the North Country*, 266.

11. *The Souvenir Industrial Edition of Plattsburgh, 1897*, 79, 102; *Le National*, 11 novembre 1886, 1, CCHA, 2013.079.0098; *Le National*, 20 janvier 1887, 3, 28 avril 1887, 3, 5 mai 1887, 3; Duane Hamilton Hurd, *History of Clinton and Franklin Counties, New York* (1880; repr., Plattsburgh, NY: Clinton County American Revolution Bicentennial Commission, 1978), 137.

12. *Sentinel*, 26 September 1902, 1; Plattsburgh City Hospital Incorporation request, 1902, Champlain Valley Hospital papers, box 7, CVPH; Corporations Book 1, pp. 409–10, CCCO.

13. Jay P. Dolan, *The American Catholic Experience: A History from Colonial times to the Present* (Garden City, NY: Doubleday, 1985), 325; Paul Starr, *The Social Transformation of American Medicine* (New York: Basic Books, 1982), 173; Florence Marie Chevalier, S.S.A., "The Role of French National Societies in the Sociocultural Evolution of the Franco-Americans of New England from 1860 to the Present: An Analytical Macro-sociological Case Study in Ethnic Integration Based on Current Social System Models" (PhD dissertation, Catholic University of America, 1972), 210–11; "A Chronology of Rhode Island Hospitals," *Rhode Island Medical Journal* (January 2017): 20, www.rimed.org.

14. *Sentinel*, 26 September 1902, 1, 3 October 1902, 4.

15. *Daily Press*, 28 April 1903, 4; *Plattsburgh Sentinel and Clinton County Farmer*, 1 May 1903, 4.

16. *Sentinel and Clinton County Farmer*, 21 August 1903, 4; Memorandum of Agreement between The Sisterhood of Gray [sic] Nuns of The State of New York and Plattsburgh City Hospital, 23 October 1903, Historique et constitution, Champlain Valley Hospital, Plattsburgh, files, ASCO, M057,SA; Deed Book 106, p. 336, CCCO.

17. *Sentinel and Clinton County Farmer*, 21 August 1903, 4.

18. Knights of Columbus 60th anniversary, 23; *Daily Press*, 28 April 1903, 4, 30 January 1906, 3, 14 April 1906, 3, 16 November 1906, 5, 13 December 1906, 5; Everest, "The Grey Nuns in Plattsburgh," 5–6.

19. "Clippings, Champlain Valley Hospital," inside front cover.

20. SCO Chroniques, vol. 2, 13 juin 1904, 82; *Daily Press*, 30 May 1905, 3, 7 March 1906, 4. In 1906, annual dues were $1 for active members and $5 for associate members, with life members paying $25. Incidentally, men could

become associate members of the auxiliary for $2 annually, honorary members for $5 annually, and life members for a $100 contribution. *Daily Press*, 7 March 1906, 4. The fee structure of course recognized the greater earnings potential of men.

21. *Daily Press*, 7 March 1906, 4.

22. *Daily Press*, 26 April 1906, 3; *Republican*, 9 June 1906, 1.

23. *Republican*, 23 March 1907, 1.

24. *Plattsburgh City Directory for 1902–'03*, 130; Taylor, *A History of Catholicism in the North Country*, 266; *The Champlain Valley Hospital in the City of Plattsburgh, New York: First Annual Report of the Board of Directors, June, 1910, to June, 1911* (Plattsburgh, NY: Robinson's Printery [1911]), 5, 47, PPL, Pam176; *Daily Press*, 3 July 1906, 3; pamphlet, "Addresses Delivered at the Laying of the Corner Stone of the Champlain Valley Hospital (Plattsburgh City Hospital, Inc.), July 2, 1906, Plattsburgh, N.Y." (Plattsburgh, NY: Sentinel, 1906), 5, Champlain Valley Hospital papers, box 7, CVPH; *Sentinel*, 18 December 1908, 7; Corporations Book 2, p. 23, CCCO; minutes, Champlain Valley Hospital Board of Directors, The Champlain Valley Hospital Records, 1910–1962, 10–11, CVPH; Champlain Valley Hospital incorporation papers, box 7, CVPH; SCO Chroniques, vol. 2, 13 juin 1910, 175.

25. *Republican*, 23 June 1906, 1; "Addresses Delivered at the Laying of the Corner Stone of the Champlain Valley Hospital," 3, 10, 12, 16, 24; *The Champlain Valley Hospital . . . First Annual Report*, 45–67.

26. *The Champlain Valley Hospital . . . First Annual Report*, 51. Stetson may have misspoken. Both parents of John Haughran, the treasurer of Champlain Valley Hospital, had emigrated from Ireland to the United States, making his lineage Irish. *The Champlain Valley Hospital . . . First Annual Report*, 5; *Sentinel*, 10 October 1919, 5.

27. *Daily Press*, 3 July 1906, 3; "Addresses Delivered at the Laying of the Corner Stone of the Champlain Valley Hospital," 5, 9.

28. *Republican*, 5 June 1909, 1; *Sentinel*, 25 June 1909, 2; *Daily Press*, 29 August 1907, 3; *Sentinel*, 9 October 1908, 1, reproduced from *Adirondack Enterprise*.

29. Corporations Book 1, pp. 410–11, CCCO; *Sentinel*, 7 June 1907, 1, 21 February 1908, sec. 1, 1. When Smith's estate was finally settled, the hospital endowment turned out not to be as large as originally promised. Champlain Valley Hospital received $183,437.15 out of the $225,000 legacy, or 81.5 percent of what it had expected. Minutes, Champlain Valley Hospital Board of Directors, 1910–1962, 84.

30. *Daily Press*, 20 December 1909, 5; Corporations Book 1, pp. 410–11, CCCO; *Plattsburgh City Directory for 1909* (Newburgh, NY: L. P. Waite, 1909), 129; *Sentinel*, 4 February 1910, 8.

31. US Department of Commerce, Bureau of the Census, *Thirteenth Census of the United States Taken in the Year 1910*, vol. 3 (Washington, DC: Government

Printing Office, 1913), 196, 246; percentages calculated from *Thirteenth Census of the United States* (1913), 196, 246.

32. *Sentinel*, 13 May 1910, 3; *Republican*, 14 May 1910, 3, 21 May 1910, 7; *Plattsburgh City Directory for 1911*, vol. 15 (Newburgh, NY: L. P. Waite, 1911), 22. Curiously enough, Dr. J. H. LaRocque was among the six doctors named to the advisory board by 1906, but he did not join the hospital's initial medical board in 1910. "Addresses Delivered at the Laying of the Corner Stone of the Champlain Valley Hospital," title page; *The Champlain Valley Hospital . . . First Annual Report*, 6.

33. *Republican*, 11 June 1910, 3.

34. Annales de la Communauté 1888, translated by Sr. Jacqueline Peloquin, Sisters of Charity Hospital Archives, Saint Mary's Regional Medical Center, Lewiston, Maine, cited in Susan P. Hudson, *The Quiet Revolutionaries: How the Grey Nuns Changed the Social Welfare Paradigm of Lewiston, Maine* (New York: Routledge, 2006), 62; Richard, *Loyal but French*, 50–51; SCO Chroniques, vol. 2, 1 janvier 1904, 71, 1 janvier 1905, 98, 1 janvier 1906, 121, 7 janvier 1907, 138, 3 janvier 1909, 165, 6 janvier 1911, 181, 1 janvier 1914, 222, 3 janvier 1915, 239. The records of the hospital and of the Grey Nuns suggest only one instance of LaRocque contributing his professional skills at the facility. When one of the doctors of Champlain Valley Hospital came down with pneumonia in February 1920, LaRocque assisted another doctor in attending to him. Annals, 15 February 1920, in "Clippings, Champlain Valley Hospital," 60. The sources vary in the use of an apostrophe with Physicians' Hospital; today, it is no longer used.

35. SCO Chroniques, vol. 2, 10 juin 1910, 175, 13 juin 1910, 175; *Sentinel*, 21 January 1910, 8; "History of the Medical Center," *10th Anniversary, CVPH Medical Center, Plattsburgh, New York*, supplement to *Plattsburgh Press-Republican*, 9–15 May 1982, 3, Champlain Valley Hospital documents, box 6, CVPH.

36. *Republican*, 25 June 1910, 3; Kauffman, *Ministry and Meaning*, 169.

37. *Republican*, 25 June 1910, 3; Kauffman, *Ministry and Meaning*, 49.

38. Judith G. Cetina, "In Times of Immigration," in Stepsis and Liptak, eds., *Pioneer Healers*, 113; *Republican*, 25 June 1910, 3.

39. History notes, 22 June 1910, November 1910, January 1911, May 1911, in "Clippings, Champlain Valley Hospital," 15, 18–22.

40. Kauffman, *Ministry and Meaning*, 158, 167; Berthold, *Les Soeurs de la Charité de Québec*, 98; Briggs, "The Grey Sisters of Canada Come to Ogdensburg," 16; "History of the Grey Nuns in Diocese of Ogdensburg," 3; history notes, "Clippings, Champlain Valley Hospital," 17; *Sentinel*, 17 March 1911, 9; Everest, "The Grey Nuns in Plattsburgh," 6.

41. *The Champlain Valley Hospital . . . First Annual Report*, 11, 31–33; *Sentinel*, 31 May 1916, 6. Reports of the first year indicate that seven to nine women pursued their nursing studies with the sisters.

42. *Sentinel*, 31 May 1916, 6.

43. History notes, "Clippings, Champlain Valley Hospital," 24–25; SCO Chroniques, vol. 2, juin 1913, 213; États de la Maison-Mère et des Autres Missions, 1897–1927, 247; List, Soeurs de la Charité d'Ottawa.
44. *NY Census, 1915.*
45. Gerianne Wright, *Press-Republican*, 4 June 1992, A-3.
46. Nelson, *Say Little, Do Much*, 13.
47. Kauffman, *Ministry and Meaning*, 135; Everest, "The Grey Nuns in Plattsburgh," 6; *Report of the Champlain Valley Hospital, Plattsburgh, New York, 1925* (Plattsburgh, NY: Clinton Press, 1925), 4, 9, CCHO.
48. *The Champlain Valley Hospital . . . First Annual Report*, 11–12, italics in original.
49. "The Champlain Valley Hospital, Plattsburg, N.Y." [1917], 1–5, Historique et constitution, Champlain Valley Hospital files, ASCO, M057,SA.
50. *NY Census, 1915.*
51. *The Champlain Valley Hospital . . . First Annual Report*, 10, 18; minutes, Champlain Valley Hospital Board of Directors, 1910–1962, 43, 55–57.
52. Suzy Farren, *A Call to Care: The Women Who Built Catholic Healthcare in America* (St. Louis, MO: The Catholic Health Association of the United States, 1996), 110, 139–40, 169; Kauffman, *Ministry and Meaning*, unnumbered page between 126 and 127; minutes, Champlain Valley Hospital Board of Directors, 1910–1962, 34–35.
53. Minutes, Champlain Valley Hospital Board of Directors, 1910–1962, 44; *Daily Press*, 12 October 1912, 5; *Sentinel*, 28 December 1920, 5.
54. *The Champlain Valley Hospital . . . First Annual Report*, 36–38; minutes, Champlain Valley Hospital Board of Directors, 1910–1962, 45; "The Champlain Valley Hospital, Plattsburg, N.Y." [1917].
55. *Daily Press*, 6 September 1913, 4; "The Champlain Valley Hospital, Plattsburgh, N.Y." [1917].
56. *Daily Press*, 11 April 1914, 6.
57. *Daily Press*, 18 June 1910, 6; *Republican*, 25 June 1910, 3; pamphlet, "Constitution and By-Laws of [the] Women's League of the Physicians Hospital" (n.d.), inserted inside front cover, Physicians' Hospital minutes, 1924–1935, 1, CVPH.
58. *Sentinel*, 30 September 1910, 5; *Plattsburgh City Directory for 1911*, 22; Articles of Incorporation, Record Book, Physicians' Hospital of Plattsburgh, 26 September 1910—February 1922, 1, and Record Book, 75, box 9, CVPH; Corporations Book 2, pp. 27–29, CCCO; *10th Anniversary, CVPH Medical Center*, 4.
59. Typology of Paul Starr, explained in Kauffman, *Ministry and Meaning*, 131. Not only the Grey Nuns but also a widow went against this pattern by founding in Plattsburgh their own hospitals run by women. The widow organized Carrie Spaulding Hospital, named after herself, on Couch Street in Plattsburgh. The *US Census, 1920* indicates that the sixty-five-year-old Spaulding served as

the matron of the hospital, a twenty-eight-year-old woman served as a nurse, and Spaulding's nineteen-year-old adopted daughter handled the custodial work. It is not clear when the hospital was founded nor how long it lasted, but mention of it can be found in local newspapers from December 1919 to November 1922, particularly when individuals underwent operations there or were convalescing at the facility following surgery. *US Census, 1920*; *Sentinel*, 30 December 1919, 4, 8 July 1921, 6, 3 November 1922, 5.

60. By-Laws of the Physicians' Hospital of Plattsburgh, 5–14, in Record Book, Physicians' Hospital of Plattsburgh, 1910–22, 14; Everest, *Briefly Told*, 10; *Republican*, 14 January 1911, 1.

61. *NY Census, 1915*.

62. *10th Anniversary, CVPH Medical Center*, 4; Chapter 566, *Laws of the State of New York, Passed at the One Hundred and Fortieth Session of the Legislature* (Albany: J. B. Lyon, 1917), 1621–1623; Record Book, Physicians' Hospital of Plattsburgh, 1910–1922, 88; Chapter 133, *Laws of the State of New York Passed at the One Hundred and Forty-Ninth Session of the Legislature* (Albany: J. B. Lyon, 1926), 287; Record Book, Physicians' Hospital of Plattsburgh, 1910–1922, 55, CVPH.

63. *Daily Press*, 29 January 1918, 4; Corporations Book 2, pp. 56–59, CCCO.

64. Minutes, Champlain Valley Hospital Board of Directors, 1910–1962, 73, 76; annals, 30 March 1917, in "Clippings, Champlain Valley Hospital," 43; États de la Maison-Mère et des Autres Missions, 1897–1927, 303; List, Soeurs de la Charité d'Ottawa; *Daily Press*, 2 April 1917, 4.

65. Minutes, Champlain Valley Hospital Board of Directors, 1910–1962, 77–78, 81; SCO Chroniques, vol. 2, 17 avril 1917, 289; Deed Book 125, pp. 2–3, CCCO.

66. Marta Danylewycz, *Taking the Veil: An Alternative to Marriage, Motherhood, and Spinsterhood in Quebec, 1840–1920*, ed. Paul-André Linteau, Alison Prentice, and William Westfall (Toronto: McClelland and Stewart, 1987), 70, 72, 96, 103, 141; Thompson, "Women, Feminism and the New Religious History," 137.

Chapter Six

1. Rumilly, "Le Bilan vers 1911," *Histoire des Franco-Américains*, 271–77.

2. *Écho des Missions*, Juin 1911, 64–65, novembre 1911, 54, 57, BCI; Tregret, "The Brothers of Christian Instruction," 14, 80; *NY Census, 1915*; Menard, "The Brothers of Christian Instruction in the United States (1903–1981)," 112; Taylor, *A History of Catholicism in the North Country*, 275.

3. Fr. Patrick Menard, "Frère Alix-Marie Fresnel," *Ménologes des Frères de l'Instruction Chrétienne de Ploërmel*, tome 5 (Bannalec [Brittany]: Imprimerie régionale, 1991), 1733, FIC; *US Census, 1910*; Laprotte, *De la Bretagne au Québec*, 49; Personnel des Missions au 1er novembre 1911, 5, 8, FIC; *Un Cinquantenaire*,

1886–1936: La Branche Canadienne des Frères de l'Instruction Chrétienne (La Prairie, PQ: Frères de l'Instruction Chrétienne, 1937), 382.

4. Tregret, "The Brothers of Christian Instruction," 15; Personnel des Missions au 1er novembre 1911, 5, FIC.

5. *Plattsburgh Daily Press*, 7 August 1911, 1. In this period, Canada used the Red Ensign, featuring both Britain's Union Jack and a shield containing the coats of arms of the provinces admitted into the Confederation, as its flag. Canadian Heritage, *The National Flag of Canada: A Profile* (Ottawa, Ontario: Canadian Heritage, 2000), 9–10.

6. *Daily Press*, 5 August 1911, 6, 7 August 1911, 1; *US Census, 1910*. For reasons that went unrecorded in the press, Platt Street property-owners petitioned the Common Council in 1908 to rename their street Montcalm Avenue, and the Council acceded. *Daily Press*, 8 July 1908, 3, 2 September 1908, 3. Montcalm Avenue, along with Champlain and Lafayette Streets, all near St. Peter's Church, formed Plattsburgh's *petit Canada* (Little Canada).

7. SCO Chroniques, vol. 2, 19 mai 1912, 195, ASCO; *Plattsburgh Sentinel*, 26 May 1914, 5, 23 May 1916, 6, 12 June 1917, 3.

8. *Sentinel*, 25 June 1918, 5; *Plattsburgh Daily Republican*, 21 June 1919, 5.

9. *Plattsburgh Republican*, 14 December 1912, 7; *Daily Republican*, 14 October 1916, 8, 25 May 1918, 3; *Sentinel*, 28 May 1918, 5; *Daily Press*, 30 August 1913, 6, 20 September 1913, 4, 15 August 1914, 4, 9 February 1918, 5.

10. Soeurs de la Charité de St-Louis, *45 ans de dévouement*, 179; Garrant, "History of Our Lady of Victory Academy"; État Financier des Maisons de la Province d'Amérique de 1908 à 1922 et 1923, Congrégation des Soeurs de la Charité de St. Louis, Maison Provinciale de Pont Rouge, vol. I, box 107, SCSL, 3110-010.

11. Soeurs de la Charité de St-Louis, *45 ans de dévouement*, 180; Garrant, "History of Our Lady of Victory Academy"; "Mère Marie-Stéphanie (1878–1959)," Congrégation de la Charité de St-Louis, "A la Mémoire de nos soeurs, 1958–1967," vol. II, 1988, 63–64, SCSL, 19,121-004; État Financier des Maisons de la Province d'Amérique de 1908 à 1922 et 1923.

12. Typescript, "L'Hirondelle d'Arvor-quelques renseignements," 26 mai 1972, SCSL, 34,001-001-001; "Juvénat de Plattsburg," *L'Hirondelle D'Arvor*, no. 8 (janvier–février 1914): 128, SCSL, 34,001-002; État Financier des Maisons de la Province d'Amérique de 1908 à 1922 et 1923.

13. Pamphlet, "Our Lady of Victory Academy, Plattsburg, N.Y." [circa 1949], SCSL, 24,025-004-002.

14. "Juvénat de Plattsburg," 127; "Mère Marie-Stéphanie (1878–1959)," 65–66.

15. "Plattsburg," *L'Hirondelle d'Arvor*, no. 18 (juillet–août 1920), 295–296, SCSL, 34,001-002.

16. *Daily Press*, 28 September 1940, 3; Knights of Columbus 60th anniversary; *Sentinel*, 22 July 1919, 4.

17. *Daily Press*, 2 October 1915, 5; Final Official Circular of Information to Delegates, Peekskill Convention Committee, B. P. O. Elks (1916), Filmore J. Columbe Business Records, 1886–1928, folder 3, FLSC, 2013.2.

18. Typescript in envelope labeled "Engagements des Soeurs pour l'école appelée Couvent d'Youville," [1910], inserted in SCO Chroniques, vol. 2, between pages 134 and 135.

19. *US Census, 1860, 1870, 1880, 1900, 1910*; *NY Census, 1892, 1905, 1915*.

20. "Engagements des Soeurs pour l'école appelée Couvent d'Youville"; SCO Chroniques, vol. 2, 11 juillet 1911, 185, 1 septembre 1911, 186–87, 30 avril 1912, 195, 4 mai 1912, 195, 3 septembre 1912, 201; *US Census, 1910*.

21. SCO Chroniques, vol. 2, 19 mai 1912, 195–96; Hogue, *Centennial*, 185; *NY Census, 1915*.

22. SCO Chroniques, vol. 2, 21 mai 1912, 196.

23. SCO Chroniques, vol. 2, 6 juin 1912, 197, 7 juin 1912, 197. Regents examiners, of course, visited the school in other years as well. In 1913, a Miss Freeman came from Albany to examine the history classes and to discuss the teaching of history with instructors. SCO Chroniques, vol. 2, 27 mai 1913, 213.

24. SCO Chroniques, vol. 2, 24 juin 1912, 197–98.

25. Thompson, "Women, Feminism and the New Religious History," 151; SCO Chroniques, vol. 2, 23 décembre 1912, 205–6, 13 mars 1913, 209; List, Soeurs de la Charité d'Ottawa; *NY Census, 1915*.

26. *US Census, 1910*; *NY Census, 1915*. Census records indicate only that Sr. Duquemin was born in Canada and do not specify whether she was originally from a French-language or English-language province. *NY Census, 1915*. Her family name, however, is French.

27. Thompson and Richard, "Canadian History in a North American Context," 50.

28. SCO Chroniques, vol. 2, 11 juillet 1914, 232, 5 septembre 1914, 235, 27 juin 1917, 291.

29. SCO Chroniques, vol. 2, 24 septembre 1915, 255.

30. SCO Chroniques, vol. 2, 29 octobre 1914, 236–37, 9 décembre 1914, 238, 14 décembre 1914, 238, 15 décembre 1914, 238–39, 16 décembre 1915, 257.

31. *US Census, 1870, 1880, 1900, 1910*; *NY Census, 1892, 1905*; SCO Chroniques, vol. 2, after entry of 20 mars 1912, 193, 16 mars 1914, 225–26, 17 mars 1914, 226, 17 mars 1916, 264, 16 mars 1917, 286.

32. SCO Chroniques, vol. 2, 29 octobre 1914, 236, 28 octobre 1915, 256, 29 octobre 1915, 256.

33. *Un Cinquantenaire, 1886–1936*, 382; Menard, "Frère Alix-Marie Fresnel," 1733; SCO Chroniques, vol. 2, 24 août 1916, 274, 25 août 1916, 275, 27 août 1916, 275; Bablée, *Autobiographie*, 46.

34. SCO Chroniques, vol. 2, 8 septembre 1914, 235, 3 septembre 1916, 276, 5 septembre 1916, 276, 11 septembre 1916, 276.

35. *Plattburgh Daily Press*, 30 March 1938, 3; H. Cormerais, Rouses Point, à Ma Révérende Mère, 9 octobre 1916, and J. A. Sirois, O.M.I., Eglise St. Pierre, Plattsburgh, NY, à la Révérende Mère M. Madeleine, Fall River, Massachusetts, 25 octobre 1916, St. Peter School, Plattsburgh, New York, box 33, folder 4, DSH, F502.10.

36. SCO Chroniques, vol. 2, 2 septembre 1917, 295, 3 septembre 1917, 296, 17 septembre 1917, 296; Tregret, "The Brothers of Christian Instruction," 56; [Frère Louis-Arsène], Visiteur Provincial, Institut des Frères de l'Instruction Chrétienne, Direction Provinciale, La Prairie, PQ, au Révérend Père J.-A. Sirois, Supérieur, Plattsburg, 14 août 1914, dossier Plattsburgh Mount Assumption Institute, Communauté, Correspondance, box 5203, FIC; Rev. Walter Plaisance, OMI, Curé, au révérend frère Provincial, 1 septembre 1917, dossier Plattsburgh Mount Assumption Institute, Communauté des FIC, Rapports financiers, box 5203, FIC; *Un Cinquantenaire, 1886–1936*, 65, 382.

37. SCO Chroniques, vol. 3, Plattsburgh, 10 octobre 1918, 5–6, ASCO.

38. Registre de la Visite des Malades, 1860–1919, 105–10.

39. SCO Chroniques, vol. 2, 3 janvier 1915, 239, 4 avril 1915, 246, 10 octobre 1915, 255, 7 octobre 1916, 277, 1 janvier 1917, 283, 26 mai 1917, 290, vol. 3, 11 août 1918, 5.

40. SCO Chroniques, vol. 3, 28 octobre 1918, 7, 18 novembre 1918, 7, décembre 1918, 8.

41. SCO Chroniques, vol. 3, 20 octobre 1918, 6, 18 décembre 1918, 8; *Daily Press*, 26 May 1937, 3.

42. [Florent] VandenBerghe, O.M.I., Montréal, à [Pierre Aubert, O.M.I., Paris], 19 janvier 1872, 420, AG-OMI, partagé par AD-NDC, GLPP3071; Soeur St-Albert, Supérieure Générale, Ottawa, au Monsignor J. H. Conroy, Ogdensburg, 6 janvier 1919, Grey Nuns of the Sacred Heart file, RCDO.

43. Jul. Racette, O.M.I., to Conroy, 31 January 1919, Grey Nuns of the Sacred Heart file, RCDO.

44. Conroy to Most Reverend Pietro di Maria, Apostolic Delegate to Canada, Ottawa, 6 February 1919, Grey Nuns of the Sacred Heart file, RCDO.

45. Conroy to Most Reverend John Bonzano, Apostolic Delegate, Washington, DC, 6 February 1919, Grey Nuns of the Sacred Heart file, RCDO.

46. Conroy to Reverend Sister St. Albert, 6 February 1919, Grey Nuns of the Sacred Heart file, RCDO.

47. Conroy to St. Albert, 6 February 1919.

48. Sister Verecunda, Sacred Heart Convent, Ogdensburg, New York, to Conroy, 30 May 1919, Grey Nuns of the Sacred Heart file, RCDO; États de la Maison-Mère et des Autres Missions, 1897–1927, 154; List, Soeurs de la Charité d'Ottawa; *NY Census, 1905*; *US Census, 1920*.

49. Conroy to Most Reverend Dennis J. Dougherty, D.D., Archbishop of Philadelphia, Philadelphia, PA, 31 May 1919, Grey Nuns of the Sacred Heart file, RCDO; Roman Catholic Diocese of Buffalo, "Diocesan Bishops of the Past," 2015, www.buffalodiocese.org.

50. Conroy to Dougherty, 31 May 1919.

51. Conroy to Dougherty, 21 July 1919, Grey Nuns of the Sacred Heart file, RCDO.

52. Roman Catholic Diocese of Buffalo, "Diocesan Bishops of the Past"; Conroy to Right Reverend William Turner, D.D., Bishop of Buffalo, Buffalo, NY, 21 November 1919, Grey Nuns of the Sacred Heart file, RCDO. The Grey Nuns had actually served in New York State since 1857, thus sixty-two years.

53. Conroy to Turner, 21 November 1919.

54. Turner to Conroy, 10 December 1919, Grey Nuns of the Sacred Heart file, RCDO; *US Census, 1920*.

55. *US Census, 1920*.

56. St-Albert to Conroy, 20 October 1919, Grey Nuns of the Sacred Heart file, RCDO.

57. St-Albert à Conroy, 8 octobre 1920, Grey Nuns of the Sacred Heart file, RCDO.

58. *Sentinel*, 5 November 1920, 8; booklet, "D'Youville Academy, Plattsburgh, New York, Convent Boarding School for Young Ladies" (1920), 2–3, 6, Couvent D'Youville, Plattsburgh, Célébrations, ASCO, M005,SG,SS4,D01.

59. *US Census, 1870, 1880, 1900, 1910, 1920; NY Census, 1892, 1905, 1915*.

60. États de la Maison-Mère et des Autres Missions, 1897–1927, 247, 303; List, Soeurs de la Charité d'Ottawa; *NY Census, 1915*; *US Census, 1920*.

61. *NY Census, 1915*; *US Census, 1920*.

62. Turner to Conroy, 27 November 1920, Grey Nuns of the Sacred Heart file, RCDO.

63. Sister Paul-Emile, *The Grey Nuns of the Cross*, 193–94, OPL; Roman Catholic Diocese of Buffalo, "Diocesan Bishops of the Past."

64. Sr. Paul-Emile, *The Grey Nuns of the Cross*, 194–95. In 1920, the Sisters of Charity of Ottawa taught at three Lowell parishes administered by the Oblates: Immaculate Conception, St. John the Baptist, and Our Lady of Lourdes. *Official Catholic Directory for the Year of Our Lord, 1920* (New York: P. J. Kenedy and Sons, 1920), 35 hathitrust.org.

65. Sr. Paul-Emile, *The Grey Nuns of the Cross*, 195.

66. Sr. Paul-Emile, *The Grey Nuns of the Cross*, 195; *Daily Republican*, 5 October 1921, 5.

67. *Daily Republican*, 12 July 1921, 5, 5 October 1921, 5; *Sentinel*, 2 September 1921, 3, 2 September 1921, 5, 9 September 1921, 5, 7 October 1921, 1; "Saint Marguerite d'Youville[,] Servant of God," St. Mary's Cathedral, Ogdensburg, New York, 10 February 1991, Grey Nuns of the Sacred Heart file, RCDO; Julien

Racette, OMI, à la Très Révérende Mère M. Madeleine, Supérieure Générale, 6 février 1923, St. Peter School, box 33, folder 4, DSH, F502.10.

68. Soeur Saint-Jean l'Evangeliste, Secrétaire Générale, Maison-Mère des Soeurs Grises de la Croix, Ottawa, à la Très Révérende Mère Prieure du Couvent des Dominicaines, 14 août 1922, St. Peter School, box 33, folder 4, DSH, F502.10.

69. Saint-Jean l'Evangeliste à la Mère Prieure, 14 août 1922. The concern of the Dominican Sisters underlay another serious clash that took place in the mid-1920s, known as the Sentinelle Affair, in which militant Franco-Americans and their clergy came into conflict with the Irish Catholic hierarchy, beginning in Rhode Island but causing rancor throughout New England. Gerard J. Brault, *The French-Canadian Heritage in New England* (Hanover, NH: University Press of New England, 1986), 87–88; Richard S. Sorrell, "Sentinelle Affair (1924–1929)—Religion and Militant Survivance in Woonsocket, Rhode Island," *Rhode Island History* 36 (1977): 67, 68.

70. P. S. Garand to Conroy, 24 April 1923, Grey Nuns of the Sacred Heart file, RCDO; Roman Catholic Diocese of Ogdensburg, "Former Bishops of Ogdensburg," rcdony.org 2020; Dougherty to Conroy, 26 April 1923, Grey Nuns of the Sacred Heart file, RCDO.

71. Dougherty to Conroy, 1 June 1923, and Conroy to Dougherty, 9 June 1923, Grey Nuns of the Sacred Heart file, RCDO; Sister Ann, Grey Nuns of the Sacred Heart, Philadelphia, PA, to Conroy, 20 August 1923, Grey Nuns of the Sacred Heart file, RCDO. By this point in time, Sr. Anne de Jésus appears to have used the English version and spelling of her name: Sr. Ann.

72. *Le Messager* (Lewiston, Maine), 25 octobre 1926, 8, 4 mars 1927, 8, 18 mars 1927, 4, 27 juillet 1927, 8; George J. Sánchez, *Becoming Mexican American: Ethnicity, Culture and Identity in Chicano Los Angeles, 1900–1945* (New York: Oxford University Press, 1993), 57; SCO Chroniques, vol. 2, 18 juillet 1917, 292.

73. Tregret, "The Brothers of Christian Instruction," 37, 42, 74–75.

74. On the differing responses of francophones on each side of the border to participation in World War I, see Robert G. LeBlanc, "The Franco-American Response to the Conscription Crisis in Canada, 1916–1918," *American Review of Canadian Studies* 23, no. 3 (Autumn 1993): 343–72. For an example of recent scholarship that challenges low enlistment figures for Canada's francophones, see Jean Martin, "Yes, French Canadians Did Their Share in the First World War," *Canadian Military Journal* 17, no. 4 (Autumn 2017): 47–55, www.journal.forces.gc.ca.

75. *Sentinel*, 13 April 1917, 1. Incidentally, the officers of the *Sentinel* were not Franco-Americans promoting their own ethnic group, for they were: Mrs. T. F. Mannix, President; M. M. Dunphy, Secretary-Treasurer; and William M. Lynch, Manager. *Sentinel*, 13 April 1917, 3. Other non-Franco organizations similarly recognized the contributions of Franco-Americans to the war effort. French names, for example, are well represented among the more than 500

compiled by the American Legion of men from Plattsburgh who served in the Great War. See "List of Men from City of Plattsburgh, N.Y. in World War," sent to George Bixby, City Historian of Plattsburgh, by letter of F. G. Eastland, Chairman, American Legion, Plattsburgh, 8 February 1923, World War I Veterans' Service Data and Photographs, 1917–1939, Series A0412-78, Box 6, Folder 20: City of Plattsburgh, NYS.

76. *Daily Republican*, 26 May 1917, 3, 28 May 1917, 3.

77. *Daily Republican*, 24 September 1917, 3.

78. *Daily Republican*, 10 November 1917, 1; *Sentinel*, 23 April 1918, 3; *Daily Press*, 25 April 1918, 4, 28 September 1940, 3. The officers of the *Daily Press*, the same as those of the *Sentinel*, also were not Franco-Americans promoting their own ethnic group. *Daily Press*, 25 April 1918, 2.

79. *Sentinel*, 23 April 1918, 3, 10 May 1918, 1. At the end of the nineteenth century appeared the first of fourteen editions of the *Guide officiel des Franco-Américains*; the volumes ran from 1899 to 1946, basically from the end of the Spanish-American War to the end of World War II. The volume published in 1921 specifically documented Franco-American involvement in the First World War to demonstrate to the United States and to the world the patriotism of this ethnic group, by proving with numbers that Franco-Americans had done their duty and were not strangers in their adopted country. In part I of the volume, one finds brief historical information on each of the French-language parishes of the United States, most centered in New England, and how many soldiers from each parish participated in the Great War. St. Peter's Church of Plattsburgh had 203 servicemen who contributed to the war effort. Bélanger, *Guide Franco-Américain* [1921], 3, 207.

80. *Sentinel*, 31 May 1918, 1.

81. *Sentinel*, 7 July 1911, 9; *Daily Republican*, 5 July 1918, 3.

82. *Sentinel*, 2 March 1920, 4.

83. "St. Peter's Parish 150th Anniversary"; *Sentinel*, 2 June 1911, 9; *US Census, 1910*; Deed Books 115, pp. 845–46, 119, pp. 836–37, 120, pp. 552–53, 122, pp. 346–47, 122, pp. 424–25, 123, pp. 144–45, 125, pp. 259–60, 127, pp. 56–57, 128, pp. 463–64, 132, pp. 194–95, 132, pp. 195–96, and Miscellaneous Records, Book 2, p. 189, CCCO; *Plattsburgh City Directory for 1913*, vol. 17 (Newburgh, NY: L. P. Waite, 1913), 111; *Plattsburgh (New York) Directory, 1914*, vol. 18 (Springfield, MA: H. A. Manning, 1914), front cover, 57; *Plattsburgh (New York) Directory, 1916*, vol. 20 (Greenfield, MA: H. A. Manning, 1916), 104, 110; *Plattsburgh (New York) Directory, 1917*, vol. 21 (Schenectady, NY: H. A. Manning, 1917), 36, 55, 56; *Plattsburgh (New York) Directory, 1919*, vol. 22 (Schenectady, NY: H. A. Manning, 1919), 33; *Plattsburgh (New York) Directory, 1920*, vol. 23 (Schenectady, NY: H. A. Manning, 1920), 124, 156.

84. *Daily Press*, 14 January 1911, 5; *Sentinel*, 12 January 1912, 5; Mark Paul Richard, "Coping before *l'État-providence:* Collective Welfare Strategies of

New England's Franco-Americans," *Québec Studies* 25 (Spring 1998): 63; Deed Book 119, p. 19, CCCO; *Daily Republican*, 7 December 1916, 3.

    85. *Daily Press*, 24 January 1920, 4; *Sentinel*, 23 January 1920, 4; *US Census, 1920*.

Chapter Seven

    1. *Plattsburgh Daily Press*, 25 November 1926, 3. On the Ku Klux Klan in the Northeast, see Richard, *Not a Catholic Nation*.

    2. US Department of Commerce, Bureau of the Census, *Fourteenth Census of the United States Taken in the Year 1920*, vol. 3 (Washington, DC: Government Printing Office, 1922), 695, 702, 704; calculations from *Fourteenth Census of the United States*, vol. 3, 695.

    3. US Department of Commerce, Bureau of the Census, *Fifteenth Census of the United States: 1930*, vol. 3, part 2 (Washington, DC: Government Printing Office, 1932), 291, 300–301.

    4. Leonard J. Moore, *Citizen Klansmen: The Ku Klux Klan in Indiana, 1921–1928* (Chapel Hill: University of North Carolina Press, 1991), xii, 1, 189–90. For a synthesis of the scholarship on the 1920s Klan, see Thomas R. Pegram, *One Hundred Percent American: The Rebirth and Decline of the Ku Klux Klan in the 1920s* (Chicago: Ivan R. Dee, 2011.)

    5. *New York Times*, 6 December 1922, 4, 23 December 1922, 1–2; Charles Drury, *Boston Herald*, 15 August 1924, 1–2; *Plattsburgh Sentinel*, 24 June 1927, 4.

    6. *Daily Press*, 30 July 1926, 3; *Plattsburgh Daily Republican*, 30 July 1926, 3; *Sentinel*, 3 August 1926, 6.

    7. *Daily Press*, 25 November 1926, 3; *Plattsburgh Press-Republican*, 10 November 1945, 1, 3; *US Census, 1920*; Taylor, *A History of Catholicism in the North Country*, 270. Eventually, St. John's parish acquired much of Conway's property, and part of it became an athletic field for the parochial school. *The Roman Catholic Church of Saint John the Baptist, 1827–2012*, 55.

    8. *Daily Press*, 25 November 1926, 3. The *Daily Republican* (9 July 1927, 1, 13 June 1928, 1) reported two other cross burnings in Plattsburgh in the 1920s, but it did not attribute either to the work of the KKK. A short cross of "but a few feet in height" that burned near the pond of the Plattsburgh Normal School one Friday night in July 1927 was blamed on "a group of youths who were playing on the campus early in the evening." The burning remnants of another cross that firefighters discovered around midnight at Cumberland Head one evening in June 1928 went unexplained.

    9. See Richard, *Not a Catholic Nation*.

    10. Note, for example, the actions of Bishop Louis Walsh of Maine in Richard, *Loyal but French*, 125–26, 137–42, 146–47, 150.

11. *Daily Republican*, 1 July 1929, 3. The newspaper did not indicate whether the speakers made their remarks in French or English.

12. "Fr. Léo Deschâtelets, O.M.I.," 2017, omiworld.org; Deschâtelets, "Notes historiques sur notre maison."

13. *Sentinel*, 26 December 1922, 2, 30 March 1926, 5, 30 November 1926, 5; *NY Census, 1925*; Annales, St. Peter, Plattsburgh, NY, vol. 1, 27 février 1924, box 34, DSH, F502.10; *Daily Press*, 16 November 1925, 3, 29 November 1927, 2; *Daily Republican*, 26 November 1928, 3.

14. *US Census, 1920, 1930*.

15. Brochure, Mount Assumption Institute Commencement Exercises, 22 June 1922, Plattsburgh Mount Assumption Institute, Juvénat, Publications, box 5203, FIC; Mount Assumption Institute Catalogue 1924, 8, 10, MAI Plattsburgh, brochures, box 5257, FIC.

16. *Sentinel*, 18 June 1926, 5, 28 February 1928, 5; Annales, St. Peter, Plattsburgh, vol. 1, 18 avril 1929, 19 décembre 1929, DSH.

17. See, for example, Mark Paul Richard, "Franco-Americans Fight World War One—Abroad and at Home," *Je Me Souviens Magazine* 43, no. 2 (April–June 2020): 39–44.

18. *Sentinel*, 28 December 1926, 5. Incidentally, St. John's also celebrated Christmas with a midnight mass that year.

19. Membership applications, 1921–1930, Association St. Jean Baptiste Collection, CCHA; Initiation de la Société St. Jean Baptiste de Plattsburgh [1920s], Miscellaneous Papers, Association St. Jean Baptiste Collection.

20. Sean T. Moore, "Law Enforcement and Prohibition in Northern New York, 1920–33," in Ouellette, ed., *Conflict and Accommodation in North Country Communities*, 84–85; Initiation de la Société St. Jean Baptiste de Plattsburgh; *Rutland (Vermont) Daily Herald*, 3 September 1924, 1, 5 September 1924, 2, 6 September 1924, 2.

21. *Sentinel*, 11 February 1921, 5; *US Census, 1920*.

22. *Sentinel*, 28 June 1921, 5.

23. *Sentinel*, 11 February 1921, 5. See, for example, Minutes de l'Assemblée de 2 août 1927, Association St. Jean Baptiste Collection.

24. *Daily Republican*, 5 May 1923, 7, 14 June 1924, 8, 17 December 1927, 3, 8 January 1930, 3; Deed Book 139, pp. 261–62, CCCO; *Sentinel*, 21 December 1923, 2, 4 May 1926, 5; *Daily Press*, 12 March 1924, 3, 10 May 1927, 11; Report of Auditing Committee, Association St. Jean Baptiste, Building Fund, 1 June 1923 to 31 March 1929, dated 30 April 1929, 2, Association St. Jean Baptiste Collection, CCHA, 88.010.0001.

25. *Sentinel*, 28 June 1927, 3; *Daily Republican*, 25 June 1928, 3.

26. Undated advertisement of L'Union St-Jean-Baptiste d'Amérique, in typescript, Walter Peter Light, Stephen Collins Light, and Keith Andrew Herkalo, "Genealogy of the Light Family of Plattsburgh, N.Y.," 2nd ed. (1993), 9,

courtesy of Stephen Light, Plattsburgh, NY; *Sentinel*, 16 April 1929, 2; Rumilly, *Histoire des Franco-Américains*, 334.

27. Mark Paul Richard, "Negotiating Ethnic Identity: St. Jean-Baptiste Day Celebrations in Francophone Lewiston, Maine," in Nelson Madore and Barry Rodrigue, eds., *Voyages: A Maine Franco-American Reader* (Gardiner, ME: Tilbury House and the University of Southern Maine Franco-American Collection, 2007), 211–23; *Sentinel*, 24 June 1924, 5.

28. *US Census, 1910, 1920, 1930*; *NY Census, 1915, 1925*; St. John the Baptist Church, Plattsburgh, New York: The First Century, 1875–1975, 15–16, PPL, Pam410.

29. Taylor, *A History of Catholicism in the North Country*, 270; St. John's Church, Plattsburgh, New York, 1868–1943, PPL, Pam415; Deed Book 129, pp. 71–72, CCCO; *Daily Republican*, 28 April 1919, 3. Celebratory publications of St. John's parish point out that it had organized Plattsburgh's first Catholic school around 1842 in the basement of the church shared by the Irish and the French Canadians on property now occupied by city hall. Organized before St. Peter's formed a parish of its own, it is unclear how long it lasted, for St. John's parish publications provide no further information on the school. See *The Roman Catholic Church of Saint John the Baptist, 1827–2012*, 45, 54.

30. *Daily Republican*, 8 September 1920, 8.

31. Taylor, *A History of Catholicism in the North Country*, 42, 262; *Daily Republican*, 14 December 1931, 3; typescript, Sister Mary Agnes, Harding, R.S.M., "A History of the Sisters of Mercy in the Ogdensburg Diocese of New York State" (1959), 45, 48, courtesy of Sr. Brian Marie Latour, R.S.M., Plattsburgh, New York; *Official Catholic Directory, Almanac and Clergy List for the Year of Our Lord, 1905*, vol. 19, no. 1 (Milwaukee: M. H. Wiltzius, 1905), 484; *Sentinel*, 17 February 1928, 3.

32. *Daily Republican*, 5 August 1920, 6, 8 September 1920, 8; *The Roman Catholic Church of Saint John the Baptist, 1827–2012*, 55; Harding, "A History of the Sisters of Mercy," 171–72; *Press Republican*, 3 July 1943, 7; *US Census, 1930*.

33. *NY Census, 1925*. Newfoundland remained a colony of Britain until 1949, when it joined the Canadian Confederation.

34. *US Census, 1930*.

35. *The Roman Catholic Church of Saint John the Baptist, 1827–2012*, 50, 53; Mary C. Kelly, "'Spiritual heirs of the great Protestants who gave their lives for Ireland': Expanding Irish American Nationalist Landscapes, 1919–1922," *Journal of American Ethnic History* 40, no. 4 (Summer 2021): 8; BBC History, "Eamon de Valera (1882–1975)," 2014, www.bbc.co.uk; Suzanne Lynch, "Éamon de Valera's US Trip that Left Irish America Divided," *The Irish Times*, 1 June 2019, www.irishtimes.com.

36. *Daily Republican*, 18 March 1924, 1; Merriam-Webster, "Erin go bragh," 2022, www.merriam-webster.com.

37. Harding, "A History of the Sisters of Mercy," 114, 188–91; *Sentinel*, 4 November 1921, 2; Deed Book 134, p. 455, CCCO; *Daily Republican*, 30 July 1931, 7; Taylor, *A History of Catholicism in the North Country*, 267; *NY Census, 1925*; *US Census, 1930*.

38. Taylor, *A History of Catholicism in the North Country*, 93; Albert A., Bélanger, dir., *Guide Officiel des Franco-Américains, 1922* (Fall River, MA: Albert A. Bélanger, 1922), 209; *Sentinel*, 21 October 1927, 5.

39. *Daily Press*, 12 June 1920, 6; *Daily Republican*, 3 June 1920, 3, 5 June 1920, 5, 28 July 1920, 7; *Sentinel*, 27 July 1920, 6, 15 October 1920, 6.

40. *Daily Republican*, 4 May 1928, 3, 7 May 1929, 2.

41. Mémorial du Monastère du Sacré-Coeur, Lewiston, Maine, 1904–1968, vol. I, 1904, 1, Archives of the Dominican Sisters, Sabattus, Maine; *Album-Souvenir: Vingt-Cinquième Anniversaire de l'arrivée des Religieuses Dominicaines à Lewiston* (Lewiston, ME: Le Messager [1929]), 3; Deed Book 137, pp. 224–225, CCCO; *Sentinel*, 20 October 1922, 3, 7 July 1925, 5; Jul. Racette, O.M.I., Eglise St. Pierre, Plattsburgh, NY, to Rt. Rev. J. H. Conroy, D.D., Ogdensburg, NY, 27 March 1923, Dominican Sisters, Fall River, file, RCDO.

42. Yearbook and Church Directory of St. Peter's Church [1931–1932]; Racette à la Très Révérende Mère M. Madeleine, Supérieur Générale, 6 février 1923, and M. Madeleine à Racette, 26 février 1923, St. Peter School, box 33, folder 4, DSH, F502.10.

43. Racette to Conroy, 27 March 1923, Dominican Sisters, Fall River, file, RCDO; Conroy to M. Madeleine, 13 April 1923 and 19 May 1923, Dominican Sisters, Fall River, file, RCDO; handwritten note from Conroy to Racette on copy of 13 April 1923 letter.

44. M. Madeleine to Conroy, 23 May 1923, Dominican Sisters, Fall River, file, RCDO.

45. M. Madeleine and Sister M. Joseph, Secretary General, to Racette, 26 July 1923, St. Peter's Plattsburgh, box 98, folder 13, DSH, F502.10 and F623.01. The Dominican Sisters proved flexible about this requirement, however, in order to meet the needs of the parish community during difficult financial times. In an undated letter, probably penned during the Great Depression, the Prioress General informed the Dominican Sisters in Plattsburgh that the parish did not have the funds necessary to pay the salaries of the Brothers of Christian Instruction and that they would have to take over the classes of boys formerly taught by the brothers. Her concluding line made apparent that this was an "obedience" they had to accept: "Each must therefore resign herself to taking a class of boys as an act of resignation." M. Madeleine to Sisters [in Plattsburgh], undated, St. Peter's Plattsburgh, box 98, folder 9, 1924–1939, DSH, F502.10 and F623.01.

46. *Daily Republican*, 1 September 1923, 8; Taylor, *A History of Catholicism in the North Country*, 261; Annales, St. Peter, Plattsburgh, vol. 1, 1923, 28 août 1923, 11 septembre 1923, 18 septembre 1923, 11 juillet 1924, DSH; history

of Couvent St. Dominique, Plattsburgh, NY, Juin 1923 à Juin 1935, St. Peter School, box 33, folder 2, DSH.

47. History of Couvent St. Dominique; Hogue, *Centennial*, 185; Annales, St. Peter, Plattsburgh, vol. 1, 27 août 1923, 15 septembre 1925, DSH.

48. Annales, St. Peter, Plattsburgh, vol. 1, 1923, 2 septembre 1923, DSH; Livre des Oeuvres, Saint Peter, Plattsburgh, NY, 1923–1959, box 33, folder 6, DSH; Mission de Plattsburg, NY, Registre du Personnel et des Oeuvres du divers Couvents de la Congrégation, 1923–1924, 44, box 71, book 36, DSH, F242.0601; St. Peter School, box 33, folder 2, DSH; Fall River Sisters Papers, box 105, DSH, 02/F0003; History of Couvent St. Dominique.

49. *NY Census, 1925*; *US Census, 1930*.

50. Annales, St. Peter, Plattsburgh, vol. 1, 10 juin 1924, 16 juin 1924, DSH; Racette à M. Madeleine, 26 juillet 1924, St. Peter School, box 33, folder 2, DSH.

51. Annales, St. Peter, Plattsburgh, vol. 1, 18 août 1924, 11 novembre 1924, 17 août 1925, 10 décembre 1925, 14 et 16 août 1926, 4 juillet 1928, DSH.

52. Conroy to the Superiors-Teaching Communities of Women, Diocese of Ogdensburg, 3 June 1927, Correspondence, Prioress General, box 58, folder 7, DSH, F205.01.

53. Annales, St. Peter, Plattsburgh, vol. 1, 31 août 1925, 8 septembre 1925, 7 septembre 1926, 6 septembre 1927, 30 août 1929, DSH; *Daily Press*, 8 September 1925, 4; *Sentinel*, 23 August 1927, 6; Yearbook and Church Directory of St. Peter's Church [1931–1932].

54. *NY Census, 1925*; *US Census, 1930*.

55. *US Census, 1920, 1930*; *NY Census, 1925*; Guilbeault-Cayer, *Les Soeurs de la Charité de Saint-Louis en Amérique*, 97–98; italics in original, Laperrière, *Les congrégations religieuses*, 469–70.

56. *NY Census, 1905, 1915, 1925*; *US Census, 1910, 1920, 1930, 1940*; Taylor, *A History of Catholicism in the North Country*, 271; Menard, "The Brothers of Christian Instruction in the United States (1903–1981)," 96, 112; Tregret, "The Brothers of Christian Instruction," 84–85; *Un Cinquantenaire, 1886–1936*, 383–84. A draft of a five-year contract beginning in September 1924 between St-Pierre parish and the Brothers of Christian Instruction reveals that St. Peter's agreed to continue paying the order $1,000 annually for parish boys who attended Mount Assumption Institute for their education after grade six. Engagement du personnel, Plattsburgh, MAI Juvénat, box 5203, FIC.

57. Menard, "The Brothers of Christian Instruction in the United States (1903–1981)," 98, 112–13; Taylor, *A History of Catholicism in the North Country*, 271; Everest, *Briefly Told*, 22.

58. Typescript, Brother Patrick Menard, F.I.C., "The Brothers of Christian Instruction in the United States (1979–1991)," vol. 2 [1991], 70; Menard, "The Brothers of Christian Instruction in the United States (1903–1981)," 99.

59. Booklet, "Mount Assumption Institute: Catholic, Coeducational High School, Grades 9–12," [1970s], 4, Parish History Folder, SPP; Menard, "The Brothers of Christian Instruction in the United States (1903–1981)," 22, 96; *US Census, 1920*; yearbook, *The Mount* (1926), 80, BCI.

60. *US Census, 1920*; *The Mount* (1926), 80; Institut des Frères de l'Instruction Chrétienne, visite regulière, établissement de Plattsburgh, NY, dossier Plattsburgh-St-Peter's School, Communauté des FIC, Rapport des visites de 1912, 1913, 1914, 1915 et 1927, box 5203, FIC; *Sentinel*, 3 May 1929, 2.

61. Deed Books 145, pp. 260–61, 153, pp. 49–50, CCCO; *The Mount* (1928), 75, PPL.

62. *The Mount* (1925), 73, PPL; Carl Wittke, *Tambo and Bones: A History of the American Minstrel Stage* (Durham, NC: Duke University Press, 1930), 6, 9, 12–13; Michael Rogin, "Making America Home: Racial Masquerade and Ethnic Assimilation in the Transition to Talking Pictures," *Journal of American History* 79, no. 3 (December 1992): 1052; Tim Rowland, *The Sun* (community newspaper), 11 May 2019, 8.

63. *Daily Press*, 23 October 1909, 5; *Sentinel*, 17 December 1909, 1; flyer, "M.A.I. Glee Club Minstrels," MAI Scrapbook, c. 1925, BCI, 49228; Stanley Brunell, "The M.A.I. Minstrel Show," *The Mount* (1925), 74.

64. Rogin, "Making America Home," 1053, 1061. For an example from ethnic groups of Massachusetts of the phenomenon Rogin describes, see John F. McClymer, "Passing from Light into Dark," *Journal for MultiMedia History* 4 (2003), www.albany.edu/jmmh/vol4/passing/passing1.html.

65. *Report of the Champlain Valley Hospital, Plattsburgh, New York, 1925* (Plattsburgh, NY: Clinton Press, 1925), ix, 60, CCHO.

66. *Report of the Champlain Valley Hospital* (1925), 60; Myra Eileen Slattery '29, Champlain Valley Hospital and School of Nursing, box 3, GNSH.

67. *Sentinel*, 18 May 1923, 4.

68. Typescript, "The Champlain Valley Hospital, Plattsburgh, N.Y., Admission Requirements" [1926], School of Nursing Memorabilia, Champlain Valley Hospital and School of Nursing, box 2, GNSH.

69. *NY Census, 1925*; *US Census, 1930*. The large majority of the hospital's patients may have been anglophone, if one can judge from a census snapshot. When census-takers came around in 1925, only about one-fourth of Champlain Valley Hospital patients had French surnames. *NY Census, 1925*.

70. Because the *US Census, 1920*, does not clearly distinguish student nurses from other hospital staff, there is no discussion here of the data from that census year.

71. *NY Census, 1915, 1925*; *US Census, 1930*.

72. *Sentinel*, 10 October 1922, 3, 18 September 1925, 4, 21 September 1926, 4, 16 September 1927, 2; *Daily Republican*, 13 September 1929, 5.

73. John Moffitt, President, "Report of the Directors of the Champlain Valley Hospital" [1921], 1, Champlain Valley Hospital papers, box 7, CVPH; brochure, Fund Raising Campaign for the Champlain Valley Hospital, August 29th—September 4th, 1921, 2, 4, Champlain Valley Hospital documents, box 6, CVPH; "Report of the Superintendent for the Year Ending June 30, 1921," 2, Champlain Valley Hospital papers, box 7; minutes, Champlain Valley Hospital Board of Directors, The Champlain Valley Hospital Records, 1910–1962, 99, CVPH; *Daily Republican*, 27 August 1921, 7.

74. Fund Raising Campaign for the Champlain Valley Hospital, 1921, 3–4; Champlain Valley Hospital Records, 1910–1962, 109; *Daily Press*, 30 July 1921, 8; *Daily Republican*, 7 August 1923, 8, 28 February 1929, 3; *Report of the Champlain Valley Hospital* (1925), 36.

75. *Sentinel*, 16 May 1922, 1, 13 June 1922, 5; email communication from Diane Merkel to the author, 13 December 2018; *Republican*, 21 May 1910, 7.

76. *Sentinel*, 31 July 1923, 4, 5 October 1928, 6; *Daily Republican*, 1 March 1929, 3; *Report of the Champlain Valley Hospital* (1925), 65–66.

77. *Daily Republican*, 15 January 1931, 3, 22 August 1933, 3; *Daily Press*, 11 December 1931, 3.

78. Champlain Valley Hospital Records, 1910–1962, 130, 150, 153.

79. Champlain Valley Hospital Records, 1910–1962, 147–49.

80. *Sentinel*, 7 August 1925, 4.

81. *Sentinel*, 4 June 1926, 2, 4 January 1927, 3, 1 February 1927, 3, 2 August 1927, 5.

82. Champlain Valley Hospital Records, 1910–1962, 200; *Manning's Plattsburgh (New York) Directory for Year beginning October 1928*, vol. 31 (Springfield, MA: H. A. Manning, 1928), 78.

83. *Daily Republican*, 8 August 1929, 3; Champlain Valley Hospital Records, 1910–1962, 203.

84. Booklet, *The Physicians Hospital School of Nursing, Plattsburgh, New York* (Plattsburgh, NY: Physicians Hospital, 1928), Alice T. Miner Museum, Chazy, New York; pamphlet, The Constitution, By-Laws, Rules and Regulations of the Champlain Valley Hospital, Plattsburgh, NY, 1927, 25, Champlain Valley Hospital papers, box 7, CVPH; *The Physicians Hospital, Plattsburgh, New York* (Plattsburgh, NY: Physicians Hospital, 1929), PPL, Pam366.

85. No enumeration of the Physicians' Hospital student nurses could be found in the *US Census, 1920*.

86. *NY Census, 1925*; *US Census, 1930*.

87. Pamphlet, William Henry Miner, Philanthropist, n.d., box 10, CVPH; LaVerne Dutcher, *Press-Republican*, 23 September 1990, C1; Directors' report [1921], 2, Champlain Valley Hospital papers, box 7, CVPH; *The Physicians Hospital School of Nursing, Plattsburgh, New York*, 1928; "History of the Medical Center,"

10th Anniversary, CVPH Medical Center, Plattsburgh, New York, supplement to the *Press-Republican*, 9–15 May 1982, 4, Champlain Valley documents, box 64, CVPH; *The Physicians Hospital, Plattsburgh, New York*, 1929; *Press-Republican*, 8 August 1952, 3, 29 August 1953, 1.

88. F. C. Dossert, comp. and ed., *The Barton Forceps* (N.p.: Free Press Printing, 1949), 115–20, 122, 124–26, 129–45; Archibald Donald Campbell, "Foreword," in Dossert, *The Barton Forceps*, vii.

89. *Republican*, 19 November 1910, 1; minutes, Physicians' Hospital Corporation Board of Directors, 1924–1935, 2, 5, CVPH.

90. *Daily Press*, 17 March 1924, 4; *Sentinel*, 21 March 1924, 5; Will of J. H. LaRocque, 28 October 1918, Dr. LaRocque Collection, CCHA, 2013.079.0072.

91. *Daily Press*, 17 March 1924, 4.

Chapter Eight

1. Yearbook and Church Directory of St. Peter's Church [1931–1932].

2. Deed Books 162, p. 292, underscoring in original, 162, p. 349, 164, pp. 279–80, CCCO; *Manning's Plattsburgh (New York) Directory for the Year beginning November, 1930*, vol. 33 (Schenectady, NY: H. A. Manning, 1930), 67, 141.

3. Arthur J. Lemire, O.M.I., treasurer, St. Peter's Rectory, Plattsburgh, New York, to Chancery Office, Ogdensburg, NY, 2 January 1934, parish correspondence, St. Peter's, 1914–1960, RCDO.

4. Yearbook and Church Directory of St. Peter's Church [1931–1932].

5. Yearbook and Church Directory of St. Peter's Church [1931–1932]; *US Census, 1930*; *Plattsburgh Sentinel*, 25 February 1930, 2; *Plattsburgh Daily Press*, 20 August 1931, 1, 9 August 1932, 7, 10 August 1932, 3; *Plattsburgh Daily Republican*, 27 July 1934, 4.

6. *Daily Press*, 2 December 1931, 3; Yearbook and Church Directory of St. Peter's Church [1931–1932]; *Daily Republican*, 7 June 1929, 3. Incidentally, this practice of sewing for the poor did not begin during the Great Depression, for women of St. Peter's parish used to gather to sew garments for the poor as early as 1908. See *Daily Press*, 28 October 1908, 3.

7. *Daily Republican*, 3 October 1931, 3, 15 December 1936, 4, 17 March 1937, 3; *Daily Press*, 14 December 1932, 3.

8. *Daily Press*, 24 November 1931, 3, 2 April 1932, 3, 18 April 1932, 10; pamphlet, "First Annual Minstrel of the St. Jean Baptiste Association and St. Peter's Church, St. Peter's Hall, April 18, 19, 20, 1932," Plattsburgh St-Peter's Church, Publications, box 5203, FIC; *Daily Republican*, 21 April 1932, 3.

9. *Daily Press*, 23 April 1936, 3; open letter of Lemire, 8 May 1936, 1–2, inserted into scrapbook, Leander Bouyea Papers, 1937–1944, box 2, PPL, B-113.

10. *Daily Republican*, 26 February 1938, 3, 1 March 1938, 3.

11. Pem Davidson Buck, "Constructing Race, Creating White Privilege," 24, in Paula S. Rothenberg with Soniya Munshi, eds., *Race, Class, and Gender in the United States: An Integrated Study*, 10th ed. (New York: Worth Publishers, 2016.)

12. Kathryn Vaggalis, "Off-White Romantics: Cross-Cultural Histories of Immigrant Picture Brides and the Process of US Race Making," *Journal of American Ethnic History* 40, no. 3 (Spring 2021): 50.

13. Yearbook and Church Directory of St. Peter's Church [1931–1932]; *Daily Republican*, 19 May 1939, 3.

14. *Daily Republican*, 12 September 1933, 3, 15 September 1933, 4.

15. *Daily Press*, 20 June 1936, 3, 24 June 1937, 3, 6 September 1938, 4; *Daily Republican*, 6 August 1934, 4, 22 June 1936, 3, 6 September 1938, 3.

16. *Daily Press*, 6 July 1931, 1.

17. *Daily Press*, 31 July 1937, 2; *Daily Republican*, 31 August 1936, 3.

18. *Daily Republican*, 23 May 1932, 3, 25 May 1935, 3, 24 May 1937, 3; *Daily Press*, 23 May 1932, 3, 11 June 1934, 3.

19. Catholic Reference Book and Church Register, Our Lady of Victory Church, Plattsburgh, New York [1931], PPL, Pam675.

20. Yearbook and Church Directory of St. Peter's Church [1931–1932]; Annales, St. Peter, Plattsburgh, NY, vol. 1, 17 juin 1931, 24 juin 1932, vol. 2, 17 juin 1936, box 34, DSH, F502.10; *Daily Republican*, 22 June 1939, 3.

21. *Daily Republican*, 27 January 1934, 11, 3 March 1934, 10.

22. Annales, St. Peter, Plattsburgh, vol. 1, 7 mars 1930, vol. 2, 25 mars 1937, DSH; *Daily Press*, 2 February 1931, 5, 24 March 1934, 7, 26 February 1936, 3, 4 March 1937, 5, 11 March 1938, 3; *Daily Republican*, 23 March 1935, 3.

23. Association St. Jean Baptiste ribbons, Association St. Jean Baptiste Collection, CCHA; *Daily Republican*, 24 June 1931, 3, 29 June 1931, 3, 16 December 1933, 3.

24. Yearbook and Church Directory of St. Peter's Church [1931–1932].

25. *Daily Republican*, 24 October 1931, 7; *Plattsburgh Press-Republican*, 6 October 1952, 3.

26. *Press-Republican*, 6 October 1952, 3; Leander A. Bouyea, Mayor, to Charles Spencer Hart, Grand Exalted Ruler, B.P.O.E., New York, NY, 9 May 1938, Leander Bouyea papers, box 1.

27. *Press-Republican*, 6 October 1952, 3; Bouyea to Hartwell Rosson, Burns & McDonnell Engineering Co., Cincinnati, Ohio, 18 October 1937, Leander Bouyea papers, box 1.

28. Bouyea to L. G. Anderson, Scotland, South Dakota, 11 July 1938, Leander Bouyea papers, box 1.

29. Bouyea to Max Wagner, Montréal, PQ, 31 May 1938, Leander Bouyea papers, box 1.

30. *Chronique des Frères de l'Instruction Chrétienne de Ploërmel dits Frères de la Mennais*, no. 105 (1er septembre 1931), 67, and no. 107 (1er janvier 1932), 61–62, BCI.

31. Yearbook and Church Directory of St. Peter's Church [1931–1932]; Menard, "The Brothers of Christian Instruction in the United States (1903–1981)," 31; *Un Cinquantenaire, 1886–1936*, 386–87.

32. Annales, St. Peter, Plattsburgh, NY, vol. 2, 6 septembre 1932, 5 septembre 1939, DSH.

33. Hogue, *Centennial*, 186; A. Veronneau, OMI, St. Peter's Rectory, Plattsburgh, NY, à la très Révérande Mère Générale, Maison Mère Des Srs. Dominicaines, Fall River, Mass., 31 août 1933, St. Peter School, box 33, folder 4, DSH; handwritten notation of M. Madeleine on Veronneau's letter.

34. Annales, St. Peter, Plattsburgh, NY, vol. 2, 9 février 1933, DSH.

35. *Daily Republican*, 31 January 1931, 3; Annales, St. Peter, Plattsburgh, NY, vol. 2, 17 décembre 1935, 20 décembre 1935, 9 décembre 1936, et 2 décembre1937, DSH.

36. Annales, St. Peter, Plattsburgh, NY, vol. 2, 19 et 21 mars 1937, 19 décembre 1937, 27 février 1938, 9, 10, 12, et 13 mars 1939, DSH.

37. "Condition for Admission of Candidates to the Community of Dominican Sisters," Membership Attestations, 1920–1951, box 93, DSH.

38. Annales, St. Peter, Plattsburgh, NY, vol. 1, 4 août 1930, vol. 2, 7 mars 1939, DSH; Report to the General Council from Couvent Saint Dominique, Plattsburg, NY, 16 juin 1933, St. Peter's, Plattsburgh, box 98, folder 8, DSH, F502.10 and F623.01; St. Peter School, box 33, folder 2, DSH; *US Census, 1940*; typescript, "Changes in the Constitutions of the Dominican Sisters of the Congregation of St. Catherine of Siena, Fall River, Mass." [1947], Dominican Sisters' Fall River file, RCDO.

39. Reports to General Council from Couvent Saint Dominique, 25 juillet 1930, [1937], and [1940], St. Peter's, Plattsburgh, box 98, folder 8, DSH; Annales, St. Peter, Plattsburgh, NY, vol. 2, 24 juillet 1936, 9 septembre 1936, DSH; *Daily Press*, 15 September 1937, 3.

40. Registre du Personnel et des Oeuvres de la Congrégation, book 36, pp. 107, 170, box 71, DSH; Fall River Sisters Papers, box 105 and box 106, DSH, 02/F0003, supplemented by archivist; Annales, St. Peter, Plattsburgh, NY, vol. 2, 7 octobre 1934, 18 septembre 1935, DSH.

41. Bouyea to Colonel Thomas Crystal, Plattsburgh Barracks, New York, 16 January 1939, Leander Bouyea papers, box 1.

42. Harding, "A History of the Sisters of Mercy," 190–91, 193; *Daily Republican*, 23 July 1931, 5, 30 July 1931, 7, 15 December 1931, 3, 25 September 1939, 5; Taylor, *A History of Catholicism in the North Country*, 268; *US Census, 1940*.

43. *Daily Press*, 21 August 1931, 3.

44. St Peter's Plattsburg, box 98, folder 8, DSH.

Notes to Chapter Eight | 325

45. *US Census, 1920, 1930, 1940; NY Census, 1925.* More specifically, in 1930, eleven of the fifteen Grey Nuns working at the hospital as administrators or nurses were born in English Canada, while two each were born in Ireland and the United States; in 1940, eight of the fifteen Grey Nuns were born in English Canada and seven were born in the United States.

46. Annals, Champlain Valley Hospital, 1937–1949, Record Group 600, box 1, GNSH.

47. *Daily Republican*, 29 June 1931, 3, 1 July 1931, 3, 18 February 1933, 3; *Daily Press*, 18 February 1933, 4.

48. *Daily Press*, 11 June 1934, 4.

49. J. H. Conroy, Bishop of Ogdensburg, to Rev. J. E. Turcotte, O.M.I., Rector, Church of St. Peter, Plattsburgh, NY, 11 June 1938, Champlain Valley Hospital Convent Correspondence, 1937–1962, Plattsburgh file, RCDO; Lemire to Bishop F. J. Monaghan, D.D., Ogdensburg, NY, 18 December 1939, and Monaghan to Lemire, 20 December 1939, underscoring in original, Parish correspondence, St. Peter's, 1914–1960, RCDO.

50. *Daily Republican*, 11 March 1932, 3, 15 September 1933, 3, 18 September 1934, 10, 19 September 1935, 10, 23 January 1939, 3.

51. *Daily Republican*, 21 December 1934, 3, 24 April 1935, 3, 19 September 1935, 10; *Daily Press*, 27 December 1934, 3, 9 August 1935, 3.

52. *Daily Republican*, 5 August 1935, 4.

53. *Daily Republican*, 25 May 1936, 3, 23 March 1937, 4, 12 April 1938, 3; *Daily Press*, 5 August 1936, 3, 5 March 1937, 3, 26 March 1937, 4.

54. Edna Marie Leroux, RSM, "In Times of Socioeconomic Crisis," in Stepsis and Liptak, eds., *Pioneer Healers*, 141; minutes, Champlain Valley Hospital Board of Directors, The Champlain Valley Hospital Records, 1910–1962, 225, 251, CVPH.

55. *STAT* (Physicians' Hospital yearbook), 1931, CCHO; *Daily Press*, 5 November 1934, 3, 22 October 1936, 3; minutes, Physicians' Hospital Corporation Board of Directors, 1924–1935, 219, 228–29, CVPH.

56. Minutes, Champlain Valley Hospital Board of Directors, 1910–1962, 213, 241, CVPH; Annals, Champlain Valley Hospital, 1937–1949, 5 March 1937, 5, GNSH. The April 1935 minutes of the Physicians' Hospital board of directors make no mention of merger discussions, suggesting the possibility that only the Champlain Valley Hospital board of directors broached the subject around that time. The two institutions did not pursue a merger until several decades later.

57. Minutes, Physicians' Hospital Corporation Board of Directors, 1924–1935, 313, CVPH; typescript, "Treasurer's Report to Board of Directors of Physicians' Hospital of Plattsburgh, New York[,] for Year 1932," 6–7, inserted between pp. 276 and 277 of the minutes; Report of Irving Haynes, Superintendent, at the 18 April 1935 special meeting of the Physicians' Hospital board of directors, 8, inserted between pp. 314 and 315 of the minutes; "History of

the Medical Center," *10th Anniversary, CVPH Medical Center, Plattsburgh, New York*, supplement to the *Press-Republican*, 9–15 May 1982, 4, Champlain Valley Hospital documents, box 6, CVPH.

Chapter Nine

1. US Department of Commerce, Bureau of the Census, *Sixteenth Census of the United States: 1940*, vol. 2, part 5 (Washington, DC: Government Printing Office, 1943), 66, 80, 113; calculations from figures on p. 80. Other immigrants living in Plattsburgh in 1940 had come from (in descending order) Italy, Russia (USSR), Germany, England, Poland, the Irish Free State (Eire), Greece, and Northern Ireland.

2. US Department of Commerce, Bureau of the Census, *Census of Population: 1950*, vol. 2, part 32 (Washington, DC: Government Printing Office, 1952), 95, 99; calculations from figures on pp. 86, 99.

3. *Plattsburgh Press-Republican*, 24 March 1947, 3.

4. *US Census, 1940, 1950*. In 1940, seven priests resided at St. Pierre rectory; of them, two had been born in French Canada, and the other five—all with French surnames—had been born in the United States. In 1950, of the six priests at the rectory, five were native of the United States, and only one had been born in French Canada. All but one of the six priests in 1950 had French surnames.

5. *Press-Republican*, 29 August 1945, 3, 10 August 1948, 3; Annales, St. Peter, Plattsburgh, NY, vol. 3, 8 mai 1949, box 34, DSH.

6. *Plattsburgh Daily Press*, 29 February 1940, 3, 10 March 1941, 3, 3 March 1942, 3; *Press-Republican*, 13 March 1944, 3, 3 July 1947, 3, 27 February 1948, 3, 10 March 1949, 3, Annales, vol. 3, 13 mars 1949, box 34, DSH.

7. *US Census, 1940*; Registre du Personnel et des Oeuvres du divers Couvents de la Congrégation, vol. 1, book 36, 1891–1947, 224–25, 276–77, box 71, DSH, F242.0601, and vol. 2, book 37, 1947–1957, 349–50, box 71, DSH, F242.061; Fall River Sisters Papers, boxes 105 and 106, DSH, 02/F0003; Hope Sisters Personal Papers, Membership H400, file cabinets 1, 2, 3, DSH, supplemented by archivist; *US Census, 1950*.

8. Annales, vol. 3, 3 mai 1942, 29 décembre 1948, 17 avril 1949, box 34, DSH.

9. Annales, vol. 2, 17 mars 1941, 17 mars 1942, box 34, DSH; Annals, Champlain Valley Hospital, 1937–1949, inserted between 11 and 13 April 1942, 25, box 1, GNSH.

10. *US Census, 1930*; *Daily Press*, 9 June 1942, 3, 10 June 1942, 4, 11 June 1942, 5; Annals, Champlain Valley Hospital, 1937–1949, 8 June 1942, 26–27, GNSH.

11. Annales, vol. 2, 8 janvier 1940, 31 mai 1940, vol. 3, 7 septembre 1943, 4 septembre 1945, 2 novembre 1948, box 34, DSH.

12. Report to General Council from Dominican Sisters, Plattsburgh, New York, mai 1946, 2 juillet 1948, St. Peter's Plattsburgh, folder 8, box 98, DSH, F502.10 and F623.01. The Dominican Sisters were not the only order to close their boarding school in the 1940s; the Sisters of Mercy at St. John's Academy closed theirs in 1944. Harding, "A History of the Sisters of Mercy," 172.

13. Prioress General to the Trustees of St. Peter's Parish, 16 July 1948, St. Peter School, folder 3, box 33, DSH.

14. Arthur J. Lemire, O.M.I., curé, St. Peter's Church, Plattsburgh, NY, à la Révérende Mère J.-Augustin, O.P., Fall River, Mass., 15 août 1949, St. Peter School, folder 3, box 33, DSH; Annales, vol. 2, 20 février 1940, box 34, DSH.

15. Sr. Jean Augustin to Lemire, 22 October 1949, and handwritten note, signed Lemire, 1 October 1949, St. Peter School, folder 3, box 33, DSH.

16. Jean Augustin to Lemire, 22 October 1949.

17. Lemire, Oblates of Mary Immaculate Retreat House, Augusta, Me., to Sr. Sybillina, 11 January 1954, St. Peter School, folder 3, box 33, DSH.

18. Annales, vol. 2, 2 avril 1941, vol. 3, 18, 20 et 21 février 1944, 17, 18, 19, 20 et 21 avril 1944, 11, 12 et 13 février 1945, 25, 26 et 27 février 1946, vol. 4, 25 février 1950, box 34, DSH.

19. Annales, vol. 3, 15 mai 1944, box 34, DSH; *Press-Republican*, 10 November 1949, 3. The Dominican Sisters organized performances of minstrel shows by their students at least through 1957. Annales, vol. 6, 13 avril 1956, vol. 7, 22–27 avril 1957, box 34, DSH.

20. Annales, vol. 5, 15 octobre 1950, box 34, DSH. For a study that examines Catholic racism in the United States from World War I to the early 1970s, see John T. McGreevy, *Parish Boundaries: The Catholic Encounter with Race in the Twentieth Century Urban North* (Chicago: University of Chicago Press, 1996.)

21. *Daily Press*, 22 June 1940, 4, 21 September 1940, 6–7.

22. Typescript, Sr. M. Joseph, O.P., Prioress General, "St. Dominic's Priory, 100 Cornelia Street, Plattsburgh, N.Y." (19 January 1946), Dominican Sisters file Fall River, RCDO; Annales, vol. 3, 2 septembre 1947, box 34, DSH.

23. Fr. Paul Cueff et Sr. Simone Morvan, *Deux Congrégations Mennaisiennes: Les Frères de l'Instruction Chrétienne de Ploërmel [et] Les Filles de la Providence de Saint-Brieuc* (n.p., 1980), 80, FIC; Menard, "The Brothers of Christian Instruction in the United States (1903–1981)," 39; *La Chronique des Frères de l'Instruction Chrétienne*, no. 165 (1er janvier 1947), 125, FIC. By 1946, when enrollments at Mount Assumption peaked at 484, there were 28 brothers in residence. Increasing enrollments led the Brothers of Christian Instruction to expand their holdings, acquiring another property adjacent to the former Vilas mansion. In 1950, twenty-two Brothers of Christian Instruction were teaching or serving as school administrators in Plattsburgh; several others kept the fires

going to heat the dormitories or worked as janitors of the buildings they owned. Taylor, *A History of Catholicism in the North Country*, 271; Deed Book 212, pp. 235–36, CCCO; *US Census, 1950*.

24. Tregret, "The Brothers of Christian Instruction," 6–7.

25. Brochure, "Mount Assumption Institute, Plattsburgh, New York" [1948], 6, 10, capitalization in original, Plattsburgh Mount Assumption Institute Juvénat, Publications, box 5203, FIC; *US Census, 1950*.

26. *US Census, 1940, 1950*.

27. *US Census, 1940, 1950*; yearbook, *The Victor, 1941*, SCSL, 24,022-003-001; *The Victor, 1947*, SCSL, 24,022-003-002; *The Victor, 1949*, SCSL, 24,022-003-003; pamphlet, "Our Lady of Victory Academy, Plattsburg, N.Y." [circa 1949], SCSL, 24,025-004-002.

28. Garrant, "History of Our Lady of Victory Academy"; *Press-Republican*, 14 March 1950, 3; Francis J. Monaghan, Bishop of Ogdensburg, to Reverend Sister St. Henry, Superior, Sisters [of Charity] of St. Louis, Plattsburg, NY, 19 November 1940, Our Lady of Victory Convent Correspondence, 1924–1979, Plattsburgh file, RCDO; "Plattsburg," *L'Hirondelle d'Arvor*, no. 21 (novembre-décembre 1953), 29/562, SCSL, 34,003-001.

29. Bishop of Ogdensburg to Mother Mary Beatrice, Our Lady of Victory Academy, Plattsburg, NY, 14 May 1948, Our Lady of Victory Convent Correspondence, 1924–1979, Plattsburgh file, RCDO, including the original Latin version and the English translation of rescript no. 15028/48 from the Apostolic Delegate in Washington, DC; Deed Books 259, pp. 447–48, 273, pp. 225–26, 228, CCCO; *Press-Republican*, 23 April 1949, 3; *Laws of the State of New York Passed at the One Hundred and Seventy-Second Session of the Legislature . . . 1949* (Albany: n.p., 1949), 1593–94.

30. *Press-Republican*, 23 October 1950, 3, 2 June 1949, 3; *Daily Press*, 12 November 1940, 3; texte dactylographié, Résumé des annales: 1952–1958, 1952, 163, SCSL, 24,026-001.

31. Plattsburg," *L'Hirondelle d'Arvor*, no. 21 (novembre-décembre 1953), 32/565, 33/566, SCSL, 34,003-001.

32. "Plattsburg," *L'Hirondelle d'Arvor*, no. 21 (novembre-décembre 1953), 30/563, SCSL, 34,003-001; Taylor, *A History of Catholicism in the North Country*, 262.

33. "Plattsburg," *L'Hirondelle d'Arvor*, no. 21 (novembre-décembre 1953), 31/564, SCSL, 34,003-001.

34. *US Census, 1940, 1950*; *Press-Republican*, 11 October 1948, 2.

35. *Daily Press*, 9 March 1942, 2; *Plattsburgh Daily Republican*, 2 May 1942, 3; Annales, vol. 3, 4 mai 1942, 12 mai 1944, box 34, DSH. Beth Israel Synagogue appears not to have sponsored basketball players for the Church League or students for the music festivals in the forties.

36. *US Census, 1940, 1950*.

37. *US Census, 1940, 1950.* Another measure, the number of Franco-American graduates in 1950, corroborates this point. *Letter Home* (Champlain Valley Hospital School of Nursing yearbook) [1950], PPL.

38. Annales, vol. 3, 17 mars 1942, box 34, DSH; Report of the Schools, September 1940–May 1943, St. Peter's Plattsburgh, folder 8, box 98, DSH, F502.10 and F623.01.

39. Annales, vol. 3, 24 janvier 1943, 12 juin 1944, box 34, DSH; Report of the Schools, 1940–1943.

40. Annals, Champlain Valley Hospital, 1937–1949, 24 and 25 December 1942, 38–39, 1943, 48–49, June 1944, 70, GNSH; *Press-Republican*, 18 October 1943, 5.

41. *Press-Republican*, 10 April 1943, 3.

42. *Daily Republican*, 21 September 1940, 3, 7 January 1942, 3, 17 January 1942, 3, 19 February 1942, 3; *Daily Press*, 5 January 1942, 4, 19 February 1942, 3.

43. *Press-Republican*, 10 May 1943, 4, 4 August 1943, 3, 2 September 1943, 7, 22 October 1959, 6; minutes, Champlain Valley Hospital Board of Directors, The Champlain Valley Hospital Records, 1910–1962, 294, CVPH.

44. *Press-Republican*, 4 August 1943, 3, 18 January 1944, 6.

45. *Press-Republican*, 7 September 1943, 3, 26 July 1944, 3, 9 September 1947, 3, 8 September 1950, 3; minutes, Champlain Valley Hospital Board of Directors, 1910–1962, 289, 294, 302, 307, 337, 17 December 1946, Champlain Valley Hospital papers, box 7, CVPH; Annals, Champlain Valley Hospital, 1937–1949, 11 August 1944, 71, GNSH; typescript on Champlain Valley Hospital stationery stapled to sheet on Bonds information, Champlain Valley Hospital papers, 1 January 1946, box 7, CVPH.

46. *Daily Press*, 3 November 1941, 3, 9 February 1942, 3; *Daily Republican*, 5 June 1942, 3; Skopp, *Bright with Promise*, 104, 106; *Press-Republican*, 2 January 1945, 5; Frost, *Plattsburgh, New York*, 84.

47. *Daily Republican*, 29 July 1942, 3; Annals, Champlain Valley Hospital, 1937–1949, 27 July 1942, 31, GNSH; *Press-Republican*, 12 September 1945, 3, 31 October 1946, 3; Annals, Champlain Valley Hospital, 1949–1955, 19 December 1949, 8, May 1950, 21, box 1, GNSH.

48. Notitiae and Financial Statement for Hospitals in the Diocese of Ogdensburg, 30 December 1940, Champlain Valley Hospital Convent Correspondence, 1937–1962, Plattsburgh file, RCDO; E. C. D. Cameron, Vice President-Secretary-Treasurer, J. & J. Rogers Company, AuSable Forks, NY, to Emmett J. Roach [President, Board of Directors, Champlain Valley Hospital], Plattsburgh, NY, 5 March 1946, 2, Champlain Valley Hospital papers, box 7, CVPH; Livre du Conseil, Plattsburgh, NY, 1924–1976, 23 décembre 1943, St. Peter School, folder 14, box 33, DSH; Sister Annunciata, Champlain Valley Hospital, Plattsburgh, NY, to Most Reverend Bryan J. McEntegart, D.D., Bishop of

Ogdensburg, 5 June 1947, Champlain Valley Hospital Convent Correspondence, 1937–1962, Plattsburgh file, RCDO.

49. *Daily Press*, 14 August 1940, 4; *Press-Republican*, 1 February 1944, 3.

50. *Press-Republican*, 5 February 1945, 3, 1 February 1946, 7, 27 February 1946, p. 4.

51. *Press-Republican*, 16 November 1944, 6, 25 September 1945, 5, 17 September 1949, 5, 27 September 1950, 3.

52. *Press-Republican*, 26 October 1945, 5, 31 October 1945, 2, 29 June 1946, 4, 30 November 1946, 3, 1 February 1947, 3, 16 October 1947, 4, 6 December 1948, 5, 12 May 1949, 3, 21 November 1949, 5; *Daily Press*, 3 August 1942, 5.

53. *Daily Press*, 3 August 1942, 5; *Press-Republican*, 1 July 1947, 3.

54. *Press-Republican*, 3 December 1942, 9, 19 October 1950, 11.

55. Annals, Champlain Valley Hospital, 1937–1949, 14 June 1942, 27, 21 June 1942, 27, 27 February 1943, 42–43, 12 June 1948, 138, GNSH.

56. "Student Handbook, School of Nursing, Champlain Valley Hospital, Plattsburg, N.Y.," 3 [1940s], and "Nurses' Morning Prayer, Champlain Valley Hospital, Plattsburg, N.Y., 1949," School of Nursing Memorabilia, Champlain Valley Hospital and School of Nursing, box 2, GNSH.

57. *Daily Press*, 25 June 1942, 2; *Press-Republican*, 26 February 1947, 3.

58. *Press-Republican*, 5 June 1946, 3, 4 August 1947, 3, 7 August 1947, 5, 16 June 1948, 3.

59. *Press-Republican*, 14 June 1946, 3.

60. *Press-Republican*, 3, 19 September 1945, 3, 12 January 1946. Correspondence and notice from St. Peter's Church file, RCDO: Rev. Charles H. Dozois, O.M.I., Hospital Chaplain, Champlain Valley Hospital, to Mother Saint Edward, GNSH, Superior General, 30 May 1946, 26 June 1946, to Most Reverend Bryan J. McEntegart, D.D., Bishop of Ogdensburg, 30 May 1946, 26 June 1946; Arthur J. Lemire, O.M.I., St. Peter's Church, Plattsburgh, to Rt. Rev. J. T. Lyng, Chancellor, Ogdensburg, Chancery, 27 June 1946; Lyng to Lemire, 4 June 1946, to Dozois, 5 July 1946; Saint Edward to Dozois, 17 June 1946; typescript, Notice to All Non-Catholic Student Nurses, from Rev. Charles H. Dozois, O.M.I., Hospital Chaplain (n.d.).

61. *Daily Press*, 22 June 1940, 4; brochure, "Mount Assumption Institute, Plattsburgh, New York" [1948], 6, Plattsburg Mount Assumption Institute Juvénat, Publications, box 5203, FIC; pamphlet, "Our Lady of Victory Academy, Plattsburg, N.Y." [circa 1949], SCSL, 24,025-004-002.

62. Richard T. Schaefer, "The Ku Klux Klan: Continuity and Change," *Phylon* 32, no. 2 (1971): 157; Philip Jenkins, *The New Anti-Catholicism: The Last Acceptable Prejudice* (New York: Oxford University Press, 2003), 33; Mark S. Massa, S.J., *Anti-Catholicism in America: The Last Acceptable Prejudice* (New York: Crossroad, 2003), 59–99.

63. Pamphlet, "'Be His Queen': An Appeal to Youth for Religious Life," 1949, SCSL, 3303-01-06.

64. "'Be His Queen,'" capitalization in original.
65. "'Be His Queen.'"
66. *Daily Press*, 7 September 1940, 3.
67. *Daily Press*, 25 June 1940, 2, 31 October 1941, 2, 14 November 1941, 5; *Press-Republican*, 28 July 1945, 3, 27 July 1948, 5.
68. Herbert H. Dewey, *Ramblings of a Convalescent: Homespun Philosophy and Dialect Tales in Prose and Verse, Reflecting Fifty Years as a Farmer, Salesman and Country Storekeeper* (Champlain, NY: Moorsfield, 1950), preface, copyright page; *Press-Republican*, 10 June 1950, 3.
69. Dewey, *Ramblings of a Convalescent*, 10–11, 68, 89.
70. Holman F. Day, "The Jumper," *Pine Tree Ballads: Rhymed Stories of Unplaned Human Natur' Up in Maine* (Boston: Small, Maynard, 1902), 251–53; Robert E. Bartholomew and Benjamin Radford, *Hoaxes, Myths, and Manias: Why We Need Critical Thinking* (Amherst, NY: Prometheus, 2003), 219–20; Stephen R. Whalen and Robert E. Bartholomew, "The Enigma of the 'Jumping Frenchmen of Maine,'" *Maine History* 43, no. 1 (January 2007): 66. For more on the Jumping Frenchmen Syndrome, see Richard, "A Peculiar Condition," 355–74. For an overview of discrimination against Franco-Americans of the northeastern states, including the involvement of colleges and universities in fomenting cultural prejudice, see C. Stewart Doty, "How Many Frenchmen Does It Take to . . . ?" *Thought and Action* 11 (Fall 1995): 85–104. For a more recent publication that explores perceptions of French-Canadian descendants in the United States over historical time, see David Vermette, *A Distinct Alien Race: The Untold Story of Franco-Americans: Industrialization, Immigration, Religious Strife* (Montréal: Baraka, 2018), especially 193–292.
71. "William Henry Drummond," *The Canadian Encyclopedia*, www.thecanadianencyclopedia.ca (2023); William Henry Drummond, *The Habitant and Other French-Canadian Poems* (Montréal, 1897; Project Gutenberg, 2006), www.gutenberg.org, ebook #9801; Jay Gitlin, "'La Confédération perdue': The Legacy of Francophone Culture in Mid-America," *The Bourgeois Frontier: French Towns, French Traders, and American Expansion* (New Haven, CT: Yale University Press, 2009), 170, ProQuest Ebook Central.

Conclusion

1. Editorial, *Plattsburgh Press-Republican*, 3 July 1943, 4; see also 6–7.

Afterword

1. Minutes, Champlain Valley Hospital Board of Directors, The Champlain Valley Hospital Records, 1910–1962, 337, 346, 17 December 1946, CVPH;

minutes, Physicians' Hospital Board of Directors, 1936–1957, 451, CVPH; resolution proposed and discussed by the Clinton County Medical Society at its meeting of 25 May 1948, Champlain Valley Hospital and School of Nursing, box 2, GNSH; *Plattsburgh Press-Republican*, 13 June 1952, 10, 16 June 1952, 3.

2. Minutes, Champlain Valley Hospital Board of Directors, 1910–1962, 361; brochure,"For Health Security: A Greater Champlain Valley Hospital, Plattsburg, New York" (1952), 5, Champlain Valley Hospital documents, box 6, CVPH; *Press-Republican*, 20 June 1952, 3, 20 January 1953, 3, 5 May 1954, 2; Reverend James J. Navagh, D.D., Bishop of Ogdensburg, to Mother Mary Ita, G.N.S.H., Superior General, 22 December 1960, Grey Nuns of the Sacred Heart file, RCDO; untitled typescript [January 1962], Emmett Roach correspondence, Champlain Valley Hospital documents, box 6, CVPH; Anthony J. J. Rourke, "Champlain Valley Hospital, Plattsburgh, New York, December, 1961," F4, F5, box 10, CVPH; Mortgages, Books 183, pp. 507–12, 197, pp. 399–404, 198, pp. 17–26, CCCO; Roy Southworth, *Press-Republican*, 8 February 1963, 1.

3. *Press-Republican*, 12 February 1958, 3, 4, 22 March 1958, 3, 19 December 1958, 3; Jim Adams, *Press-Republican*, 11 February 1958, 3; pamphlet, "Champlain Valley Physicians Hospital Medical Center School of Nursing, 1910–1979," in possession of Stephen G. Baughn, Plattsburgh, New York.

4. Annals, Champlain Valley Hospital, 1956–1963, 28 April 1961, 2 July 1962, 5 August 1963, box 1, GNSH; Rourke, "Champlain Valley Hospital," F22; Mother Mary Ita to the Board of Directors, Champlain Valley Hospital, 20 February 1962, to Emmett Roach, President, Board of Directors, Champlain Valley Hospital, 27 June 1962, and Roach to Mother Mary Ita, 14 August 1963, Roach correspondence; Roy Southworth, *Press-Republican*, 8 February 1963, 1; Kathy Everly, *Press-Republican*, 10 April 1963, 1; *Press-Republican*, 10 June 1963, 3.

5. Minutes, Physicians' Hospital Board of Directors, 1957–1962, 20 April 1965, 106–7, CVPH; Roy Southworth, *Press-Republican*, 24 June 1965, 1, 3, and 13 May 1966, 3; "History of the Medical Center," *10th Anniversary, CVPH Medical Center, Plattsburgh, New York*, supplement to the *Press-Republican*, 9–15 May 1982, 5, Champlain Valley Hospital documents, box 6, CVPH; Supreme Court Orders, Book 44, pp. 525–27, CCCO; Frost, *Plattsburgh, New York*, 69–70; Deed Book 506, pp. 439–42, and Satisfaction of Mortgages, Book 70, pp. 44–45, CCCO; George W. Angell, President, State University College, to Emmett Roach, 30 April 1964, Roach correspondence; Helen McLeod, *Press-Republican*, 21 March 1979, 6; *Press-Republican*, 28 March 1980, 17A.

6. *Press-Republican*, 7 June 1969, 5; brochure, "Champlain Valley Physicians Hospital Medical Center School of Nursing, Plattsburgh, New York" [1975], 3, box 10, CVPH; *North Countryman* (Rouses Point, NY), 19 August 1976, 11; minutes, Board of Directors of the Champlain Valley Physicians Hospital Medical Center, 1973–1996, 374, CVPH.

7. Taylor, *A History of Catholicism in the North Country*, 270; Sr. Mary Salome, R.S.M., Loretta Residence, Plattsburgh, NY, to "Dear Father" [Chancery in

Ogdensburg], 11 December 1955, St. John's Convent Correspondence, 1919–1979, Plattsburgh file, RCDO; Harding, "A History of the Sisters of Mercy," 195.

8. Taylor, *A History of Catholicism in the North Country*, 273; Jean Mockry, *North Country Catholic*, 12 May 1993, 12, RCDO; Everest, *Briefly Told*, 22; Robin Caudell, *Press-Republican*, 23 April 2021, online; Guilbeault-Cayer, *Les Soeurs de la Charité de Saint-Louis en Amérique*, 141–43; newspaper clipping, most likely from *North Country Catholic* [1993], Our Lady of Victory Plattsburgh file, RCDO.

9. Menard, "The Brothers of Christian Instruction in the United States (1903–1981)," 68; Guilbeault-Cayer, *Les Soeurs de la Charité de Saint-Louis en Amérique*, 215; Mary Carol Conroy, SCL, "The Transition Years," in Stepsis and Liptak, eds., *Pioneer Healers*, 155–56; Kauffman, *Ministry and Meaning*, 283.

10. Taylor, *A History of Catholicism in the North Country*, 208, 271; Menard, "The Brothers of Christian Instruction in the United States (1903–1981)," 55–56. From 1983 to 1989, two Brothers of Christian Instruction worked as administrators of St. Peter's School. Menard, "The Brothers of Christian Instruction in the United States (1979–1991)," 84.

11. Taylor, *A History of Catholicism in the North Country*, 208, 271; Mother Theresa of Jesus, O.P., Prioress General, St. Catherine of Siena Convent, Fall River, Massachusetts, to Reverend Thomas A. Donnellan, Bishop of Ogdensburg, 20 May 1966, Dominican Sisters Fall River file, RCDO; press release of the Diocese of Ogdensburg, 2 June 1966, St. Peter's Plattsburgh, box 98, folder 13, DSH, F502.10 and F623.01; "St. Peter's Parish 150th Anniversary."

12. Taylor, *A History of Catholicism in the North Country*, 208, 270; texte dactylographié, "SCSL USA" (s.d.) 4, SCSL, 24,026-007-003.

13. Typescript history attached to a diocesan historical report [1972], Sisters of Charity of St. Louis file, RCDO; Taylor, *A History of Catholicism in the North Country*, 267; Frost, *Plattsburgh, New York*, 72; "SCSL USA," 7.

14. "St. Peter's Parish 150th Anniversary"; Frost, *Plattsburgh, New York*, 28.

15. Supreme Court Orders, Book 54, pp. 1065–66, Deed Book 562, pp. 712–15, CCCO. Two other Franco-American societies appear to have met their demise two decades earlier. Judging from the meeting notices published in the press, it is likely that the Montcalm and Sainte-Cécile councils of Union Saint-Jean-Baptiste d'Amérique ceased functioning as mutual-benefit societies in 1953 and 1954, respectively. The last meeting announcements for each appeared in the *Press-Republican* on 29 September 1953, 6, and 29 September 1954, 3.

16. Taylor, *A History of Catholicism in the North Country*, 270; Record, 23 September 1970–1 January 1998 (journal of the Brothers of Christian Instruction in Plattsburgh), 1975–1976, 43–44, BCI; Menard, "The Brothers of Christian Instruction in the United States (1903–1981)," 81, and "The Brothers of Christian Instruction in the United States (1979–1991)," 71.

17. Typescript, Rev. David W. Stinebrickner, Chancellor, Letter to Priests Regarding Champlain Valley Physicians Hospital, 22 November 1977, Oblates of Mary Immaculate Pre 1990 file, RCDO; Rev. Stanislaus J. Brzana, S.T.D.,

Bishop of Ogdensburg, to Rev. Norman J. Parent, O.M.I., Provincial Office, Oblates of Mary Immaculate, Worcester, MA, 2 June 1978, 13 December 1978, Oblates of Mary Immaculate Pre 1990 file, RCDO.

18. Agreement between the Roman Catholic Diocese of Ogdensburg and the Provincial of the Oblates of Mary Immaculate of the St. John the Baptist Province, 1986, Oblates of Mary Immaculate Pre 1990 file, RCDO; *Press-Republican*, 15 April 1989, 9; "St. Peter's Parish 150th Anniversary."

19. "Mount Assumption Institute, Plattsburgh, New York, 1919–1989," in brochure, Br. Charles Thomas, comp., "We Remember, 1903–2003: The Brothers of Christian Instruction in the United States" [2003], BCI; brochure, "Seton Catholic Central Coeducational High School, Grades 9–12" [1989], Journal scolaire, Seton Catholic Central, box 5257, FIC; Menard, "The Brothers of Christian Instruction in the United States (1979–1991)," 80; deed record 2017-00002030, CCCO.

20. Michael Marois, *Press-Republican*, 15 June 1992, 3; Mary Lou Kilian, *North Country Catholic* online, 23 January 2002, 3; Scott Wilson, *North Country Catholic* online, 1 February 2006, 3.

21. Mary Beth Bracy, *North Country Catholic* online, 23 September 2020.

Index

Acadians, 2, 68
Acculturation: of Joseph Chapleau, 78, 82; measures of, 18–19, 24, 32, 43, 106, 117, 149; process of, 4
American Legion, 245, 313n75
Anne de Jésus, Sr., 122, 126, 131, 136, 137, 150, 157, 313n71
assimilation, 4, 25, 74, 87, 107, 174

Bachand, J. H. A., 146, 174, 182, 209, 238
Barnabé, Fabien, 67–68
Barton, Lyman, 204–205
bazaar: in Champlain, 54; in Dannemora, 126; at Our Lady of Victory, 239; at St. John's, 41; at St. Peter's, 9, 13, 15, 54, 92, 151, 152
bilingualism: of Dominican Sisters, 233; at D'Youville Academy, 56, 59, 94; during excursion, 91; of Grey Nuns, 12, 59, 120; at Our Lady of Victory Academy, 107, 148, 214; at Our Lady of Victory Church, 146; in Plattsburgh, 179; of Sisters of Charity of St. Louis, 108; at St. Peter's Church, 9, 10, 43, 92; at St. Peter's parish school, 43, 101, 149
Boire, Victor, 92, 148, 171, 178, 182, 183

borderlands: Canada-U.S., 3, 4, 32, 60, 169, 255, 284n70; New York-Québec, xi, 1, 4, 89
Bourget, Ignace, 8, 28
Bournigalle, Charles: conflict with Bishop of Albany, 36; conflict with Canadian Union, 24, 25; founder of St. Joseph Society, 25, 27; relations with Grey Nuns, 20, 36, 38; at St. Peter's Church, 37, 39, 41, 286n21
Bouyea, Leander, 215, 216–17, 219, 221
British North America, 2, 11, 277n2
Brothers of Christian Instruction: American district, 236; arrival in Plattsburgh, 95, 96, 236; ethnic origins, 100, 165; during Great War, 169; juvenate, 143, 144, 217; migration to Québec, 95; at Mount Assumption Institute, 97, 193–94, 195, 206, 319n56, 327n23; reception of, 98, 101, 221; recruitment of students, 217; scholasticate, 99, 100, 217; at St. Peter's parish schools, 104, 105, 117, 144, 154, 155, 236, 261, 263, 318n45, 333n10; teaching certification, 99
Brown, John, 79–80
Brown, Nelson, 79–80

335

Brown, Peter, 78–80, 82
Bruyère, Elisabeth: as foundress, 12, 15; and Plattsburgh mission, 12–13, 14, 16, 17, 31; relations with Oblates, 12, 20, 38, 158

Canadian Union, 21–29, 32, 37, 40
Catholic Summer School, 60, 115, 186, 192
Champlain, New York, 48, 54, 70, 71, 110, 114, 143, 176
Champlain, Samuel de, 1, 18, 48, 255; commemorations of, 48, 52, 89, 110, 112; monument to, 113–17
Champlain Tercentenary, 110–13, 116–17
Champlain Valley Hospital: administrators of, 129, 130, 133, 141, 164–65, 166, 198, 222–23, 232, 240, 242, 243, 245; assisting poor, 136, 140; financing of, 128, 129, 137, 140, 141, 199, 200, 201, 204, 224, 225, 227, 246, 259, 305n29; founding of, 127, 131, 156; merger of, 226, 259, 260, 325n56; mission of, 127; nonsectarian nature of, 130, 131, 135–36, 197, 223, 249; patients of, 136, 139, 251, 320n69; religious nature of, 131–32, 136, 224, 247, 248; trustees, 123, 125, 127–31, 141
Champlain Valley Hospital Junior League, 225, 246
Champlain Valley Hospital School of Nursing, 133–35, 141, 157, 197–98, 206, 241, 243–45, 247–48, 259–60, 306n41
Champlain Valley Hospital Women's Auxiliary, 126–27, 128, 137–38, 199, 200, 224–25, 227, 245–46, 304n20
Chapleau, Eliza, 77–78, 81, 294n45
Chapleau, Joseph: background of, 77–78, 82–83, 295n49; judicial leniency towards, 295n47; significance of murder case, 63, 73–74, 77, 82, 85; trial of, 78–80; visits of Grey Nuns, 81
Children of Mary. See *Enfants de Marie*
Christmas: at Champlain Valley Hospital, 242; dances, 224–25; at D'Youville Convent and Academy, 20, 92; in order of Sisters of Charity of St. Louis, 250; at Our Lady of Victory, 178, 180; at St. John's, 316n18; at St. Peter's, 20, 43, 54, 55, 91, 180, 220
Cleveland, Grover, 72–73, 75, 76, 77, 293n20, 302n64
Clinton Community College, 260, 261
Clinton County Medical Society, 123, 129, 130, 205, 259, 260
Cold War, 229, 248, 254
Collège St. Pierre, 94, 101, 104, 105, 117. See also St. Peter's Academy
Conroy, J. H., 145, 150, 151, 158–63, 165, 168–69, 178, 189–90, 192, 197
Conroy, John, 34, 35, 37, 279n9
Conseil Montcalm, 105, 183, 184, 211, 333n15
Conseil Sainte-Cécile, 105, 183, 184, 211, 333n15
Conway, Thomas, 114, 177, 219, 315n7
Côté, Cyrille, 3
Council of Baltimore, 56, 57
Crete, Israel, 85, 106, 296n57, 300n52
cross burnings, 175, 177, 180, 206, 315n8

Decoration Day, 39–40, 52, 288n53
Democratic Party, 22, 28, 44, 63, 72–73, 75, 76–77, 86, 88, 216, 262, 290n74, 293n20
Democrats, 29, 72, 75, 76, 80, 85, 88, 113, 216, 262, 290n74, 302n64
Desjardins, Joseph Ludger, 106, 107, 173
de Valera, Éamon, 186
Dewey, Herbert, 251–54
Diocese of Ogdensburg, foundation, 35, 37, 39
Dominican Sisters: arrival of, 190–91, 205; contact with Grey Nuns, 167; contracts with parish, 233–34; 318n45; ethnicity, 191, 221, 231–32; fundraising activities of, 234–35, 327n19; in Great Depression, 218, 219–20, 221, 222; priory of, 220; recruitment to St. Peter's, 154–55, 189; schools of, 180, 192, 221, 233, 236, 261, 327n12; state certification, 191–92, 221; in World War II, 241–42
Dougherty, Dennis, 160, 163, 165–68
Draper, A. S., 102–103
Driscoll, J. H., 95, 145, 185, 186, 187
Duvernay, Ludger, 3, 143
D'Youville Academy, 56, 59, 92–95, 149, 151, 152, 236; closure, 163–64, 166–67
D'Youville Convent, 13, 125, 153, 157, 164, 189

Elks Club, 88, 90, 110, 112, 126, 148–49, 216, 245
Enfants de Marie, 37, 43, 171
epidemic: influenza, 156, 157; smallpox, 42, 120
Erno, Edward, 23, 24, 25, 27, 287n36

Fall River, Massachusetts, 4, 47, 74, 112; Dominican Sisters in, 155, 167, 189, 191, 233, 235, 261
fire-hose companies, 48, 110, 111, 114, 287n41
flag: Canadian, 40, 101, 145, 309n5; French, 39, 40, 50, 51, 101, 110, 113, 115, 145, 148; Irish, 39; Papal, 242; U.S., 22, 39, 40, 48, 50, 51, 101, 110, 113, 115, 145, 180, 183, 185, 242
Fournier, Joseph A., 51, 58–59
Fourth of July, 18, 19, 25, 26, 27, 29, 32, 39, 41, 52, 90, 110, 114, 172, 213
French and Indian War, 1, 2

Gabriels, Henry, 84, 99, 100, 106, 122, 123, 145, 151, 173
Gallant, Edward, 171, 172
Garand, P. S., 166, 168, 169
Garin, André, 12–13, 14, 19, 35
Girard, P., 27, 28, 41, 287n36
Grand Army of the Republic, 39, 48, 52, 90, 113, 114, 170, 171, 172
Great Depression, 187, 201, 207–42, 318n45
Great War, 134, 140, 143, 145, 155, 157, 165, 169–70, 172, 174, 177, 314n79. *See also* World War I
Grey Nuns of the Cross: boarding school, 12–13, 16, 21, 43, 92–94, 164; certification, 60, 98; conflict with bishop, 158–63, 165–66, 168–69; conflicts with Oblates, 21, 32, 37–38, 149–56, 158; division and departure, 143–44, 166–68, 174, 189–90, 198, 234, 236; end of public-school teaching, 101–103, 117; ethnicity, 164–65; fundraising, 15–16, 29, 55, 153; hospital

Grey Nuns of the Cross *(continued)* founding, 96, 307n59; hospital work, 119–36, 141; intermixing with the Irish, 19–20, 41, 256; missions with Oblates, 11–12, 121; parish school of, 14, 30–31, 43, 55, 59, 60, 92, 104; student recruitment, 14, 56, 152; work with sick and poor, 14, 42, 156. *See also* Sisters of Charity of Ottawa

Grey Nuns of the Sacred Heart: ethnicity, 222, 240, 325n45; formation of, 166, 168–69; hospital management, 177, 201, 226–27, 245, 260; during World War II, 242–43

Guigues, J. E., 11, 12, 20

Harrison, Benjamin, 50, 72, 77
Hartwell, William, 30, 31, 43
Hill, David, 50, 75, 80, 295n47

immigration: from Canada, 1, 83–84, 87–88, 89, 256; mass, 182; restrictions, 1, 75, 169, 211, 217, 229

incorporation: Brothers of Christian Instruction, 100, 263; Canadian Union, 24; Grey Nuns, 33–35, 44; Notre-Dame des Victoires, 106; Oblates, 35; Physicians' Hospital, 140; Plattsburgh City Hospital 124; Sisters of Charity of St. Louis, 239; St. Peter's parish, 53–54, 288n57

Independence Day. *See* Fourth of July
Indians, 18, 40, 48, 114. *See also* Iroquois; Native peoples
integration, cultural, 21, 29, 52, 78, 105, 214
Irish Settlement, 14, 15
Iroquois, 1, 18, 48, 113, 114

Jews, 15, 21, 102, 127, 146, 177, 188, 196, 199, 245

Keeseville, NY, 65, 66–68, 109, 126, 148, 186
Kelley, William, 121, 123, 127
Knights of Columbus, 88, 90, 110, 125, 148, 149, 172, 184, 205, 213, 216
Ku Klux Klan, 160, 175–77, 180, 181, 189, 196–97, 198, 205–206, 249, 257, 299n37, 315n8

Labor Day, 90, 104, 212
Lake Champlain, 2, 40, 54, 76, 87, 91, 113
LaMoy, William, 24, 25, 27, 28
Lavoie, Eléonore, 13, 34
Lenthier, Benjamin, 46, 49–50, 56, 57, 70–71, 76, 77, 293n20
Lewis, L. V., 92, 104, 178
Loretta residence, 187, 222, 240, 260
Lower Canada, x, 2–3, 7, 17, 26

Maccabees, 90–91, 114, 120, 172
Mallet, Edmond, 64, 66–68, 71, 76–77, 83
Marie de la Victoire, 150, 151, 155
"La Marseillaise," 171, 172
McCloskey, John, 8, 12
McKeever, Bernard, 14, 19, 31–32, 281n21
McMillan, Marie, 55, 81, 150–51
Memorial Day, 52, 90, 170, 171, 288n53. *See also* Decoration Day
Métis, ix, 12, 64–69, 70, 71
Miner Foundation, 204, 225, 226, 227
Miner, William, 203–204
minstrels, 107, 195–96, 209–11, 235, 239, 254, 257, 327n19

Moloney, Richard, 13, 19, 35–37, 38, 40, 42
Monaghan, F. J., 224, 238
Mount Assumption Institute: curriculum, 194–95, 237, 249; finances, 236, 319n56; founding, 97, 193; merger, 262, 263; physical plant, 206; school, 179, 194, 327n23; sports, 240; students, 194–95, 217–18, 235
Mount Carmel Cemetery, 105, 117, 232
mutual-benefit society, 22, 182, 184; St. John Baptist Association, 41, 120, 173, 181, 183; Union Saint-Jean-Baptiste d'Amérique, 104, 105, 183–84, 211–12, 333n15

Native peoples, 12, 18, 50, 64, 114, 116, 287n43. *See also* Indians; Iroquois
naturalization, 68; of Canadians, 69, 70, 74, 240
Nelson, Robert, 3
New England, comparisons with, ix–xi, 1, 4, 19, 26, 52, 167, 177, 184, 256, 314n79
Northwest Territories, ix, 12, 64–65, 68–69, 70, 71
Notre-Dame des Victoires, 105–106, 107, 117, 146, 147, 172. *See also* Our Lady of Victory

Oblates: arrival, 8–9; creating community, 7, 50, 61; ethnicity, 11, 13, 20, 25, 149, 179, 230; ethnic retention and, 32; founding secondary school, 57; library, 91–92; property of, 34; at St. John parish, 13, 42; withdrawal, 262–63
Order of Mary Immaculate. *See* Oblates

Our Lady of Victory Academy, 146–48, 214, 236–40, 249, 262; ethnicity of students, 192
Our Lady of Victory: fundraising, 239; merger, 263; parish, 178, 180, 188, 213. *See also* Notre-Dame des Victoires

parades: Champlain Monument unveiling, 114–15; Champlain Tercentenary, 110–13; Decoration/Memorial Day, 52, 90, 171; French-Canadian convention, 47–48, 183; Fourth of July, 26, 52, 90, 172, 213; Labor Day, 90, 104; in Montréal, 89; New Deal, 212; of paramilitary groups, 145, 212; Saint-Jean-Baptiste Day, 18, 25–26, 40, 50; St. John Baptist Association anniversary, 182, 215; war bond, 242; welcoming bishop, 39
Patriotes, x, 2–3, 9, 26
Pelletier, Joseph, 91, 94–96, 100, 104, 105, 111, 123, 208
Physicians' Hospital: founding, 130, 138–39; funding, 140, 204, 226–27; merger, 259–60, 325n56; Nursing School, 203, 243, 244, 260; secular nature, 140; trustees, 139–40; Women's League, 138, 140, 141
Plaisance, Walter, 146, 155–56, 157, 171
Plattsburgh Board of Education, 29–32, 38, 43, 55, 57–60, 92, 101–103
Plattsburgh City Hospital, 122–27. *See also* Champlain Valley Hospital
Plattsburgh National Bank, 88, 129, 202
Plattsburgh Normal School, 94, 98–100, 152, 193, 222, 240, 299n29, 315n8

Plattsburgh State Teacher's College, 244, 247
population, of Plattsburgh, 4, 21, 57, 87, 98, 129, 175–76, 211, 229–30
Prohibition, 173, 176, 181
Protestants: in Canada, 64, 68; cemeteries, 40, 52; churches, 21, 279n2; Dutch, 2; intermixing with Catholics, 53, 60, 101, 102, 121, 125, 177, 188; in Ireland, 186; in Plattsburgh, 96–97, 98, 99, 232; students, 21, 99; in the United States, 73, 77, 124, 130, 147, 175–76, 249; women, 13, 55, 81, 119, 121, 132

Québec: Catholic institutions of, 28, 53, 176, 249; economy, 3; education in, 82, 95, 99, 155, 260; emigration from, 23, 48, 64, 109, 191; French Canadians in, 64–69; hospitals in, 122, 133; migration from France to, 95, 100, 107, 298n21; national song, 26; Province of, 2, 141, 213, 236; repatriation to, 23, 46, 205, 282n49; visits to, 9, 91, 107. *See also* Lower Canada

Racette, Julien, 157–58, 189–91
Rebellion of 1837–1838, x, 2–3, 9, 26, 231
Regents: Board of, 59, 133, 147, 164, 191, 194, 214, 260; curriculum, 104, 147, 237, 239, 249; examiners, 92, 150, 310n23; exams, 59, 92, 101, 147, 164, 191
Republicans, 28, 29, 44, 63, 72, 73, 75, 85, 216, 262, 302n67
Revolutionary War, 2, 52, 195
Riel, Louis, 63–73, 86, 231, 291n6
Riley, J. B., 102, 104, 126, 127

Rouses Point, NY, 3, 8, 126, 155, 169, 176, 185
Rumilly, Robert, 143, 184

Saint-Jean-Baptiste Day, celebrations, 13, 17, 18–19, 25, 26, 32, 40, 48, 50, 51, 58, 89, 184, 288n51
Sallaz, Claude, 13, 16–17, 19, 24, 30, 31, 34, 35, 38
séance, 29, 43, 180, 214, 220, 221, 234
Senecal, Andrew, 113–14, 215
Sharron, Albert, 88–89, 90, 123, 215
Silver, Cassius, 130, 138–39, 204
Sirois, J. A., 150, 151, 153–54, 155
Sisters of Charity of Ottawa: in Buffalo, NY, 12; division of, 165–66; founding hospital, 119–22, 128, 131, 141; founding nursing school, 133–34; linguistic tensions within, 160, 165; in Lowell, Mass., 56, 312n64; Mother House, 15; in Ogdensburg, NY, 121, 124–25, 133, 157, 159–60, 162, 163, 166–67; in Plattsburgh, NY, 8, 11, 12, 14, 60; teaching, 102, 103, 156, 158, 163, 256. *See also* Grey Nuns of the Cross
Sisters of Charity of St. Louis: arrival, 107–109; emigration from France, 107, 117; ethnicity, 192–93, 237; founding of order, 107; home for aged, 239, 261; funding, 108, 146, 196, 209, 238–39; juvenate, 147; parish school and academy, 147, 240, 249, 261, 263; recruitment to order, 249–50; secretarial school, 260–61
Sisters of Mercy, 177, 185–87, 205–206, 211, 221–22, 240, 260
St. Albert, Mother, 165–68

"Star Spangled Banner," 51, 115, 171, 172, 179–80
St. Dominique Convent/Priory, 220–21
Stetson, Francis Lynde, 116, 127–28, 130, 199, 305n26
St. John Baptist Association: attempted secularization, 57–58; as ethnic society, 50, 61, 89, 174, 181–82; financial challenges, 182–83, 262; formation, 27, 41; during Great War, 170, 171; Guard of Honor, 110–14, 170–72, 173, 183, 212–13, 250; hall, 56; members, 46, 90, 92, 123, 173, 183, 205, 215, 216; nonethnic activities, 188, 213; women's auxiliary, 182–83, 215
St. John the Baptist Church, 19, 36, 40, 41–42, 95, 105, 106, 117, 185, 186, 187, 232, 240, 255
St. Joseph Society, 25, 26–27
St. Patrick's Day, 19, 32, 42, 94, 153, 186, 209, 232
St. Peter's Academy, 100, 105, 144, 146, 154, 155, 194; band, 110, 111, 173
St. Pierre Cemetery, 105, 117, 173, 207
St. Peter's Church: building, 9, 54; masses, 17–18, 25, 41, 43, 47; members, 54; rectory, 13; trustees, 8–11, 18, 24, 31, 53, 88, 29, 96, 233, 236, 279n9, 288n57
St. Vincent de Paul Society, 208, 209, 219, 234; women's auxiliary, 208
survivance, 149, 181

Tabor, Irwin: conflict with Chapleau, 78–79, 83, 295n47; murder, 73–74, 77, 79–83; property, 78, 83
Tilden, Samuel, 45, 302n64
transnationalism, 5, 64, 255
Tregret, Cyprius-Celestine, 96–99, 144, 155, 169, 236–37
Trudeau, Alexandre, 43, 286n21
trustees, village of Plattsburgh, 85, 123, 296n57
Turner, William, 162–63, 165

Union Saint-Jean-Baptiste d'Amérique. *See* mutual-benefit society
U.S. Cadet Nursing Corps, 243–45

VandenBerghe, Florent, 36–37
Verecunda, Sr., 160, 163
Vincent de Paul, Sr., 162–63, 168

Wadhams, Edgar, 24–25, 35, 39, 42, 47, 53, 57, 76, 121
War for Independence. *See* Revolutionary War
Weed, Roswell, 9, 29
Weed, Smith: assisting hospital foundation, 122, 124–25, 130; as politician, 113, 123, 290n74, 302n64; on school board, 30, 31–32, 55, 59, 103
World War I, 141, 169, 170, 177, 180, 185. *See also* Great War
World War II: effect on religious orders, 236, 238; Franco-Americans during, 251, 254
Wright, Carroll, 47, 84